THE COMPANION GUIDE TO PARIS

THE COMPANION GUIDES

*It is the aim of these guides to provide a Companion
in the person of the author; who knows
intimately the places and people of whom he writes, and is able to
communicate this knowledge and affection to his readers.
It is hoped that the text and pictures will aid them
in their preparations and in their travels, and will
help them remember on their return.*

BURGUNDY · THE COUNTRY ROUND PARIS
DEVON · EDINBURGH AND THE BORDER COUNTRY
FLORENCE · GASCONY AND THE DORDOGNE
GREEK ISLANDS · ISTANBUL · KENT AND SUSSEX
LAKE DISTRICT · LONDON
MADRID AND CENTRAL SPAIN
NEW YORK · ROME
SICILY · SOUTH OF SPAIN · VENICE

THE COMPANION GUIDE TO

PARIS

ANTHONY GLYN
Revised by Susan Glyn

COMPANION GUIDES

First published 2000
Companion Guides, Woodbridge

ISBN 1 900639 31 9

*The publishers and author have done their best to ensure
the accuracy and currency of all the information in
The Companion Guide to Paris.
However, they can accept no responsibility for any loss, injury,
or inconvenience sustained by any traveller as a result
of information or advice contained in the guide.*

Companion Guides is an imprint of Boydell & Brewer Ltd
PO Box 9, Woodbridge, Suffolk IP12 3DF, UK
and of Boydell & Brewer Inc.
PO Box 41026, Rochester, NY 14604–4126, USA
website: http://www.boydell.co.uk

A catalogue record for this book is available
from the British Library

Printed in Great Britain by
St Edmundsbury Press Ltd, Bury St Edmunds, Suffolk

Contents

PART THREE: THE LEFT BANK

Maps and Plans

Illustrations

Introduction

This is not a guidebook for the faint-hearted. Within its pages you will not find neutral descriptions of every major feature of the city, politically correct assessments of the characters who have walked its streets, half-hearted endorsements of architects and city planners who have done so much to shape the French capital city which we see today. You will find something else – passionate opinion, deep and abiding historical curiosity and a wonderfully lively 'feel' for Parisians and others who have lived, worked, loved, fought, intrigued, revolted and created in the hundred or so square kilometres which make up this extraordinary city.

The book's author has a point of view. He feels a sense of history as he takes you on your journey through Paris, whether on a wide and crowded boulevard or down a narrow, quiet and empty sidestreet. Those of us who have discovered Paris without Anthony Glyn at our elbow will feel the urge, as we turn these pages, to go back – immediately! – and see the sight described with such erudition and dry, laconic wit. Those of us who do not know Paris have countless treats in store, and can be all the more envied for that. If there is joy in discovery there is almost as much in sharing that discovery with others: this book informs, entertains and creates that joyous feeling, whether enticing you into forgotten corners of the (incredibly small) Ile de la Cité or marching you through the still debated Pyramid to unlock treasures galore in the Grand Louvre.

The author uses the first person plural throughout. It may disconcert at first, but go with him – he has much to tell you, much to make you try to see for yourself and the 'we' form is appropriate for a companion, after all. Wisely he does not try to tell you where you ought to eat and drink, where is 'in' and where is 'out' – these aspects of a city change so rapidly that any guidebook treading such paths becomes out of date almost as soon as it is printed. His bill of fare is different. Look at the city around you, explore its quirkiness, its glorious originality. Why does that building over there attract you and what lies behind it? Let me tell you something of its history…

As a penniless Sorbonne student over thirty years ago I sacrificed a meal and bought instead a well-thumbed *Connaissance du vieux Paris* by Jacques Hillairet, three volumes and 800 pages in dry as dust style, street by street, house by house, the facts – nothing but the facts! Years later I quarried its pages to conduct tour groups on nocturnal rambles of the Latin Quarter, improvising the bits I did not know and generally masking (I hope) lack of scholarship with empathy and lively imagination. How I could have done with this *Companion Guide* at that time. How I would have hated anyone in my audience who had one! For the great achievement of the book is to wear its erudition lightly, to give us words which we later realise are knowledge and finally perceive as wisdom and discernment. About Paris there may be more to say, but this book takes us to the heart of the city and its own *point de départ* is the author's love of his subject. May it prosper!

MIKE REYNOLDS

The publishers would like to acknowledge the assistance of
Mr Mike Reynolds, Professor Nigel Wilkins
and Mr George Chowdharay-Best
in the updating of this Guide.

PART ONE

The Seine

1

Ile de la Cité

THE FRENCH HAVE a phrase for it – *le point de départ*. With the right departure point, you will have a good journey and arrive finally at the right place. With the wrong departure point, you will never arrive at the right destination, no matter how many changes you may make on the way. The phrase applies not only to journeys but to writing books, decorating rooms, going into battle or founding companies. And for an exploration of Paris, or for a book about Paris, the departure point is obviously very important. For us, it is Point Zéro.

Point Zéro is a compass star set in the pavement in front of the main façade of Notre-Dame Cathedral (Metro Cité). It is the point from which all distances are measured in France, but it is clearly far older and more significant than that. It is the centre of the centre of the centre of the city, of France and, arguably, of Western civilization. Not the geographical centre, of course, but the spiritual, emotional and administrative heart of France. A few yards to the south stands a huge equestrian statue of Charlemagne and his vassals (erected in 1882), reminding us of the long-standing connection with Germany. Charlemagne, a Frank, was the first Holy Roman Emperor (AD 800) and, in his way, the founder of a united Europe. Immediately to the east is Notre-Dame where Henry VI was crowned King of England and France, emphasizing cross-Channel ties. A few feet below us are the remains of the Roman civilization, recalling the eternal link with Italy. Ile de la Cité was the centre of it all.

But it is much older than that. Somewhere below Point Zéro was one of the entrances to the Underworld. It was guarded by a god called Cernunnos, whose cult probably dates back to the reindeer-hunters of about 20,000 BC. He wore antlers on his head and sat cross-legged, yoga-style, an unusual position for a Western deity.

Over thirty altars to him have been found in various parts of France, guarding Underworld entrances, but it seems that Ile de la

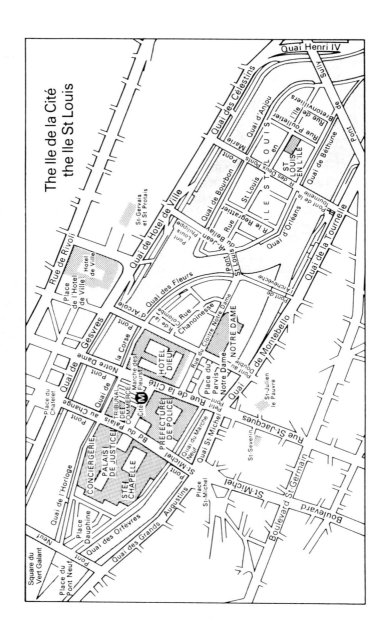

The Ile de la Cité
the Ile St Louis

Cité was one of his most important sites and it has remained an important religious centre to this day.

This point is not only associated with the Underworld; other cults go back just as far. The star is slightly worn by the feet of people standing on it to wish. Many of them were young women and, as they were standing between the statue of Mother and Child in the cathedral and the maternity wards of the Hôtel-Dieu Hospital, it is easy to guess what they were wishing for.

Ile de la Cité has changed its shape and its height many times since Cernunnos. In the pre-Roman era it was a sandbank and a primitive village, where the Seine boatmen and fishermen could find shelter and were protected on their river island from marauders. Later the local tribe, the Parisii, moved in and built a small town with massive bulwarks against other Gaulish tribes (third century BC). Things changed with the Roman expansion. Vercingétorix, the hero of Gaul, rose in revolt, but he was defeated by Labienus, Cæsar's lieutenant, who burnt and then abandoned Ile de la Cité, a smoking ruin.

Reconstruction began in the first century AD. The Gallo-Romans have left many traces of their civilization. They expanded on to the Left Bank, where they built, among other things, a large forum, three thermal baths, theatres, arenas and a fifteen-kilometre-long aqueduct, which brought clean water to the town, now renamed Lutetia Parisiorum. Temples sprouted on the island, the one on the site of Notre-Dame being dedicated to various Roman gods, including Jupiter and the Emperor Tiberius.

All this lasted until the third century when Lutetia Parisiorum was destroyed by German invaders. Later these invaders turned Ile de la Cité into a small defensive fortress with ramparts, traces of which still remain. In 508 a major event occurred. Clovis, King of the Franks, established his capital and his seat in Paris, now officially the capital of France, though France itself did not extend very far, scarcely more than the area now known as Ile de France.

Christianity had some rather controversial appearances in Paris before that: the Bishop of Paris, St Denis, had been martyred, Julian the Apostate, the Prefect of Gaul, had been proclaimed Roman Emperor by his legions, and Ste Geneviève had turned away the Hun invasion under Attila. But now Christianity became irresistible and Romanesque basilicas, rather small ones apparently, were built on the island in honour of the Virgin Mary, St Etienne (St Stephen, the first martyr), Ste Geneviève herself and St Christopher, who possibly replaced Hercules. The foundations of several of these can still be seen in the Archæological Crypt.

Saint-Etienne was the earliest, a few feet north of Point Zéro, but Notre-Dame, farther east, followed soon afterwards. There was naturally a certain conflict between the two, but gradually Notre-Dame expanded and enclosed Saint-Etienne. Long before the first stone of the present cathedral was laid, in 1163, the Virgin Mary reigned supreme in the area. She has done so ever since, except for a period during the Revolution when a Mademoiselle Maillard was enthroned on the high altar as Goddess of Reason, a surprising experience for a ballet dancer.

In the Middle Ages Ile de la Cité was a crowded, congested little town and the streets were unbelievably narrow. One of them, Rue de Venise, was only a metre wide. (Its former position is engraved on the paving, near the cathedral entrance.) The great stones from the Gallo-Roman period were re-used in the housing, with wooden upper storeys. Notre-Dame, either the earlier basilica or the later Gothic cathedral, was scarcely visible. A narrow glimpse could be had along Rue Neuve, which ran along the island, over Point Zéro, to the great west door. A closer look, cricking the neck, could be had from the little square, called the Parvis (a corruption of Paradisus) immediately in front of Notre-Dame.

Many dramatic events have had their setting here and it does not require much imagination to see Hugo's Quasimodo, the deaf hunchback of Notre-Dame, on the gallery under the rose window, throwing back the scaling ladders and hurling down abuse at the crowd below. The Parvis was used for processions and mystery plays, and there the *amende honorable* took place. A small platform was erected and the criminal, heavily guarded and noosed, was led there. Kneeling, wearing a white penitential sheet, and holding a candle, he would mouth the formal words of penitence before being led away to a slow and horrible death across the river in Place de Grève (now Place de l'Hôtel de Ville) on the Right Bank; the most notorious of these was Ravaillac, the hot-eyed fanatic who had murdered the great and popular French king, Henri IV. Lesser criminals were left on the platform to be pelted and abused by the crowd, pillory-style.

Apart from churches, houses and taverns, the island had two hospitals: the Hôtel-Dieu, on the south side, where the Charlemagne statue now stands, and a Foundlings Hospital on the north side, on the site of the present Hôtel-Dieu, which is the big building we see on our left. This last, in the eighteenth century, was an attractive neo-classical building by Boffrand, Mansart's partner in building Place Vendôme. When the Hôtel-Dieu was burnt down in 1772, Boffrand planned to replace it with a twin building to his Foundlings Hospital, and widen Rue Neuve, so that Notre-Dame could be seen better, without creating the huge empty square, the so-called 'paved prairie' which we now have. But Boffrand's excellent plans were never carried out, and indeed nothing remains above ground level of his Foundlings Hospital, except for some engravings.

Much of this has only come to light in recent years. In the course of excavating a new underground car park in front of Notre-Dame, the foundations of Gallo-Roman and mediæval Paris were unearthed and preserved, thus greatly reducing the size of the proposed car park. The **Archæological Crypt** is well worth a visit. The entrance is at the western end of the present Parvis. It tells the story of Paris in mainly visual terms. Not a museum (the coins and pots have been moved elsewhere, some to Cluny), it is intelligently and rather spookily lit. Here we can study again the ground-plan of old Paris, examine the foundations of Saint-Etienne and Sainte-Geneviève, look at the heating arrangements for these old houses, and speculate on exactly where Cernunnos must have sat. We can also look with wonder at the old Rue de Venise and try to imagine why a distinguished man like Commissionaire Delamare, colleague of Colbert, should have chosen to live there, within touching distance of a noisy tavern, when he could have been in a country château or at Versailles. Perhaps it was the island or the Seine which called him.

In the nineteenth century the Ile de la Cité was completely changed. Baron Haussmann, Napoleon III's Prefect of the Seine (the title Mayor of Paris had been abolished by Napoleon I, and has only relatively recently been restored – the man might have become too powerful), rebuilt Paris almost completely. Haussmann disliked poky little streets and small corners where revolutionaries could plot together; better were wide avenues and big squares, which could, if necessary, be swept by bullets. However, in his defence, it can be claimed that he created the boulevards, a great benefit to modern traffic, pavements where people could saunter *(flâner),* and with them the pavement cafés, so much a part of the Paris scene nowadays. In any event his ideas were more glorious, more suitable to a great capital, than a huddle of mediæval houses, however picturesque.

On Ile de la Cité he was quite ruthless. He removed twenty-five thousand people and about ninety streets, with their homes, shops and taverns, all in the cause of opening up the views of Notre-Dame. In their place he built the huge modern Parvis, and four enormous buildings of functional value, but of no architectural interest – the Hôtel-Dieu Hospital; the Préfecture de Police; the Tribunal of Commerce; and the Palais de Justice (the Law Courts). The first two of these can be seen from the Parvis. He was dismissed for extravagance before he could finish the work, and the part of the island which was not swept away by his cleansing operation is the area lying north of Rue du Cloître Notre-Dame, between the cathedral and the Seine. We shall return to look more closely at some of the houses here.

To reach Point Zéro, the easiest way, short of emerging from the Underworld, is by the underground railway, the Paris metro, at Station Cité. The metro runs deep here, under the Seine, and we ascend by a lift. The entrance to the metro station is worth more than a glance. This is real Art Nouveau, with curly wrought-iron moulded into bushes and leaves, the lamps being amber tulips, or perhaps pears. No lines are straight, even on the lettering. Built by Guimard in 1900, this is the romantic line which took hungry Modigliani from Montmartre to Montparnasse and back. It is still one of the quickest and most efficient underground systems in the world, but many of the original entrances have gone elsewhere; one, Metro Raspail, is in the sculpture section of the Museum of Modern Art in New York.

In front of us lies the flower market, the Marché des Fleurs, a covered garden of cut flowers all the year round, a delight to the eye and very convenient for visitors to the Hôtel-Dieu. On Sundays it changes to a caged-bird market, but gifts of these may be less acceptable to the hospital. Various plans to move the market to make more room for police cars have so far been resisted successfully.

Having walked round the market we return to Metro Cité and follow the sign 'Notre-Dame' into Rue de la Cité and round the corner of the Préfecture de Police. There, suddenly making us catch our breath, is the Parvis and the great west façade of Notre-Dame, as Haussmann intended us to see it. Whether the original architects had any such grandiose notions is not known, but perhaps they did; it was built in an age of great faith on the part of everyone from expert stonemason to humble labourer. The original plans have hardly been altered despite many vicissitudes in the meantime.

Notre-Dame remains one of the glories of French Gothic art, its shape and proportions in perfect harmony. Some may regret that its height appears to be lower by being seen from a long distance, others that the towers were not, in the end, topped with steeples, as was at one time mooted. Some find it too perfect, too cold, too symmetrical and there are those who prefer the asymmetry of most French cathedrals, the feeling of random harmony which exists in Chartres, Rouen and elsewhere. But Notre-Dame is nonetheless one of the masterpieces of art and architecture, a worthy centre for the life, faith and culture of the French people, and Paris in particular.

We approach Notre-Dame across the **Parvis.** Far from being an 'asphalt skating-rink', as it has sometimes been called, it is a pleasant place to stroll or to sit on one of the stone benches. There we can enjoy not only the great façade but also the view across to the Left Bank, old houses on the far quay, the distant dome of the Panthéon and, from some angles, the Eiffel Tower. And above everything the huge expanse of Paris sky, which could have been painted by Sisley, and which is always changing: blue, white, pink, grey.

For those who prefer wooden benches and the shade, these are on the south side, under the plane trees. The view from here is more limited, but much of the Hôtel-Dieu is concealed by a double line of chestnuts; these are some of the first trees to come out in the springtime and they turn a beautiful colour in September. In summer the view may be obscured by a mass of scaffolding. A temporary theatre is often built on the Parvis for mystery plays, ballets and other spectacles, performed against the backcloth of the floodlit cathedral. This, of course, continues the mediæval tradition.

The Parvis has one more claim to our attention; it was the site of a battle. On 19 August 1944 the French police revolted. A thousand of them assembled in the courtyard of the Préfecture and sang the *Marseillaise*, a song not heard in France for four years. Then they sallied forth to fight. The Germans counter-attacked ferociously with tanks, field guns and armoured cars. The battle lasted for four days, with volunteers from the Hôtel-Dieu crawling out under fire to drag in the wounded. But with the Allied armies encircling Paris, the Germans were forced to withdraw, and the Tricolore was hoisted over the Préfecture and many other places. The police, who lost 280 men in the fight, found themselves (temporarily) the heroes of France. Bullet holes can still be seen on the buildings, the scars of honour.

Before taking a closer look at Notre-Dame or going inside, we would do well to walk round the cathedral or, even better, the island itself and get the feel of the place. From Point Zéro we cross the road and skirt Notre-Dame to the south, into a garden. This is a lovely place in the spring, the cherry trees in white blossom, the great rose window hanging above and, on the other side, the Seine with its barges. Moving on, we find that the garden widens into the Place Jean XXIII, where we can sit again, if we wish.

We are now at the east end of Notre-Dame and have one of its most beautiful (and most painted) views. It stands, or lies, as has been said, like a great ship becalmed in the flowing waters. The flying buttresses soar out of the chestnuts, which are white-flowering and, as they belong to the cathedral, have not as yet been pollarded. In summer the lime trees are in flower, and sitting there we can catch their sweet elusive scent. The children play on the swings, the tourists walk anxiously to and fro; it is a very Parisian place.

From the heights to the depths, from exaltation to degradation, is a matter of seconds, of inches. We cross the road into another small gravelly garden, the 'stern' or east end of the island. And there we have the **Mémorial de la Déportation**, beside the Passerelle Bridge.

Underground (like so many other things on Ile de la Cité), suitably on the site of the one-time morgue, it is a worthy and much visited monument to the two hundred thousand Frenchmen who died in the Nazi camps. The Unknown Victim lies in state, but otherwise everything is understated. The surroundings are simply cells, prison bars and chains; on the walls just the names of the camps (so many!) and the phrase *'Pardonne mais n'oublie pas'*. We, like others, emerge deeply moved.

Continuing to circle Notre-Dame, we are now on Rue du Cloître Notre-Dame. On the left is the cathedral, on the right a line of cafés and souvenir shops and the small Museum of Notre-Dame. This is the part of the island which Haussmann left untouched, and unfortunately much of it has been redeveloped piecemeal during the last century – note the fire station and the police motorcycle garage. We turn off, therefore, into Rue Chanoinesse and pause before the door of no. 10. A plaque tells us that a comic singer lived there in the last century, but that is not why we are there. The site was the temporary home of Héloïse and Abelard – a plaque commemorating them is on the other (river) side of the house.

Peter Abelard (1079–1142) is a fashionable figure nowadays, the prototype of the with-it clergyman; not that he was ever a priest. In his private life he practised extreme permissiveness; 'I feared no refusal from whatever woman I might deem worthy of my love,' he wrote. In public he preached against the Establishment, embodied in the person of St Bernard, abbot of Clairvaux.

In an age of faith and certainty Abelard was a questioner. Although not an atheist, doubt was his *point de départ*. In particular he had no use for abstractions, for certain types of thought and words, derived from Plato, which were then accepted.

For instance, Paris was (and still is) inhabited by thousands of dogs. But, if we take Abelard's view, they are all just separate animals; the idea of 'dogginess' as such is simply a name, without any reality of its own. As Abelard put it, it is a *nomen* and can be a *vox* (bow-wow!) but can never be a *res* or real thing. (For more about Abelard's thinking, see pp. 220–221.)

This down-to-earth type of thought, with its threads back to Aristotle, both undermined and renewed the scholastic Church. Abelard had a profound and long-lasting effect, both on philosophy and on Paris. He was one of the founders of the University of Paris which was at first orthodox enough, but later, permeated with his and parallel ideas, became the great Temple of Doubt, which it remains. When Abelard was finally forced to leave the precincts of Notre-Dame, he moved several times, finally ending up on the Left Bank. His followers went with him and the Left Bank was established as the intellectual centre of Paris and of France, which it still is.

But, standing before no. 10 Rue Chanoinesse, we tend to think more about his private than his academic life. The house (1849) is of no interest in itself. It must have looked very different in 1118 when Canon Fulbert of Notre-Dame lived there with his niece, Héloïse (probably 'niece' was a euphemism for 'daughter'). He was, it is said, pleased when the famous teacher of theology came to tutor his niece and encouraged Abelard, who was then thirty-nine. Héloïse was a pretty seventeen-year-old and it is uncertain how interested she was in the problem of *nomen* and *res*. Abelard wrote later: 'The lesson-times were spent in hidden places chosen by our love. We dealt more in kisses than words'.

The story of Héloïse and Abelard never seems to die, an ill-fated love that was doomed from the start. Héloïse became pregnant and was sent away by Abelard to Brittany, where she bore him a son, whom she named, curiously, Astrolabe (an instrument used in astronomy). This suggests unperceived depths in Héloïse or, possibly, that Abelard's teaching was indeed unorthodox. She abandoned her baby and returned to Paris. At her uncle's instigation, she married Abelard in a ceremony which she insisted must be kept secret, to protect her husband's future career in the Church. This, however, was not enough for Abelard or, in the opposite sense, for the canon. Abelard sent her away to a convent, the first of many, where she dutifully took her vows, and he then went on a long carouse through the taverns of the city in search of women and wine. This was too much for the canon, who organized his famous revenge. Two thugs came to Abelard's bedroom at night and 'their knives separated me from those members of my body which were guilty of the error they resented'.

Abelard survived the attack, but vengeance was swift. The two thugs were caught, castrated and blinded; the canon was deprived of his home, his position and his possessions. But Abelard was very sorry for himself. Since he was mutilated, he could no longer consider entering the Church. St Bernard taunted him cruelly with no longer being a man 'and Peter is a man's name'. He died aged sixty-three, soon after hearing that his latest book, a treatise on logic, was to be burnt by order of the Lateran Council. Héloïse, twenty-two years younger, outlived him by many years, becoming an abbess, dying in 1164. Their bodies, after many removals, now lie together in Père Lachaise cemetery.

Other personalities, perhaps less colourful, have been associated with the street and the area, among them the American writer Ludwig Bemelmans and the Aga Khan. The street has been too much rebuilt in the last century to be attractive but we catch occasional glimpses of Notre-Dame through the side streets and the sound of bells can be heard everywhere; the deep one, the only one to survive the Revolution, is called Emmanuel. The most pleasant building is no. 24, in fact several houses with an old coaching entrance, now the restaurant *La Lieutenance*. It was an old *hôtel* of the canons, sixteenth century, but much altered since.

Turning right, we are in Rue de la Colombe, a much prettier street than Rue Chanoinesse. Many old houses, or parts of them, still survive. In particular we should look at no. 5, a private house. Under it, in the cellar, is the old chapel of St Aignan. Mass was celebrated there secretly during the Revolution, but it was obviously a place of hidden worship long before that. Little remains except rounded arches, columns with acanthus leaves on their capitals, a graceful plaque of the Madonna, a dignified head of the saint. It still has an atmosphere of secret religion and long-forgotten mysteries. Holy wells are usually very much a part of such places, and the well here is in *La Lieutenance*, a few yards away.

At the end of the street are flights of steps, leading to the quay and the river, a reminder of the changing height of the island. We walk along the Seine past the Hôtel-Dieu. The hospital was founded in AD 651 by St Landry, Bishop of Paris, who sheltered the sick in part of his palace. The name might be translated as 'God's hostel'.

We turn back into the flower market, to Metro Cité. This is the moment to take a brief glimpse inside the Préfecture de Police. The immediate reaction is, how few police! What you are more likely to see are thousands of ladies in mauve overalls, carrying files. No matter which entrance you choose, there they are, harassed but usually polite. There are also several thousand foreigners, mainly Algerian, waiting for work or residence permits, usually polite too. But the experience is Kafka-esque. Anyone, for instance a foreigner resident in France, who has business there, must have calm, patience, a good book and an ability to read standing up; a sharp eye for queue-jumpers is also useful. Reorganization to diminish queueing is regularly undertaken, but never succeeds.

Emerging, we pause on the pavement in front of Metro Cité, and turn left. There, before us, are the gilded gates and great staircase of the **Palais de Justice.** This is the ancient seat of authority in Paris and France. It was the palace of the Roman prefects, of King Clovis and his Frankish followers, of Hugues Capet and the Capetian kings, of St Louis and Philip the Fair. From Roman to Valois times it was the government centre of Paris, until King Charles V in 1358, following the bloody uprising of Etienne Marcel, moved the court to the Marais and then to the Louvre. Justice, however, remained.

The gilded gates are seldom open; justice is free for all-comers, but getting in means another check by the police. We enter and climb the stairs where St Louis administered palm-tree justice (not the same staircase, of course; little of his palace survived Haussmann). At the top we are in a world of vast marble corridors. Advocates in robes and bands (but not wigs) walk to and fro talking to each other or to their clients, sometimes perching on the pedestal or toe of a statue. We are free to enter any of the court-rooms and listen to the proceedings. The civil courts can be rather dull, a long mumbling of wills or leases. The criminal courts (*chambres correctionnelles*) are usually more dramatic, but even here, it seems, much of the traditional rhetoric has gone out of French legal pleading in modern times.

The most beautiful and one of the best-known pictures of St Louis's palace is in the fifteenth-century Book of Hours (*Les Très Riches Heures du Duc de Berry*). The originals are in the museum at Chantilly, but have been reproduced many times in art books and calendars. The picture illustrates 'June', and the palace is seen from the Left Bank, from Hôtel de Nesle, the Duc de Berry's town house, now the site of the Bibliothèque Mazarine. In the foreground are peasants haymaking. Beyond the Seine the towers and walls of the palace are clearly seen against the blue sky, and can be easily identified. The whole complex of buildings is dominated by that soaring masterpiece, the Sainte-Chapelle. Alas, it no longer dominates the present Palais de Justice.

Nowadays the towers of St Louis are best seen from the north bank of the island or from across the river. The easternmost tower, square-built, is the Tour de l'Horloge, which dates from the fourteenth century and has a clock of the same date which is claimed to be the oldest public clock in the world. Much restored and redecorated, it still keeps remarkably good time; it has a rather cryptic Latin quotation about time and justice. The next two towers, steepled, form the entrance to the Conciergerie, but the last one, the Tour Bonbec, is not open to the public. Thought to be a torture chamber, the name means 'babbling', which anyone might do under duress.

We have, however, come to the Palais de Justice to see its most famous monument, the **Sainte-Chapelle.** We enter next to the main gates (survivors of the eighteenth century) but do not climb the stairs. We follow the signs through a tunnel, round the chapel to the west end and enter the vaulted lower chapel, gaudily painted in pseudo-mediæval colours. This was where the servants worshipped. We climb a narrow winding stair, and at the top the great glory awaits us.

It is dazzling and must look today much as it did on the day it was finished in 1248. A church built entirely of stained glass! Henry III of England was overwhelmed by it. Even on a cloudy day it is like being inside a huge jewel. The very idea of such a building was new – churches had often been used as fortresses, but how to defend a glass shrine? How to keep the roof up without any supporting walls? The achievement of the architect, Pierre de Montereau, was immense and, seven hundred difficult years later, the slender buttresses show no cracks, the chapel no sign of collapsing. Immense too was the cost, eight hundred thousand *livres d'or*, and we cannot think that St Louis grudged a penny of it.

There are fifteen hundred square yards of stained glass in the chapel, all of it (except for the later rose window) predominantly in red and blue. But there are so many shades of red and blue, carefully and harmoniously blended, that there is no monotony. The windows are a series of Bible scenes, a vast illustrated Bible, like the illuminated manuscripts. We can, if we wish, follow it round, up and down, scene to scene, window to window. We may notice the emphasis on kings and law-givers, for instance St Louis himself receiving the Holy Relics, on the immediate right as we enter, or Solomon on his throne, second window from right. This suits the chapel's theme of the Crown – it is possible to see the building itself as shaped like a mediæval crown. Most of the subjects are from the Old Testament, but the life of the Virgin, Christ's Passion and John the Baptist can be seen at the far end.

If we wish to study the scenes in full detail, we may get books and charts at the desk, or join a guided tour. But to concentrate only on detail is to miss the great design.

All art students learning stained-glass design in Paris are taught, of course, to find first their *point de départ*. This, which is usually dictated partly by the architect or stonemason, is made by the black interstices, the shape like black lace, the *dentelle*. Only after this has been designed can the glass be planned. Standing in front of one of these windows, our eyes and minds closed to the Bible scenes, we can see the *dentelle,* the shape and construction of the window. Every one is different, but all are carefully harmonized. And then we step back and let the whole mediæval, mystical glory overcome us as it overcame the kings of France and England.

The west rose window was added over a hundred years later. Like many windows facing the sunset, it shows the Apocalypse. But it is very different in mood from the other windows. The lines of the *dentelle* are curly, not straight; the main colours are not red and blue, but green and yellow. It does not fit very comfortably with the rest of the chapel. Yet it is a masterpiece in its own right and shows very clearly in the scene from the Book of Hours as the dominant feature of the chapel.

St Louis built the Sainte-Chapelle to be a worthy shrine for the Crown of Thorns, which he had acquired on his first crusade. In fact, he bought the Crown, for an enormous sum, from the Venetians, to whom Baldwin of Constantinople had pledged it as security for a loan. Later Baldwin sold St Louis directly a fragment of the True Cross and some more questionable relics, such as a feather from the wing of the Archangel Gabriel. These he adored in Notre-Dame, but the Crown of Thorns was apart and required special veneration.

The twelve statues of the apostles against the pillars have great quality. Six of them are originals and one is thought to be a portrait of St Louis. Others, unfortunately, have been removed to the Mediæval Museum at Cluny.

St Louis (King Louis IX, 1214–70) has indeed left his mark on Ile de la Cité, on France and on continents of which he was unaware. His austere life was dominated by two principles: one was Christian piety, which he doubtless learned from his mother, Blanche of Castile; the other was the ideal of kingship (what would Abelard have said!). St Louis has been called the embodiment of this mediæval ideal. To him, it meant not only to wear a crown, to reign, to rule, but to make peace everywhere and to dispense justice fairly. His principle in justice was a determination that every man should have his due. Coupled with this was an idea that, until the truth could be ascertained, the poorer man should be preferred – an arguable point, and startling indeed in feudal times.

In international affairs his principle was to make peace, imposing it, if necessary, by force. He succeeded in this in France, in Flanders and in Catalonia. In England he arbitrated between King Henry III and Simon de Montfort and his parliament, giving judgment, naturally, for the king. As a king, he was a man of peace. What is paradoxical is that his other principle, piety, required him to bring war to the Middle East. Most of his time, his treasure, and finally his life were devoted to his two crusades.

But we must return to the Sainte-Chapelle, where the original services were splendid affairs, conducted by twelve canons and many chaplains. The king himself mounted a special stair to show the Crown to the faithful. Gradually things changed. A later king, Louis Xl, a more secretive monarch but, all the same, the man who put France together, had a side oratory built where he could observe mass without being seen. In the seventeenth century the Couperins played the organ. Even before the Revolution it had become a storehouse for flour. It was planned to demolish it, but it was found to be a convenient storehouse for legal files. Much of the glass was damaged.

Restoration began in the nineteenth century under Haussmann and his architect Viollet-le-Duc. The glass was painstakingly repaired by Steinheil (a friend of Balzac and Baudelaire) so that now it is difficult for us to tell the recent from the original. But secularization continued. In the present century the chapel was cleared, the relics being taken to Notre-Dame (the Crown of Thorns can be seen there on Good Friday), the altar, the organ and the furniture being removed. The chapel is now used for choral and orchestral concerts and mediæval music is often performed. The windows are floodlit from the outside and the sense of being inside a luminous jewel is intense. St Louis would have been amazed.

Only one Mass a year is now said, in May, for the feast-day of St Ivo (or Yves), a bishop of Chartres and an expert on canon law, the patron saint of lawyers. Admission is by invitation only.

Forty years later another king made his mark on the palace. Philip the Fair was far from being another St Louis. Indeed, he spent seven years of his reign quarrelling with the Pope (the same Pope, Boniface VIII, who canonized St Louis). The difficulty was over authority. The Pope claimed complete authority, temporal as well as spiritual, over all creatures on earth. The king retaliated by blocking the transport of all gold and valuables to Rome and attempting to bring the Pope to trial. The Pope replied by preparing a papal bull excommunicating the king, but was forestalled by the king sending a commando under the Chevalier de Nogaret to arrest and imprison the Pope. The Pope was released by Italian troops after a few days, but the shock was too much for him and he died a month later. His successor, Clement V, was more co-operative and King Philip was free to continue his own ambitions. These were to create the most sumptuous royal apartments yet seen in France (his Sainte-Chapelle!) and to destroy the Templars.

He did not care for St Louis's bleak apartments, and it must have been agreeable to look out of his windows at the Templars being burnt at the stake, and reflect that it was their wealth which was financing his palace. However, the Grand Master, Jacques de Molay, called out from the stake, summoning the king, the Pope and the Chevalier de Nogaret to appear before the throne of God within the year to answer for their misdeeds. Their deaths duly happened on time; and history's verdict is that the Templars were largely blameless of the crimes of which they were accused.

The sumptuous apartments are no longer sumptuous; they are part of the Palais de Justice. The Great Hall is the so-called Salle des Pas-perdus. But below it is the **Conciergerie**, 1 Boulevard du Palais (Metro Cité) and, in particular, the Salle des Gens d'Armes, where the guards and servants of the royal household lived. It is a vast and splendid Gothic room, about 20,000 square feet, supported by three lines of Gothic pillars. Adjoining it are the kitchens, with four great corner ovens which could serve up to three thousand people in the Salle and upstairs (a winding stair) in the Great Hall. At the west end of the Salle, separated by a grille, is a passage called Rue de Paris, so-called because the public executioner, known anonymously as Monsieur de Paris, had his rooms adjoining.

The Conciergerie was originally the dungeon of the palace. Many well-known prisoners spent a brief time there, and gradually they took the place over. Even by the standards of mediæval prisons the vileness and filth were notorious. Twice it was swept by plague and had to be cleared and cleansed. But its most famous time was during the Revolution, when it was filled to overflowing. The main activity, however, was in Rue de Paris, and beyond it in the Salle des Prisonniers. This was always full, not only with aristocrats, but with soldiers, gaolers and lawyers.

On the left, leading off it, is the small room where the condemned had their final preparation – neck-cloths removed, hair cut and hands tied behind the back. From here they went through the dreary little courtyard, the Cour des Femmes, out through the main gates of the palace, twelve at a time, into the street, where the jeering public and the *tricoteuses* awaited them and the tumbrils took them to the guillotine. Nearby is a small cell where Queen Marie Antoinette was held for a time after the execution of her husband, Louis XVI. But after a rash escapade to rescue her through a door from the palace, she was moved to another cell, equally small but more secure, at the other end of the Salle des Prisonniers. In these barbarous conditions she existed from August to October 1793 (she was executed on 16 October – 'the Capet woman' or 'widow', as she was contemptuously called).

Next door is another tiny cell, occupied in turn, it is said, by Danton and Robespierre. Beyond is a chapel, which was turned into a prison for the twenty-two Girondins, who were moderate reformists and were guillotined in 1793. The prison has now been turned into a kind of shrine for Marie Antoinette – an altar, her crucifix, a letter trying to make provision for her children, and – grim reminders – a cell door and a guillotine blade (rather blunt!). These solemn relics seem pathetically unsuited to the Austrian queen's real character, frivolous, bewildered and sad.

The Public Prosecutor, Fouquier-Tinville, had his offices in the twin towers above the entrance to the Conciergerie; this was indeed convenient for the Tribunal next door. In due course he was led down to the Conciergerie, protesting volubly, and onwards to the tumbrils. He was followed by the members of his Tribunal, judges, juries and lawyers. It was 1794 and the Terror was over.

The Conciergerie can be hired for private parties and so may be closed to the public without notice. Some of these parties are held by wine-growers for their retailers and café-proprietors to taste (*déguster*) the new wine of the year, in particular Beaujolais Nouveau. If we can arrange an invitation, we should certainly go. The great hall is full of barrels of wine, from which we help ourselves liberally; there are trestle tables piled with plates of cheese (including a rarity, blue Camembert), pâtés, sausages and bread. The throng, mostly male, talks about the new wine and café trade in particular. In our conversation we should hint that we are *courtiers-gourmets* (which means middlemen in the wine and food trade, and not what might be expected). Many candles light up the hall, the atmosphere is convivial, the wine flows but nothing can overcome the macabre feeling of past horrors. Even after many glasses, the Terror still has us in its grip.

Emerging into the street, where no tumbrils await us, we walk along the quai and turn into the little funnel-shaped Place Dauphine. The east end is dominated by the Palais de Justice, but the rest includes a number of old houses, many of them restored. There are several restaurants, art galleries and many parked cars. We emerge through the narrow end of the funnel between two beautiful houses (seventeenth century, but well restored) of brick and stone. These are the houses which André Maurois thought about every night during his wartime exile in England; to him they embodied Paris and France.

Beyond is Pont Neuf, and there facing us in the middle of his bridge rides Henricus Magnus, Henry of Navarre, the Vert Galant, Henri IV of France. But he requires more space than is available in this first chapter. And so does his beautiful bridge, the oldest in Paris despite its name.

Beyond Pont Neuf we reach the tip of the island, the bows, so to speak, of the Paris ship. We descend stairs to a little park, the Square du Vert Galant. (Vert Galant means 'gay old dog' or Merry Monarch, a reference to the many mistresses and illegitimate children of this popular king; the 'square' is in fact a triangle.) It is the only part of the island at river level, a quiet place full of worn cobblestones and chestnuts and dappled light from the river all round us. (It is sometimes under water in the spring.) It is a favourite area for young loving couples and the Vert Galant himself would have approved strongly.

Unable to go any farther, we return along one or other of the quais, in search, probably, of refreshment. There are two groups of cafés on the island: one lot, in the Boulevard du Palais, between the Palais de Justice and the Préfecture de Police, is where clerks and secretaries take their midday meals or snacks. The other group is, naturally, near Notre-Dame, either in Rue du Cloître Notre-Dame or in Rue d'Arcole which meets it at right-angles. Cameras rather than briefcases are the impedimenta here and the cafés provide souvenirs, drinks and snacks.

A word of warning is required about all these cafés. Ile de la Cité is almost uninhabited. Tourists and clerks depart, and at night it is virtually a desert island. All the cafés without exception close at about eight o'clock, which can be dispiriting for those who come to see Notre-Dame floodlit. The restaurants, however, remain open for dinner, unless they are closed on Monday or for the summer holidays.

And now it is time to take a closer look at Notre-Dame itself. We must hope that it is a fine day, with the afternoon sun blazing on the rose windows.

2

Notre-Dame

THE FOUNDATION STONE of the Cathedral of **Notre-Dame-de-Paris** was laid in 1163 by the Pope (Alexander III) and it was finished about 1345. The site architects were Pierre de Montereau (who built the Sainte-Chapelle) and Jean de Chelles and doubtless many others; much of the labour was done by enthusiastic volunteers. But, in the end, it looked very like the original sketches of Bishop Maurice de Sully in 1159, and as it looks today.

There were, however, certain conspicuous though temporary differences. The statues on the west and north portals were painted in brilliant mediæval colours: blue, scarlet, green and yellow, all against a background of gold. The cathedral glowed with colour. Inside, instead of the present reverent hush, was a combination of a bazaar and a hostel for the homeless. Here was the whole cavalcade of mediæval life: merchants calling from their stalls to the passers-by, travellers from overseas showing or selling their souvenirs, crusaders taking their vows and fugitives in search of sanctuary. At one period there was also St Louis, who did not at all object to the hubbub of the people, adoring his relics.

But the French tired of Gothic in the Renaissance. First Mansart and then Soufflot were put in to modernize the building. The tombs, statues, some of the stained glass, choir stalls, rood screen and even the high altar were removed and replaced by some mock-classical statues of the Virtues. The colour was removed, the portals and the inside were whitewashed and the idea was to make the building look as much like a classical temple as possible. Then came the Revolution and its period as the Temple of Reason, after which it fell into decay.

Robespierre in 1793, finding that Revolution and Reason were not enough, pronounced his doctrine of the Supreme Being. As he was guillotined soon afterwards, he had no time to explain exactly what he meant; whether the Supreme Being was an Immortal, a great leader, or even possibly himself. But the great leader was already there, waiting in the wings for his cue. When General Bonaparte became the Emperor Napoleon, it was natural for him to wish to be crowned in Notre-Dame.

After Napoleon's fall, the cathedral again fell fast into decay. The whole once-great building was sold to a demolition contractor. That it was ever saved and restored was largely due to one man – Victor Hugo, a professed atheist, though pantheist would seem to describe his faith more exactly. His long novel *Notre-Dame-de-Paris* (*The Hunchback of Notre-Dame*) aroused popular feeling about the derelict masterpiece in their midst. Napoleon III and Haussmann felt justified in the large effort and expenditure involved in restoring it. Viollet-le-Duc, an expert restorer was given the job, and in general it is felt that he overdid it. In every century, and particularly the nineteenth, there are those who prefer a building to be in ruins. In fact Viollet-le-Duc made Notre-Dame look very much as it does in the mediæval engravings. Apart from much-needed repairs, he replaced the missing statues and glass and he added very little of his own.

We should look carefully at the **west front.** At the rose window level are statues of Adam and Eve and, between them, in front of the huge window, the redeeming Virgin and Child. On the next level, above the graceful columns, is a veritable carved zoo of monsters, gryphons and demons, but these can only be seen by the tower-climbers. They are, in fact, nineteenth century, the idea of Viollet-le-Duc.

It is the **three main portals** which should claim our closest attention. Even without the intended colours they remain master-pieces of mediæval sculpture. The central portal shows the Last Judgment. The tympanum above the doors shows the Resurrection and the Weighing of Souls, with Christ in Majesty, the Virgin and St John, at the apex. The statues in the embrasures are mostly recent, the originals (like the kings of Israel and Judah higher up) having been destroyed in 1871 by the Communards, who took them mistakenly for the kings of France. The left portal is dedicated to the Virgin. The tympanum, virtually unchanged for centuries, is a glory of mediæval art, full of flowers, fruit, angels, prophets and, by way of a change, the signs of the zodiac. The right portal is dedicated to St Anne, the mother of the Virgin. There in the congregation of Heaven, we can see St Marcel killing the dragon, Bishop de Sully (standing) and King Louis VII (kneeling) consecrating the cathedral.

In Rue du Cloître Notre-Dame we have another way of entering the cathedral, **the cloister portal.** This was built about 1250 by Jean de Chelles and is another major example of thirteenth-century sculpture. Later in date than the west portals, it is more elaborate and decorated with more detail, designed to harmonize with the rose window above. The tympanum illustrates the life of the Virgin together with scenes from a mystery play. In the centre is a fine thirteenth-century Virgin, a gentle Lady – though it is sad that her Child was lost during the Revolution.

The equivalent portal on the south side is equally elaborate in design, and illustrates the life and death of St Stephen. We can, however, only see it from a distance, because of the sacristy railings.

On the north side, also, is the **Porte Rouge,** now closed, but once the private entrance of the canons. The tympanum shows the coronation of the Virgin by her Son, assisted by St Louis and Marguerite de Provence.

We must now enter Notre-Dame through one of the portal doors and immediately we are struck by the beauty and the size of the soaring **nave**. It is in fact not the longest mediæval cathedral or abbey (Winchester) nor the tallest (Beauvais), but it can hold a congregation or a concert audience of about nine thousand. What impress us, however, are its beautiful proportions, its grace and lightness.

We can be grateful again that it was spared in some later ordeals. In May 1871 the Communards, fashionable revolutionaries of the moment, vowed to destroy all Paris in two hours. They piled the chairs in the centre aisle, poured on petrol and set fire. Fortunately for us, one of them had second thoughts and returned to put out the fire. Notre-Dame also survived the Liberation and Hitler's order to burn it down, together with much else. On 26 August 1944 the famous Liberation *Te Deum* was held there, with bullets whizzing about the nave and the tall figure of General de Gaulle refusing, typically, to duck. Much may be still to come, but at the moment what we find there is peace and beauty.

We walk up one of the side aisles to the transepts, where we can see the **rose windows.** The south one, of course, gets the sunlight. It has been much restored and portrays Christ surrounded by saints and angels. These details are not discernible from floor level and we are left to admire the shape, size and colours of the much-photographed window. The colours are mainly blue and red, as in the Sainte-Chapelle, and they blend into a many-toned purple. Another good time to see the window is at dusk, *l'heure bleue,* when the reds fade and we are left with a huge round-cut sapphire glowing in the twilight.

The north rose window, which never catches the sun, has been almost undamaged and unrestored since the thirteenth century. Said to be the personal gift of St Louis to the cathedral, it is also said to show the Virgin surrounded by personalities from the Old Testament. To me it is even more beautiful than the south window, a study in blues of many different shades, the whole being more cobalt than ultramarine.

The windows of the nave at ground level need not detain us, but we should look carefully at the windows in the triforia and clerestories (one and two storeys up) in the nave and transepts. These are modern, the work of Le Chevallier. One can appreciate his problems, his difficult *point de départ*. Both the shapes of his windows and the general colour scale were unalterable. His designs are purely abstract, but he used mediæval colours and techniques, and the result is admirable. We should note particularly the blue window in the triforium of the north transept, a good example of modern glass. All these windows are visible from ground level.

Beside the central altar, at the chancel steps, are two statues, one of St Denis, the other (spotlit) a lovely Virgin and Child, Notre-Dame-de-Paris. This dates from the thirteenth century and was for many centuries in the nearby chapel of St Aignan, which is why it has survived. It shows a young, happy Madonna. There are three other Virgins in Notre-Dame, one on the high altar, and the other two either side of the entrance, surrounded by the lighted candles of the faithful. But – a curious thing for a Christian church – there is no conspicuous Crucifix or Cross. We are reminded again to venerate the Lady to whom the cathedral is consecrated.

Napoleon's coronation took place in front of the high altar on 2 December 1804. The occasion was unusual in many ways. French kings had normally been crowned in Reims Cathedral: coronations in Notre-Dame had been few, only Henry VI of England in 1430, and Mary Queen of Scots as Queen Consort to François II. Napoleon found the cathedral almost in ruins, but it was magnificently decked out with tapestries for the great occasion. The Pope was summoned from Rome to perform the crowning, but at the last moment the emperor decided that the Pope was unworthy of the honour, and he seized the crown and crowned himself, and then his empress Josephine, leaving the Pope with nothing to do. The whole scene has been vigorously portrayed by David in his huge painting which we can see when we go to the Louvre.

24

On the pillar immediately to the west of Notre-Dame-de-Paris is a plaque, in English and French, commemorating the million British and Commonwealth dead from the First World War, who are mostly buried in France. On 11 November every year the Royal British Legion holds a service in their memory, complete with the Last Post. Once, the veteran trumpeter sounding this call dropped dead in the middle – a newsworthy item for the French and, doubtless, how he might have wished to die.

The ambulatory, behind the high altar, has memorials to various bishops of Paris. On the south side is the entry to the **Treasury** (entrance fee required). Apart from an illuminated manuscript, some pieces from the eighteenth century (later gifts) and a grandfather clock, the treasure is mainly nineteenth century, chalices and platters. Gold, however, always attracts a sizeable crowd.

From the central altar we can look backwards, along the nave, to the west rose window. Unfortunately the lower half is blocked from view by the **organ.** This is a beautiful piece of sculpture, the masterpiece of France's best organ-builder, Aristide Cavaillé-Col (d. 1899), who built many of France's organs. One could wish that he could have found a different position for his great work but it is a marvellous organ, France's biggest, with over six thousand pipes, and it makes a great and very varied sound.

France has produced and attracted many great organists, and Paris has drawn organ students from everywhere, studying at the Conservatoire, playing publicly whenever they can and hoping to follow in the footsteps of the Couperins, César Franck, Widor, Schweitzer, Marchal, Dupré, Messiaen, and Cochereau. Improvising at the organ goes back to Bach and beyond, but it was Charles-Marie Widor (d. 1937, composer of the well-known Toccata) who transformed it into the complex art-form which it now is, rather a French speciality. Improvisation is very much a part of the French character and way of life. Anyone who has heard the late Pierre Cochereau in Notre-Dame improvising *aux grandes orgues,* creating an elaborate suite containing, probably, a fugue and a resounding climax, will not soon forget it. It was an experience made all the more poignant, for the large hushed audience, because the music was temporary, lost for ever in the air even as it was being played.

Even more memorable is one of the great services in Notre-Dame, for instance the Easter Eve vigil. The windows are dark but the cathedral is lit, mainly by thousands of lighted candles carried by the congregation. The choir peal out their alleluias, the organ sounds in triumph, and we are reminded that Notre-Dame is not only an art museum and a concert hall, but a place of worship, as it has been for thousands of years.

Those who are more interested in the architecture than the Easter vigil will, of course, visit Notre-Dame in daylight, although many bus-loads come at night for the floodlighting alone. Parisians may say, with local pride, that Gothic architecture originated at Notre-Dame. But in fact the style developed gradually, in several places at once. In England, Gothic was evolved locally from the Norman tradition, but there were some major exceptions such as Westminster Abbey; when French bishops were appointed, they brought French ideas with them. Italy too produced an indigenous Gothic, retaining the wooden roofs of the old basilicas, except in parts of the North, where French influence can be seen, for example in Milan, imitating Bourges.

The much higher buildings, characteristic of Gothic in the 'Anglo-Norman area' where it took hold, and which became almost an obsession in France, were made possible by the development of the ribbed vault. Previous barrel or groin vaults could not hold up such high naves and choirs. The ribbed vault was based on joining arches, which provided a framework, to be filled in later. It has been likened to an umbrella frame, but it is possible to see it as a palm-tree shape. At all events, the use of pointed arches, which was introduced with it, is thought to have been brought back from Syria or Palestine by returning Crusaders. The ribbed vault first appeared in Lombardy, Normandy and Durham, all at about the same time; the earliest survivor is in Durham (1093).

In France, transition from Romanesque to Gothic was gradual. The first cathedral classed as truly Gothic (although still transitional) was Abbot Suger's at Saint-Denis (1135–40). Chartres came next, but that building was burnt down in 1194 and replaced. Several others followed, all together, but Notre-Dame-de-Paris was the first to develop fully the ideas which were to dominate Gothic architecture in France, and spread to Belgium and Germany. In particular Notre-Dame perfected flying buttresses, here seen at their best, and its other glories are the rose windows and the *chevet* – the forest of stone at the east end. In these, Parisian pride is justified and Notre-Dame was a pioneer of the great period of church-building in France. This only lasted until the fourteenth century, when the Hundred Years' War brought it to an end. When building resumed in the fifteenth century, it was in the 'Flamboyant' style, which many think exaggerated and less successful.

Superimposed on the original Gothic, Notre-Dame has, of course, the work of restoration by Eugène-Emmanuel **Viollet-le-Duc** (1814–79), architect and writer. He also restored many other cathedrals, abbey-churches and churches throughout France, notably Amiens, Vézelay and Saint-Denis, and the walls of the old town at Carcassonne. His books about architecture include the ten-volume *Dictionnaire de l'Architecture française du XIe au XVIe Siècle.* In 1863 he was made Professor of Artistic and Aesthetic History at the Ecole des Beaux-Arts.

Viollet-le-Duc was a specialist in Gothic architecture and one of the figures in the 'Gothic Revival'. He claimed that integration of form and structure was the chief virtue of the style. He also propounded the dubious theory that an analytical study of the past, combined with the application of constructive principles to modern building materials, can create a new contemporary style, a theory which inspired Auguste Perret to build his pseudo-classical façades in reinforced concrete. Viollet-le-Duc is also credited with having influenced many later architects, including Gaudí and Frank Lloyd Wright – temporarily, one must think. His work and ideas have not been generally admired for some time now, but enthusiasts for Victorian Gothic have seen new virtues in him.

Viollet-le-Duc at Notre-Dame also introduced the popular gargoyles, of which replicas and photographs can be found in all the souvenir shops. Less forgivably, he added the sixteen green copper statues which surround the base of the central spire – apostles and evangelists, among whom he included himself. The spire rises to nearly three hundred feet and tapers more gracefully than it does in mediæval engravings, where it seems more of a sharpened pencil stood on end. Sometimes at night intrepid revolutionaries climb the spire – an airy experience, indeed! – to hoist the flag of their particular cause at the masthead, above the crow's nest. They are followed the next morning by equally intrepid policemen or alpinists, removing the offending emblem. On one occasion a fireman was lowered from a helicopter to remove the flag of North Vietnam, to the entertainment of thousands of spectators.

For those who wish to see the view legally, the way is up the towers (entrance outside the **north tower** in Rue du Cloître Notre-Dame). It is a long climb. We traverse the front of the cathedral and finally emerge on to the roof of the south tower, surrounded by a wonderful roofscape of towers, belfries, gargoyles and the spire. We also have a great view of the Seine and most of Paris.

3

Ile Saint-Louis

ILE SAINT-LOUIS (4me) is the second of the two Paris islands, the smaller; the dinghy, it is sometimes said, towed behind the ship of the line. If we are on Ile de la Cité, we simply walk across Pont Saint-Louis. Or else we can go to Metro Pont Marie and walk across the beautiful bridge of the same name. The two islands are in great contrast: one an almost uninhabited ancient centre of religion and administration; the other a secluded and compact island village, dating back only to the seventeenth century. And although about six thousand people live there, it is still a village in spirit, where everyone knows everyone and neighbours greet each other daily in the shops and cafés.

An island in the heart of Paris! The thought is still scarcely believable, and so romantic. It is not possible to leave it without crossing water by a bridge, and it is this which has kept Ile Saint-Louis a little different from the rest of Paris during its three centuries of existence. There used to be plenty of Louisiens who prided themselves on never having been to the 'mainland'. They were usually very small, with mediæval names like Basseporte or Crèvecœur, and they seemed to spend much of their time on games of skill. Even fifty years ago there were at least four cafés with billiard tables for the customers, and one with chess facilities.

Things have changed a little since then, since the island was 'rediscovered'. The Louisiens have grown taller and have acquired a taste for travel, going to the mainland to work or to shop – prices in the markets of Place Maubert or Rue Saint-Antoine are noticeably lower. Strangers (like the present writer) have moved in, the billiard tables and chess sets have given way to candlelit restaurant tables; Crèvecœur and Basseporte have gone. But the atmosphere of a secluded island still remains, with its narrow streets and old houses, and even relative newcomers have a feeling of 'belonging', of being members of a special community, rare nowadays in a great city.

One of the remaining glories of the island is its **river quays.** At a time when so many of the famous quays of the Seine were given over to motorways, including the whole of the Right Bank, Ile Saint-Louis still retained its charm and it is possible to walk almost round the island at river level. We descend from the upper level by one of the many flights of stairs and immediately we are on cobbles, away from the traffic, a few inches from the Seine (which in spring sometimes floods the lower quays). Here we find loving couples kissing, fishermen, sunbathers, students reading Bergson or Lévi-Strauss, *clochards** (the old-established tramps of Paris) sleeping under the bridges, families picnicking, and hundreds of poplars, replanted during the 1990s. From time to time we may also find a fishing competition or film-makers shooting a film on location or models posing for the fashion magazines, their clothes always six months ahead of the weather. And beside us the Seine with its unceasing procession of barges and *bateaux-mouches;* around us the dappled light from the trees and the river.

Ile Saint-Louis is delightful at any time of day or year. But one can single out one or two highlights: a hot June afternoon, ourselves eating ice-cream, and the whole island in a cloud of cottonseed from the poplars, a pleasure to those who identify it with summer and the approaching holidays, a misery to those afflicted with carpet-brushing or sneezing; or a misty autumn morning with the river scarcely visible, and the sun coming through in a pearly light, gradually revealing the Seine and, beyond, the towers, spires and domes; a wet night, with the cafés and restaurants glowing with light and life; or indeed night at any time, with the lights from the mainland shimmering across the water – in their path the Seine always seems to be fizzing like champagne. An island in the centre of Paris! Balzac said that the place made him feel uneasy. But he came often, just the same.

The island was originally two (a third was incorporated into the Right Bank to form Quai Henri IV); Ile Notre-Dame with Ile des Vaches upstream, the divide coming at what is now Rue Poulletier. They were uninhabited and frequently flooded, but people came to them for occasional fairs or duels. St Louis visited them on occasion and a temporary oratory was erected for his frequent devotions. The islands belonged to the canons of Notre-Dame, but early in the

---

* Now primly referred to by the media as 'SDF's, 'sans domicile fixe' or 'of no fixed abode'.

seventeenth century they sold the land, to their later regret, to three architects, Marie, Le Regrattier and Poulletier. The king, Louis XIII, approved and himself laid the first stone of Pont Marie in 1614. The islands were joined together and embanked, and building began. The oldest buildings (1616) are at the corner of Rue Saint-Louis-en-l'Ile and Rue Le Regrattier.

The island is laid out on a simple grid plan. The houses on the quays naturally face the Seine; down the centre runs a straight narrow street, **Rue Saint-Louis-en-l'Ile,** the commercial street, dominated by the almost transparent spire and hanging clock of the church, Saint-Louis-en-l'Ile. There are fine great houses on both quays and in the central street. Crossing the island at right-angles are narrow side streets, with more modest but equally attractive houses. Behind these houses, particularly the big ones, are large courtyards, originally for coaches and horses, and these courtyards give a further depth of secrecy to an already secret island.

The architecture of the big houses (*hôtels*) deserves our attention. The seventeenth century was a particularly good period of French building and many of these splendid *hôtels* (including one for himself) were built by Louis Le Vau, certainly one of the greatest of French architects. The island was not a place for the aristocracy, who already had their *hôtels* and châteaux elsewhere. They were the homes of ambitious bourgeois who had made their fortunes in the Royal Chamber or the Royal Accounts, and became the ancestors of a new generation of aristocrats.

The north quay (Quai de Bourbon, Quai d'Anjou) was the fashionable side, being protected from the sun. In the seventeenth century its inhabitants included the Corrector of Accounts in the Royal Chamber, one of the twelve hautbois players in the Royal Chamber, the Grand Master of Waters and Forests, the Queen Mother's private portrait-painter and valet (a versatile man, it seems), the Captain of the Queen's Regiment, an iron merchant, the Governor of the Bastille, the President of the Chamber of Accounts, a gentleman with the baffling title of Lieutenant de la Robe Longue à la Connétablie de France, the Professor of Arabic at the Collège de France and Le Vau himself. Many talents, much ambition, a certain lack of incorruptibility – but we may wonder what they talked about on social evenings.

In the eighteenth and nineteenth centuries the island became less fashionable, though still the home of some interesting people. Except at the western, downstream, end in the nineteenth century, there was little rebuilding. The island was 'rediscovered' in the present century, after World War Two. But now it was the south-facing quays (Quai d'Orléans, Quai de Béthune) which became fashionable in a sun-loving time. Among the personalities who have lived there since then we find Georges Pompidou, Helena Rubinstein, the writers Francis Carco and James Jones, the famous French actor Claude Dauphin, and the distinguished couple Mr and Madame William Aspenwall Bradley, literary agents of Proust and Hemingway, whose work and friendships covered over half a century. Their Saturday-night receptions were a welcome rendezvous for writers from France, Britain and America.

Pont Saint-Louis is a modern prefabricated affair, linking the two islands. As it is chained off from traffic at both ends, it provides a pleasant viewpoint for walkers and a paradise for roller-skaters.

Pont Saint-Louis is the ninth bridge on the site, a series of disasters having destroyed previous ones. There is, perhaps, a reason for this. In 1472 a group of swarthy people encamped round Notre-Dame. They were, it is said, a duke, a count and ten knights from Lower Egypt, Christian refugees from the Saracens. They had confessed their sins to the Pope, who ordered them as a penance to wander the world for seven years without sleeping in a bed. With their wives, families and hangers-on, they numbered, remarkably, twelve hundred people. They had black hair, wore earrings and masses of jewellery and told fortunes, and it seems clear that they were gypsies. The canons of Notre-Dame, weary of their presence, which both fascinated and annoyed the faithful, drove them away (17 April 1472), and, as they crossed to Ile Saint-Louis in boats, they cursed the strip of water beneath them.

The curse seems to have been effective. The first permanent bridge between the islands, built by Marie in 1634, collapsed on its opening day, drowning twenty and injuring forty more. A later bridge, Pont Rouge (painted red to protect it from the weather) was destroyed by floods. Others were severely damaged by barges or blocks of ice, or became inexplicably shaky. So perhaps there is a grain of truth in the old legend.

Crossing the bridge, we find ourselves in a little square, the junction of the quays and Rue Jean-du-Bellay, the only street wide enough in the island to have pavement cafés (it is named after the sixteenth-century cardinal, bishop and writer, the uncle of Joachim, the poet). We are surrounded by parked cars, cafés, restaurants and brasseries. *Brasserie de l'Ile Saint-Louis* is on the site of the old *Taverne du Pont Rouge*. It is nicknamed '*The Oasis*'.

We, however, turn sharply left either at street level or down a flight of steps to river level, in order to reach the western tip of the island, downstream, with its trees, cobblestones and old lamps. From here we get a fine view of the splendid seventeenth-century house by François Le Vau, younger brother of Louis, which dominates the Seine here (45 Quai de Bourbon), home for a long time of the Princess Bibesco, uncrowned 'Queen' of the island; and later used by her descendants, mostly British.

From here to the other end of the island we have a choice of three routes, on the north or south bank or down the middle. But it would be a mistake to confine ourselves to one or the other; better to feel free to wander, to find the buildings, the shops and the views which appeal most. We can suggest a few.

Ile Saint-Louis was not planned as a symmetrical whole like Place Vendôme or Place des Vosges. But there is a feeling of harmony and of place which is appealing. The *hôtels* which face Quai de Bourbon (facing north) are remarkable for their stateliness and their pediments. They are now all converted into flats, with wide stone staircases and tall rooms with painted ceilings between the old oak beams. At night we can get many glimpses inside, as the French do not often draw their curtains. The inhabitants usually seem to be sitting at tables or desks, writing. These *hôtels* are in contrast to the Polish Library on Quai d'Orléans (south side), a severe neo-classical façade, which is much admired. Ile Saint-Louis has been for centuries the centre of Polish culture in Paris.

Walking along the centre street, Rue Saint-Louis-en-l'Ile, we find butchers, bakers, hairdressers, boutiques and many antique shops, where devotees can browse. But above no. 51 we must note the florid pediment of **Hôtel Chénizot,** supported by two elaborate gryphons and a sea-god. The *hôtel* was at one time the residence of the archbishops of Paris; one of them was fatally wounded at the barricades of Faubourg Saint-Antoine during the 1848 revolution, and was brought home to die. But its most famous inhabitant was undoubtedly Theresia Cabarrus, sex symbol of the 1789 Revolution, nicknamed Notre-Dame de Thermidor.

She lived there with her first husband, the Chevalier de Fontenay, and they were an ill-matched and unhappy couple. The marriage had been arranged by their parents to unite two family fortunes. She was only fourteen, partly Spanish, luscious; the curves of her bosom and hips, which were later to become so famous, were already conspicuous. He was small, red-faced and ugly, and she was ashamed to be seen about with him. His main interest was in raising himself in the aristocracy (the title Chevalier was self-awarded), and in the month of August 1789, when some of the nobility were thinking of packing and leaving, he finally succeeded in buying a genuine marquisate. His young marquise was not interested in this sort of thing, and her drawing-room was full of young cocktail-party revolutionaries, at least theoretically so; they included the La Rochefoucauld brothers and Lafayette, the more progressive nobility. Theresia even joined the reformist Club des Feuillants and, it is said, played with the Revolution like a child with a toy.

It could not last, of course. The moderates were swept away by the Terror. The couple parted and left, the marquis to America, she to Spain and her relations. However, she never got there. She was captured and put in a dungeon in Bordeaux. She did not remain there long; her intelligence and her attractions were too great. She soon became the mistress of Citizen Tallien, the bloodthirsty dictator of Bordeaux, and from there she returned to Paris, to her famous rôles in the Revolution. She was usually dressed as Liberty or Calypso, or just vaguely in gold and ostrich feathers, appearing at galas or riding in carriages. She was, however, frequently pregnant and had eleven children altogether. Napoleon said that she had the bastards of the whole world, though it is unlikely that he was one of the fathers. She made a last return to Ile Saint-Louis, to the bedside of her eldest son, Antoine de Fontenay, who was dying of wounds received in 1815.

Rue Le Regrattier was named after one of the original developers of the island. It is a narrow cross-street where Coffinhall, friend and colleague of Robespierre, lived until their execution on the same day in 1793. The northern half of the street was for some time known as Rue de la Femme Sans Tête, a more pronounceable name than the original and present one. Her statue stands in a niche on the corner overlooking the Seine. 'Headless' seems a mild way of describing a lady who was decapitated, apparently, at her knees. She was probably a Virgin or Sequana, the goddess of the Seine, fished out of the river, and nothing to do with the guillotine.

Half way down the island we find Rue des Deux Ponts, which connects Pont Marie and Pont de la Tournelle and funnels a great stream of traffic across the island, dividing it in two.

Crossing the street, but still in Rue Saint-Louis-en-l'Ile, we find a long-established attraction of the island, *Berthillon*'s ice-cream shop (no. 31). It sells ice-cream or *sorbets,* including a delicious passion-fruit, to take away or eat on the premises, and it attracts a long queue in hot weather. It is closed on Mondays and Tuesdays, holidays, and at other less predictable times. When it is closed the same ices can be bought, for consumption on the premises, at the *Café Louis IX,* a few yards away on the other side of the cross-roads.

The spire of **Saint-Louis-en-l'Ile** dominates the narrow street. It is one of the few spires in Paris which defies the Renaissance's obsession with Greek columns and Roman domes. The spire is pierced with a pattern of ovals which, seen from the side, gives a strange asymmetrical, almost kinetic effect, as we walk by. It was built in 1765 to replace Le Vau's original campanile, destroyed by lightning. The clock, which chimes the half-hours loudly (at night too), is worthy of attention. To an Englishman the whole building says 'Wren' and it would not look out of place in the City of London. Similarly, the carved wooden doors remind us of Grinling Gibbons, and, indeed, both the church and its doors are contemporary with the English masters.

Saint-Louis-en-l'Ile was begun in 1664 to the designs of Le Vau, but it was not finished until 1726, which perhaps explains the more elaborate baroque interior, with its decoration, gilded scrollwork and marble. It is a fashionable church for weddings, not only for islanders but for those living farther afield. It is also used for concerts, attractive candlelit occasions.

Crossing Rue Poulletier (another of the developers of the island), we find the **Arch of Bretonvilliers,** which spans the short street of the same name. It was originally part of the huge Hôtel de Bretonvilliers (another developer), which has been demolished to make the Boulevard Henri IV. But much remains to show the splendid style of the seventeenth century. The building and the arch are now pierced with windows, out of which schoolgirls looked, giggling, until 1984, when the school closed.

Madame de Bretonvilliers, the wife of the *nouveau riche* contractor, was also mistress to the Archbishop of Paris. For some reason her husband objected to this and, when the archbishop tried to slip away discreetly, he was escorted to his residence by many servants in full livery carrying torches, as was fitting to a personage of his rank. The archbishop, it is said, did not return.

Strolling down the short street to Quai de Béthune, we find two houses on the corner. The left-hand one is reputed to be haunted by a ghost – whose and why is not known. The right-hand one carries a plaque, recording that the Princesse de Poix, *'très haute et très puissante'*, bequeathed the house in 1728 to the Maréchal de Richelieu. The military achievements of the marshal and duke (a great-nephew of the cardinal) were mainly against the British in Minorca. But his more famous victories were in the bedroom. His sexual appetite was almost inexhaustible, and there were no lengths he would not go to, even tunnelling through walls, to get the girl. Duchesses, actresses, servants, he pursued them all tirelessly, though he was often plagued by jealous husbands, duels and, occasionally, marriages. With such vitality it is hardly surprising that he lived to the age of ninety-two, and his final score, it is said, was three wives, forty-four 'official' mistresses and an uncountable number of more informal seductions.

Returning to Rue Saint-Louis-en-l'Ile, we find several galleries. Most of these cater for the tourist and have a general show of 'souvenir art'. Others are more serious, if often more macabre. But on one occasion there was an exhibition of artists who lived on the island (there were seventy-five, including at that time Chagall). The result was a varied and surprising revelation of the artistic depths of the islanders. It is to be hoped that one day one of the bookshops will do the same for the writers.

At Quai d'Anjou, 17, north side, we find the refurbished **Hôtel de Lauzun,** sadly very rarely open to the public. Apart from the gutters, the outside is rather severe, and is incomplete, as the contractor was arrested for selling non-existent fuel to the army. It is built with the principal rooms on the first and second floors, to avoid flooding. This allowed secret exits onto the Seine for clandestine visitors. It also allowed, during the Terror, the young son of the house to escape while his father, the Marquis de Pimodan, was arrested upstairs by patrols of the Committee of Public Safety.

The house was known at the time as Hôtel de Pimodan. Lauzun replaced it in 1850, when the then owner put up the present plaque which has both Lauzun's name and date wrong. Lauzun in fact only lived there for three years (1682–85), escaping from his enormous, dominating wife, La Grande Mademoiselle, the king's niece (for more about this extraordinary couple, see p. 234). The first floor is fairly plain seventeenth century, the second a riot of French baroque, covered with clouds, rivers, swathes of flowers, trumpets, goddesses, masks and false perspectives.

Hôtel de Lauzun looked like that when its most distinguished tenant, **Baudelaire,** lived there in 1843, in a small room under the roof. His friends were amazed when he abandoned his usual haunts on the Left Bank and went to live in outer darkness. It was the river which drew Baudelaire. Water without limit symbolized genius without form. The fixed quays symbolized (symbols were very important to him) the form and the discipline necessary to his poetry and his life, which he found so hard to find. He would stare at the Seine for hours from his window, and one day he saw, bathing in the river, the beautiful mulatto girl, Jeanne Duval (*la Vénus noire*). (The Seine was relatively unpolluted and bathing was permitted.)

Jeanne's origins are mysterious. She is supposed to have come from the West Indies, and there are conflicting accounts of her appearance: tall, crinkly-haired, graceful, *farouche*, full-breasted, though others have described her as of medium height, ungainly, queen-like and flat-chested. Baudelaire fell passionately in love and installed her nearby in Rue Le Regrattier; she became for him the symbol of carnal and profane love. Baudelaire's two years in Hôtel de Lauzun were the happiest years of his life, and the longest he ever spent in one lodging.

But troubles were crowding in – lack of recognition, debt, the sea of madness like the Seine without banks. He stabbed himself in her presence. It was ineffective and he recovered in a few days, but the romance was over. So was his life on Ile Saint-Louis.

But he returned many times to Ile Saint-Louis, to Hôtel de Lauzun for meetings of the Club des Haschichiens. The Hashish Club met in the small east room of Hôtel de Lauzun, where one could get a good smoky fug very quickly. The chairwoman (La Présidente, as she was known) was 'Madame' Sabatier, a demi-mondaine and courtesan and, like others (La Dame aux Camélias, for example), an important influence in French literary and artistic life. Aglaë-Apollonie Sabatier was a jolly, pretty girl of twenty-four, but she became for Baudelaire his symbolic angel of purity (*la Vénus blanche*), his chaste guardian, his embodiment of sacred love, to be contrasted with Jeanne – not that there was anything very chaste about Madame Sabatier.

The Hashish Club, however, was neither brothel nor merely a den for drug-takers. Among its distinguished members were many who came for the company and not for the hashish. Théophile Gautier (who wrote the preface to Baudelaire's *Fleurs du Mal*) presumably smoked, judging from his own hallucinatory writings. So did Boissard, who introduced the cult and was the real president. Balzac, on the other hand, inspected the spoonful of yellow-green paste, which gave out a strong smell of rancid butter, and declined. He had, he explained, consumed so much alcohol and coffee that he was immune to such stuff. We do not know about the habits of the others – Delacroix, the Goncourt brothers, Daumier (who drew caricatures of the smokers and lived almost next door), Meissonier, Steinheil (who restored the glass of the Sainte-Chapelle) and, of course, Baudelaire himself. Visitors from abroad included Sickert, Rilke and Wagner. The East Room has long since been redecorated, but a small, very black patch has been preserved, a reminder of what hashish-smoking does to the wallpaper and, presumably, to the human lung.

Hôtel de Lauzun was bought by the City of Paris in 1928 and has since been used for official receptions. One of the most famous was in 1957 for Queen Elizabeth II and the Duke of Edinburgh on a state visit. Powdered footmen waited on the glittering guests and, above, musicians in eighteenth-century clothes played suitable music.

Moving along the quay, we pass Daumier's modest house and Le Vau's own *hôtel* with its convex front, shaped to the river line. And there we meet Le Vau's masterpiece, **Hôtel Lambert,** with its bow windows overlooking the *hôtel* garden and the river. It was built for Lambert *le riche,* who had studied the art of embezzlement under Louis XIII's superintendent of finance, named (suitably) Claude de Bullion. After Lambert, it was owned by a Monsieur Dupin, whose wife's lover was Jean-Jacques Rousseau, and then by the Marquis du Châtelet, whose wife's lover was Voltaire, briefly. In the nineteenth century it was owned by Prince Czartoryski and it became the centre of Polish life; among its distinguished guests was Chopin, who often played there. During the Second World War it became the secret hide-out of Allied airmen shot down over France. When Germans searched the house, the concierge would give a special ring on the bell, and the airmen would lose themselves in the complicated cellars until the danger was over. When they needed a breath of fresh air, other than the gravelly and rather bare garden, they would be allowed to wander about Paris on strict condition that they did not speak a word. Later they would start on the long secret journey to Spain.

Later the *hôtel* became famous for parties given by the Comte de Rédy. The guests, who never arrived before midnight, would be greeted in the courtyard by enormous floodlit papier-maché elephants. It then became the town-house of the Baron de Rothschild and was closed to the public. But we can admire the main entrance (at 2 Rue Saint-Louis-en-l'Ile), with its big, plain but beautifully proportioned portico. If the doors are open, we can look in at the court-yard. On the far side is the double staircase, and, behind it, Le Sueur's fresco of the Seine (seen as a very old man) being rejuvenated by Ile Saint-Louis (rather a fierce young woman); this is a curious concept, the Seine being normally shown as a chaste young goddess, Sequana, and St Louis as his royal self. Le Sueur also did the frescoes and ceiling, which show the labours of Hercules, of the upper bow window overlooking the Seine. These can be glimpsed from a distance.

Crossing the last boulevard, we find another gravelly garden, typically French, and we take the steps down to the river level, the upstream point of the island, a pleasant place for sunbathing – were it not for passing *bateaux-mouches* of ever-increasing size, with their amplified commentaries.

We cross to the mainland, the Right Bank, by the unattractive Pont Sully. But, half way across, we should pause and look downstream at one of the finest views in Paris: the curving Seine, old houses, poplars, distant towers and Pont Marie, the most graceful bridge in Paris. On the mainland, near the entrance of Metro Sully-Morland, we should pause beside the *Café Sully*. From here we have a pleasant view of Hôtel Lambert with its harmonious lines; perhaps the lights are coming on in the Hercules Salon and we can see, romantically, glittering chandeliers and the painted ceiling. Across Boulevard Henri IV we have a closer sight of the ruins of the Bastille prison, moved from the original site. But that is for another chapter.

Or perhaps we remain on Ile Saint-Louis and eat there. When last counted, there were thirty-six restaurants on the island – this included brasseries, cafés and tea-shops offering light lunches. They are much frequented by visitors from all parts of Paris and the suburbs. Some are closed on Mondays, some on Wednesdays, some close in the evening, others only open then and stay open late. But, with such a choice, we shall not go hungry, whether we want *haute cuisine,* simpler grills, provincial dishes (Alsace, Auvergne, Burgundy), exotic food from other countries or just a pancake (*crêpe*). The price range is wide too, but we can study the menus posted outside, before we commit ourselves.

4

The Seine

THE SEINE IS the heart of Paris – or rather, the great artery that feeds everything else. It is hardly possible to move about the centre of Paris without travelling along or across the river at some point. All streets, even if they do not actually lead to the river, are numbered from their river end. Paris, despite its size and growth, is still 'on the Seine'.

The seven miles of the Seine in Paris are without doubt the most famous river-front in the world, celebrated in paint, romanticized in song. Just as the Seine originally created Paris, so Parisians have cherished the Seine, turning it into a long park or garden, full of trees and water. Unlike the Seine at Rouen, its course through Paris has been designed for pleasure, for strolling, cruising, fishing, loving, sunbathing, sprawling, picnicking, drinking, living and, for some, sleeping sous *les ponts de Paris.*

Keen Seine-watchers will notice its colour – that special blend of green and grey which was captured so successfully by Sisley and Monet. It is, of course, heavily polluted, but its colour and appearance have hardly changed since the time of the Impressionists. Another curiosity should be noted; the Seine often seems to be flowing upstream. This is not romantic fantasy. The Seine is a very slow-moving river. The total drop between the source near Dijon and the sea is only 470 metres, and most of this takes place in the Côte d'Or when the river is still only a trickle. There are no snow mountains to give it spate and the tributaries are all equally gentle. The Seine is not like the rushing Rhône. At its widest at Rouen it only reaches an average of 500 cubic feet a second (compare the Danube's 9,000 at Vienna). It meanders gently across the plain of Ile de France, making enormous bends, most of them downstream from Paris. It is, as nearly as such a thing exists, a stationary river and the slightest breeze is enough to move the surface of the water downwind, upstream. And with a winding river like the Seine, every breeze blows upstream somewhere.

There are, of course, many locks and weirs, mostly very shallow, and the Seine is a very useful waterway. Paris is the fourth largest port of France (after Marseilles, Le Havre and Dunkirk). Barge traffic increases every year, but most of these unload at Gennevilliers, downstream, or at Charenton, and beyond, upstream. It is rare nowadays to see a barge moored in central Paris. Instead we have a picturesque and almost continuous procession of boats, many of them carrying petrol or sand. Some of them have Belgian, Dutch or German flags, for the Seine is connected to the canal systems of the Low Countries and the canals of France. But they all fly, gaily like flags in a regatta, an almost unbelievable amount of washing, particularly children's knickers.

The life of a French bargee is rather separated from that of his brothers on land. For one thing, he takes pride in setting foot as little as possible on the soil of France. So do all his friends, relations and future sons-in-law; they wave as they pass, meet briefly in the locks (where there is usually a shop), and for longer periods in the two great centres of Saint-Mammés (upstream) and Conflans-Sainte-Honorine (downstream). In the latter the church is on an old barge, so that the bargee and his large family can attend mass without setting foot on shore.

But the life is changing, naturally. The Impressionists showed us strings of barges, each separately steered and towed by a small tug. Puccini depicted the drama of barge life on the Seine in his extraordinarily evocative one-act opera *Il Tabarro* (*The Cloak*). But with labour costs rising (and social security contributions for employees) single barges arrived, self-propelled and probably owned by the skipper, and these still form the greater part of Seine river-traffic. Then came the *pousseurs* (pushers). These powerful boats, owned by the big oil, chemical and construction companies, can push up to six barges, two abreast, before them. With a fine disregard of the old nautical principle of sharp-end first, they consume a great deal of fuel and save a great deal of manpower. Whether this will prove finally to be economic is uncertain. The mayor dislikes their pollution and hopes to see this freight traffic transferred to road or rail.

Barges are not allowed to carry passengers, but bargees are hospitable people and if we find one moored, they may invite us on board and show us over their immaculate and highly-polished boat. There can be up to fourteen people living on board in extremely cramped conditions; it is thought lucky for a baby to be born on the barge. If they are about to leave, they will perhaps give us a ride to the next stop or lock. Their life, however, is changing. The demands of education and midwifery are forcing them to have more contact with the mainland. Most now have television and many carry their owners' cars, made fast on the hatches. But they still remain an essential part of the Paris scene.

There are river cruise-boats which ply up and down, and we should certainly take one of these trips, preferably on a fine day when we can sit on deck. We have a beautiful view of the Seine and its incomparable architecture, though we may be irritated on some trips by the loudspeaker commentary, which seems obsessed by the weight of the bridges and the names of the visible ministries. The biggest boats (*bateaux-mouches*) look like huge insects made of glass. These also run at night, offering a longer cruise, a leisurely candlelit dinner (rather expensive) and a view of the buildings, floodlit by the boat itself. The view may be partly obscured by condensation, in which case we can console ourselves with the food and wine.

But the best way of exploring the Seine, like the rest of Paris, is on foot. The quays of the Seine are tree-lined double-decker affairs, plane trees above, poplars below. The walk along the Right Bank at river level has been obliterated by a barbarous motorway (named Voie Georges Pompidou, after the politician who authorized it) which channels another hundred thousand vehicles a day beside the Seine, through the centre of Paris. The project to build a similar motorway along the Left Bank was vetoed by President Giscard d'Estaing and so we can still enjoy a walk of several miles along the bank of the Seine, shaded and in parts still cobbled. It extends from near Gare d'Austerlitz to Gare des Invalides (both metro stations), at which point an older motorway takes over. On our way we can admire not only the river scene, but many of the most beautiful buildings of Paris.

Or we can take the upper level along either bank. The traffic is daunting but there are many compensations: the chance to see the buildings more closely, glimpses down narrow streets into the Marais (Right Bank) or the Latin Quarter (Left Bank), and, especially, the bookstalls. These are mainly in the Notre-Dame area and years ago were frequented by those who wished to buy porn novels forbidden in other countries. Things have changed with time and now the bookstalls sell old books, prints, maps, posters and inescapable, international pictures of doll-like children with huge eyes. Even if we do not wish to buy (and prices are not cheap), we can enjoy browsing. The stall-owners, though keen to make a sale, are tolerant.

The buildings along the Right Bank will be described in later chapters, but here we are walking along the upper level of the Left Bank, starting at Quai Saint-Bernard. The first thing we notice is the smell of animals; we are passing the **Zoo** and the **Botanical Gardens.** These contain Paris's celebrated Cedar of Lebanon which the botanist Jussieu is said to have brought back from the Middle East, watering it with his own drinking water. In fact it was a gift from Kew Gardens. The Zoo, 3 Quai Saint-Bernard (Metro Gare d'Austerlitz) was originally stocked with animals 'borrowed' from travelling circuses. The arrival of the first giraffe, a present from the Pasha of Egypt in 1827, caused a sensation. The animals were all slaughtered for food during the Siege of Paris in 1870, but it has since been amply restocked. The animals are kept in more or less natural surroundings and we can see the antelopes through the railings as we walk by.

On our left was the Halle aux Vins, the wine market of Paris. This has been replaced by the Science Faculty of the University (Jussieu), a modern glassy building with a dominating tower, another of Pompidou's gifts to the city – he was one of its few admirers.

Crossing the end of Boulevard Saint-Germain (which continues across Pont Sully to the tip of Ile Saint-Louis and the Right Bank, Boulevard Henri IV and the Bastille), we find ourselves on Quai de la Tournelle. The Tournelle was originally a fort guarding the entrance to Paris, part of the walls of Paris which King Philippe-Auguste built in 1190. There was another tournelle on the Right Bank and a chain was hung between them. The forts were also used as transit posts for galley-slaves on their way to Marseilles, but happily nothing of this remains except the name of the quay.

We are now beside **Pont de la Tournelle,** one of the most graceful in Paris. It is a modern bridge, replacing the old wooden footbridge mentioned by Hemingway in his first novel, *Fiesta.* In a single span it reaches Ile Saint-Louis, allowing plenty of room for modern barges and also, shaped like a flying buttress, repeats the flying buttresses of Notre-Dame. The simple statue of Ste Geneviève, facing east towards the invading Huns she defied, is placed off-centre so as not to interfere with the view of the cathedral.

The other bridge, **Pont Marie** (Metro Pont Marie), connecting the Ile Saint-Louis with the Right Bank, is also beautiful but much older.

Designed by Marie, the original developer of the island, its first stone was laid by Louis XIII in 1614. On either side of the road were rows of four-storey houses and shops and these can be seen in old prints. Two of the arches and twenty-two of the houses were destroyed in 1658 by floods, many inhabitants being drowned. The arches were rebuilt without houses and, following more floods, the remaining houses were removed in 1740. The spans of Pont Marie are too narrow for modern barges so the bridge is left to the cruise-boats. From them we can enjoy the proportions of the bridge and its mellow stone, which is floodlit at night.

The other bridges of the two islands are, except Pont Neuf, useful pieces of nineteenth-century engineering and need not excite our curiosity. We should concentrate, rather, on the riverside buildings as we walk along the Seine on the edge of the Latin Quarter. Passing restaurants, cafés and shops, we reach Place Saint-Michel, a large square on the river, surrounded by student bookshops, cafés, restaurants and traffic (Metro Saint Michel).

Crossing the Place, still beside the river, we are on Quai des Grands Augustins, site of a sixteenth-century monastery, now with a line of fine eighteenth-century houses; fashionable apartments, though the roar of traffic has made them less desirable. Only a few paces away, is one of the great monuments of Paris, Pont Neuf.

Despite its name, **Pont Neuf** is the oldest bridge across the Seine; the most famous, the grandest, the solidest and a triumph of bridge design. It crosses the river at its widest point in Paris, with five arches to the tip of Ile de la Cité and seven more to the Right Bank. The piers supporting the bridge are surmounted by round bays with stone seats – the bridge was always intended for leisure as well as traffic. Below the rim a theatrical frieze of grimacing masks runs right round the bridge.

Pont Neuf is always associated with Henri IV, whose statue stands in the middle (a nineteenth-century replica, the original was melted down during the Revolution). But the idea had been mooted for a long time without anything happening. The first stone was laid in 1578 by Henri III. It was a sad occasion: the king was in deep mourning and tears; three of his favourite *mignons* (boyfriends) had recently been killed in a duel with the Guises and he was almost speechless with grief. Nothing more happened for twenty years until Henri IV, his cousin, and brother-in-law for a time, ordered the bridge to be finished. He made two changes in its design: there were to be no houses built on it and there were to be pavements for those on foot. He himself opened the bridge in 1607, riding across it on his charger.

Immediately it became the promenade of Paris. The city was not a pleasant place for walking. The streets were narrow, deep in filth, crowded with horses, wagons and the carriages of the great. The unfortunate pedestrian would be jostled by lackeys and footmen, possibly set on by thieves. But now at last Paris had a pedestrian precinct. It was, in a sense, Paris's first boulevard and it was thronged, day and night, by a crowd endlessly moving up and down, the first *flâneurs*.

It was also a permanent fair. The bays were occupied by booths, stalls and merchants crying their wares, including plenty of prostitutes. A carillon played every quarter of an hour; jugglers, acrobats and strolling players entertained the passers-by. Under one of the arches was a large pump and statue, *La Samaritaine*, which provided water for the Louvre. It was the social centre of Paris and it continued for nearly two hundred years until the Revolution, which swept the fair away. Jugglers, singers, actors, prostitutes and bookstalls can still be found plentifully in Paris, but no longer on Pont Neuf.

One of the traders who cried his wares on the bridge was a Monsieur Cognacq-Jay, who prospered, founded a museum, now at 8 Rue Elzévir (Metro Saint-Paul) in the Marais and, in particular, transferred his business to the end of the bridge on the Right Bank, where he renamed it **La Samaritaine,** after the fountain. It is now one of Paris's largest department stores and it is there that we should now go. Crossing the quay, we enter the big building, Magasin Deux; we ignore the attractions round us, the heat and the crowds, and head for the lift to the ninth floor, the roof terrace. Here, over a drink, we can enjoy one of the finest views of Paris: not as remote as the Eiffel Tower or Montmartre terrace, not as exhausting as the Notre-Dame towers or the Arc de Triomphe, but we can see them all from here and much else. Below us lies the Seine and its bridges and beyond it the façades of the Left Bank. On every side are the domes, towers and spires of Paris, and we can identify them all from a helpful circular map on the turret above, reached by a small winding stair. Is the Panthéon dome more beautiful than those of the Invalides or the Institut below us? Is the Monnaie more beautiful than the Louvre? Is Montparnasse Tower an eyesore or a masterpiece? Is the Pompidou Centre at Beaubourg the most startling building we have ever seen? We can decide it all over a cool drink under an awning.

(The terrace is open during the store's shopping hours, but the café is closed from the end of October till April.)

We descend and re-cross Pont Neuf. It is the moment to consider the personality of **King Henri IV,** Henry of Navarre (1553–1610). In a long line of mediocre kings. he stands out like a star. Soldier, statesman, man of ideas, he became France's most popular king since St Louis – though the two men had little in common except a concern for the welfare of ordinary people. The leader of the much-persecuted Protestant Huguenots, he believed in freedom of worship, which he achieved in the Edict of Nantes (13 April 1598).

His economic idea was summarized in his hope that there would be no Frenchman too poor to have a chicken in his pot every Sunday. This *poule au pot* philosophy was to be achieved by ending the Wars of Religion and giving peasants time to breed chickens and grow vegetables. He was helped in this by his able minister and closest friend, the Duc de Sully. Sully said, 'Grazing and ploughing are the two breasts from which France is fed, the true mines and treasures of Peru'. This was a crack against rich Spain, whose wealth came, temporarily, from the looted altars of South America. Sully also forbade the gentry to ride over growing crops and vines, and introduced a close season for hunting. He reorganized taxation; many rich people had bought themselves out of the system. He reconstructed roads, built bridges and started the Canal de Briare, joining the Seine and the Loire. The royal treasury overflowed.

But ending the Wars of Religion was a hard task. The Huguenots were outnumbered by the Catholic League, led by the powerful Guise family and able commanders such as Mayenne and Farnese. Henri IV was often outnumbered two to one; on one occasion his cavalry were outnumbered five to one. Several times he took refuge on the coast, where he received help from England; indeed, he even considered marrying Queen Elizabeth I. In the end he won, and the treaty of Vervins was signed (1598). It was a generous peace; Henry was a man to forgive and forget.

But the problem of Paris, firmly Catholic, remained. 'What can I do?' the king in tears asked Sully. 'If I do not forswear Protestantism, there will be no more France.' This question is often misquoted as the cynical 'Paris is worth a Mass'. In 1594 he became, in Chartres, a Catholic for the second time. A month later Paris opened her gates to him and he was given a rousing welcome. It was not, however, completely unanimous. Some, like the mad Ravaillac, thought it was all part of a cunning plan to murder the Pope; others were suspicious of his conversion and thought that he was still at heart a Protestant. There was some reason for this. In his last year he was preparing an army to prevent Austria from imposing Catholic princes on the Protestant Rhineland.

Despite the Massacre of St Bartholomew, the long years of civil war and two unhappy marriages, Henry was a man who enjoyed life. He liked riding his horses down the corridors of the Louvre. Especially he enjoyed the feel of female flesh, preferably unwashed. His favourite mistress, Gabrielle d'Estrées, bore him two children, but this did not prevent him having children by her sister and by many other young women. At one moment he parked fourteen of his children with their various mothers at Saint-Germain-en-Laye, which brought a moment's quietness to the Louvre. He also liked riding through the narrow streets in his carriage, greeting ordinary people, a habit which made him an easy target for assassination.

But beyond all this was his vision of peace. He dreamed of a federal Europe, a *république chrétienne,* with a Senate which would settle all international disputes of frontiers and religion. He was foreseeing and trying to prevent the horrors of the Thirty Years' War, which lay just ahead. As an idea it was three hundred years in advance of its time, and it was not to be fulfilled. When Ravaillac stabbed him in his carriage in Rue de la Ferronnerie on 14 May 1610, everything changed. All France was in tears. He was remembered, and still is, as Henri le Grand, who brought peace, prosperity and reconciliation to the country.

Regaining the Left Bank, we reach **l'Institut du Monde Arabe**, (Institute of Arab Culture) 1 rue des Fossés St-Bernard (opposite Ile Saint-Louis, overlooking Quai Saint-Bernard), Metro Sully-Morland or Jussieu.

It was founded in 1987 with the object of explaining the high quality of Arab culture to French people and encouraging cultural communication and co-operation between France and the Arab world. It has a library with 55,000 books in French and Arabic, a museum worth seeing, a bookshop and a restaurant. The centre runs language-courses, holds lectures and presents films, music and folk songs. There are guided visits. High-level cultural exchanges are organised, with the help of the French government and the City of Paris. This is all done in a very civilized spirit and carefully avoids contentious matters, past or present.

The outside of the building is glistening and attractive, showing just what art can do for a plain glass nine-storey block. The architects, Jean Nouvel, Gilbert Légénès and the Studio group, have fixed 242 panels of aluminium sculpture, in a modern Islamic-style design, inside the glass outer wall of the southern façade. These panels open and close by themselves according to the intensity of the sunlight, to regulate conditions inside. The façade on the river side is curved, in a plain style. The interior seems to be all-metal, with a striking modern hall for the lift. A tempting bookshop invites us to travel to Samarkand or Lebanon, and features art books about Delacroix, who loved and painted Morocco.

The museum starts on the seventh floor and works downwards, in date order. The best things are at the end.

We see pleasing earthenware vases and amphorae from Carthage (Tunisia), third century BC, and designs on ostrich-eggs. These were votive offerings in the tombs. Later works show Greek influence, followed by Roman, notably a head of the good-looking Emperor Lucius Verus, second century AD.

From Iran we see pottery of the ninth and tenth centuries; from Syria part of an elaborate balustrade, twelfth century; from Damascus a thirteenth-century stone funeral stele, engraved with Arab lettering; from Egypt and Syria fourteenth-century pots of copper encrusted with silver.

Suddenly we find, in the last room, a whole series of glorious wall-hangings, spot-lit to show their intricate designs. These are on loan from private French collections. The oldest items are tenth-century prayer-mats from Palestine whose patterns had religious significance, including the theme of the door into the next world. The sixteenth century is described as 'the golden age of carpets'. It was the highpoint of the Ottoman Empire in Turkey, coinciding with the arrival of the Safavi in Persia and the Mogul dynasty in India.

The first Indian carpets date from 1556. There were many tribal designs, handed on in their own districts, from one generation to another. The ones we see were reproduced in nineteenth-century Turkey. They show scenes of the chase and floral 'court' designs. There are also carpets from the Caucasus, of the seventeenth and eighteenth centuries, with floral patterns and some splendid dragons.

We end our visit on the **Rooftop Terrace** on the ninth floor. This is open to everyone, whether we place an order in the little open-air café or not. It is often too windy to stay for long, but the view is memorable. We look down on Notre-Dame and its chestnuts, surrounded by the Seine; opposite, we see Ile Saint-Louis, with its quays planted with poplars; we see Ste Geneviève on her bridge close by; on the river, the cruise-boats pass below us. This must rank as one of the sights of Paris.

We next find ourselves on Quai Conti, in front of the **Monnaie, the Mint.** There has been much rebuilding on the site, which was originally Hôtel de Nesle, town house of the Duc de Berry. In 1670 it was the Paris residence of the Princesse de Conti. In the eighteenth century Louis XV moved the Mint there and an unknown architect, Antoine, was commissioned to make the necessary alterations between 1771 and 1776. The façade which we now see is plain and almost severe, but pleasing in its formality. In the age of baroque it was a surprising addition to Paris. But it pleased the Parisians, who were beginning to tire of ornamentation; it also pleased the architect who, disconcertingly, decided to live there.

Coins, like graves, are often the chief witnesses of the past. The **Musée de la Monnaie** owns 30,000 antique coins, but only 2,000 are on view. We learn that the Gauls had their own coinage, much influenced in design by Greece and Rome, but making a special feature of legendary beasts. The great currency-reformers, bringing in new coins, were Charlemagne (AD 800), whose empire was so large that his coins were fore-runners of the Euro; Saint Louis; Jean II "Le Bon", who invented the franc; Louis XIII; Napoleon; and, finally, de Gaulle, who brought in the Nouveau Franc, worth 100 of the old. The artist Matthieu's ten-new-franc-piece was such a success that it remained in use for many years, and is now a collector's piece. The minting of coins for current use was transferred from Paris to Pessac, Gironde, in 1974 and now includes the Euro.

Besides coins, the museum possesses a superb collection of medallions. These are small bronze reliefs, quite distinct from coinage or military medals. This art-form was developed in Italy in the fifteenth century, notably by Pisanello, but soon became a feature in France too. From the start, these pieces could be either cast in a foundry or hammered. They were much used in the time of Henri IV, Louis XIV, the Revolution and Napoleon. In the nineteenth century they changed to recording the arts of peace, rather than martial glory. In the twentieth century they had a remarkable renewal; for twenty years, from the mid-1960s to the mid-1980s, La Monnaie became an important centre of contemporary art, and its generous patron. They commissioned models for bronze medallions from independent sculptors (chosen from dossiers submitted) and gave them a free hand. The mint's own expert craftsmen produced them on the premises, where they were put on sale. They made excellent gifts, at reasonable prices. The Club Français de la Médaille nominated 'choices' among the pieces, which carried high prestige and helped with sales through its catalogue and membership. When the museum was reconstructed in 1988, these "Choices" sculptors were invited to the opening. They received a shock. Out of La Monnaie's collection of 75,000 medallions, only 450 were on view. In its long catalogue the new museum only acknowledged the existence of the independent contributors in half a line. Future purchases were to be of historic or commemorative pieces only. The honeymoon was over.

However, the 450 on view are very well mounted and so well lit that they appear three-dimensional. They show the wide scope of this art-form and the excellence it attained, especially in a marvellous one of New York. We should certainly go to see them.

Much of the space in the museum is taken up by huge antique presses (looking like Anne Hathaway's famous 'second-best bed') which were part of past machinery in the Mint, now disused. School groups are taken round these in such detail that they do not seem to have time for much else. Happily, it was announced in a reform of school programmes, on 30 October 1998, that lycée students were no longer to have their time taken up by the study of obsolete machinery, so we must hope that the 'bedsteads' will soon disappear, allowing space for more of the Monnaie's treasure of beautiful pieces, ancient and modern, to be put on view again.

The next building is the **Institut de France**, 23 Quai de Conti (Metro Pont Neuf), a landmark for its fine gold-ribbed dome, and the Mazarin Chapel, containing the cardinal's tomb but otherwise secularized. Originally part of Philippe-Auguste's fortifications, and later the Hôtel de Nesle, it was completely rebuilt in the late seventeenth century by order of Mazarin on his death-bed (1661). He had ruled France during the boyhood of Louis XIV and amassed a huge fortune; he left two million *livres* for the building of his memorial chapel and a college and library for students from four 'acquired' provinces. The two curved wings end in square pavilions on the Seine and were designed by Le Vau, although not actually built by him; the Corinthian columns are not typical of his style.

The east wing contains the **Bibliothèque Mazarine**, originally the cardinal's own library, but with many later bequests. It is a lovely room, with its leather-bound books, especially manuscripts, and its view over the river.

The rest of the building is given over to the **Académie Française**. It is closed to the public, but the dome and courtyards may be seen during the guided tours organised by the Institut. The French Academy was founded by Richelieu in 1635 in the Louvre and moved to its present site, on Napoleon's orders, in 1806. Its members include distinguished people from all the professions, but it has a strong literary flavour and is responsible for the official French Dictionary. Its meetings are spectacular and widely publicised, members wearing knee-breeches, swords and green robes. It was exclusively male, but a woman was finally admitted (the novelist Marguerite Yourcenar); it was reported that she did not wear a sword. The members think highly of themselves and write '*de l'Académie Française*' after their names, even, it is wickedly said, on cheques. They are called 'the Immortals', though the majority were and are rather obscure. The list of those, from Descartes to Proust, who have been refused admission, is starry indeed. The Parisians regard the Academy with a mingled awe and amusement which is typically French.

Crossing the Seine in front of the Institut is **Pont des Arts**, a footbridge opened in 1803. The first iron bridge in Paris, it attracted a huge crowd, about sixty thousand, and the pattern of the curved arches is very pleasing. Unfortunately the task of navigating it and Pont Neuf in rapid succession was too much for many bargees and it was increasingly damaged by collisions. The bridge has recently been rebuilt on the old design, but with fewer (seven) and wider arches. There are no longer seats and flowers, but we have pavement artists and, in particular, the wonderful view. We are poised in air above the Seine between the Mazarin Dome of the Institut and the classical Cour Carrée of the Louvre, upstream are Pont Neuf and Ile de la Cité, downstream the river and its bridges. Elsewhere there are pleasant houses with well-proportioned façades. Add trees, water and sky and we have what Lord Clark, speaking of this view, called a humane and reasonable solution of what town architecture should be.

After Quai Conti we are on Quai Malaquais (6me). Queen Marguerite de Valois, known popularly as Fat Margot, the estranged first wife of Henri IV, built herself a sumptuous palace here, deliberately facing the Louvre and her former husband. She lived a debauched life, but much may be forgiven her (except perhaps strangling her lovers with her garters); she was the daughter of Catherine de Medici and had had a sad life, including the St Bartholomew massacre on her wedding-day and a long period of house arrest in the provinces. Nothing now remains of her mansion except the name Malaquais (ill-acquired) – the means by which she got her estate from the University of Paris, which owned the land, were very suspect.

Now we have, here and on Quai Voltaire (Metro Musée d'Orsay), a pleasant line of eighteenth-century houses, and the enjoyment of looking at them is much increased by recalling what a distinguished collection of writers, painters and composers lived here beside the Seine, sometimes briefly, sometimes for long periods: Anatole France (at no. 19 Quai Malaquais), Ingres (no. 11 Quai Voltaire), Delacroix and Corot (at no. 13 in the same studio, but not of course at the same time). At no. 19 Quai Voltaire, in the same hôtel, were, at various times, Baudelaire, still gazing at the Seine, Wagner finishing *Die Meistersinger,* and Oscar Wilde in exile. Voltaire himself was at no. 27 in 1724, aged thirty. Fifty-four years later, after years of exile in Geneva, he returned in triumph to the same house and died a few weeks later.

Pont de Carrousel, joining the Left Bank and the Louvre, carries much traffic, but our admiration should be reserved for the next one, **Pont Royal,** Louis XIV's gift to the river. Its simple grace and curve are an example to bridge-builders. It is in strong contrast to the Pavillon de Flore on the Right Bank, the downstream end of the Louvre, built in the nineteenth century under the Second Empire, dignity without beauty.

On our left is the dark hulk of the former Gare d'Orsay. Scheduled for demolition, it was rescued and became the Musée d'Orsay (see Chapter 5). Across the river are the formal Tuileries Gardens.

We also pass Piscine Deligny, a floating swimming pool moored in the Seine. The idea of a floating swimming pool is intriguing. The pool has been there since 1842 and has proved to be immensely popular in recent years.

Pont de la Concorde is a plain austere bridge, which does not take the eye from its surroundings. It merely joins the Chambre des Députés with Place de la Concorde and carries a huge amount of traffic. The Chambre, Assemblée Nationale or **Palais Bourbon** as it is often called, is the French parliament, but architecturally it is a Roman temple built by order of Napoleon, who saw Paris as another Rome. The façade of columns is false; the real entrance is on the far side of the building. Since a presidential system of government was adopted by the French under de Gaulle, the Chambre des Députés has lost much of its power and newsworthiness.

When the Finance Ministry was forced out of the Louvre to make way for the Grand Louvre, during the 1990s, and banished to its new fortress in Bercy, senior officials insisted on having their own fleet of motor-launches, to take them to meetings in central Paris. So we may see them going by in regal style like the old Doges of Venice, or Cardinal Wolsey going from Hampton Court to Westminster. Their fleet is rumoured to cost as much as the Navy.

But, as Seine-watchers, we should reserve our attention for the next bridge, **Pont Alexandre III.** It was built for the 1900 World Exhibition and named after a tsar. It is the most sumptuous and the most flamboyant of all the Seine's bridges. Every spare centimetre is encrusted with decoration: cupids, scrolls, garlands of flowers, wreaths, shells, birds, shields, trumpets, lions – they are all there, some in stone, some in bronze, some gilded. It is a supreme example of the architecture of the Third Republic and the Belle Epoque. At the Exhibition and ever since it has been a popular promenade, and, if we tire of the decoration, we can enjoy a superb view of the dome of the Invalides, Hardouin-Mansart's great golden bubble floating over the Esplanade, and meditate on changes in architectural fashion in little over a hundred years.

We can no longer stroll along the water's edge except on Sundays; a motorway took over at Gare d'Orsay, but on the quays we can still enjoy fine and famous views. On the right we have the huge glass mound of the Grand Palais; on the left we are increasingly aware of the Eiffel Tower. We pass Quai d'Orsay, the French Foreign Office, and Pont des Invalides, built at the turn of the century, but since rebuilt. We should, however, notice **Pont de l'Alma.** Originally nineteenth century, it is remarkable for the huge statue of a *zouave,* a French-Algerian soldier. This is popular as a marker for the height of the Seine. Has it reached his waist? His neck?

Pont d'Iéna is also encrusted with eagles and horses, and was built at the start of the nineteenth century, though it has been much altered since. On the Right Bank is the Palais de Chaillot and its gardens; the bridge is a fine place to see the fireworks which are let off on 14 July and other national occasions. On the Left Bank we can see the Champ-de-Mars and, distantly, the Ecole Militaire. Overtopping everything is the Eiffel Tower, at whose foot we now stand.

The cruise-boats do not go further than this, but on foot we can persevere a little longer. On the left is Grenelle, a working-class area once full of factories, builders' yards and the Citroën works. The

Citroën site is now a delightful garden and the mayor of Paris hopes to induce all the remaining industries to remove from the Seine, to cut down pollution. Efforts have been made to raise the '*standing*' of the area by building seven high-rise apartment blocks, two of which are reserved for low-rent tenants ('Where our servants will live,' it was explained to me). On the right is the Seizième Arrondissement, full of fashionable homes and small gardens. The circular white building beside Pont de Grenelle is the Maison de la Radio, the Broadcasting House of Paris. The Seizième spreads down the hill from the Arc de Triomphe to the Bois de Boulogne and Auteuil. At Auteuil we are at the city limits and the Seine leaves Paris.

We need not walk as far as this, but we could continue as far as Pont Mirabeau before descending into Metro Javel. There we should recite, if we can, the opening lines of Apollinaire's celebrated poem:

> *Sous le pont Mirabeau coule la Seine*
> *Et nos amours*
> *Faut-il qu'il m'en souvienne*
> *La joie venait toujours après la peine...*

5

The Musée d'Orsay

THE MUSÉE D'ORSAY was formerly a railway station, the 'Gare d'Orsay', and has an RER station at the entrance, so we can arrive, suitably, by train and emerge from the underworld into a pleasant paved courtyard, overhung by a big chestnut tree. The Seine and its boats are just across the road. Lulled by this, we may bump straight into a giant rhinoceros at bay by Pierre Rouillard, or his great horse rearing over a spiky harrow. Nearby is a trumpeting young elephant trapped by a foot-rope, by Emmanuel Fremet. These were a set made for the Expo at Trocadéro in 1878, and they show a conscience about ecology which was then a novelty (or perhaps they were still celebrating man's triumph over nature). Young people eating sandwiches sit on the rhino's plinth.

If we want to go back into the past, the Grand Louvre will take us far back, at lurching speed, or the Musée de l'Homme even further, hence its popularity. But if we are romantic about the near past, the Musée d'Orsay will take us into it. The museum aims to show us French art of all sorts, including architecture, photography and furniture, of the period 1848 to 1914, in association with its historical and political background. There are lectures and debates, concerts, film projections and cultural history courses, to achieve this object. But we have probably come to see the art itself, particularly the paintings, so a good place to start is the library, near the entrance where, amongst much else, we can buy the official guide, if we can afford it. But we are not bound to do so, as every work has its date and the name of the artist clearly labelled. The Musée d'Orsay's scope is too vast to be compassed in one visit, so we should next decide what our chief interest is, and go straight to that section. Most of the Impressionists are on the upper level, section 9.[*] If they are

---

[*] Direct access to the upper level is from the far end of the ground floor; there is a lift for the handicapped only.

our first choice, we should ignore official advice and begin at the top, at the upper level, where we can look down at the great hall below. Under its arched glass roof, we can almost feel that it is a station still and that a train will soon run in. It is remarkable that the whole building was completed in two years. It opened in 1900. The central ground floor we are looking down on shows large statues of the rather heavy style typical of the date and very suitable for a station. This period was the high time of the Railway Age, so we are in just the right place to see its art.

The Impressionists

This group was formerly housed in the 'Jeu de Paume' gallery, but security was not good enough to house such treasures and they were transferred as soon as possible to the Musée d'Orsay. There is a smaller, although excellent, collection of them in the Marmottan Gallery, and it seems a pity that the opportunity was not taken to put them all together when the Musée d'Orsay opened. But the Marmottan belongs to the City of Paris and the Musée d'Orsay is a national museum; there has always been a rivalry. Sadly, even the Jeu de Paume collection has not been kept together. This museum is rigidly laid out according to decades with the idea of relating the political events of each period to the works of that date. The result is that long-lived painters such as Monet appear in three different rooms on the upper level, with a further (pre–1870) selection on the ground floor. Dégas, Monet and Renoir also appear on the ground floor as well. This may seem barbarous to art-lovers who would like to see one room for each principal artist, where his development could be followed through his life. Some spirit of the old railway timetables seems to have taken control of the Musée d'Orsay. Trains ran to time in those days and clocks were everywhere.

Time is still the theme. We shall therefore stroll through this floor of the museum, pausing every time we see something which gives us pleasure. Myself, I can never see enough pictures of the Seine valley, of huge skies with moving clouds, of the reflections of light on water. Others may prefer to linger in front of race-horses, circuses, ballerinas and portraits of interesting people, both famous and unknown. The range of subjects for the Impressionists was wide.

But not wide enough for many contemporaries. The Impressionists deliberately rejected all the traditional subjects of art. We shall not find any Annunciations, any scenes from the Bible or classical mythology, any court portraits, battlefields or disembowelled horses. We are a long way from David and Delacroix; in size, too, these pictures are generally much smaller. What we have are pictures of everyday life: a bridge over the Seine, a cottage, a pretty girl in a smart dress (or nude, probably bathing), someone in a café, lunch, a boating party, a plate of fruit, a glass of wine. The artists were trying to avoid both the classical and the romantic, but we may well find their works romantic in our nostalgia over a hundred years later.

The word 'impressionism' derives from an early picture of Monet, *Impression of Sunrise at Le Havre*, which gave the name to the whole movement. But it is a mistake to imagine the artists are a coherent group, inspired only by the idea of painting light effects – this was confined to the 'hard-core' Impressionists, Monet (1840– 1926), Sisley (1830–1900) and Pissarro (1860–1903). They were a group of individualists, held together by rejection of traditional art, of rigid laws of design, content and colour laid down by the Ecole des Beaux-Arts and by the jury of the Paris Salon, which rejected their works again and again. This meant that they were deprived of public recognition and success; it was a permanent battle against loneliness, poverty and usually ill health. When Monet took refuge in London from the 1870 war, it is thought that he was influenced by Turner; certainly there is something Turneresque about his paintings of Westminster, with light filtering through the mists. We may compare Turner's *Rain, Steam and Speed* in London with Monet's *Gare Saint-Lazare* (1877) which he painted seven times. Nobody had ever thought of painting a train before. Frith's *Paddington Station* concentrates on the passengers. But there was a great difference in their lives. Turner was given commissions and honoured; Monet did not win recognition for his work until he was 50. Yet the quality which emerges from so many Impressionist canvasses, whatever their subjects and techniques, is joy and happiness.

So, rejected by the conventional art world, they fell back on each other, encouraging each other, exchanging ideas and even teaching each other – they were nearly all self-taught. Some were country-lovers, some town-birds, some gregarious, some solitary, but they were held together by their wish to paint their own pictures in their own way. For ten years after 1871 seven of them Monet, Renoir (1841–1919), Sisley, Dégas (1834–1917), Manet (1832–1885), Caillebotte (1848–1894) and Berthe Morisot (1841–1895) lived at

Argenteuil, meeting, talking, and painting each other; the year 1872 was a high point of their collective achievement. However it was an on-and-off business; they did not all share the countryside vision. The real meeting point was in Paris, at the Café Guerbois in Avenue de Clichy, near Montmartre; or else they were entertained by Manet in his Paris home; he was better off than the others and became unofficial president of the group. Others who helped were the photographer Nadar, who lent his studio in Boulevard des Capucines for their first show on 15 May 1874; the dealer Durand-Ruel who bought many of their pictures, and thereby made himself a fortune; and their fellow-painter Gustave Caillebotte who was persuaded to think that he had more money than talent and contented himself with buying their work. His paintings are much more highly valued now. We see here his painting of workmen planing some of the acres of parquet laid in the Haussmann buildings. A shy bachelor, he bequeathed his collection to the Louvre, with Renoir as executor. An acrimonious debate followed, with Clemenceau intervening on behalf of the Impressionists. The Louvre even then accepted only half of the pictures.

Édouard Manet's rejection can be seen most spectacularly in his *Déjeuner sur l'herbe* This large picture shows a picnic in a wood, the girl being naked. It was rejected by the Paris Salon and finally shown in the *Salon des Refusés* (sic) where it caused a scandal. It is not especially 'impressionist' and there had been plenty of nudes in French art before that girl. The trouble was that she was not labelled Venus or Justice, but was quite anonymous. (Incidentally, the talkative young man on the right is Manet's son.) Two years later, in 1865, the Salon again rejected Manet's *Olympia*, a marvellous study in black and white (ground floor) for the same reason. After that he became, temporarily, a true Impressionist, as his pictures of the Monet family in a garden or boating at Argenteuil show. However, his heart was in Paris and in portraits; note his portrait of Clemenceau (1879). Other notable pictures in the museum are *The Balcony* – equally rejected (the girl is Berthe Morisot), and *The Fife Player* (ground floor). Denied the popular and critical success for which he longed, Manet died prematurely of locomotor ataxia. His last work was the well-known *Bar aux Folies Bergère*s, now in London. In 1890 Monet raised a fund by public subscription which bought *Olympia* for the nation.

Claude Monet, however, was the true leader of the Impressionists and he really was obsessed by light; light on water (his *Bridge at*

Argenteuil, his *Regatta*, his lily-pond at Giverny) light in the sky, light on buildings. He was reacting to the sombre colours of the Barbizon School and to the dark-varnished masterpieces of earlier centuries. He preferred not to mix his colours on his palette, but to apply them plain in juxtaposition. The blending and the vividness come in the viewer's eye and for this reason we should stand well back from them – a difficult thing to do in an always-crowded gallery. His compositions are those of a child snap-shotter; he did not often bother to include the end of the bridge, the top of the palazzo, the side of the cathedral. It was the light he was interested in, the rippled Seine, sun coming through the mist, the ever-changing façade of Rouen Cathedral. He painted parts of this building twenty times, going from one canvas to another as the light moved. Five of them hang together in the Musée d'Orsay and we should remember that they are not pictures of the cathedral, but studies of changing light on the same stones. Also here are one of his Westminster series, his *Gare Saint-Lazare*, a murky triumph, and also his *Haystacks*, arguably the finest picture in the whole museum. It really glows with light.

Alfred Sisley, of British parentage although he lived all his life in France, was also obsessed with light, in the sky and on snow. He was a solitary man, withdrawn and irritable, too poor to buy shoes – he wore clogs. There are rarely any people in his pictures, and then only in the distance. But his works give great pleasure and we should enjoy his *Floods at Port-Marly*, his *Snow at Louveciennes*, and his many pictures of the Seine with its barges and regattas. Nor should we miss his picture of Argenteuil, that white little town, as it then was.

Camille Pissarro, another true Impressionist (born in St Thomas, Virgin Islands in 1830), was less interested in water. Instead he preferred country lanes, orchards, gardens, trees and cottages (note his *Village of Voisins* and his *Red Roofs*). Finally he returned to Paris where he was fascinated by the streets especially when wet. His well-known *Boulevard des Italiens at night* evokes the dark, lamplit city, but that is now in London.

Coming to the Semi-Impressionists, we reach Pierre-Auguste Renoir, a painter whom we either love or hate. His flirtation with Impressionism was comparatively brief (note his *Hillside Path*). A cheerful, gregarious man, he preferred painting people to landscapes; in particular he enjoyed painting female flesh and returned to eighteenth-century colour, seeing himself as the successor to

Boucher and Fragonard, whom he greatly admired. But whatever we feel about his too, too fleshy flesh (did those girls never use powder?) nobody can fail to enjoy his big picture *Le Moulin de la Galette*, with its happy, dancing, drinking crowd.

Paul Cézanne was only an intermittent Impressionist. He lived, from 1872–74, in Auvers-sur-Oise, near to Argenteuil, where his close neighbour, Pissarro, influenced him strongly, particularly by the idea of working in the open air. He knew most of the others in the group and his *House of the Hanged Man* was shown in the group exhibition at Nadar's studio. But his tendency was towards geometrical construction, very different from Monet, as were his preferred colours, which were not at all to the taste of juries. His shy, fierce temperament made it hard for him to make friends, and rejections by the Salon hurt him. He was happier in his native Provence, to which he returned for a yearly visit. He was in the end officially accepted by the Salon, but it no longer meant much to him. He was trying to move beyond Impressionism to a kind of new classicism, and in this area he did his greatest work. The Salon d'Automne showed many of his works in 1907, but he only commented that he was making slow progress. The Musée d'Orsay has few of his works, but we should notice two of his still lifes (bottles and apples, of course); his Provençal landscapes, full of sunshine and warmth; and a wonderful but rather grim double-portrait, *The Cardplayers*.

Next we have Vincent Van Gogh and Paul Gauguin. The Impressionists normally stayed on friendly terms, but these two quarrelled so bitterly (about what we do not know) that Van Gogh cut off his own ear. His *Restaurant de la Sirène* reminds us that he was once an Impressionist, but most of the works shown are from his final period, after his return from Provence to Auvers-sur-Oise and momentary peace in the house of Dr Gachet, whose portrait hangs here. There is also a picture of the local church, very wavy. But the two pictures here which remain in the mind are both portraits. One is a *Self-Portrait*, a haunted, agonised man on the edge of suicide; the other is an earlier work from Provence, *L'Arlésienne*, a formidable woman, seated against a yellow background.

Paul Gauguin (1848–1903) is represented by some works from his Impressionist period, but the others are in his well-known Tahiti style, with its vivid colours, its total rejection of perspective and his flat-nosed women. Some of them command our notice: *Tahitian Women* and *Arearea*, two girls and a dog beside a blue tree.

Compelling, but a very long way from Monet, whom he had rejected. We also see his two nudes *Et l'Or de leurs Corps*. The museum has reconstructed his sequoia wood painted and carved doorway, the *Maison du Jouir*. He painted *Soyez mystérieuses* on one side, and on the other *Soyez amoureuses et vous serez heureuses*.

Now transferred to the Musée d'Orsay from the Louvre, we see the famous portrait of his mother by the American James McNeill Whistler (1834–1905). It shows her in black, wearing a lace cap, beside a black curtain and a grey wall. It is a face of great sadness and dignity. He was influenced by the Japanese style in restricting his colour-scale.

There is no space here to consider the others – Bazille, Boudin, Jongkind and Fantin-Latour. But we should take time to study Edgar Dégas (1834–1913). For Dégas an impression was a picture of movement, not of light. It was said of him that his idea of the countryside was a racecourse. Certainly he liked painting horses and also ballerinas, on stage or in their dressing rooms. Or people at work, laundresses yawning, a moment in time, an impression captured. Yet the picture which will surely remain in our minds is *Absinthe*, a sad picture of stillness, a man and a woman sitting motionless at a plain table, the glasses before them.

This collection is a big Salon des Refusés, the life's work of men of genius, disappointed, often ignored and sometimes coming to sad ends. Yet, as we walk out into the Paris scene and see the skies of Monet and Sisley, the streets of Pissarro, our feeling is one of exhilaration, as if we had just had a glass of champagne. These men had something inside themselves, a *joie de vivre*, which could not be extinguished by any failure, any illness or any jury or critic.

Excellent lighting is obtained on the upper level by a combination of daylight and good artificial light. Since watercolours, pastels and drawings have to be spared from bright light, these are in galleries by themselves. If we plunge into a room which seems to be completely dark, we shall know that we are looking at Odilon Redon (1840–1916), even if we can't see his work. The room of Dégas' pastels is more visible.

If we eat in the modest but pleasant *Café des Hauteurs*, between Impressionists and Post-Impressionists, we find ourselves, delightfully, using the huge face of the old station clock as a window. We can walk out onto the station roof, flanked by vast statues of women which have presided over the station all along. In the basement lurk terrifying heads of even more gigantic female statues (apparently guillotined). But we must not grudge this temple of the Railway Age its goddesses. On such a site as this there must have been many others before them. We look out on Paris, seeing the river below, lined with trees, and above these typical Paris roofs, rising up to domes on the skyline, and the Sacré Cœur Basilica, topping it all from Montmartre.

Before we go to the ground floor, to find the rest of the Impressionists' work, we should visit the rooms on this upper level which show their successors. Dealers are fond of telling us that the Impressionists have been 'over-exposed', and that the later work should be valued just as highly. We can now judge this for ourselves.

'Post-Impressionist' is a vague phrase which embraces several distinct schools: Symbolism and Art Nouveau, with the school of Pont-Aven (Gauguin, Bernard, Serusier etc); the 'Nabis' ('prophets' in Hebrew), admirers of Gauguin (Bonnard, Vuillard, Denis, Maillol, Vallotton) a band of friends who formed the avant-garde of the last decade of the nineteenth century; and Neo-Impressionists (Seurat, Signac, Cross and some works by Pissarro). These are usually known as *pointillistes*, because of their technique of using small adjoining dots or cubes of primary colour to convey light. The technique is based on the mosaic rather than on sweeps of the brush, and it is certainly effective; the canvases seem to glow with light and heat. But it is also restricting to the human face, which, when they bothered to paint it at all, has to be much simplified. Both Georges Seurat (1859–1891) and Monet (whom he attacked) were trying to find a scientific way of rendering light, water and the Seine countryside. Which succeeded better is a matter of choice; we can enjoy them both. We see here Seurat's sketch for his famous painting of boys bathing, *La Grande Jatte*, which is in Chicago. We may also like Maximilien Luce's (1858–1941) pointilliste *The Louvre and the Pont Neuf by Night*, as a view of Paris.

We glimpse Pierre Bonnard (1867–1947), nicknamed the 'Japanese Nabi' because he shared the vogue for Japan of the time, with his ferocious arching cat *Le Chat Blanc* in the '*Petit Format*' room and *Le Corsage à Carreaux* (*The Checked Blouse*) 1892, but his larger works are on the middle level, where we can see them at the end of our visit.

It seems to be a good idea to separate Henri de Toulouse-Lautrec (1864–1901) from the Impressionists, with whom he has often been grouped. Apart from a slight acquaintance with Van Gogh, he did not know them and his aims were indeed different. Not for him long hours of studying light on the Seine. His days were spent racing, his nights at the *Moulin Rouge* or the *Mirliton*, where he painted the dancers and singers, designed posters for 'La Goulue' and the singer Aristide Bruant, and drank far too much, which brought about his early death. One of his best-known paintings is here, *La Clownesse Cha-U-Kao*. But personally I am drawn to a small portrait *La Femme aux Gants* (*The Woman in Gloves*). It is an extraordinary likeness of my grandmother Elinor Glyn, face, posture, clothes, gloves and all. She lived in Paris then, and I have always believed it must be her. One of her novels had a crippled artist (like Lautrec) who was a genius. But the Musée d'Orsay now tells us that the sitter's name was Platzer. Elinor must have had a double. It's a good picture anyway.

We must also study Henri 'Douanier' Rousseau, 1844–1910. At first sight we may think his work is childish, because he was so obviously self-taught; his figures and animals, even a tiger, look like toys, and the jungle he never saw but studied in the Botanical Gardens is like a giant aspidistra. But the more we look into his work the more it grips us. He was ahead of his time in painting from such an intense interior vision. We are sharing his dream world, and it can be frightening, as dreams so often are.

He was nicknamed 'Douanier' (Customs-Officer) because he had a minor clerical job to do with the tollgates. But painting was his life and his originality won him support from other artists and writers including Gauguin and Picasso who acquired some of his works. Signac introduced him to the Salon des Indépendants in 1886. When Rousseau retired from his job in 1893 he was able to undertake the large canvases with strange themes for which he became famous. His *War* of 1894, normally shown here, is one of two paintings chosen to frame the entrance to the modern art section of the reopened Centre Georges Pompidou. The work which stays most in our minds was one of his last, *The Snake-Charmer* of 1907. Here the dark figure playing a pipe in the moonlight is full of mystery. She has a snake curled round her neck.

Ground Floor

Reaching the ground floor, we must not be dismayed by the mass of gesticulating sculpture ahead but turn into the side-aisles, where we find the paintings. We are moving back in time, because this level starts in 1848, the Musée d'Orsay's first years.

Near us, on the right are Eugène Delacroix (1798–1863), and Ingres (1780–1867) and his school, the great rivals of their period. Their earlier works are in the Grand Louvre, their late works here. Delacroix was praised for his glowing colours, Ingres for his flowing lines. But we may see many other differences between them. Delacroix's huge energy is so far from Ingres' static calm. We only see the sketch here for Delacroix's *The Lion Hunt* (1854) with its lionskin and blood colouring, but it is enough to explain why he was called powerful and uninhibited. His paintings are full of action, as in his *Arab stallions fighting in a stable* and *Crossing a ford in Morocco.*

We will be pleased to find one of the best known of Ingres' rhythmically balanced nudes *La Source* (*The Spring*), completed in 1856, a nymph pouring out a ewer of water held on her shoulder. Many artists have been inspired by this and have produced their own versions, including Seurat, Picasso and even René Magritte. *Venus at Paphos* is another typical Ingres nude.

In the series of rooms in the left aisle, almost the first painting we see is a large canvas by Rosa Bonheur (1822–1899), one of the very few women artists shown in the Musée d'Orsay. The Impressionist Berthe Morisot, whom we saw on the upper level, was not bashful about painting a baby in a cot and children in a garden, while Vigée-Lebrun (1755–1841) in the Grand Louvre hugs her little girl affectionately. But Rosa Bonheur was made of sterner stuff and paints as though she had her name as well as her sex to live down. She shows us a team of working oxen, a thoroughly down-to-earth picture, and she also carried commissions for monumental sculpture on public buildings. Long after her time, Rosa was honoured at the centenary exhibition of the Salon des Femmes Peintres et Sculpteurs as the first person to persuade the reluctant Ecole des Beaux-Arts to admit girls as students.

We cannot study all the work on this floor in a short visit but can pick out the best known. In section 6 we see Jean-François Millet, (1814–1875) Barbizon School (a village on the edge of the forest of Fontainebleau), and find his famous painting *The Angelus* (1858/59).

What a *little* picture this is, to have made such a great impact on the general public of its day. It was very widely reproduced, not only all over France but in Britain too, and American collectors tried hard to buy the original. The Musée d'Orsay cannot begin to explain its popularity. There are just two peasant figures, at dusk in a harvest field, hearing the bell from the far off church spire, which tells them that their day's work is over, and calls them to prayer. It is certainly time to stop work, as it is nearly dark. In fact the painting seems so completely dark that we must wonder if it needs cleaning. The reproduction which some ancestor had hung in my nursery was much brighter and looked frankly better. But the quality is still there, and it is the quality of prayer: something which, in all the galleries of religious paintings by great masters in the Grand Louvre, we very rarely find. *The Gleaners* (1857) is here too. Millet's *L'Eglise de Gréville* is said to have had a strong influence on Van Gogh, who made a copy of it. This was one of his last works and captures a great sense of peace.

Nymphs Dancing (1850) by Jean-Baptiste-Camille Corot (1796–1875) nearby, seems to be almost as dark as Millet, but perhaps we are all dazed by the sunblaze of the Impressionists we have seen on the upper level. And here, at last, we find them again, with the pre-1870 works of Manet, Renoir, Monet, Bazille and Dégas (sections bewilderingly numbered 14, 18 and 13, although they are next door to each other).

Here we see at last Manet's *Olympia* of 1863 and *The Fife-player,* refused by the Salon of 1866 but later widely popular. This is an uneven collection, but we may note his portrait of Zola (1868), his *Lola de Valence* (1862), full of Spanish pride, and his *White Peonies* (1864), so beautifully painted that we can almost catch their scent.

Frédéric Bazille's *Family Reunion* studies the light falling through the trees onto the group, and on the ground. It is a surprisingly assured work for such a young artist. He was killed in the defence of Paris in 1870, aged only 29. We see Renoir's portrait of Bazille painting (1867). Monet was only beginning to find his touch. But *La Pie* (*The Magpie*) – a fine snowscene dominated by a single magpie – is a real Monet. His delightful *Femmes au Jardin* (*Women in a Garden*) of 1866 was refused by the Salon but Zola wrote defending it.

It is difficult to recognise Dégas in his early work. He lived in Italy and studied the composition of early Italian painters; his work was curiously static. But by the end of the 1860s he was settling into racecourses and opera in his subjects and beginning to capture the movement and colour which have made him famous.

We go up a few steps on the left side of the aisle to find Gustave Courbet (1819–1877). How relieved the Grand Louvre management must have been when Courbet was transferred to the Musée d'Orsay. He was always very badly hung there, perhaps because his landscapes looked so much more real than those of their favourite, Corot. The Musée d'Orsay gives him a very large room to himself (ground floor, section 7), up a few steps close to the early Impressionists, and values him as a 'Social Realist' – considered a crime in his own day. His huge canvas *Burial at Ornans* caused an uproar when it was shown in 1850, because he had not idealised the people but painted them as they were.

Courbet may have attended a real funeral in this graveyard, because Ornans was his grandfather's home. Perhaps this is what made the whole scene live in his mind, and why the grief in the faces of the women (the group on the right) seems so deeply felt. We must wonder why the critics of the time described these simple country people as 'hideous'. Even Delacroix deplored their 'vulgarity'.

The construction is elaborate, light concentrated on the draped coffin and the men's sashes for lowering it, in such a way as to lead the eye to the small crucifix, high over the grave. But there are in fact three complete circles made by the groups and the light picks this out on the Breton caps of the women too, allowing us to notice the contrast between the uncaring faces of the officials, for whom this is just another job, and the sorrow of the family.

Opposite, another long, enormous canvas by Courbet, *L'Atelier* (*The Studio*) was described by himself as 'a realist allegory completing 7 years of my artistic life'. The principal feature is a very beautiful girl, nude except for a modestly held shawl. The studio is crowded with people, once again grouped into three separate circles. If we study them, we find that no one at all notices the girl, even the artist himself, sitting on a chair with his back to her, hard at work painting a landscape. The girl seems to be invisible. She looks over his shoulder so keenly, and with so much love, watching his work, that we may think she is not his model after all but his Muse. Equally unnoticed is a canvas of the Crucifixion, stacked behind the painter's landscape.

Middle Level – Sculpture

France has always had generous patrons for sculpture. When British people tease them that their ideal garden is a gravel-patch with a statue, they see nothing wrong. The 'Musée d'Orsay period' produced many sculptors who are still valued in France, although they have not achieved international fame. They are all here. Some even have museums of their own, for example Aristide Maillol (1861–1944), with soft-looking marble nudes and Emile-Antoine Bourdelle (1861–1929), whose bronze *Hercules the Archer* of 1909 uses simple lines to express great strength. But we may decide to head straight for the Auguste Rodin (1840–1917) terrace (middle level, arrival end). In the Rodin Museum we will have the chance to see his work more fully but here we may see some of his most famous works, in plaster, for example his *Balzac* (1897) and his *Gate of Hell*, in which he combined between 1880 and 1890, various of his former well-known works such as *Le Penseur* (*The Thinker*) and *Le Baiser* (*The Kiss*). This gate is based on Dante, but was first inspired by the gates of the Baptistery at Florence. It was commissioned in 1880 for a proposed new Museum of Decorative Arts, planned on this very site. But the Gare d'Orsay was built here instead.

Paintings

We may see more of Pierre Bonnard (1867–1947), in section 72, among his fellow Nabis, Valloton Denis and Vuillard (1868–1940), and enjoy his *Woman in a Cape* (1891), which uses a restricted colour-scale to effect. It glows with golden warmth. Another Bonnard, *The Box* (1908) is in a later style. It shows his friends the Bernheim brothers (gallery owners), with their wives, at what seems to be the opera. But it must have been a dull opera – or perhaps the wives were dull women. The piece has been described as 'distinguished boredom'. In *En Barque* (1907) the passengers in the boat gaze away from the shore, thinking their own thoughts and seeing nothing of what goes by. The landscape is almost completely effaced, because it is unnoticed. Yet it is there, with its houses and people, existing, and leading its own, scarcely discernible, life. This is painted with great skill. The artist appears to be musing over the old philosophical conundrum: 'If an object does not exist in the mind of an observer, has it any existence at all?'

We may find it a little hard to see what the Symbolists had in common, as they were not united in time, place or style. The Musée d'Orsay breaks out from showing only French art, at this point, and stuns us by grouping Edward Burne-Jones, Gustav Klimt and the Norwegian Edward Munch (1863–1944) together. Nice though it is to see some of our favourite artists turn up in Paris, it's hard not to feel a lurch of culture gap between Burne-Jones (1835–1898) and the Austrian Klimt (1862–1918). The Musée d'Orsay gives credit to British Pre-Raphaelites for being among the first to react against both Realism and Impressionism and to set out to translate their thoughts and dreams. They show us Burne-Jones' *The Wheel of Fortune* (1883), and Klimt's *Roses under the Trees* (1905). Klimt was one of the founder members of the Vienna 'Secession' movement, opposed to the artistic establishment of its time, as artists and intellectuals in many countries were, especially in France. The connection between him and Burne-Jones still seems rather tenuous.

The middle level includes Decorative Arts, including ceramics and Lalique glass, and Art Nouveau furniture. We must see Alexandre Charpentier's (1856–1909) whole dining-room of mahogany panels, elaborately carved with climbing plants in the true, drooping Art Nouveau style of 1900, reminding us of the old Metro entrances of the date by Guimard. He cleverly integrated sideboards and cupboards, and designed a whole set of furniture to match, but only the table survives.

Apart from this ensemble, all by one artist, the museum has decided against putting together rooms where furniture is combined with other art to make a whole period room, such as we shall see in the Jacquemart-André Museum. The exception is the *Ball Room*, which has been preserved as it was in 1900 and filled with the type of sculpture and painting most admired at its date. This, of course, was not in the new Art Nouveau style, but was designed in the neo-Rococo style popular at the end of the century. This ballroom is a revelation, and not to be missed. The walls are encrusted with garlands and shells in gold relief and huge ornate mirrors, opposite and beside the window. The painted ceiling is also encrusted with gold and cherubs. Six great chandeliers multiply in the mirrors, making a 'Palais-des-Glaces'. What magnificence! And the pictures show us lavish women's clothes as well. In Alfred Besuard's (1849–1934) full-length portrait, the dress is of wonderfully glinting white satin, with a bodice and underdress of pink – daring at that time with red hair. This was accepted by the Salon des Artistes Français of 1886 and shows us what their taste was. But, alas, the face is quite outshone by the ball-dress and has no character. The lady needn't have bothered to pose – the artist could just as well have painted the clothes on a stand. Perhaps he did. Dress was everything. Caillebotte's stripped-to-the-waist, sweating workmen, and laundresses as drunk as Maxim Gorky's in *My Apprenticeship* may not have lived well, but some people in those days certainly did, and in luxury never seen again.

We are near the end of our visit and should remember that the museum starts to close half an hour ahead of its official time. But if it is a late opening night and the 'Restaurant du Musée d'Orsay' is open for dinner (it is nearby, on this level), we may see that it is decorated, as far as a modern budget permits, to match the *Ball Room*.

There we can dream ourselves back into the nineteenth century, feeling opulent over a good dinner and French wine. The service is excellent and rapid. From the windows we can see the lights of Paris. It still looks much as it did then. This would be a romantic and not too expensive place to bring a party, even if we were not visiting the museum.

PART TWO

The Right Bank

6

The Champs-Elysées

W E TAKE OUR *point de départ*, once again, from a star, but this time from a much bigger star, the Etoile. The circle round it has now been renamed Place Charles de Gaulle, but everyone, Gaullist or anti-Gaullist, still refers to it as the Etoile – the star. In the centre of it stands the Arc de Triomphe, one of the best-known monuments in the world (Metro Charles-de-Gaulle-Etoile). From here, or better still from the top, we can see twelve avenues radiating out in all directions. Nine of them are not very interesting, unless we have business there. Two of them, Victor Hugo and Foch, are fashionable residential streets leading to the Bois de Boulogne, and we shall come to them later. The one we are concerned with at the moment is the main one leading down the hill to Place de la Concorde and the Louvre, Avenue des Champs-Elysées. The whole area and idea is generally thought, in France and abroad, to be the high point of French town-planning.

However, it was not planned like that. Outside the city limits, it was simply fields and marshes in the time of Henri IV. In 1616 his wife, Marie de Medici, created the Cours-la-Reine, a fashionable carriage-drive. But it led, not through the fields, but along the Seine to what is now Place de l'Alma. In 1667 the great landscape-gardener, Le Nôtre, who loved distant prospects and formal perspectives, planted chestnut trees in rows and named the area the Elysian Fields. In 1724 the Director of the Royal Gardens, the Duke of Antin, prolonged the avenue to the top of the Butte de Chaillot, now the Etoile. His successor extended it to the Seine at Neuilly. To improve the perspective and make the avenue easier for horses, Soufflot, in 1774, reduced the height of the Butte by sixteen feet (five metres), the spare earth being dumped in the nearby Rue Balzac, where it remains. The top of the hill became a grass lawn and it was Napoleon, in 1806, who had the idea of placing a huge triumphal arch on the summit.

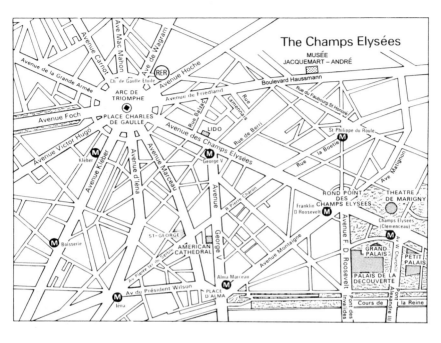

The Champs Elysées

MUSÉE
JACQUEMART – ANDRÉ

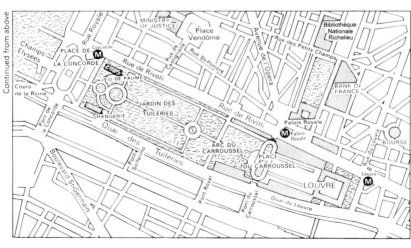

His choice of architect for the **Arc de Triomphe** was Chalgrin whose ideas were monumental indeed. The arch was to be fifty metres high and forty-five metres wide, encrusted with large flamboyant sculptures, friezes, shields and hundreds of names. Less elegant than Arc de Carrousel at the other end of the Champs-Elysées, it dominates the Etoile and the avenues, as it was intended to, particularly at night when it is floodlit.

We reach the arch by the underground passage (from the north side of the Champs-Elysées); no one dares to cross Place Charles de Gaulle on foot. Beneath the arch lies the Unknown Soldier with his flame, and several other plaques record historical events. In the very centre, worn by many feet, is a bronze Napoleonic eagle.

Outside we should note the four sculptured reliefs. Facing the Champs-Elysées, the one immediately on our left is generally considered the finest of the four; by Rude, it shows the departure of the volunteers in 1792 and is usually called *La Marseillaise.* It is full of life and revolutionary vigour, but it may seem rather too flamboyant for some tastes. The other three sculptures have less life and are less admired. On our right is the Treaty of 1810 (*La Triomphe*) by Cortot. On the other side of the arch, facing Avenue de la Grande Armée, we have *Peace* on the right, *Resistance* on the left, both by Etex. On a higher level are six panels showing battles and funerals. The battle of Austerlitz faces Avenue Wagram, the battle of Jemmappes Avenue Kléber.

We re-enter the arch and there, standing between the imperial eagle and the flame of the Unknown Soldier, we realize that we are, in a sense, in a cathedral. The Arc de Triomphe is Napoleon's Notre-Dame, his Sainte-Chapelle, great in size and dedicated to the glory of the Grande Armée. On the walls round us are the names of battles, marshals and generals, founders of the Napoleonic Empire.

Some well-known names are, of course, missing and many of the battles may be unknown to us. Which of us could write an impromptu essay on the battle of Dietikon? (Near Zürich in September 1799, French troops and Swiss levies under Masséna checked the advancing Russians under Suvarov. Switzerland, *la république helvétienne,* had been quietly absorbed into the French Empire, a shocking thought for those who fondly imagine that the little neutral country has been independent and free of foreign invasions for five hundred years.)

Standing in the middle of the arch, we can certainly find it an awe-inspiring building and forgive its ungainliness, its megalomania.

It dominates the avenues and the landscape, much as Napoleon dominated continental Europe for fifteen years.

However, the arch got off to a shaky start. The Empress Josephine had not produced an heir, though she had children by her first marriage. In 1810 he divorced her, to the disapproval of the Pope, Pius VII, who was taken into captivity, in Valence and elsewhere. As his second wife, Napoleon took a prize of war, the young Princess Marie-Louise of Austria. On her way from Vienna to Paris she was unexpectedly waylaid by Napoleon himself, who virtually raped her – in her carriage, some say. He then returned to Paris. The nineteen-year-old princess made her way to the arch, through which she was supposed to make her triumphal entry, and so down the Champs-Elysées to the Tuileries. Unfortunately the arch was only a few feet high, Chalgrin having had problems with the foundations. A false arch of canvas was hastily erected and the future empress passed through this in her procession down to her bridal bed. She produced an heir the following year, Napoleon François, King of Rome whose short, sad life has been eloquently described in Rostand's weepy play *L'Aiglon* (*The Eaglet*).

The arch was finally finished in 1836, after years of neglect. Four years later Napoleon's body, brought home from St Helena by permission of the British (Palmerston), passed through it on its way to the Invalides. Since then there have been many moving events there: the Victory procession through the arch in 1919; the crowd of enthusiasts, led by de Gaulle, in 1944; the annual large ceremony held there every 11 November, in memory of the Unknown Soldier. On major festivals and state occasions, a huge Tricolore flag hangs and billows inside the arch, reminding us that it is an arch of celebration as well as a cenotaph.

The summit platform is open to the public during daylight hours. It is an ascent of two hundred and eighty-four steps; there is also a lift and a queue. But it is an ascent which we must certainly make, one way or the other. Around us lies Paris, or at least the Right Bank, which most visitors consider to be Paris. The Champs-Elysées, beneath us, leads to the Place de la Concorde, the Tuileries Gardens and the Louvre. We are in the centre of the Etoile, the star with its twelve radiating avenues. It is a memorable, panoramic experience.

The **Etoile** itself was completed in 1854 under Haussmann (who else?). He added seven further avenues to complete the twelve-pointed star and commissioned Hittorff to design the uniform façades which ring the Place between the avenues. It is majestic town-planning which the French admire, though some visitors prefer narrow streets and picturesque corners elsewhere, which time has forgotten to develop.

We return through the tunnel to the 'mainland'. Two addresses nearby may be useful to the British visitor. One is St George's Anglican (high) Church at 7 Rue Auguste Vacquerie (Metro George V). It is not easy to find, although it is only a short walk from the Etoile (up Avenue Iéna). It has a tradition of good music and an excellent choir, but the great organ which Susan Landale used to play has gone, along with the nineteenth-century building. The site has now been redeveloped into a block of flats, with the church squeezed into part of the underground garage. It is always full and many people stay for wine and cheese, or lunch, on Sundays, after the 10.30 a.m. service. Social activities include the Cardew Club for young people and study-groups. A few yards away, at 5 Rue de Presbourg, we find the *Sir Winston Churchill* pub.

Remontons les Champs-Elysées! – though in fact we shall be going downhill. The phrase was much used at the turn of the century, when carriages of the well-to-do, several abreast, passed up and down the avenue, greeting each other and strollers on the pavements. The ladies wore large hats, the gentlemen top-hats, unless they were alongside on horseback. Above them were the chestnuts, nostalgically always in candle; the world of Gigi and her admirers. It is not quite like that now. The chestnuts have been replaced by planes, supposedly more resistant to traffic fumes. The carriages and horsemen are now cars, going much too fast to greet anybody, but often honking their horns. But the magic remains. It is partly due to wide pavements and the vast crowds which wander up and down, all day and most of the night, French as well as visitors. It is still the great Promenade of Paris. *Remontons les Champs-Elysées!*

In addition to an ever-moving cavalcade, the **Champs-Elysées** is also a street of more formally organized events; for instance, the big parade on 14 July, the moving procession on 11 November, state visits of foreign potentates, when the avenue is hung with flags; and lighter events such as the summer day when the avenue is closed for the Tour de France bicycle race and sweating riders go up and down for more than two hours. There is talk of a grand prix rally there, similar to the one through the streets of Monte Carlo. A simpler spectacle, though not without its dangers, is to cross the Avenue on a wet winter night and pause at a traffic island; from here we can watch the twinkling red tail-lights of the cars, and their reflections, as they mount to Etoile or descend to Place de la Concorde, also floodlit. And at Christmas there are lights in the trees along the whole avenue.

But there is more to it than that. The Champs-Elysées has become an idea, an emotional rallying-point for Parisians. We can mention such spontaneous and unorganized events as the huge demonstration on 30 May 1968, when the long avenue was crowded from end to end with thousands of Frenchmen, waving Tricolores and singing the *Marseillaise*. It was a counterblast by the silent majority to the much-publicized riots in the Boulevard Saint-Michel, which preached anarchy and revolution. The *événements* on the Left Bank, as they are tactfully called, petered out soon after. Two years later there was a big silent march, equally unorganized, in memory of de Gaulle. When France won the World Football Cup in 1998, the biggest crowd seen since the Liberation gathered in the Champs-Elysées (an estimated two million) and celebrated all night.

When we stroll down the Champs-Elysées on a summer afternoon, we are not only making the scene; we are also, in a small way, part of history.

Architecturally it is not much, apart from the two perspectives up and down, and an occasional glimpse through a side avenue at the Invalides dome. It is a commercial street of banks, airline offices, car showrooms, cafés, cinemas and hamburger bars. It is another Piccadilly. But recently it has become a good shopping area, especially for women. Less expensive than the Faubourg Saint-Honoré, less way-out than Saint-Germain-des-Prés, it is popular with those wanting fashionable clothes and shoes. Many of the boutiques are in shopping arcades, leading off the main avenue and often on several levels.

Many avenues and streets lead off the Champs-Elysées and we cannot explore them all. But we can note the main ones and their points of interest. Descending from Etoile, we find on the right, leading down to the river, **Avenue George V,** named after the English king. Lined by chestnuts (which seem to survive the traffic without difficulty), its most prominent feature is the spire of the **American Episcopalian Cathedral.** This is a nineteenth-century Gothic building, dignified inside as well as out. Its services, always crowded and not only by Americans, are noted for their music; each one is almost a concert and the choir is very well rehearsed.

Otherwise the avenue is very typical of this part of Paris, the eighth Arrondissement. It contains fashion houses, an embassy (China), two luxury hotels, a popular night-spot (the *Crazy Horse*

Saloon), any number of banks and offices, cafés, restaurants.
boutiques and the Paris office of a big firm of British chartered
accountants. Such a mixture is very Parisian and we shall meet it
again in the Opéra area, but it is scarcely conceivable in London or
New York. The avenue ends at the Seine, at Place de l'Alma, a semi-
circular area of cafés and restaurants, where four avenues meet the
quay and the Right Bank expressway. This is also the embarking
point for the *bateaux-mouches,* the big boats which provide evening
dinner cruises.

Back on the Champs-Elysées, we find ourselves at *Fouquet*, the
famous old café and restaurant. At the bar, there is a celebrated notice
that unaccompanied women are not admitted; this has given much
annoyance to Women's Lib and female journalists. From Avenue
George V, under the chestnuts, we can see guests eating out on the
terrace, open in summer. We pass the long Rue La Boétie. In a café here
I once saw a man order a cheese soufflé and then give it to his dog.

We are now at the **Rond-Point,** a roundabout where six avenues
meet, a point bright with fountains and flowers and trees, and
splendid views in all directions. Two good façades remain here; on
the south side the buildings of the magazine *Jours de France* (behind
the big black and gold railings); on the other, the buildings occupied
until recently by the newspaper *Le Figaro.* It was planned to
demolish both and replace them by high-rise developments. This was
prevented. The façades were retained and restored, while the
buildings behind them were rebuilt – a typical French compromise,
and one pleasing to the eye.

The first avenue on our right at the Rond-Point is **Avenue
Montaigne** (8me). Formerly Ruelle des Veuves, it was a bright spot
with many 'dancings' and three thousand gas-lights. Many people
went to the Winter Garden there to hear Monsieur Sax play his new
instrument, the saxophone. The avenue is now very like Avenue
George V, and it also leads down to Place de l'Alma and the river.
Apart from hundreds of big business addresses, it has high fashion,
the Canadian Embassy, a luxury hotel and two theatres, the Comédie
des Champs-Elysées and the **Théâtre des Champs-Elysées,** almost
on Place de l'Alma (Metro Alma-Marceau).

We should note the théâtre, one of the first reinforced concrete
buildings to be built in Paris, completed in 1912. It was designed by
Auguste Perret and he tried to soften the bleakness of the material
with pilasters and reliefs (by Bourdelle). His reputation soared and,
many years later, he was commissioned to replan and rebuild the city

of Le Havre, totally destroyed in 1944 by the Germans, who wanted to deny the Allies a Channel port. Le Havre is the only modern city in Europe planned and designed by one man and, whatever we may think of it now, we have a foretaste and sample of his architecture here in the Avenue Montaigne. Grandiose, we may think, and uninspired.

The Théâtre des Champs-Elysées is now almost wholly given over to concerts; it is the main concert hall of central Paris. It is also used by visiting ballet companies, and it was here that the Diaghilev Ballet gave the notorious first performance, on 29 May 1913, of *Le Sacre du Printemps*. The conductor, Pierre Monteux, had prophesied that the work would cause a scandal, but even he did not foresee the riot that actually occurred. Stravinsky, it was said, was trying to destroy music, though little of his score could be heard through the booing and catcalling. After the performance Diaghilev, Stravinsky, Nijinsky and Cocteau took a cab and drove round the Bois de Boulogne, to calm themselves. Diaghilev wept, nobody spoke. By 1921 the work had achieved respectability and was placidly received at a London concert, conducted by Goossens. Fifty years after the first performance the music was performed with Monteux still conducting, and Stravinsky present, and this time it was the coronation of a masterpiece.

Also leading off the Rond-Point is **Avenue Franklin D. Roosevelt**, reaching the Seine at Pont des Invalides. This is another typical avenue of the area. Of note are the restaurant *Lasserre*, the stark German Embassy and the France-Amérique club, a pleasant mansion, often used for public events. (We must not confuse the avenue with Rue Franklin, called after Benjamin, which is in the sixteenth Arrondissement.) Here is the **Palais de la Découverte**, which has been the Science Museum of Paris since 1937 and is sponsored by the City of Paris, as well as receiving public funds. It adjoins the Grand Palais and is a palatial neo-Rococo building, put up for the 'Expo Universelle' of 1900, at the same time as the Eiffel Tower.

There is a rivalry between this museum and the much more recent 'Cité des Sciences' at Villette; they are both intended for schoolchildren and both have a planetarium, but they are quite different in their approach. 'Découverte' is intended for serious study, taking school groups aged 10 to 18, or over, and it also admits adult students, particularly in chemistry. It publishes a science magazine. Its sections are divided into Astronomy, Chemistry, Mathematics, Physics, Meteorology and Biology. In each section there are not only exhibitions but workshops, where the pupils take an active part in simple experiments at levels suited to their age. These are 50-minute programmes.

For museum lovers, a detour from the Rond-Point down the other part of Avenue Franklin Roosevelt brings us to the Musée Jacquemart-André and the Musée Nissim de Camondo.

The **Musée Jacquemart-André** (Metro Saint-Philippe-du-Roule, RER Etoile) is at 158 Boulevard Haussmann, which crosses the end of Avenue Franklin Roosevelt. Parisians are even more fascinated than tourists by this high-quality museum, because they understand that the sumptuous palace, of 'Second Empire' style (architect Henri Parent, finished in 1875), was a private house which was still lived in, not so long ago, and has been left just as it was. It was built for a member of a Protestant banking family, Edouard André, whose portrait we see, in military uniform, painted by Winterhalter in 1857. It must have been a highly successful bank, as its owners, Edouard André and his wife Nélie Jacquemart, a well-known portrait-painter, were able to travel all over Europe and the East buying art treasures for their home which now make up a priceless collection. It has been compared with the Frick Collection in New York and the Wallace Collection in London. Nélie Jacquemart bequeathed it to the Institut de France in 1912 on condition that nothing was to be moved from its place, as the arrangement of each room was an expression of the personal taste of the owners. French people, even if they are not art-lovers, go to see what it used to be like to be *really* rich.

We may go in a more artistic spirit. The museum houses fine works, by some of the greatest masters, which would be quite at home in the Louvre or the National Gallery. And so many of them! Part of its charm is that every room is done in its own style, with furnishings of its period, which produce an 'all-round environment'. We can dream ourselves into the time, in each room, even Nélie's own splendid bedroom.

We see a gracious 'Grand Salon' with gilding on the pilasters and painted ceiling. Next door to it we find splendid Beauvais tapestries. There are three Tiepolo ceilings; it's hard to imagine how they were transferred onto canvas for removal (or who could have been willing to part with them), but they are just what we expect Tiepolo (1696–1770) to be. The former dining-room, now open as a café, selling light, good quality, refreshments, has tapestries on the walls and the palest of the Tiepolo ceilings. The old library hangs great Flemish and Dutch masters, such as Van Dyck, Rembrandt, Ruysdael and

Hals. In the smoking-room we discover, unexpectedly, some good portraits of the English eighteenth-century school, which the Louvre must envy: Lawrence, Reynolds and Hopner (1756–1810). The French guide does not mention them.

There is a unique collection of French eighteenth-century paintings; Nélie Jacquemart was naturally interested in the work of another woman portrait-painter, Vigée-Lebrun; a Fragonard *Tête de Vieillard* is arresting; he seems to be hearing a call. We find a charming Greuze, plus Boucher, Oudry, Nathier and Chardin. The sculpture is by the well known Houdon and Lemoyne.

The first-floor 'Italian Museum' is even finer, with favourite painters from the fourteenth to sixteenth centuries, whom we shall meet again in the Louvre: Mantegna, Bellini, Uccello (St George killing a lovable dragon). There is also work by della Robbia, and a Carpaccio.

The monumental double-turn marble staircase of the winter garden with gilded ornate banisters, is a main feature. At its head a very fine Tiepolo fresco runs the whole length of the wall. It depicts Henri III of France being greeted by the Doge Contarini. Its beautiful pastel colouring has been faithfully restored.

One period of French painting seems to have been almost entirely avoided, although so much pressed on our view in the Louvre, and that is the art between the 1792 and 1848 revolutions, just before Edouard André's time. Bankers don't like revolutions.

If we take Rue du Téhéran from Boulevard Haussmann to Rue de Monceau, we come to **Musée Nissim de Camondo** (Metro Villiers). This is a private collection of antiques in an eighteenth-century style *hôtel* (rebuilt in 1913), specializing in furniture of the reigns of Louis XV and Louis XVI, the last French kings before the revolution of 1792. At this date furniture had developed into an important art form. There are keen partisans both of the highly ornate and curvaceous Louis XV style and of the lighter, straighter and more elegant Louis XVI pieces. The brocades which covered them were also elaborate and beautiful, originally in brilliant colours.

In this building, richly decorated in eighteenth-century style, with white and gold wainscot in the 'Salon Doré', and Aubusson carpets, the furniture has a perfect setting. It was the home of the Nissim de Camondo family, who formed the collection; they had been bankers in Constantinople. There are paintings too, notably by Francesco Guardi (1712–1793).

From Rond-Point to Place de la Concorde, the Champs-Elysées has quite a different character. Buildings are few and set well back from the avenue. We are in a garden, or perhaps a wood, with avenues of mature chestnuts, azaleas and other shrubs and no fences. We (and dogs) are free to roam as we wish. On the left side, almost hidden among the trees, are the Théâtre de Marigny and the well known **Espace Cardin,** once the Théâtre des Ambassadeurs. It is now in two parts. One is a television studio (visitors admitted after queueing) where we can watch our favourite programmes going out live. The other is a large hall, with plate-glass windows, used for exhibitions and sometimes for ballet. If we happen to go in May, our eyes may be distracted from the works of art displayed for us to the view through the windows, chestnuts in candle, azaleas in flower, the Champs-Elysées in spring. Concentration on the works on show can be an effort

On the right side, at the statue of Clemenceau (by Cogné, 1932), we find another avenue, **Avenue Winston Churchill**[*]. This is quite different from the other avenues we have seen. For one thing it has no houses. Instead it has two palaces, the Grand Palais and the Petit Palais, one on either side. It also has a superb view, down to the Seine, across Pont Alexandre III, over the Esplanade to the final dome of the Invalides. It is the kind of formal perspective which the French love and which they do so well.

At the opposite end of the avenue from Georges Clemenceau's statue (the river end, near the junction with Rue Albert Ier), we should look at the fine bronze statue of Sir Winston Churchill, unveiled by Queen Elizabeth II on 11 November 1998. Funds for this were raised by subscription in France in response to a request by President Jacques Chirac. It honours Churchill as a great statesman who was a friend of France.

London had got in first, by putting up a statue to General de Gaulle, in 1993. The part they played together, between 1940 and 1945, to bring about the liberation of France is emphasized, in this statue, by the choice of dress for it. Churchill is shown striding forward, wearing the uniform of an RAF Air Commodore which (rather puzzlingly) he wore when he walked down the Champs-Elysées beside de Gaulle in the famous parade of 11 November

---

[*] Paris has honoured many well-known Englishmen by naming streets after them. Apart from George V and Churchill, Queen Victoria has an avenue, Edward VII a square and an equestrian statue. Streets are also named after Roger Bacon, Byron, Dickens, Newton and Stephenson. There is also a Rue des Anglais and a Rue de Londres. More recently a humorous Cockney sculptor called Roy Adzak has had a museum named after him. He once advised a friend 'Don't jump onto every band-wagon: stick to every other'.

1944. It is by a French sculptor, Jean Cardot, born in 1930, a member of the Académie des Beaux-Arts.

The **Grand Palais,** built for the 1900 World Exhibition, is a huge building of stone, glass and steel. The north end, nearest to the Champs-Elysées, used to be an art museum devoted to one-man shows of the great. Retrospective exhibitions of Picasso, Léger, Chagalle, Miró and Cézanne attracted enormous crowds. At times the Grand Palais provided space for big commercial exhibitions such as the Motor Show and the Boat Show; it was the Earls Court or Olympia of Paris before it was supplanted by the Palais Omnisports de Paris at Bercy.

The central part used to be the regular home of many of the independent exhibitions so well known in Paris such as the long-established Salon des Indépendants and the huge Salon d'Automne, always thronged with artists and visitors; also more occasional salons such as the Triennale Européenne de Sculpture and the Biennale des Femmes (a large international show launched in 1988). The important autumn dealer's trade fair of contemporary art, the FIAC, was there too, each year, drawing huge crowds. The Grand Palais kept open late, and it became a habit of Parisians, especially young people, to stroll in in the evening, to see 'what's new this year', and to talk to the artists; sometimes with unnerving knowledge and discrimination, sometimes with a high-voltage booster of enthusiasm. The Palais, dominated inside by a huge ornamental clock, had an exciting atmosphere.

All this was suddenly closed down. The salons were told that the roof was about to fall in. Whether this was true or not, the free salons thought they were just being suppressed by authority. They had already been thrown out of the old Musée d'Art Moderne and denied access to the Centre Pompidou. So they went on their travels again, either to the exhibition centre at Porte de Versailles, or to Villette, and the Grand Palais was draped lugubriously in dustsheets and closed, its future unknown.

The Ministry of Culture puts on high-quality exhibitions of Old Masters borrowed from other museums in two of the wings (entrances in Square Jean-Perri and Avenue Georges Clemenceau). But at these shows the public cannot talk to the artists.

Opposite it is the **Petit Palais,** built mainly of stone, best known for its temporary exhibitions. I specially recall the Tutankhamen treasures which attracted long queues. Frescoes from Florence and Pompeii have also been shown with success. The Petit Palais also has the Palais des Beaux Arts de la Ville de Paris. This covers the long period from antiquity to the Renaissance, also Flemish and Dutch paintings. Two other collections, Tack and Dutuit, consist mainly of objects – enamels, porcelain, books, drawings and furniture, also tapestries.

At the end of the Champs-Elysées, on the right, we find restaurant *Ledoyen*, a pavilion set on a lawn. It was once a country inn where people went to drink milk still warm from the cows which grazed outside. It is not like that now, but is still one of the best-sited restaurants in Paris. *Fouquet* and *Ledoyen* are the only major restaurants on the Champs-Elysées itself. But if we explore the quarter a little further, we shall find three further restaurants: one of these, *Lasserre*, no. 17 Avenue Franklin D. Roosevelt, is best known for its first-floor dining-room, where the painted ceiling (by Touchagues, who also did the murals) can be rolled back in warm weather, so that guests can dine under the stars and look out on a roof garden. The décor has been compared to a transatlantic liner of the 1930s. But if all these restaurants are rather above our budget, there are plenty of cheaper places to eat. The Champs-Elysées caters for everyone.

As we enter **Place de la Concorde** (Metro Concorde) we should pause to admire the **Marly horses.** These superb statues flank and, in a sense, guard the entrance of the Champs-Elysées. They are eighteenth century, the work of Guillaume Coustou, and originally in the Château de Marly, one of Louis XIV's houses destroyed in the Revolution. The horses were brought to the Champs-Elysées in 1795, dragged by sixteen live horses. The statues, magnificent wild animals, rearing, are shown being tamed by Africans. There is a delightful description of a small boy riding one in Nancy Mitford's novel *The Blessing.* The marble horses have been replaced by exact, pollution-proof replicas; the originals are housed in the Louvre.

We are now in the huge square. It was intended to impress, and impress it does, by its size and by its position beside the Seine, between the Gardens of the Champs-Elysées, framed by the Marly horses, and the Tuileries Gardens, framed by two winged horses by Coysevox, erected in 1719. Replicas have replaced these too. The one on the north side is called *Mercure*, the other *La Renommée*. Everywhere there are long vistas, great perspectives. André Maurois went so far as to write: 'There is not on this planet a more beautiful architectural ensemble than that which leads from the Arc de Triomphe to the Louvre and from the Madeleine to the Palais Bourbon' (the Chambre des Députés, across the river). There are certainly plenty of columns and arches to be seen: Rome in the heart of Paris.

The best place for seeing these vistas is at the centre, on the island by the obelisk. Getting there is hazardous, as thousands of cars cross the square every hour (or minute). While waiting for a chance to return to the 'mainland', we can pass the time by counting the lamps – I have got as far as two hundred. More romantically, we can look at the distant skyline of towers and domes, and the huge sky with its sailing clouds, which might have been painted by Monet. In spring and summer we can enjoy the flood of fresh green from both gardens, turning to gold in the autumn. Even in winter the square has its charm, especially on a wet night when the buildings and fountains are floodlit.

The square also has eight large statue groups, dedicated to French cities, and two statue-fountains (copied from St Peter's Square, Rome), in honour of River Navigation and Maritime Navigation. It is difficult to tell these last apart, but River Navigation is, surprisingly, the one farther from the Seine. The French love to fill their squares with statues of large, semi-nude, full-breasted, gesticulating ladies representing Peace, Liberty, Eloquence, Consular Jurisdiction, the city of Bordeaux, Lyric Poesy and Maritime Navigation – to name but a few. Personally I find them lovable and am sad that this type of art has been discontinued.

The square was originally given by the bourgeois of Paris to King Louis XV, *le bien-aimé,* with a statue of him by Bouchardon in the centre. A competition to design the square was won by Jean Gabriel, ahead of Soufflot, Servandoni and others. However, famous events intervened and the square was only finished in the reign of Louis-Philippe (1830–48) by Hittorff. Gabriel's two immense buildings remain on the north side of the square. Neo-classical in design, they deliberately remind us of the Louvre and of Italy and, with their arcades, their colonnades, and their pediments, they are justifiably admired as masterpieces of eighteenth-century architecture.

They are, however, simply façades, flanking Rue Royale. To an eighteenth-century architect, a building meant a façade. The idea of 'the use of space' or the *'machine à habiter'* (Le Corbusier's phrase) is modern. Gabriel himself had no idea what was to be behind his great façades, nor what the buildings were to be used for. At the present time, the right-hand building houses the Navy and Environment Ministries, the left the French Automobile Club and the **Hôtel Crillon.** This building has long been associated with French-

American relations. It was here that the Treaty of Friendship (1778), recognizing the independence of the thirteen states, was signed by Louis XVI and a number of American diplomats, including Benjamin Franklin. The Hôtel Crillon has kept its American connection; it is a convenient place for distinguished American guests, the embassy being only a few yards away. The bar is also a rendezvous for international visitors.

But, back in the great square, our minds naturally turn to history, in particular those events which took place between 1792 and 1795. It was Place Louis XV, but his statue was toppled and the square renamed Place de la Révolution. On Sunday, 21 January 1793, the first guillotine was erected there, on the west side near the present statue of Brest. The king, Louis XVI, walked calmly down Rue Royale to his death. He tried to make his last words heard above the rolling drums; something about his blood assuring the future happiness of France. But blood-lust was now high and, four months later, the guillotine was re-erected near the present statue of Strasbourg and the march of the tumbrils, the Terror, began. The guillotine was a portable machine and it moved, like a travelling circus, to Place du Carrousel, Place des Grèves (Hôtel de Ville), the Bastille area and Place de la Nation, where in fact most of the executions took place.

However, the guillotine was moved back to Place de la Révolution for the execution of Robespierre. Robespierre, the austere tyrant, whom Danton had teased for never having been drunk, for never having laid a woman, whom Carlyle nicknamed 'the Sea-Green Incorruptible', was thrown unceremoniously on to the guillotine platform, as if he had been a mere marquis or fellow-politician. It was seven o'clock in the evening of 28 July 1794. Over 1300 people had been beheaded in that square before him.

After the Revolution the Directoire tried to cleanse the blood-soaked square. The guillotine was removed and the square renamed Place de la Concorde. (It was temporarily renamed Place Louis XVI in 1823.) The square became a place for celebrations and festivities. The statues were erected on unfinished plinths originally designed by Gabriel, and the **Egyptian obelisk** from Luxor raised in the centre. Louis-Philippe, a king who liked to keep a low profile, thought that an antique obelisk would be less controversial than a statue. The obelisk, over 3000 years old, was a gift to France from Mehemet Ali, Viceroy of Egypt (he also gave Cleopatra's Needle to London). The obelisk, made of rose-red stone, is covered with hieroglyphs recording the achievements of Rameses II, too obscure to excite popular wrath. Twenty-three metres high and weighing 230 tonnes, its transport from Luxor to Paris was a great engineering achievement, the details of which are recorded at its base and in the Musée de la Marine in the Palais de Chaillot.

Place de la Concorde is now a great sea of cars, except on certain festive occasions. On 14 July there is dancing there to live bands. The square also had one of the main entrances to the sewers of Paris. This has been closed and the main entrance for visitors is now on the left bank of Pont de l'Alma. There are plans to reduce the traffic and increase the public space.

We climb the steps to the **Tuileries Gardens** and pause for a moment on the terrace to admire the view. The Tuileries are sometimes called, and often thought of as, 'the noblest gardens in Paris'. They extend for a kilometre, from Place de la Concorde to Place du Carrousel and the Louvre, between the Seine and Rue de Rivoli; much of the Tuileries has been remade, with delightful flower beds.

We have to remember that this is a formal, symmetrical garden, intended for strolling and the contemplation of distant views, in the Italian manner. Indeed, the gardens were first planned by Queen Catherine de Medici on the site of an old tileworks (*tuileries*). However, the present gardens owe everything to Le Nôtre, who designed or redesigned so many gardens for Louis XIV. His passion for geometry, for straight avenues and formal ponds and patterns, for clipped trees and regular statues, found its expression here. And we should take it, as the French do, in the spirit in which it was planned, rather than wonder what an English gardener like Capability Brown would have done with the site. Anyway, we can admire many of the statues, especially those by Coustou, Coysevox and Maillol.

The gardens were first opened to the public, reluctantly, by Colbert at the beginning of the eighteenth century and have been a popular promenade ever since, especially during summer lunch hours. The **Tuileries Palace** was at the far end, almost adjoining the Louvre and many historic personalities have gazed out on these gardens.

Louis XVI was brought there ignominiously from Versailles by the Parisians, who thought it was time that their king lived among them. Later, after his abortive flight abroad, which was stopped at Varennes, he was brought back to the Tuileries in ignominy. On 10 August 1792 he again escaped from the palace, across the gardens to a temporary haven in the Palais Bourbon; most of his Swiss guards were massacred in the gardens by the mob. After the Revolution the palace was Napoleon's home in Paris, where he held court with his marshals and other leading Bonapartists. The Bourbon kings lived there after the Restoration (except for the Hundred Days in 1815, when Louis XVIII fled to Ghent). The Tuileries was also the home of that unloved emperor, Napoleon III, whose bones the French are happy to let lie in England. (But in his defence we can claim that he created the modern Paris that we love.) The palace was destroyed by the Commune in 1871, and nothing now remains of it, except the gardens.

We can stroll along the south side beside the Seine and above the expressway, Voie Georges Pompidou, which is hidden below us, the noise partly diminished. On the main avenue, we turn and admire once again the long view up to the Arc de Triomphe. From here, however, the vista is slightly marred by the off-centre high-rise buildings of La Défense far beyond. Pompidou said that this did not bother him, but it bothers many French people.

Before returning to Place de la Concorde we should look out on the north side at **Rue de Rivoli,** a very long street running from Concorde almost to the Bastille, getting shabbier and seedier as it goes on. The street was laid out in 1804 and named after Napoleon's first great victory, in Italy. The present buildings facing the Tuileries Gardens are grandiose enough for any emperor. Built in the early nineteenth century, they are suitably Italianate, with a long formal arcade and lighting. The arcade allows us to window-shop, sheltered from the rain or the sun. *Angelina*'s tea-shop, at no. 226, was called Rumpelmayer when it was founded in 1903, but changed its name after the last war. The style is still luxurious, with its red carpet, marble, gilt decor and wrought-iron, and it is always crowded. It is close to the **Hôtel Meurice**, which was German military head-quarters during the Occupation of France. Here, in August 1944, the commandant, General von Cholitz, after much heart-searching, took the decision to disobey Hitler's order to burn down Paris. Lovers of Paris should remember his name with gratitude.

However, back in the Tuileries Gardens, we may have noticed two large pavilions on the edge of Place de la Concorde. The one beside the Seine is the **Orangerie,** the greenhouse of the gardens; the other, beside Rue de Rivoli, is the **Jeu de Paume,** the tennis court. Both are now art galleries. The Orangerie, closed for refurbishment until the end of 2001, is the permanent home of Monet's *Nymphéas* and an interesting modern art collection. The Jeu de Paume used to be the home of the French Impressionist painters, before their transfer to the Musée d'Orsay (see Chapter 5). Now known as the Galerie Nationale du Jeu de Paume, it is used for temporary exhibitions.

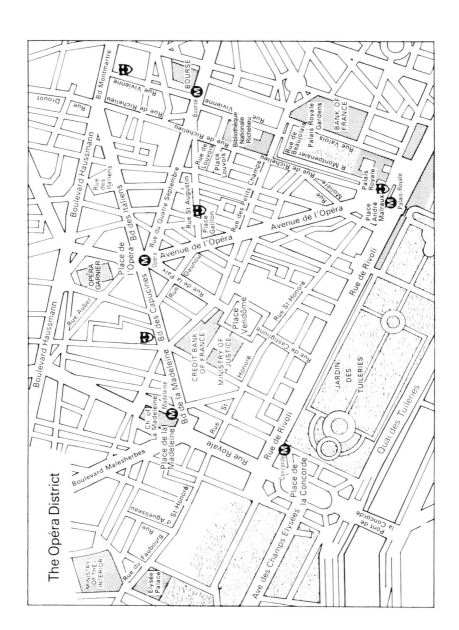

The Opéra District

7

The Opéra District

THE NORTH SIDE of Place de la Concorde is filled by Gabriel's two great façades, described in the last chapter. They form a kind of portal, framing yet another of Paris's perspectives, Rue Royale leading to the Madeleine; and Rue Royale is the start of our walk (Metro Concorde). Almost immediately, on our left, we find one of the landmarks, the restaurant *Maxim*'s.

Originally an eating-house for cabmen waiting in Place de la Concorde, it moved a long way to become a rendezvous of the international jet-set. In other ways it has not moved at all, preserving its original turn-of-the-century décor, which we call Art Nouveau and the French call Belle Epoque or Style Rétro – the Beardsley-like world of mauve, Pernod-green and mustard, dim mirrors and drooping exotic flowers. As we enter, we step back into another century. The food is not always the main attraction here: cloakroom facilities for ladies are opulent and memorable.

Moving along Rue Royale, we find ourselves at a crossroads. On the right is Rue Saint-Honoré (8me), a long narrow street of shops and business offices. On the left is **Rue du Faubourg Saint-Honoré**, which has more to interest us.

At no. 33 is the Cercle d'Union Interallié, grandly placed in the old Rothschild Palace, now an international businessmen's club. Next door (35–39) is the **British Embassy**. It is an eighteenth-century building, the former Hôtel de Charost. In 1800 it was bought by Napoleon's sister, Pauline, who, after a stormy life of loves and marriages, had become the Princess Borghese. Fourteen years later she sold the Palais Borghese to Wellington, who moved in immediately, though his stay was interrupted by Waterloo. Now, as the British Embassy, it is not open to the public, but we can sometimes peer in through the gates at the gatehouse (the comfortable residence of a diplomat) and the courtyard, a fine piece of architecture, described by Nancy Mitford in her last novel, *Don't*

Tell Alfred. The history of the house as an embassy is vividly portrayed by Lady Gladwyn in her book *The Paris Embassy.* Those who visit Paris as part of a grander European tour may wish to make a mental note that it is inextricably linked both by history and its contents with the Farnese Palace in Rome.

If we get the chance to go inside, we shall see immediately busts of Napoleon and Wellington, side by side, with Winston Churchill at the foot of the marble staircase. There are imposing reception rooms covered with crimson brocade, used for lunches and parties; and even Queen Victoria's throne-room, now used mainly for embassy entertainments and when the annual garden-party is rained out. Upstairs are more reception rooms and, finally, the bedrooms and Pauline Bonaparte's bed. This is a splendid affair, with gilded curtains hanging from the claws of a Napoleonic eagle. Some ambassadresses enjoy sleeping in it, others find it intimidating and have it put downstairs. Outside is the garden, leading down to the Avenue Gabriel. This is a true English garden with lawns, borders and unclipped trees. Many an ambassadorial dog has been buried here.

Almost opposite the embassy, at 5 Rue d'Aguesseau, is the **Embassy Church, St Michael's** (Metro Madeleine). Like St George's Anglican Church, it has been rebuilt as a modern block, with the 'church' in the basement. It looks rather like a small boardroom and the altar can be screened off to allow meetings. The 'low' services are crowded and emphasis is on youth, informal dress and Christian names. Gone are the days when the ambassador sat in the front and read the lesson. Meetings and outings are organized.

The American ambassador's residence is at 41 Rue du Faubourg Saint-Honoré. Farther along we find the portico of the **Elysée Palace** (Metro Champs-Elysées), official home of French presidents. Another eighteenth-century building, it was at one time the home of another of Napoleon's sisters, Caroline, and then of his first wife, the Empress Josephine. Napoleon's nephew, Louis-Napoleon, lived there, planning the 1851 *coup d'état,* after which he became the Emperor Napoleon III and moved to the Tuileries. The Elysée has only been the presidential palace since 1873 and for much of this time the president was only a figurehead, choosing prime ministers, often in the middle of the night. It is only since the introduction of presidential government by de Gaulle in 1958 that the Elysée has become the centre of power. But, even now, some presidents, including Mitterrand, have preferred to live at home and visit the Elysée daily for work and entertaining. The fear of being 'A Prisoner of the Elysée', out of touch with Paris and France, is one that haunts French rulers.

The principal attraction of the street for us may be the three fine buildings described or it may be the large number of fashionable boutiques which cluster between Rue Royale and Avenue Matignon. These expensive shops deal mainly in clothes for men and women, scent, beauty and hairdressing. There are also a number of art galleries here and in Avenue Matignon, which show and sell what is called 'Right Bank' art: recently painted works in fairly traditional style, landscapes and still lifes, all in big gilt frames. For more avant-garde art we have to go to the Beaubourg area or the Left Bank.

Back in Rue Royale, we approach the **Madeleine** (Place de la Madeleine, Metro Madeleine), the huge Roman temple which has been dominating us ever since we left Concorde. There had been at least two attempts to build a church there before (one was to be another Panthéon dome), but neither got very far. In 1806 Napoleon decreed that it was to be a temple to glorify the Grande Armée and the chosen architect was Vignon. But it was not finished till 1842 and by then the original idea had evaporated; the Grande Armée, it was felt, was already sufficiently glorified in the Arc de Triomphe and the Invalides. One can imagine the problem of the French in finding a use for the huge brand-new Roman temple in their midst. As a church it would be (and is) a discouraging place, pagan and windowless. As a railway station, another suggestion, it would be too small, despite its size. There had also been thoughts of using the place for the Banque de France, the Bourse or the National Library. However, it was finally consecrated to St Mary Magdalen, whose picture is above the high altar.

Vignon had produced an enormously inflated version of the charming Maison Carrée at Nîmes and, even if nobody could call the Madeleine charming, we can be struck by its dimensions and dominating site, by the twenty-eight steps which lead to the entrance, by the fifty-two Corinthian columns, each over sixty feet high, which support the frieze. We can even bring ourselves to admire the vast bronze door, inspired by the Ten Commandments, and the huge pediment above it, by Lemaire. It shows the Last Judgment and has one of the fattest Christs in Europe.

The Madeleine is set in a large square and a flower-market brings happy memories to many British people of weekends or honeymoons in Paris. For it is a place of memories and ghosts and we should have the eyes and the imagination to see them. On the corner of Rue

Royale, where the shirt shop now is, we can see the portly figure of King Edward VII, a great lover of Paris and French food, emerging, after a large lunch, from *Larue*, his favourite restaurant. On the other corner we can imagine men in top hats entering Thomas Cook's to book their *wagon-lit* on the Blue Train or the Orient Express. A few yards away, no. 4, a jeweller's shop, was once *Durand*, the well-known music publishers. It was here that Chopin first met Liszt in 1831, but the story that they played the A-Flat Polonaise as a duet, shaking hands in the middle, is probably mythical. Chopin's funeral was held in the Madeleine; the Conservatoire performed Mozart's *Requiem* before a congregation of four thousand.

At no. 26 Place de la Madeleine, the far end, is a shop which is definitely not for ghosts – *Fauchon*, the most sophisticated food shop in Paris. The smell from the kitchen ventilators of baking tarts and cooking chocolates is worth a visit for itself alone, even if we are not planning to buy anything. *Fauchon* is closed on Mondays, but the cafeteria and pâtisserie are open.

We stroll along **Boulevard de la Madeleine**, the start of the long boulevard which, though often changing its name and its style, would eventually lead us to Place de la Bastille, should we wish to walk so far. This part is a street of banks, boutiques, shoe shops and airline offices and we may prefer to observe our fellow boulevardiers – and the ghosts. Passing *Aux Trois Quartiers*, Paris's most expensive department store, we can glance at no. 11. Here lived and died a fashionable courtesan, Mlle Plessis, who was the original of the younger Dumas's *La Dame aux Camélias* and Verdi's *La Traviata*.

The street becomes Boulevard des Capucines (Metro Opéra) and on our left is the site of the **Olympia music-hall**, once a mecca for successful pop singers, French and international. The Beatles played here when they started on their world travels. But the ghost is surely Edith Piaf, probably singing 'Milord', the never-forgotten *chanteuse,* who held all France in her spell and who is now honoured with her own memorabilia museum in the Belleville quarter.

The Impressionists held their first group show on 15 May 1874 at no. 35, then Nadar's photographic studio.

On the corner of Place de l'Opéra is *Café de la Paix*, a well-known rendezvous for people from many lands. When it was completely restored, the Beaux-Arts insisted that the original style be followed faithfully. Inside, it still has Ionic columns in green and gold and painted-sky ceilings; and it looks very much as it must have looked when Oscar Wilde tried unsuccessfully to borrow money from Lord Alfred Douglas there. The terrace still keeps its old style. It has been said that if you sit there long enough, you will see someone you know walk by. The experience has only happened to me twice and on the second occasion the man did not recognize me. I recalled later that he was the man who sometimes made announcements from the stage at Covent Garden, and my face must have been quite unknown to him.

We are now at Place de l'Opéra (Metro Opéra), dominated by the enormous **Opéra Garnier,** the brainchild of the Emperor Napoleon III and Haussmann. It has sometimes been called a gigantic wedding-cake; and, though it does resemble a cake, we can appreciate the pale stone, the pink and green colours, the gold frills, as something festive and a part of its time. The architect was Charles Garnier, a fairly unknown young man, who won the qualifying competition; a golden bust of him stands on the Rue Auber side of the theatre. The Empress Eugénie complained that the still unfinished opera house had no style, it was neither Greek nor Roman. Garnier answered that it was the style 'Napoleon III'. Indeed, Garnier hoped to found a new school of architecture, but his work, a mishmash of many styles and lands, could have no followers. Nevertheless the Opéra remains as the most grandiose monument of the Second Empire, even though it was only finished in 1875, after the fall of Napoleon III.

From the start the Opéra was intended as much for balls as for opera and ballet. The annual Polytechnic Ball and occasional presidential galas are still held there. It is also a place of many statues; hundreds inside, some outside. From the entrance hall we can glimpse the great staircase, steps made of marble, banisters of onyx; framing the entrance to the auditorium are two huge caryatids. But, to see the house properly, we should really attend a performance. Then we can climb the staircase to the Grand Foyer, fifty-four metres long, with mirrors and allegorical paintings; we can step out on to the big balcony to look at Place de l'Opéra at night, and then head for the ridiculously small bar for a sandwich and a bottle of beer.

Or we can descend to the basement where we find a vast cavern of mirrors, reflecting us from all sides, fountains and pools. It was this underground grotto which gave Leroux the idea of *The Phantom of the Opera*.

The bells ring, we leave the caverns and return to our pleasure-dome. The auditorium is as sumptuous as everything else. Five tiers of boxes rise round us. In front of us is the famous painted curtain, behind which is one of the biggest stages in the world, capable of holding the most extravagant productions. Above us is a chandelier, weighing six tonnes, and above that a false ceiling painted by Chagall in 1964. This shows sketches of scenes from well-known operas and ballets mingled with the tourist monuments of Paris. Some find it childish, others typically Chagall. A thorough renovation has added very welcome air-conditioning.

The big **Place de l'Opéra** was planned by Haussmann to be an imposing junction; the buildings round it are of uniform style, nineteenth-century classical, complete with pilasters, and only tasteful white neon signs are permitted. The Place seethes with traffic and pedestrians; six main thoroughfares meet there. The metro station underneath is also a main junction where several lines meet.

But Place de l'Opéra is more than a traffic junction. It is a meeting place of three different Parisian worlds, who mingle, even if they do not actually meet, in the many restaurants and cafés of the neighbourhood. The ladies at the next table may be buying leather goods or watches, or having their pearls restrung; or they may have been shopping in one or more of the big department stores in the Boulevard Haussmann, immediately behind the opera house. The area is an attractive shopping quarter for the rich and the thrifty alike – and especially for window-shoppers. At the table on the other side the men in their dark suits are probably businessmen. The Opéra is the business area of Paris. There are big banks everywhere, the head offices of the main French banks, the Paris branches of foreign banks: the Bourse is nearby. The buildings are filled with offices, commercial law firms, accountants, brokers and agencies. The area is also Paris's theatre-land. There are many theatres here besides the Opéra and at night our restaurant will be filled with theatre-goers. Three different worlds, shopping, business and theatres, all in the same place! This gives the area an extraordinary variety and vitality; it also means that Place de l'Opéra is as lively at midnight as it is at midday – something which cannot be said of Threadneedle Street or Wall Street.

Now we should window-shop our way down the smart **Rue de la Paix**. It was originally called Rue Napoléon; he had ordered its construction in 1806. (There is, incidentally, no Rue Napoléon now in Paris although there is a Rue Bonaparte.) However, as we stroll down the 'Street of Peace', our minds will be less on battles than on luxury, and we shall pass many familiar names. At the end we find ourselves in that masterpiece of French seventeenth-century architecture, **Place Vendôme** (Metro Tuileries). The square was originally conceived as a backdrop for a huge equestrian statue of Louis XIV by Girardon. The Duke of Vendôme's town house and the Capuchin convent were bought in 1685 and demolished, and Jules Hardouin-Mansart was commissioned to build the new square. The nephew by marriage of the distinguished architect François Mansart, Hardouin had added his surname to his own and, confusingly, is often simply referred to as 'Mansart'. The square was finished in 1699 and named Place des Conquêtes.

It is built of pink-grey limestone and is completely formal and symmetrical. Above an arcade, Corinthian pilasters rise for two storeys between the windows. The roof is steeply pitched and broken by curved dormer windows. These are replaced by classical pediments in the middle of the two long sides and on the four buildings which cut off the corners. Such a rigid formality could easily be monotonous, but instead it is pleasing and graceful. The style of the architecture, the size and shape of the square, and the proportions of the façades add up to an artistic achievement, typical of its century. A sense of proportion was one of Hardouin-Mansart's greatest gifts as an architect; we have another example of it in the Invalides dome.

He was, however, only building a façade. The buildings behind it were added later and could be entered only from the back. Nothing was allowed to spoil the uniformity of the square. But, on a prime site, such a state of affairs could not last indefinitely and now every building opens onto the square; many of them have shop windows showing diamonds glittering on black velvet. Place Vendôme has long been known as a centre of jewellery and fashion and there are still a number of jewellers. But fashion and beauty are being squeezed out by yet more banks and offices. The west side of the square is mainly occupied by the Ministry of Justice and the Ritz Hotel, a contrasting pair to find behind the same façade. In a different key, Chopin died in 1849 at no. 12; a plaque reminds us of the composer and of the time when people actually lived in the square.

The central statue of Louis XIV was destroyed in the Revolution. A Rome-style column was erected by Napoleon as yet another monument to the Grande Armée. It is covered with a spiral of bronze plaques made from guns captured at the battle of Austerlitz (1805) which are said to show scenes from the campaigns. The column was toppled by the Commune in 1871 and many of the plaques had to be recast when the column was re-erected by the Third Republic. Several statues have stood on its top – Napoleon in military uniform, Henri IV, a giant fleur-de-lys. The present incumbent is Napoleon dressed as Julius Cæsar, in accordance with his original order.

On the south side of the square Rue de Castiglione leads across Rue Saint-Honoré to Rue de Rivoli. This too is a window-shopper's paradise, but the jewellery here is more likely to be costume jewellery than diamonds.

We should, however, retrace our steps up Rue de la Paix and turn right into Rue Daunou. At no. 5 we find a popular landmark for businessmen and visiting Anglo-Saxons, *Harry's Bar*, known to the owner, and many Americans as 'Sank Roo Doe Noo'. It is decorated with British and American college shields and pennants, to remind us of our youth, and it was for a long time the only bar in France to serve Californian wine. The bar was started early in the century by a successful American jockey, who went broke and sold it to his bartender, Harry MacElhone. It became a fashionable supper club downstairs, its clients including Gloria Swanson (then a marquise), the Duke of Windsor (in his young princely days), Noel Coward and Charles Chaplin. Upstairs, writers and sportsmen mingled near the bar, among them Jack Dempsey, Big Bill Tilden, Hemingway, James Joyce (usually at a secluded table), Marcel Achard, O'Flaherty, Thornton Wilder, James Jones and Jean-Paul Sartre during his pro-American phase. The bar is open until dawn.

We continue our walk along Rue Daunou to Avenue de l'Opéra, a long dull street, one of Haussmann's lesser achievements, and now filled with banks and airline offices. Its best feature is its view of the Opéra and to this we should now return, turning right at *Clerc* into Boulevard des Capucines (Metro Opéra).

There are many boulevards in Paris, but the phrase **Grands Boulevards** is usually only applied to the string of streets and boulevards which, under different names, lie between Opéra and Place de la République and Bastille. The names are: Capucines, Italiens, Montmartre, Poissonnière, Bonne Nouvelle, Saint-Denis, Saint-Martin, Temple, Filles de Calvaire and Beaumarchais. The total distance is about three miles. The smart end is near the Opéra; it gets seedier as we go east – not that we shall go so far today.

The Grands Boulevards, originally 'The Boulevard', were constructed in the reign of Louis XIV on the site of old ramparts and moats which had fallen into decay. The boulevard was wide and lined with trees; triumphal arches replaced the old gates of Paris, Porte Saint-Denis and Porte Saint-Martin. It became a fashionable place to drive in carriages or ride, though it was not till 1828 that the first bus travelled the length of the Grands Boulevards. Capucines and Italiens became fashionable places to live in the eighteenth and nineteenth centuries and many theatres were built. The eastern end seemed to be a non-stop fairground and circus.

Much changed with the arrival of Haussmann, the motor car, the cinema and neon lighting. Boulevard des Italiens may not still look as it did in Pissarro's picture of the boulevard at night. But, though much has gone, including fashionability, much still remains, the vitality, the people. To sit on a café terrace on a warm summer evening and watch the crowds walking up and down on pleasure or business is an enjoyable and interesting experience. These are the real Parisians, descendants of Gauls and Franks.

At no. 8 Boulevard des Capucines, almost beside the Opéra, Offenbach composed *The Tales of Hoffmann,* but he died there before the work, on which he rightly set great store, could be performed. *Le Grand Café*, at no. 4, was another of Wilde's haunts during his prosperous years, before his fall.

We are now on Boulevard des Italiens and trying not to see the ugly Berlitz building. Why 'Italiens'? In 1782 the Duc de Choiseul built a theatre in the grounds of his house to attract people to the area, where he was a big landowner, and to house the Italian Comic Opera Company. This became eventually the Opéra-Comique, performing operettas, particularly the works of Offenbach and Johann Strauss.

On the north side of the boulevard, we find the dog-legged Rue des Italiens and the premises of **Le Monde,** France's most respected and influential daily newspaper. In theory an evening paper, its first edition is on the news stands at eight o'clock in the morning. It used to sell half a million copies a day and was one of France's few papers to make a profit. Later it lost money and was threatened with closure. It is a journalists' cooperative, electing its own editors but remaining faithful to the principles of its founder, Hubert Beuve-Méry. There are few concessions to popular attraction such as headlines, photographs, gossip columns, strip cartoons or crossword puzzles. Officially it is independent of all party politics, but behind its sober exterior and the solid pages of print, we can detect a strong left-wing slant; many of its readers never notice this, regarding it as objective and impartial, which it often is. But *Le Monde* was one of the few Western newspapers which could be bought in Moscow in the strict Communist era.

At the end of Boulevard des Italiens, we are joined by Boulevard Haussmann. On the left is Rue Drouot; no. 9 is Hôtel Drouot, one of Paris's main auction rooms, where you may, if you are lucky and in ample funds, pick up a Louis XV chair or a Fragonard painting being sold by an impoverished marquis. In stark contrast is the **Musée Grévin** in Boulevard Montmartre; full of waxworks, distorting mirrors and conjurors, it attracts many children and reminds us of the old Grands Boulevards, as does the Wrestling Theatre ('Catch') a little farther on.

We should, however, turn right into Rue Vivienne, leaving the Grands Boulevards. On the left, the Théâtre des Variétés was for a long time the stage home of Sacha Guitry; the theatre is still associated with light comedy. A little farther on we find the **Bourse,** the Stock Exchange, another Roman temple. There are galleries inside which we can visit, if we like, to watch the market; there are also guided tours in the mornings for those who are interested. Round the Bourse there are plenty of cafés and restaurants, full of stockbrokers; there are also sometimes demos by anti-capitalist factions.

We will leave the Bourse by Rue Saint-Augustin, avoiding Rue du Quatre Septembre, a business street which leads back to Opéra. The Théâtre de la Michodière, nearby, was for many years associated with Yvonne Printemps and Pierre Fresnay. But our goal is the charming Place Gaillon (a triangle more than a square), which was reconstructed by Visconti in 1827, and we should note the fountain with a boy on a dolphin which was erected in 1707. However, the dominating feature of the little square is the restaurant *Drouant*.

Drouant is best known for the November morning each year when the Goncourt Academy meets there to award the Prix Goncourt, France's most prestigious literary prize. A crowd gathers in the rain to watch the great men arrive, something which one can scarcely imagine in another city. On one occasion one of the academicians paused to address the damp crowd. 'Have no fear!' he said. 'We shall be at lunch within an hour.' This was not to reassure them about his possible starvation, but to tell them that the short list was short indeed that year. The choice made, the jury is served with a large lunch, ending traditionally with Reblochon cheese from the Savoy mountains. Meanwhile, telephones ring, reporters interview the happy winner and booksellers rearrange their windows.

The prize is still only fifty francs and most winners prefer to frame the cheque rather than cash it. The real reward comes with the vast sales and fame which follow; the French respect the judgments of their seniors and dutifully buy their choices. But during the 1980s some controversial choices, involving resignations, damaged the prestige of the prize and its value. Revelations were made about how the winner was chosen; the book almost always came from one of the same three publishers. Nobody can win the Goncourt twice, yet Romain Gary is said to have done this, with the help of a pseudonym. Advice was published to aspirants telling them where to be seen lunching (*Lipp*'s) and how to dress (prosperously). Favourites boasted openly of their friends on the jury; it was desirable to have parents or ancestors who lived in a distant country and endured great hardships, though the author himself now lived comfortably on the Left Bank.

All this was saddening, though perhaps inevitable where so much money was involved. Yet a good deal of glamour still remains in Place Gaillon on that damp morning in November. The ordinary Frenchman who rarely buys a book still regards the Goncourt with awe. Edmond de Goncourt wrote: '*il n'y a de bon que les choses exquises*'. A better period began for the prize with the selection of Marguerite Duras suggesting a newer trend. Another woman writer was chosen in 1996, Pascale Rozel.

Leaving Place Gaillon, we make our way to the pleasant Square Louvois and to the **Bibliothèque Nationale Richelieu,** facing us at 58 Rue de Richelieu (Metro Palais-Royal, also Meteor Line). The façade is eighteenth century, by Robert de Cotte, but the building is of many dates. The old Hôtel Tubeuf was rebuilt in the seventeenth century by François Mansart, whose additions included the Mansart and Mazarin Galleries. The former reading room and the rest of the library are mainly Second Empire.

The library originated as the royal library in the Louvre, Blois and Fontainebleau. In 1537 François I, a great book collector, brought in a law that the royal library must possess a copy of every book printed. When the library reached two hundred thousand books, Colbert decided to move it to his own house in Rue Vivienne; fifty years later it was moved across the street to Hôtel Tubeuf, its next home, which held Cardinal Mazarin's personal collection of pictures and works of art. In the 1980s this library had about seven million printed books, including two Gutenberg Bibles and first editions from Villon onwards; manuscripts dating back to AD 600; prints and engravings; newspapers and periodicals; maps, photographs, music, records. Everyone was sad when this beautiful old building became overwhelmed by the growing number of books, and of book-thieves, and the problem, as the years went by, of precious pages becoming worn through by too many thumbs. In fifteen years the number of books grew from seven million to ten million. A bigger building had to be built, using 'high-tech' methods to present rare books projected onto screens. More room for readers was needed, too: the Richelieu reading room has only 400 seats. A new site was found, in the thirteenth Arrondissement, and the new Bibliothèque Nationale de France, combining both the Tolbiac building (from then onwards the principal site) and the Richelieu building, was established by decree in 1994.

All the printed books and other printed works, including periodicals, were transferred to Tolbiac, including 150,000 rare books, but the Richelieu site retains its other treasures, and is to house a National Institute of Art History as well. The **Médailles Collection** is open to the public and is well worth a visit. This is not purely a collection of coins or military medals. The medallion, as an art form distinct from coinage, was developed in the fifteenth century in Italy and France. One of the earliest medallions shows a knight on a galloping horse and commemorates the expulsion of the English from France in 1455. Other good examples are shown here, notably portrait medallions of Erasmus (1519), Catherine de Medici, Henri IV (1602), Monet by E. Rousseau and Stravinsky by Berthe Camus (1972). The collection also contains fine small works of art from prehistoric fragments (spirals) to the present day. As we go in, there are urns, heads, small figures, vases and wrought-silver ewers. One of the finest bigger pieces is an amphora of 470 BC, found in Agrigento, Sicily, and representing Poseidon and Theseus. A head of Nero as a baby is improbably cherubic and innocent-looking, but a great silver platter is very fine: fourth century BC, it shows the death of Patrocles at Troy, and was discovered in 1656 between Arles and Avignon.

We should look at the **State Room** on the ground floor, which is open to the public. The eighteenth-century wooden panelling is remarkable. So is Houdon's famous seated statue of Voltaire (1787). Here we have the original plaster statue – the bronze cast from it is in the foyer of the Comédie Française. In both we can glimpse the wry, cynical philosopher, the essayist, novelist and satirist; not the serious writer of solemn (and now forgotten) tragedies – Voltaire's own image of himself. His heart is buried in the pedestal, the strangest object in the whole bibliothèque. One would have expected his brain to be of more interest.

Leaving the library, we turn left into Rue des Petits Champs. Here we can see the Hôtel Tubeuf as François Mansart left it, a pleasant brick and stone courtyard with a steeply-pitched roof. Turning left again into Rue Vivienne, we can see through the railings the Library Gardens and the façade of Mansart's library, which contain the two galleries – a fine example of seventeenth-century architecture.

Returning to Rue des Petits Champs we cross into Rue de Beaujolais, one of three streets built in 1780 by Philippe-Egalité when he enclosed and 'developed' the gardens of Palais-Royal. (The other two streets are called Montpensier and Valois, good Bourbon and Orléans names.) Almost facing us is the house where Colette lived for much of her life. The house faces the **Palais-Royal Gardens** (Metro Palais-Royal), and Colette used to love looking out at them, when she was too crippled to walk any more. We turn right and, passing the restaurant *Le Grand Véfour*, enter the gardens.

The façades here are far more pretentious than the simple buildings in the three surrounding streets. Here we have royal grandeur, stonework, pilasters, arcades; an out-of-proportion imitation of Place Vendôme a hundred years earlier. The gardens themselves – trees and a fountain – are a huge courtyard of peace and silence in one of the busiest parts of Paris. A few, very few, strollers, readers and pram-pushers – that is all. The shops in the arcades are mostly empty; those still in business seem to deal mainly in philately, a quiet trade. At night the arcades are silent to the point of eeriness, despite two theatres, a busy restaurant and a café. It is as if the customers were overawed by their surroundings; time, we may feel, has passed Palais-Royal by.

It was not always thus. Philippe-Egalité (Prince Louis-Philippe of Orléans) was a man who liked to have it both ways. On inheriting the palace and the gardens, he found himself one of the richest men in France and he saw a good commercial outlet for his money in his gardens and the streets he built round them. But the façades had to look royal, even if the arcades below them were full of gambling houses and brothels. He lived in the palace, renamed it Palais-Egalité and as a good revolutionary, called himself Citoyen Egalité. He was one of those who signed the death warrant of Louis XVI, his cousin. None of this saved him from the guillotine himself in 1793.

The gardens were at first a fashionable promenade and meeting place for Parisians, but standards deteriorated quickly. Revolutionaries gathered there to hear the inflammatory speeches of

Camille Desmoulins. The palace became, like the arcades, a big gambling den and brothel, and the gardens held not only revolutionaries and prostitutes but also circuses, dance-halls and all the attractions of a funfair. It is said that Napoleon had his first sexual experience there; it was certainly he who later had the gardens and the palace cleaned up. But the gambling houses in the arcades continued until 1838, when they were closed by Louis-Philippe and, with them gone, the popularity of the arcade shops began to fade away and the gardens to assume their present respectability.

An attempt has been made to brighten things up by putting in modern sculpture by Baren. The courtyard, as we enter, is full of short fat striped tubes, varying from ankle to shoulder-height. A few are even taller. They prevent cars from parking, but provide, unintentionally, a fun obstacle-race-course for cyclists. They are perhaps meant to remind us of the columns of the Forum in Rome, but may seem to us more like sad tree-stumps – or execution blocks. The fountain makes up for this. On its raised platform the basin is filled with huge mirror globes of varying sizes, which reflect the sky and ourselves. There are sixteen of them (or is it seventeen? we can amuse ourselves counting them). As the water covers them, we have a happy effect of submerged bubbles.

The palace itself is at the south end of the gardens. It is now occupied by the Council of State (a mysterious body) and closed to the public. It was originally built in 1624 by Jacques Le Mercier (born in 1585) for Cardinal Richelieu and called the Palais Cardinal. Le Mercier was also the architect of the Sorbonne Chapel. After Richelieu's death and that of King Louis XIII, the Queen Mother, Anne of Austria, lived there with her young sons Louis XIV and Philippe, Duke of Orléans; and the palace was renamed Palais-Royal. Louis XIV, grown up, had, however, grander ideas and moved back to the Louvre for a while. In the Palais-Royal lived Henrietta-Maria, widow of Charles I of England, and her daughter Henrietta, who later married Philippe of Orléans. The palace remained in the Orléans family for many generations. Altered by Philippe-Egalité and the Bourbon Restoration after Napoleon, burnt by the Commune in 1871, restored by the Third Republic, nothing now remains of Richelieu's palace except a gallery on the Rue de Valois side.

Richelieu, as well as running the country, took a great interest in the theatre and indeed had ambitions, but not the talents, to be a playwright himself. It is said that he asked Corneille to write a play for him, but insisted on dictating its contents. Corneille naturally declined; he never regained official favour. The east wing of Palais-Cardinal contained a theatre which at last gave a permanent home to Molière and his troupe of comedians, after many years of wandering on the Left Bank and in the provinces. Molière's major works were first performed in the Théâtre Richelieu, from 1661 to 1673, when he collapsed on stage and died a few hours later. He was only fifty-one and the part he was acting was *Le Malade Imaginaire* – an ironic end indeed for the ironist.

The statue of Molière nearby, at the corner of Rue de Richelieu and Rue Molière is nineteenth century, by Visconti. The figure of the playwright, seated, pen in hand, by Seurre, is compelling; his bluff face and his big moustache I prefer to the surrounding muses and cherub.

Seven years after Molière's death, Louis XIV founded the **Comédie-Française** from the remains of Molière's troupe and the company at the Hôtel de Bourgogne. The new company and the irreverence of the works they performed brought it much anger, both from the conservative-minded and the universities. However, it continued to enjoy the support of the all-powerful king. Napoleon also supported them, perhaps because of his *tendresse* for the leading lady, Mademoiselle Mars. At any rate he gave the company state patronage, a subsidy and a measure of state control, all of which it still has.

The name Comédie-Française is now applied less to the company, some of whose leading members are frequently lured away by film and television contracts, than to the theatre itself. This is at the south-west corner of Palais-Royal, built for Philippe-Egalité by Victor Louis and restored in the nineteenth century. It faces on to Place André Malraux (formerly Place du Théâtre Français) at the southern end of Avenue de l'Opéra (Metro Palais-Royal). It is dignified without being overwhelming; indeed it is rather small for France's most prestigious theatre, though it manages some lavish productions. It also has an enormous collection of wigs and costumes; in the foyer are the chair in which Molière collapsed on stage and Houdon's bronze statue of Voltaire, referred to earlier. But Voltaire's plays are no longer performed.

The Comédie-Française has always been the home of French 'classical acting'. In this a couple stand on the stage, scarcely moving, never touching each other, while they confess, in rhythmical alexandrines, their uncontrollable, and probably incestuous, love.

Although this style is used for Corneille and Racine, French acting is not always so static. The great Sarah Bernhardt, as Cleopatra, on hearing the news of the defeat of Actium, stabbed the messenger, smashed much of the scenery, raved and howled, and finally collapsed in a shuddering heap in the centre of the stage. (In the silence after the applause an English lady was heard to remark, 'How very different from the home life of our own dear Queen!')

The Comédie-Française has for centuries specialized in the classics (though Molière's plays were contemporary enough – he would have been surprised to find himself a classic). Apart from those playwrights already mentioned, the theatre stages Marivaux, de Musset, Beaumarchais, Hugo and Rostand. Modern plays produced here include works by Montherlant, Pirandello, Giraudoux and Ionesco. Claudel's *Le Soulier de Satin* was first produced here during the war, with the approval of the German military governor. A poetic drama about sin, set in sixteenth-century Spain and lasting eight hours, should, it was thought, be quite harmless and nothing to do with the Resistance. (Gide commented that we must be grateful that he did not also write about the other slipper too.) But eventually the governor realized that the play was not as innocuous as was at first thought and it was dropped from the repertory. It was, however, revived, in a shortened version and the production was seen in London as well as Paris.

The revival was at the Odéon, not at the Comédie-Française, which seemed then to be devoted to the farces of Feydeau, as de Gaulle pointed out to his minister of culture, Malraux. It was time to revive the classics. But Corneille and Racine were no longer the draw they had once been; they were for exams only, the dilemma of any national theatre. Since then the Comédie Française has concentrated on the French classics and new productions are rare. The great standby is Rostand's *Cyrano de Bergerac,* popular with both French and foreigners.

Place André Malraux (Metro Palais Royal) is the end of our walk and we are back in the nineteenth century. It is an attractive square, as Pissarro knew, with its fountains, globe-lights, the perspective to the floodlit Opéra and the ponderous bulk of the Louvre. But before descending into Metro Palais-Royal, we could glance at *Rue-Univers*, once a well-known literary café. And we can consider where to eat.

The whole area is full of restaurants. At *Le Grand Véfour*, 17 Rue de Beaujolais, the décor has hardly changed since it was the rendezvous of the fashionable world in the Palais-Royal Gardens. A glass plate tells us that it was once the *Café de Chartres*; another advertises 'Sherry Goblets'. Inside, copper plates remind us of the celebrities, including Napoleon, with Josephine, who have been there. Prior booking, sometimes weeks in advance, makes a meal here an event rather than a spontaneous enjoyment.

8

The Louvre

The Palace

The Louvre is the largest palace in Europe, some say upon earth. It took six hundred and sixty-six years to build and spans the history of France from mediæval fortress to Second Empire folly. Seventeen sovereigns and innumerable numbers of architects were involved in its construction. The size is breathtaking – on and on it goes beside the Seine and Rue de Rivoli. One is scarcely surprised that so many of France's rulers decided to live elsewhere.

Originally it was part of the walls of Paris. Like the Tournelle, which protected Paris from upstream invasion, the Louvre guarded the downstream end, which was vulnerable to attacks by pirates and other invaders. The original tower was enlarged and in 1200 King Philippe-Auguste completed the military fortress, of which no traces now remain above ground. Although several kings lived there, it seems to have been an uncomfortable place, occupying less than a quarter of the present Cour Carrée. The word 'Louvre' is of obscure origin, but the theory most generally held is that it comes from an old Flemish word meaning fortress.

It was François I, contemporary with England's Henry VIII, who decided to reside in the Louvre, as part of an agreement, it is said, with the Parisians, who had paid his ransom when he was captured in Italy. The king ordered much demolition and rebuilding: in particular the Renaissance façade of the Cour Carrée. Catherine de Medici built a new palace, the Tuileries, at the far end of the present Louvre and the two palaces were joined together by Henri IV. Artists were allowed to live and work there – an example of state patronage of the arts unsurpassed even in our times – and it is entirely appropriate that this should be the site of the Grande Salle and other galleries, where many of the great works of the Louvre are still hung.

Louis XIV decided to reconstruct the Cour Carrée and various architects submitted plans, including Le Vau, Bernini and Claude Perrault, and it is the latter's work, mainly, that we can see and admire there now. Napoleon made further alterations to the palace, including the addition of the Arc du Carrousel, at the western end. In the Second Empire, Napoleon III and Haussmann decided finally to complete the building with the north wing and the two pavilions, Flore and Marsan, which ended the palace and joined it to the Tuileries. Much reconstruction was unfortunately carried out elsewhere. In 1871 the Commune burned down the Tuileries, damaging the two pavilions, but these were rebuilt under the Third Republic. Soon afterwards the Ministry of Finance installed itself 'temporarily' in the north wing.

Architecturally, the Louvre (Pyramide entrance, Place du Carrousel, Metro Palais-Royal or Louvre: for Rue de Rivoli entrance, Metro Palais-Royal) has only two parts which we can enjoy. Facing Place du Louvre at the extreme eastern end of the building, Perrault's colonnade (1673) is a good example of neo-classical style. Behind it is the finest part of the Louvre, the **Cour Carrée;** the façade on the left has changed little since Pierre Lescot designed it in the sixteenth century, a fine piece of graceful and harmonious Renaissance architecture. The sculptures are by Goujon.

At the other end of the palace stands the **Arc du Carrousel,** erected in 1806 to celebrate Austerlitz and other victories. The columns, however, are older, from Château de Meudon. At one time it was even decorated with the famous horses of St Mark, looted from Venice by Napoleon. But, even without these, it is a delightful work of art, relatively small and well proportioned, and many people prefer it to the Arc de Triomphe. The famous vista of the Concorde obelisk, the Champs-Elysées and the Arc de Triomphe can be seen at its greatest length through the Carrousel arch.

Otherwise the palace of the Louvre is monstrous and mediocre and our reason for visiting it, of course, is to see the art treasures inside.

The Museum

The original art collection was plundered by the English after Agincourt, but in the following century a new collection was started by François I, partly by looting in Italy and partly by encouraging artists to live and work in France. One of those who profited by this invitation was Leonardo da Vinci (1452–1519), who brought the *Mona Lisa* with him, among other works. Art, like music, was then thought to be a specifically Italian product, and the Italian collection in the Louvre is among the finest in the world. Later kings, usually discerning art collectors, added further acquisitions, but the idea of letting the public see them, first mooted by the Encyclopédistes, was stalled by Louis XVI's ministers. However, the palace was opened in 1793 housing royal collections from various palaces, the collections of émigré aristocrats and works taken from the suppressed church. Napoleon looted the art of Europe for the Louvre, but after his defeat it all had to be returned, except for *The Wedding Feast at Cana* by Veronese and a few other pieces. After the Restoration many more works were acquired by purchase or bequest. The museum now lists 2,700 donors.

The Louvre rapidly became not only a museum for the people, but a shrine of the Revolution and Napoleonic periods. Earlier, and in particular French, art was frowned on as either religious or decadent, pre-Revolutionary painters having been far too interested in aristocratic life and in the female body. Female nudes, as in Boucher's paintings were 'out', but male nudes, as in Delacroix's works, were 'in' because they were classical. This helps to explain the enormous amount of space given to the vast canvases of David and Delacroix and their contemporaries; moreover these were hung in the first gallery we reached, through which we had to pass if we wished to see anything else. So we arrived at Leonardo or Van Eyck, our eyes already dazed by dozens of battlefield or Revolution corpses, rearing cavalry horses seen from the back, gesticulating generals and goddesses.

Some distinguished modern art historians, among them René Huyghe and Pierre Quoniam, both Louvre curators, reminded us that French art flourished before the Revolution. Huyghe pointed out 'the almost unique quality of self-renewal' in French art. There was a growing feeling that insufficient emphasis and pride of place had been given to the art of earlier centuries.

The 'Grand Louvre'

It was fortunate that this change of mood coincided with one of France's periodical fits of 'folie de grandeur'. This came in the 1980s, when François Mitterrand was president. His plans for Paris were ambitious, and included the high-rise Bibliothèque Nationale, the Bastille Opera, and the transformation of the Louvre into 'the biggest museum in the world', complete with a pyramid in the Cour Napoléon. Mitterrand was accused of having a 'Pharaoh complex', but he was a great benefactor of the Louvre. A column as we enter the expanded 'Grand Louvre' records that it was he who removed the Ministry of Finance, at last, from the large 'Aile Richelieu' which it had occupied since 1871. This was a heroic task, in which many strong men before him had failed, and it was done at the cost of putting up a huge new building for the Ministry of Finance. It freed space for a great number of new galleries, permitting all the French paintings to be hung together, and many works in the Louvre's vast reserves to be exhibited. Its three interior courtyards now have glass roofs and house large-scale French sculpture in the Marly and Puget courtyards and Assyrian sculptures in the Khorsabad courtyard.

Only the façade of Visconti's building was preserved, plus the monumental staircases and the grandiose Napoleon III Apartments. Perhaps the unhappy emperor deserves at least this memorial, because he actually bought a whole gallery, the Campana, in 1861, bringing in to the Louvre fourteenth- and fifteenth-century Italian paintings, until then neglected, as well as Greek ceramic art and major antique sculptures. The Richelieu Wing was officially opened in 1993, two hundred years after the first opening of the Louvre to the public.

But all this was not enough. A major expansion was needed to make the Louvre 'the biggest'. It was realized that this could only be made underground, and excavation began under the Cour Napoléon. Much archaeological material was discovered, and is now on view in the 'Crypt of Saint-Louis' (twelfth century) including plenty of bric-a-brac left by the hangers-on of the court in the eighteenth century. More interesting was the unearthing of the base of the keep of Philippe-Auguste's original fortress, which was destroyed by François I in 1527. (Other dungeons, moats and cellars can be seen under the Cour Carrée, with access from the Pyramid's entrance-hall, entresol level, Sully Wing.)

The total exhibition space of the old Louvre was doubled from 31,000 square metres to more than 60,000 square metres. The reception area for the public was multiplied by ten. Fifteen hundred employees, polite, efficient and polyglot, cope with five million visitors a year.

The main entrance is through the glass Pyramid. There are entrances for groups and pass-holders in Passage Richelieu. Direct entrance can be made via the Napoleon Hall in Galerie du Carrousel, accessible from staircases near Arc du Carrousel at 99 rue de Rivoli, the Palais Royal metro station, and the underground parking area on Avenue du General Lemounier.

Perhaps this is the moment for some practical advice. One guidebook recommends comfortable shoes and a light breakfast – as if a Paris breakfast were ever anything else. The whole museum is much too hot in summer; perhaps the entrance fees of five million visitors can finance an improvement, but meanwhile we should wear thin clothes. More to the point is to allow as much time as possible; queues can be long and there is much ground to cover. The rooms begin to close half an hour before the official time.

The Pyramid in Cour Napoléon, facing Arc du Carrousel, acts as a skylight for the great hall excavated below. It was designed by an American architect of Chinese origin, I. M. Pei. There are three small pyramids beside it and seven triangular granite basins of water, with fountains and lights at night. The plan for this was much opposed at first. A leading critic called it 'perfectly useless, expensive, inaesthetic, out of place and degrading to the surrounding architecture'. But it fits in unexpectedly well after all, because its size (20 metres high) is not so large as to dwarf the buildings. It reflects the sky, to the point of seeming almost invisible, as we sit on the edge of the pool beside it. The water and glass give a luminosity which this huge empty courtyard never had before. Parisians have become quite fond of it. (However the lime oval screen in front of it, with a silvery metal frame, looks like a stand for a cake and is unworthy of its setting.)

Louis XIV, a statue by G. L. Bernini (1598–1680) turns his back on it all. This is not Louis XIV as we know him from his portraits, a proudly-dressed man unlikely to ride his charger in a toga and sandals, but Bernini makes a fine flourish with the cloak. It was cast in lead in 1988. Bernini's designs for the Louvre were rejected, and only this remains.

We go in through a door in the Pyramid, but may first have to endure a long queue. (Those with 'handicapped' passes can go straight to the front.) We go down an escalator into the huge reception area, which looks much like an airport, but more welcoming. There are bookstalls in many languages and an expert and helpful staff at the Information Desk, who can tell us about guided tours. But it is depressing to find that we have to queue all over again for our tickets. Looking up, we see the sky and the

Louvre buildings through the Pyramid. Its framework looks like a giant cobweb from below.

Once we have our ticket, we are faced by three escalators, the Richelieu, the Sully and the Denon and this is our moment of decision. There are rooms, mainly of sculpture, on our own level. Once the neo-classical obsession of humanism dominated the planning of the Louvre, but in our questioning age, these boundaries no longer hold good. The past has become a new dimension for us, especially the far past, and the further the better. As public interest in the ancient Roman and Greek galleries has declined, the crowds are now going towards the most ancient cultures, particularly Ancient Egypt.

Rose Macaulay, the well-known traveller and expert on antiquity, was once overheard remarking to a classical scholar 'You Classics men are simply ignorant, you know nothing at all about all the great civilizations of the past, long before your Greece and Rome. What about the Etruscans? And what about the *Hittites*?' The man was struck dumb.

In the Grand Louvre we may discover the Hittites of Anatolia at once, from a spectacular new excavation, and there are many other ancient treasures in the huge galleries near the entrances. The new trend has been reflected in the planning of the extended areas and the choice of sections to place foremost in presentation to the public. Most of them are devoted to antiquities from many cultures. There is also an important section of Islamic art occupying thirteen rooms in the Richelieu, most of which has never been shown before. The Louvre's own book about all this admits, rather ruefully, that the mainspring of the art of past times was nearly always religious. But we may notice, for example in the splendid wall relief of the royal archers of Nineveh (668 BC) that religion and martial glory were apt to get confused. This makes them seem very contemporary.

In this new order of the Louvre, European art comes last. The most famous and often reproduced works, particularly the Italian paintings, remain much as they always were, squashed into overcrowded rooms. Instead of being a section easily reached from the entrance, as it used to be, the huge underground extension has now made it one of the farthest away. The greater the Louvre the farther we have to walk, and we have never had more need of those stout walking-shoes. The present organizers evidently wish to discourage the old bad habit of looking-in on the Louvre, just before closing-time, to take a (forbidden) flash-photograph of the *Mona Lisa* and then go home. She has become very hard to find, and the

Louvre means to show us every one of its treasures before we get there.

We must now choose where to go, and the free chart of the museum available in the reception area is very useful for the details. In broad terms, the layout of the museum is on four floors and in three wings. The floors are entresol, at the level of the reception area, where we are now, ground floor, first and second floor. There are two oblong wings, Richelieu and Denon to left and right of the main courtyard, linked by Sully, which is square with a large internal courtyard of its own.

In terms of subjects, the entresol is used for **sculpture**. Both archaic Greek and later European are in the Denon wing. We may find the Marly Horses by G. Coustou in the French sculpture courtyards in the Richelieu wing, with the new Islamic art section placed, rather curiously, next door. Further sculpture is on the ground floor. In the Denon wing are sixteenth- to nineteenth-century Italian works, with North European (we find Michelangelo here), and also Etruscan and Roman antiquities. In the Sully wing are Greek antiquities, a thematic display on Pharaonic Egypt, and antiquities from Iran and the Levant. On the first floor of the Sully wing is the second half of the Pharaonic Egypt section, this time in chronological order, in which we can find the *Squatting Scribe* and three sculptures of Akhnaton. The rest of Sully at this level is Greek earthenware and Roman bronzes.

Paintings begin on the first floor. A large part of this level is taken up by the 'Grande Galerie', and its side-rooms, in the Denon wing, where the Italian paintings have always been. We cannot get to them without arriving in a huge room of large-format French paintings, whichever escalator we take. Italian drawings are also here. The Richelieu wing shows the Napoleon III Apartments and a large section of *objets d'art*, spreading over into the Sully wing. On the second floor we find the huge collection of French paintings, hung at last together in chronological order. The early works are in the Richelieu wing, so we should start there and follow them through into the Sully wing. They occupy it all. The rest of Richelieu, to which we return, houses Dutch, Flemish and German paintings.

If we had a month or a lifetime to spend, it would be very pleasant just to get lost in the maze of the Grand Louvre and see what we find. We might come upon the delightful little corner of della Robbia and Donatello ceramics which are hidden away, or enjoy the Buhl cabinets among the *objets d'art*. If we have only one day, or less, we must concentrate on the section which appeals to us most. But there are three works – the three Mediterranean ladies – which are obligatory. If we have not seen them, we have not been to the Louvre: the *Venus de Milo*, the *Winged Victory of Samothrace* and the *Mona Lisa*.

The **Venus de Milo** has now been relegated to the farthest end of the Greek Antiquities gallery (Sully wing, ground floor, section 12–13). This is a controversial work. It was discovered by a French archaeologist on the island of Milos in the nineteenth century. He proclaimed it to be the masterpiece of classical Athens, even of Praxiteles himself, and on this basis he sold it to the Louvre. There was consternation when it was found that, far from being classical, it was of late date (second century BC) and was not from Athens. It was then thought that the statue was the ideal of feminine beauty; but larger-than-life pear-shaped bodies, long noses and big feet are not at the moment thought to be signs of great beauty. What we can genuinely admire is the contrast of spirals between the smooth body and the folds of the draperies which are slipping down. We can also appreciate the feeling of balance and serenity, and also of softness; the goddess seems to be made of some material much less hard than marble. But this said, it can be added that a large number of distinguished people would gladly see it sent back to Greece.

The **Winged Victory** is still splendidly placed at the top of a staircase (which we find by going to the near end of Greek Antiquities in section 4). This superb work dates from the third or early second century BC. Found in many pieces, it has been carefully put together in its present (and original) soaring lines; the hand and finger alongside it were discovered in 1950. Like a ship's figurehead, it stands on a prow, though, being made of marble, it was never on any ship. It stood on a cliff overlooking the sea at Samothrace, erected to commemorate a naval victory. While admiring its lines as they are now, we should also try to imagine how it looked originally, with its head and arms, startling eyes and bright paintwork, like all Greek statues.

On the landing near her we see Fra Angelico's (1387–1466) *Crucifixion*. This is a large fresco from the convent of Fiesole. His Christ looks down in love on the Virgin and St John.

The **Mona Lisa** (*La Gioconde* as she is known in France) is in the hottest and most overcrowded room of all (section 6 off the Grande Galerie), and in an alcove. We have to stand well back and look through a glass protective screen, placed to avoid vandalism. This screen reflects our faces and the goggling bewildered eyes and cameras of the crowd around us. We see the picture dimly through a ghostly mirror of our own selves, which adds greatly to the sense of mystery and religious awe which surrounds the experience. But if we wish to examine the picture closely, we would do better to buy a good reproduction.

Its origins, like everything else about it, are mysterious. Leonardo finished it about 1505 after four years' work (some say seven). He brought it with him when he came to live at the Louvre, and the portrait was one of the first pictures in François I's collection. The lady is thought to have been the wife of a rich Florentine merchant, Francesco di Zanobi del Giocondo. The name *Mona Lisa* is a contraction of Madonna Elisabetta, and *La Gioconda* has a double meaning. She was, so to speak, 'Lady Elizabeth Smiley', and the portrait is a visual pun, one which perhaps Messer Giocondo and his wife had grown rather tired of.

As we gaze at the picture, a number of questions must jump into our minds. Who is this lady really? What is the picture about? Why did Leonardo take so long to paint it? Why did it remain in the painter's possession, rather than in that of the Giocondo family? Why is she sitting in a wild, uninhabited landscape, unlike that of Tuscany, rather than in her own home or garden? And, finally, why should this small, drably-coloured portrait of a not very beautiful woman have become the most famous picture in the world?

'Hers is the head upon which all the ends of the world are come', wrote Walter Pater in his *Renaissance Studies* (1873). An ambiguous sentence, but suggesting finality and universality. Pater continued, in his purple style: 'She is older than the rocks among which she sits; like the vampire, she has been dead many times, and learned the secrets of the grave; and has been a diver in deep seas, and keeps their fallen day about her, and trafficked for strange webs with Eastern merchants; and, as Leda, was the mother of Helen of Troy, and, as Saint Anne, the mother of Mary; and all this has been to her but as the sound of lyres and flutes, and lives only in the delicacy with which it has moulded the changing lineaments, and tinged the eyelids and the hands'.

A master of a very different prose style, P. G. Wodehouse, often used her nickname to describe a sorrowful girl: 'You're looking like the Mona Lisa today'.

In 1934 Cole Porter wrote the lines:

> You're the Nile, you're the Tower of Pisa
> You're the smile on the Mona Lisa ...

The picture has also been used as an advertisement for a laxative, perhaps because of the lady's greenish complexion. It is an enigmatic smile indeed!

Smiling portraits are rare and usually famous (Murillo; Franz Hals, whose *La Bohémienne* hangs in the Louvre). But there is something special about the *Gioconda* smile. It is not the toothy grin of a modern politician or television personality. It is not the mocking smile of Voltaire, nor is it brave or false. *La Gioconda* is smiling at some inner thought, which we shall never know.

The background is also mysterious. Men have obviously been there, making roads and bridges, but nobody is there any more. If we ignore for a moment the central figure, we can see that it is in fact two landscapes, which can never meet. What does this mean? Past and future? Left hand and right hand? Possibility and achievement? Leonardo, of course, does not tell us. Mystery was an integral part of his own many-sided, volatile genius, as is shown by his passion for mirror-writing.

Leonardo has several other works in the Louvre, nearby, unguarded and relatively ignored. Commissioned in 1483 but rejected and re-copied in Italy, *The Virgin of the Rocks* is a beautiful, imaginative work, showing a young, fair girl, seated in a fantastic Dolomite setting, holding out her hands to an angel and two cherubs. It is almost exactly the same as the picture in the National Gallery, London. *The Virgin and Child with St Anne* was begun in 1509 but never delivered, and is the same as the cartoon in London. He worked through several designs and cartoons. It is rather a spooky work, and some have identified the figure of St Anne with the apparition of Death.

All these works give good examples of Leonardo's *sfumato* style. This is a painter's skill, making use of light to make the figures seem alive and even in motion. But this is a technical point. We shall be more interested in the subjects and the cryptic meaning of the pictures.

In the same room as the *Mona Lisa* a whole wall is taken up by Veronese's (1528–1588) *Marriage of Cana,* 1562. His central Christ, although a tiny figure on the huge canvas, looks straight at us, and we scarcely notice the gorgeously clothed foreground figures, or the great colonnades which flank them.

The **Italian School** is the old heart of the Louvre and the chief reason why it became so famous as a museum. Still in the Grande Galerie, its collection spans the centuries from Cimabue (1272–

1302) and Giotto, in the thirteenth and fourteenth centuries, through the Renaissance to Titian who died in 1576, aged ninety-nine, and, in the eighteenth century, Guardi. There is no space here to write an essay on the development of Renaissance art, nor is this the book for that. All I can do here is to show you some works which I find particularly attractive and some artists which I find of special interest. You may well have other views.

The Primitives are now more admired than they once were and we may well pause before Giotto's (1265–1337) *St Francis receiving the Stigmata*. Painted mainly in white and gold, it is basically a Byzantine icon (painted about 1320). A hundred years later Fra Angelico's (1417–1455) *Coronation of the Virgin* (c. 1430) glows with colour, in particular cobalt blue. The simple theme is complicated by the large crowd, and the artist did not know about perspective. This technique was developed by Paolo Uccello (1397–1475), who never seemed to tire of painting the battle of San Romano (1435) – there are other pictures of it in London and Florence – and the profusion of lances, horses and bodies gave ample opportunities for his skill. Perspective, creating a third dimension in a two-dimensional art, with its vanishing points and in-going lines, was an essential part of painting from then on. One cannot imagine Vermeer or Velázquez without it – until our own times, when it was eliminated by Matisse and some of his contemporaries.

Botticelli (1445–1510) is represented here by a *Madonna and Child with the young St John Baptist* (c.1470–75) and his *Virgin and Child with five Angels* (1470). Although they are beautifully drawn, and full of grace and charm, I personally find them rather wan, and much prefer the works of Mantegna (1431–1506). His *St Sebastian* (1480) is much reproduced and in his *Crucifixion* (painted about 1456) we should note the fine rock formations, a Renaissance speciality. Ghirlandaio's (1449–1494) *Old Man and his Grandson* remains one of my favourite pictures; apart from the old man's comic nose, it is a touching portrayal of mutual affection (1490). There are several good Peruginos (1450–1523).

Raphael (1483–1520) is represented by several religious works. The *Madonna and Child*, popularly known as *'La Belle Jardinière'*, is very typical both of Raphael and of the high Renaissance (1507). There is the fine draughtsmanship, the formal construction (triangular in this case), the colour, especially Madonna blue, the distant hilly landscape. But there are those who find it sugary, and personally I much prefer his fine portrait of Balthazar Castiglione and his

116

Notre-Dame from the south

A corner of the Place des Vosges

Façade of the Musée du Louvre

The Tuileries Gardens

A Paris shopkeeper and his client

rt Nouveau Metro sign Overleaf: *The Quais and the Ile dé la Cité*

The Bastille Opéra

Bouquinistes on the Left Bank

Les Invalides

Sacré Coeur

Place de la Concorde: a fountain at night

Millennium fireworks at the Eiffel Tower

contemporary Giovanni Bellini's (1459–1516) *Portrait of a Man* c.1490–95.

Venice was a long way, artistically, from Florence. Titian's splendid *Entombment* (1525) is full of energy and movement very far from Raphael's calm. Giorgioni's *Pastoral concert* brings in secular sensuality, in particular the female nude, even if the two couples are doing nothing sexier than playing music. We should note the sky, a speciality of this artist. And so to Tintoretto (*Susanna Bathing*) and Veronese, whose *Wedding Feast at Cana*, already noticed, occupies so much space and manages to include such unlikely wedding guests as the Emperor Charles V, nobles from Venetian society and the artist himself playing the cello (late sixteenth century). Italian art had moved far away from the times of Giotto and Fra Angelico.

The French School is on the first and second floors in the Denon and Richelieu wings. Two-thirds of the paintings in the old Louvre were French. However, French art is not uniformly presented over the centuries. The nineteenth-century collection is its pride and its largest feature, in numbers and size. Those who hoped that this emphasis would be changed with the re-hanging done for the Grand Louvre were disappointed. There are three great rooms of large-format nineteenth-century canvases, two of them strategically placed at the tops of both the escalators as we reach the first floor (Denon wing), and the third occupying the principal gallery among the French paintings on the second floor. We may as well submit and start our tour, chronologically at the wrong end, because all the earlier French works are upstairs. We should remember that the Revolutionary and Napoleonic periods provided the keynote of the Louvre when it was opened to the public in 1793, and works of that date have been a rallying-point for French patriotism ever since.

Whether this is still true may be questioned. As we watch the guided tours going round the paintings on the first floor, we may notice that the Americans are by far the best informed, the Japanese the most disciplined; the Italians are much the most enthusiastic (and the noisiest); the French are the most bored. The individualistic British usually go round alone.

Some of the most sanguinary battle-scenes have been removed, perhaps in deference to a more united Europe, but there are still pictures just as melodramatic and gruesome. The huge romantic *Raft of the Medusa* by T. Géricault, showing shipwreck survivors who became cannibals and ate each other, was a political attack on the incompetence of the government who had indirectly caused the disaster; it has retained its political overtones, and Hans Werner Henze's oratorio of the same title aroused similar controversy. Julian Barnes' *History of the World in 8½ Chapters* explores every aspect of this extraordinary painting.

Jacques-Louis David (1748–1825) was the foremost French painter of his time and ruled French art 'with an iron hand', laying down classical laws of art, derived theoretically from Rome. He was a talented portrait-painter, as we can see from his famous picture of Madame Récamier on her sofa, from his Pope Pius VII and from his self-portrait. But his political theories inspired him to attempt huge canvases on classical or military themes. A close friend of Robespierre, they were together in prison and David was lucky to escape the guillotine in 1793. He was visited in prison by his estranged wife, a royalist, and he was so touched by this that he was later inspired to paint his *Sabine Women*. In this the women are shown stopping the fight between the Romans and the Sabines. This is not the popular angle on the legend and indeed is surprising from an artist devoted to martial glory. But it is a powerful work, full of sincerity, especially the pleading women. David became a Bonapartist and official painter to Napoleon. We see his coronation here, but he also painted Napoleon in battle, and riding across the Alps, showing a remarkable skill in horsemanship. After 1815 David went into exile and painted no more.

The men in the *Sabine Women* were all naked, as indeed are all his soldiers, except Napoleon. This was partly due to his early training by Boucher and partly due to his studies of classical statues. But it introduces a certain credibility gap. Do all soldiers always go into battle naked? And, if so, would they have been quite so pale-skinned? David would have us think so. The Louvre has thirty-nine of his works, and, for one visitor at least, that is quite enough.

As we gaze at the enormous canvas of David's *Coronation of Napoleon* 1807, we may feel something compelling us to look over our shoulders. There, through an archway, we suddenly catch sight of the *Winged Victory of Samothrace*. In a battle of wills she seems to draw us towards her. After all, she was a goddess able to crown others with victory. Napoleon had to crown himself.

David had many pupils, but his mantle fell upon Delacroix, who was not one of them. Once again we have the huge violent canvases, full of corpses, massacres and heroism, some of it mythical or classical, some of it more contemporary. We can certainly admire the energy, the feeling of line and construction, though this sometimes seems to be a little repetitive. But *Liberty leading the people* (1830) is a powerful and striking picture. Here the bare-breasted goddess of Liberty (the one whose face was on the postage stamps), barefoot, waving a Tricolore, strides across the corpses, followed by a street urchin (like 'Le petit Gavroche') waving pistols, a bourgeois in a top hat brandishing a shotgun, and other revolutionaries. In the distance, through the smoke of the barricades, we can see the towers of Notre-Dame. The contrast in styles, in realism and, especially in clothes, is startling, as Delacroix doubtless intended it to be. The obvious comparison is with Victor Hugo, who held similar views and wrote about the same revolution and barricades. But Delacroix much disliked being compared with his literary counterpart; he also resented being called a Romantic, when he insisted that he was a 'pure classicist'.

The French paintings continue on the second floor, where as a change from all this vast violence, we can move to the Sully wing. Here a lift will take us to the second floor to contemplate the classical nudes of Dominique Ingres (sections 50 to 73). His work after 1848 is now in the Musée d'Orsay. A follower of Raphael, a pupil of David, he spent most of his life in Rome where he became Director of the French Academy. Draughtsmanship was all-important to him, colour of far less importance. Line and shape were supreme and his figures based on classical statues sometimes seem rather lifeless. Not that there is anything asexual about his *Odalisque*, a seductive girl indeed. His portrait of M. Bertin, too, is very living.

With Corot's landscapes we are back with the eye of the artist, muddy colours, blurred shapes and diffused woodland. But, in a long career, his early and his last works show a clarity and an interest in light which he lost for a while. Some have even seen him as an early Impressionist. But we cannot see his *Bridge at Mantes* (1870) here: his post-1848 works, with those of Ingres and Delacroix, are on the ground floor of the Musée d'Orsay. It would have surprised them all to know that they would one day share a roof with the Impressionists. The Louvre never accepted them and never repented of the policy of its Salon, which rejected them. They show us with pride a painting of their Salon jury giving the verdicts which meant make or break for young artists.

Although the Louvre's nineteenth-century painters may seem to us to have a good deal in common, it must not be thought that they were a mutual admiration society like the Impressionists. David's pupils attacked Delacroix for breaking the Laws of Art, a very French offence. Ingres attacked him savagely for being a Romantic and not a Classicist – Ingres himself, despite his draughtsmanship, was criticized for deforming the human body. Courbet (now in the Musée d'Orsay) was attacked for being self-taught and for making trees look like trees, instead of feather-dusters. And it is this conflict of strongly held, if rather esoteric, views which has provided the mainspring for so much of French art. At one time, the Louvre possessed a hundred Corots, not all, of course, on view.

Having disposed of the nineteenth century we are now not far from the point where the early French painters start, just round the corner in the nearest galleries of the Richelieu wing, still on the second floor. It is well worthwhile to follow them right through in date order, which is now possible for the first time. These are sections 1 to 49, which run on into the Sully wing. Some of the best works are at the start.

Much of **mediæval art**, at a time when France was supreme artistically, has been lost, some of it in the Hundred Years' War, some of it by the periodic French wish to destroy their own heritage. However, some has survived. The round *Pietà*, by Malouel, about 1400, painted for Philippe le Hardi, duke of Burgundy and the *Pietà* by Euguerrand Quarton (c.1444–66) from Villeneuve-lès-Avignon are masterpieces of the end of the Middle Ages. The first-known individual portrait since antiquity is a canvas of *King John II (the Good)* of France, c.1360.

Sixteenth-century French art, especially portrait painting, has benefited from France's central geographical position, touching both North and South, Flemish and Italian. There is a sharp break between the early religious painting of the fourteenth and fifteenth centuries and the secular painting of the sixteenth century. The North provided, it is said, the verisimilitude, the South the intellectual content. France has also benefited much from its traditional hospitality to foreign artists, begun by François I, which still continues. So it is right that one of the finest French portraits should be of that king, by Jean Clouet, 1524 (room 8). This shows the king's sumptuous tastes, his intelligence and education, and also his cunning.

The **seventeenth century**, 'Le Grand siècle', begins with the magnificent portrait of Cardinal Richelieu by Philippe de Champaigne (1602–1644) in room 12. (An identical copy of this portrait may be seen in London.) There is also a fine portrait of Louis XIII (1635). On a lower social level are the characters in the works of Le Nain (1600–1648), and especially Georges de la Tour (room 28). The latter's candle-lit groups, the faces alive in the light of the flame, are rightly admired. No one knows for certain how he did them; it is said that he used wooden boxes with slits for his dramatic effects, but others think that he worked from sketches made in the low poorly-lit taverns which he liked to haunt. Card-sharpers, pick-pockets, sneak-thieves – these were his models. The picaresque, I feel, inspired him more than religion, and his Bethlehem scenes in the Louvre I find less exciting, though the *Adoration of the Shepherds* and *St Joseph the Carpenter* (1642), being down to earth, are fine pictures.

The seventeenth century did not only produce portraits and groups. It also produced a great nostalgia for the classical world, an alternative to the too-established Church. Nicolas Poussin (1594–1665, room 13) was a Norman who spent most of his life in Rome, painting imaginary classical scenes. Some discerning art critics find these very great, particularly the *Bacchanale* (1627); I fear I am not among them. Equally 'classical' – that is to say full of buildings with columns – are the pictures of Claude Le Lorrain (1602–1682). Here the architectural landscapes are bathed in an agreeable sunset haze and populated by figures in seventeenth-century clothes. We see a whole room of them (15).

The passion for ancient Rome had gone to extremes. Poussin produced 'laws' of Nature and Art which were rigidly applied by Louis XIV's expert, Le Brun. René Huyghe, not a man to undervalue his fellow-countrymen, wrote that the reign of Le Brun at Versailles produced, artistically, 'almost nothing of value'. Yet we see room after room of his works here. But the fine portraitists escaped his influence; the Louvre shows many good examples: Hyacinthe Rigaud (1659–1743) painted the sculptor Desjardins in 1692 and a truly regal portrait of Louis XIV in 1701 (room 34).

The **eighteenth century** reacted, going from the grandeur of Rome to what Huyghe called 'frivolity' – nudes and shepherdesses. Madame de Pompadour's artist, Boucher, may well be so criticized, but it is a little unfair on Fragonard (1732–1806, rooms 48 and 49) whose landscapes often have a pastoral, fairytale quality. In a different category is Watteau (1684–1721) the first of the Romantics, a movement which was to find its climax in Delacroix. His *Embarkation for Cythère*, 1717, is full of romantic yearnings and nostalgia, and so well painted that the Beaux Arts accepted the unknown young man immediately (room 36). Portrait painting did not flourish in Louis XV's reign. French creative genius during the eighteenth century was best expressed in architecture, furniture and interior decoration. The pastel of the Marquise de Pompadour by Quentin de la Tour (1704–1788) seems to find more interest in her dress, furniture and books than in her face – pardonably, perhaps (room 45).

Flemish art (second floor, Richelieu wing) has been almost as important and influential in France as Italian, and the Louvre has a good, although not very large, collection representing most of the great masters. Van Eyck's *The Virgin and Chancellor Rolin* (1433) is rightly famous, though we must regard it as more of a conversation piece or an interior scene then a religious picture. The chancellor, who commissioned the work, is clearly reading the Madonna a stern lecture, while she meekly sits with her eyes closed (note her red hair and red robe, a daring innovation). But our eyes will be mainly caught by the details – the tiled floor, the clothes, the capitals on the columns. All the lines lead us to the arches, the garden and the landscape beyond, with its river, little town and distant mountains. The two main figures do not hold the centre of the stage.

The same cannot be said of *The Annunciation*, probably by Rogier Van der Weyden, 1432. The Virgin and the Archangel dominate the picture. But, although it is of the same date as *Chancellor Rolin*, it is a simpler, more Gothic work. The domestic details, however, are painted with the same fidelity; we shall enjoy the angel's gold cope, worthy of an archbishop. Memling, a little later, is represented by a *Madonna and Child with St James and St Dominic*. She is not in her traditional blue but, surprisingly, in bright red on an elaborate throne. The usual Flemish domestic details are missing apart from the Virgin's oval Flemish face.

With Gérard David's *Marriage at Cana* (1505) we are back among the pots and pans, or at least among the platters and goblets. We are at a pleasant family party in Bruges, some of which is visible outside. There is no sense of wonder at the miracle. Hieronymus Bosch's *Ship of Fools* (early sixteenth century) and two Breughels are also shown here. Van Dyck has a superb portrait of Charles of England, painted in 1635. This is possibly the finest of Van Dyck's royal portraits, capturing so many facets of the king's character, his dignity, his stubbornness and his elegance. How it came to France is not known, but it was, ironically, much admired by Louis XVI.

The **Medici Gallery** has been specially rebuilt to house the twenty-four pictures which Marie de Medici commissioned from

Rubens for the Luxembourg Palace (1622–1625). This series was intended to show the life of the queen in historical terms; an unpromising commission, but one which turned out to be a masterpiece. It is thought that much of the detailed work was done by his apprentices, among them Van Dyck. Apart from Marie de Medici, we can also see his *Adoration of the Magi* (1626) and a late, great work *The Country Fair* (1635) in which he contrasts a peaceful evening countryside with the crowd of drunken peasants, in Breughel style.

Dutch seventeenth-century painting (second floor, Richelieu ing) is admired in France as elsewhere. The collection may not be large, but it contains several masterpieces. No one will want to miss the four Rembrandt self-portraits but we should also notice his *Bathsheba* (painted in 1654). This is in fact a portrait of his servant-mistress Hendrickje Stoffels, nude in her bath. As Bathsheba she is reading a letter telling her of the death planned for her husband, Uriah the Hittite. It is difficult to imagine that King David should have so much desired her heavy, unshapely body, but her face is moving, so full of love and sadness.

At the other end of the emotional scale is Franz Hals's *La Bohémienne* (about 1626). Daringly painted in red and white, the girl's smile is far from enigmatic and her sidelong glance has a come-hither look. A merry peasant, she is a contrast to Van Eyck's *Madonna*. More serious is the girl in Vermeer's *The Lacemaker* (1670), a quiet picture of someone ruining her eyesight. Hobbema's *Watermill* is a typical Dutch landscape full of sky, trees, water and perspective.

The small but important section of **German paintings** is hung near the early French paintings on the second floor of the Richelieu ing. Here we shall find a Dürer self-portrait (1493), an excellent picture of himself as a young man. Holbein's *Anne of Cleves* (1439), the cast-off wife of the English king Henry VIII, and *Erasmus* (1523) catch the eye, but the Elder Cranach's *Venus* (1529) seems rather mannered.

Compared with Italian, Flemish and French painting, the Spanish and English have always been dismissed as 'peripheral'. The last French king, Louis Philippe, made a collection, belatedly, of four hundred and fifty Spanish works, but when he was removed in 1848, these turned out to be his personal property and he sold them in London. Efforts have been made to put this right, but the English and

Spanish sections were the last to be housed in the Grand Louvre and were only hung in temporary rooms when it opened.

Among the **Spanish paintings,** we shall find a typical EI Greco *Crucifixion* (1585) and a good portrait of the old architect Covarrubias, a study in black, grey and elongation (1600). Zurbarán's *Burial of St Bonaventure* (1629) is a dramatic construction; the diagonally placed corpse robed in white, with a green decomposing face and a scarlet hat, is surrounded by mourners, some sorrowing, some like the Pope and emperor, uncaring. Ribera's *Clubfoot* (1652) is an attractive picture, the boy so merry despite his deformity. There are good Goyas, the *Woman in Grey* and the portrait of the proud Marquesa of Solana, thought by some to be his finest.

The **English School,** delightfully low-key as it seems to us, is so far from the more dramatic French tradition that they have found it impenetrable. It is impossible for them to imagine an aristocrat who was not a court intriguer or on his way to the guillotine, but quietly enjoying rural peace on his country estate. However Turner, regarded in a new light as a forerunner of the Impressionists, started to attract attention, and the section was then enlarged by some Constables and a fine portrait of Lady Alston by Gainsborough, presented by Baron Robert de Rothschild. The collection includes portraits by Reynolds (*Master Hare*), Lawrence and Raeburn and landscapes by Bonington.

Having seen all the European paintings on the second floor of the Richelieu wing, we may take the staircase down, through the *objets d'art* on the first floor (some of it excellent French furniture but also ivory, enamel, bronze and porcelain) to the ground floor rooms of French sculpture (still in Richelieu).

Sculpture

In the Grand Louvre, great emphasis has been placed on sculpture, perhaps in an effort to hold on to the Humanist tradition, which they value so much. The best of it may be found in the Antiquities sections; among the relatively modern sculpture, most of the works are French, many of a 'stereotyped' neo-classical kind. We may prefer to see the source of their inspiration among the ancient Romans and Greeks themselves. But there are a few outstanding pieces. We must not miss *The Horses of Marly* by G. Coustou, 1745, marble, so our tour begins at the entresol in the Richelieu wing, where we will find the Marly courtyards. A passage leads us from here into the great entrance hall. At the far side, opposite us in the Denon wing and still in the entresol, we may find eleventh- to fifteenth-century Italian and Spanish sculptures, and behind them twelfth- to sixteenth-century North European sculptures. But if we are looking for Michelangelo, we have to climb upstairs again to the sections on sixteenth- to nineteenth-century Italian sculptures on the ground floor. There are a lot of stairs in the new Louvre, and far too few lifts. Michelangelo's *Captives* are famous (sixteenth century, unfinished marble). They have muscular, though somewhat heavyweight, bodies but seem weighed down by lethargy. Much has been written about them: one theory is that they are captive to their own sensuality. It is surprising to learn that they were intended for the tomb of a pope (Julius II).

By now we may realise that we just can't see the whole Grand Louvre in one visit. We should plan another complete tour of the antiquities, starting with the Ancient Egyptians, and we may find that many others, especially young people, have made this their first day's tour, ahead of European art. Meanwhile, there are snackbars and cafés in the museum itself, and a variety of restaurants, as well as gift-shops, in the Louvre Carrousel, which is a big underground area, with a car-park, between the Louvre Pyramid and Arc de Triomphe du Carrousel (entrance 99 rue de Rivoli). Our Louvre tickets are valid all day and allow us to re-enter, if we feel strong enough to come back after lunch.

The Grand Louvre's collection of **Egyptian antiquities** does not date, as all good Frenchmen believe, from Napoleon's invasion of Egypt, but was formed in 1826 under the influence of Jean-François Champollion, the man who deciphered the Rosetta Stone. It has become one of the finest collections in the world, at first by purchases from other collections but later mainly as a result of 'equal share' agreements by which the Egyptian governments allowed French archaeological expeditions to keep half of their finds. This system is now under review, but it seems to have suited both France and Egypt in the past; the pride of the Louvre's collection is the compelling head of Amenhotep IV (Akhnaton, the first monotheist), which was presented by the Egyptian government not long ago as a goodwill gesture. It dates from about 1360 BC. This is specially lit, in the Pharaonic Egypt chronological circuit, in the Sully wing, first floor, towards the far end of the gallery (section 25). Examine his fine mystical face. This sculpture does not show the curiously elongated back of his head, noticeable in some portraits of him, but we may compare it with two other sculptures of Akhnaton in the same room marked 'The New Kingdom: 1353–1337 BC'. One, in 1350 BC, is a fragment of a pillar from a building east of Karnak. The other is a small stone bust, formerly painted, in which the shape of the head is quite clear. Nefertiti, with her delightful figure, is also here.

In section 22 we find the famous *Squatting Scribe*. The small stone figure is Old Kingdom (between 2750 and 2625 BC) and represents the governor of a province. We should note the eyes, which are opaque white, with quartz cornea, rock-crystal iris and ebony pupils; they stare over our right shoulders in a most disconcerting way.

Many visitors are fascinated by the Book of the Dead of the Nabqed Papyrus, *The Funerary Cortege*, about 1500–1300 BC. These books were large papyri placed near the corpse with hymns to the gods and magical formulae meant to help the deceased through the obstacles he might have to overcome in the afterlife. (Such obstacles didn't, apparently, include the problem of reading in the dark.) Two further sections show Coptic Egypt and Roman Egypt in the Denon wing, entresol level, beside pre-classical Greece.

Following on from the Egyptian thematic circuit, a series of galleries show us **Near Eastern antiquities,** from the ancient civilizations of the countries of the Levant, ancient Iran and Mesopotamia (in the Cour Khorsabad). These date back as far as 7000 BC. This section covers an area from India to North Africa and presents seven thousand objects. If we are still looking for the Hittites, we find them here. It's not possible to do justice to such a remarkably interesting display in a few pages, but the glamorous names of the past, Nineveh, Carthage, Babylon, Sumeria and Phoenicia, are enough in themselves to draw us into this world of its own. We can't miss, for example, King Darius I's palace in Susa (c. 500 BC) with its splendid archer (enamelled brick) and the bulls which were the capitals on top of the columns.

There is a great variety of style. In Sumeria as long ago as 2400 BC there was a smiling realism in the bearded figure of the administrator of the temple of Ishtar, goddess of love. He obviously enjoyed the job. From the Yemen, we may admire a carved alabaster stele showing camel-drivers making a raid. In Iran they had highly skilled craftsmen in 1200 BC who made carved goblets with designs full of fantasy. The quality of all these works is excellent. Has there ever been a place or a time without its own art? (If we answer 'our own', we cannot have visited the permanent collection of modern art in the Centre Pompidou, Beaubourg.)

The Islamic section (Richelieu wing, entresol) shows art from the seventh century to the nineteenth from all parts of the huge Islamic area, stretching from old Spain to Central Asia. This is of particular interest because much of it has never been shown before. We find it by going down a staircase from the Mesopotamian section in the Cour Khorsabad. It occupies thirteen rooms which have been laid out to show divergences of style over the various areas and periods. The museum's own experts do not even mention the word 'carpets'; they wish us to notice the delicate designs of thirteenth-century Syria; a great basin of hammered brass inlaid with silver and gold, from Syria or Egypt thirteenth–fourteenth century; sixteenth-century painted and glazed mosque tiles from Istanbul (c. 1573) and a finely-carved ivory box from Cordoba, Spain (968). But if we really care about good carpet designs we can appreciate a 'Kilim' in silk and silver thread from Kashan, Iran (sixteenth–seventeenth century), illustrating poems by a twelfth-century Persian author. It would be worth finding this section even for that alone.

The old Louvre used to pride itself on its **Greek and Roman sculpture** and the collection was declared to be one of the best in the world. But perhaps because of a decline in public interest (which would have amazed the artist David) and the discovery that many of the statues were replicas, the Grand Louvre has made the astonishing decision to disperse its Greek collection on to three different levels, in two different wings. At the same time the area has been expanded from 900 sq. metres to 7,140 sq. metres, and Roman and Etruscan works have been combined with it, producing 4,500 objects on display, many drawn from reserve collections. The result is an endurance test for the visitor. If we can spot her in the confusion, we may like to study the *Lady of Auxerre,* one of the oldest known Greek statues, a very stern work. There is also a fragment of the Parthenon frieze, confiscated from the Comte de Choisel-Gouffier in the 1792 Revolution. How he got it is obscure, but the Greeks do not seem to object if their frieze is in the Louvre. Earthenware and bronze are in the Sully wing.

One of the last Greek statues was the *Borghese Gladiator*, which was in the Borghese collection bought by Napoleon in 1808 (section 8, Denon wing, ground floor). It has been much admired for its fine, muscular body, very well modelled, especially the legs. But the stupid, scared face makes the figure a sad one. He obviously knows he is going to lose his fight and die; muscles are not enough.

The **Roman antiquities** have also been dispersed. Roman Egypt is in the entresol, and the most striking statues are alongside the escalator where we see them as we go up. These are four great caryatids, *Satyrs in Atlanta,* from the imperial period of Rome, once a set similar to those found in the Theatre of Dionysus in Athens. They have great dignity and quiet, more Grecian than Roman.

Mixed with the ancient Romans, we find the Etruscans, an older civilization which they eclipsed, like so many others. If we have visited Rome and admired the double-spiral staircase in the Vatican, said to be of Etruscan design, we must have longed to see more of their work. They were clearly unique people – who else in the Louvre ever had their sense of fun? We may see it in their dancing bronze figures, and even in the wonderful sarcophagus of the Carveteri Couple (late sixth century BC, painted terracotta) on which a life-like couple are sculpted, leaning on it as a couch for their feast in the next world. They are smiling, in the face of death, with a much happier smile than La Gioconda's.

Near the Louvre, at 107 Rue de Rivoli, is a very different collection, the **Musée des Arts Décoratifs.** This is not so much a museum as a record of the way of life of people who liked to have beautiful things round them, presented to us as a series covering seven hundred years, from the thirteenth to twentieth centuries, produced by Europeans at their most civilized. It is part of a group of museums, art schools and libraries, under one management (the Union Centrale des Arts Décoratifs) but not all on the same site. It has been an unfairly neglected little sister of the Louvre, although it has its principal site in the Palais du Louvre itself.

The name has been a sad handicap to tourism from English-speaking countries. The directors seem to be quite unaware that 'decorative' tends to suggest to us 'pretty but poor quality' and that 'art deco' means an outdated style used in restaurants. We should dismiss all this from our minds at once and go there to discover its treasures, many of which can equal those in the top museums of London, New York and Vienna. The replanning for the year 2000 caused a long closure, but the mediæval section 'Moyen Age– Renaissance' jumped the gun by opening in 1998. This was a surprise, because the museum's special feature used to be its present-day collection (they distinguish between 'Modern' and 'Contemporary' as two different periods). But the twentieth century has gone into history with all the others. The museum has also been almost overwhelmed by legacies, of astonishing quality and value, from a series of benefactors, which have taken their collection farther and farther back into the past.

The museum describes itself as 'bourgeois' because, unlike the Louvre, it has not acquired its exhibits from kings, conquests and revolutionary confiscations. Its antiques have come from discerning collectors, who travelled round Europe finding them and presented them to the museum for the enjoyment of people like us.

There are nine rooms devoted to the **Medieval and Renaissance** section (thirteenth to sixteenth centuries). These are divided between the secular and the religious life of the time, in a series of 'period rooms' which evoke the style of each date. We begin with tapestries, which are the pride of the collection. These will be shown in rotation because they are fragile, being hung in groups to illustrate different mediæval themes such as the combat between Vice and Virtue. A painted panel *The Virgin and Child with St Andrew and St James* by the Master of the Madeleine, from Florence in the late thirteenth century, is the oldest in any public collection in France. Another very early work is part of a fourteenth-century reredos by Benabarre of Catalonia.

There is a room full of furniture from a castle in Auvergne, with linen-fold carving and other typical motifs of Flamboyant Gothic style. Another room shows large tapestries, with foresters, shepherds and vineyards, of the fifteenth century. There is a fine collection (in show cases) of Venetian glass, faiences from Moorish Spain, enamel-work and small bronzes, shown beside a notable enamelled terracotta *Virgin of Mercy* from Florence, contemporary with those of della Robbia. A whole gallery is mounted as if inside a church, with church furnishings; its central feature is a reredos by the Spanish painter Borassa. Another room has 55 painted ceiling-panels from a monastery in Cremona.

The Renaissance style is shown in marquetry panels, ornate furniture and portraits, and the large final room is filled with Flemish tapestry, French and Italian furniture, paintings, stained glass and *objets d'art*.

To celebrate its renewal and reopening in 1998, the museum acquired a new treasure, a Venetian glass banqueting-goblet of the early sixteenth century, one of a set which belonged to a Medici pope. Others of this set are in the British Museum and the Metropolitan in New York. It is finely decorated with polychrome enamel and gilding. Works of this type are rare and are as much valued as gold cups.

The museum has similar departments for the seventeenth, eighteenth and nineteenth centuries, but is best known for its highly original twentieth-century collection. We can tell how much importance is attached to this when we find that the seventeenth and eighteenth centuries only have one curator between them, whereas the twentieth has no less than three curators, a chief researcher and a documentalist. Renovation of all departments is to be completed by 2001. There is also a centre for glass, a department of toys, centres for drawings and *papiers peints* and an oriental collection.

Associated in the same group is the **Musée de la Mode et du Textile** (Fashion and Fabrics), ancient and modern, in the same building (107 rue de Rivoli), inaugurated in 1997, with the support of the fashion world. The **Musée de la Publicité** was started in 1999 and tells us that it is for the perpetually renewed surprises of publicity creation.

9

Eastern Paris

PLACE DU LOUVRE (1er, Metro Louvre) is an old and attractive square. It was here that the Roman general Labienus had his headquarters when he defeated the Parisii in 52 BC. The Norsemen in AD 885 were checked here when they sailed up the Seine. But the square does not look the same now. On the west side is the neo-classical façade of the Louvre; on the east side the old church of Saint-Germain-l'Auxerrois; and to the south, the Seine flowing by.

It must have looked very pleasant too on the night of 23 August 1572, a hot Paris summer night, the eve of St Bartholomew's Day. Paris was *en fête;* there was to be a royal wedding the following day. Princess Marguerite (Margot) of Valois was to marry her cousin Henry of Navarre in Notre-Dame. Royal weddings are normally joyful occasions, but this one was especially important. Margot was a Catholic, Henry a Huguenot, and the marriage would end the civil wars of religion which were plaguing France. The planning, however, was slightly odd. The bride would be at the high altar, while the bridegroom, being a Protestant, would have to wait outside the main door. The rings, presumably would be taken to and fro by messengers. But nobody was troubled by this and thousands of Huguenots were in Paris to support their leader at the great event.

During the night the Queen Mother, Catherine de Medici, looked out of her window in the Louvre and gave a signal to watchers in Saint-Germain-l'Auxerrois opposite. The bell in the church tower began to peal and other belfries across Paris took up the signal. The massacre had begun. It had been carefully plotted by Catherine de Medici, her sons King Charles IX and Prince Henri (later King Henri III) and the Cardinal Duke of Guise, the head of the powerful Catholic family. For three days the French were overtaken by a frenzy of killing, which spread rapidly to towns. In that time about eight thousand Huguenots were killed, the ghastliest wedding

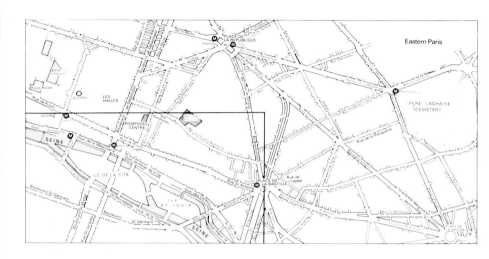

Eastern Paris

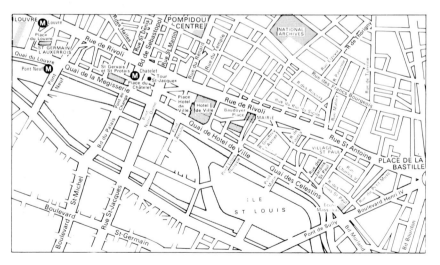

present ever given by a mother to her daughter. Henry of Navarre saved himself by kneeling before the king and swearing to abandon Protestantism. In due course the marriage took place but it is hardly surprising that it was brief, unhappy and childless.

The signal was given from the church tower which we can see from the side street; and not, as is often thought, from the big belfry which stands conspicuously in the square beside the church. This is a nineteenth-century mock-Gothic erection whose great interest is its carillon of thirty-eight bells, which weigh in total ten thousand kilos. The thirteen small bells are all of the same diameter, the different notes being caused by varying thicknesses of metal. There are carillon recitals, the secular music being mainly improvisations on popular tunes. The belfry is controlled, not by the church, but by the Mairie on the other side (housed in a mixed style nineteenth-century building by Hittorff).

The church of **Saint-Germain-l'Auxerrois,** 2 Place du Louvre (Metro Louvre) is very old, built on the site of a sanctuary destroyed by the Norsemen. St Germanus, Bishop of Auxerre (378–448 AD), was himself a remarkable man. He was originally trained as a Roman advocate and died in Ravenna while pleading the cause of the rebellious Armoricae. St Patrick of Ireland, St Illtyd of Wales and Ste Geneviève of Paris are claimed as his pupils. He came to Britain twice; in 447 he led British troops to victory over the invading Saxons and Picts, shouting his war-cry 'Alleluia!'

Apart from the older Romanesque bell-tower, his church is mainly Gothic, spread over several centuries. The centre doorway is thirteenth century but the rest of the porch was built between 1435 and 1439. Lovers of Gothic architecture will enjoy the porch vaulting, Flamboyant in the central bays, simpler at the ends. The church was much damaged in the Revolution and the statues are modern replicas.

The internal proportions are unusual. Gothic churches are normally tall, but this one is wide and comparatively low, with double aisles running right round the church. In the transepts the vaulting is late Gothic; the stained glass, including two rose windows, late fifteenth century. Two painted statues, one on wood, one on stone, flanking the chancel grille are of the same date and represent St Germanus and St Vincent. The chancel columns were given their classical aspect in the eighteenth century – regrettably, one may think. The big wooden churchwardens' pew dates from 1684 and was probably used by members of the royal family living in the Louvre. Behind it we should note a good Flemish altarpiece from the fifteenth century. In the Chapel of the Holy Sacrament, to the right of the entrance, we can see a coloured stone statue of the Virgin from the fourteenth century and an older statue of St Germanus, together with other statues and a modern *Last Supper* by Van Elsen.

The church is the centre of a 'Community of Fine Arts' which aims to encourage a continuing Christian tradition both in music and the visual arts. Organ recitals are held on an organ originally in the Sainte-Chapelle. Note the striking modern altar and lectern and a series of bold carved figures by Albert Dubos, particularly a fine 'Resurrection' in the north transept. A special service for artists is held on Ash Wednesday, according to the will of the painter and caricaturist, Adolphe Willette (d. 1926). Those present receive ashes and pray for the souls of those artists who will die in the coming year. This gloomy event is, it seems, well attended.

Outside, we get a good view of the east end and the bell-tower from the side street near the *Samaritaine* department store. Many will enjoy the gargoyles and the elaborate carvings. And then we are back beside the Seine at Pont Neuf. Leaving, for the time being, the three big stores here, we continue along **Quai de la Mégisserie,** one of the most delightful strolls in Paris. On the right is the river and Ile de la Cité. On the left is a line of pet shops; the pavement used to be lined with parrakeets, cocks, guinea-fowls, white rabbits and tropical fish, but such displays have now been banned by the authorities. A friend of mine bought a swan here, a present to the Seine and to a solitary errant swan which had become attached to Ile Saint-Louis. Once a cuddly black bear with very sharp claws escaped from a cage here and made its way through pedestrians and traffic to nearby Avenue Victoria, where it climbed a plane tree, to be brought down some hours later by an intrepid fireman.

Place du Châtelet (Metro Châtelet) is on the site of a mediæval prison, said to be even viler and more horrible than the Conciergerie, where the poet François Villon was imprisoned in the fifteenth century. Nothing now remains of this. Instead we have a square overlooking the Seine and Pont au Change (once a haunt of money-changers). In the centre is another monument to the Grande Armée. On either side are two symmetrical theatres, built by Davioud in 1862, both state-owned but quite separate. The Théâtre du Châtelet had the largest auditorium in Paris, seating half as many again as the Garnier Opéra. It reopened in 1999 after a complete overhaul.

Opposite, the Théâtre de la Ville, originally the Théâtre Sarah Bernhardt, caters for more popular culture.

Below the square is the world's biggest underground station. The junction of several metro lines, including the RER, it is really four stations joined together. It is possible to cross a great deal of Paris here without seeing daylight and it can be said that if you have not changed at Châtelet, you have not really experienced Paris

Perhaps it is part of Parisian fascination with their underground world, something which goes back to the Roman catacombs or even beyond. Catacombs, sewers, three metro systems, underground car parks, nightclubs, the Carrousel shopping area, modern churches, the Bibliothèque Nationale at Tolbiac, the Forum des Halles – the ground beneath Paris is honeycombed with tunnels and mines.

However, we should continue our walk in daylight. Behind Hôtel de Ville we find Avenue Victoria, named after the British queen. Here also is **Tour Saint-Jacques,** one of the landmarks of the Seine. The Gothic belfry is all that remains of the sixteenth-century church of Saint-Jacques, one of the starting points of the pilgrimage, by way of Rue Saint-Jacques on the Left Bank, to Santiago in Spain. From here we may want to continue to Beaubourg and Centre Georges Pompidou, the subject of the next chapter.

At the end of Avenue Victoria we emerge into **Place de l'Hôtel de Ville** (Metro Hôtel de Ville). Architecturally it is not very interesting, but it has seen much of Paris's tumultuous history. Indeed, for many centuries it was the only big square in the city. Until 1830 it was called Place de Grève; *grève* means foreshore and it was here that unemployed longshoremen and others would gather. The phrase *faire la grève* meant first to be unemployed, now to be on strike.

It was in Place de Grève that public floggings and executions took place, among them the execution of Ravaillac, murderer of Henri IV. The flesh of the condemned man would be slit at several points and boiling lead poured in, to give a foretaste of things to come. Finally the body, still alive, would be pulled in pieces by four strong horses. It was no worse than the English method of 'hanged, drawn and quartered', but the merciful invention of Dr Guillotin did not come a moment too soon.

Place de l'Hôtel de Ville has been the centre of municipal authority for a long time. Etienne Marcel in 1357 established the assembly in the Pillared House in the square; he raised the whole of France against the monarchy, sacked the palace on Ile de la Cité, encouraged the English and Navarrese invaders, and was killed by the Parisians the following year. However, the mayor of Paris and the municipal assembly did not have much authority under the Valois or Bourbons, nor indeed until the Revolution, when the Committee of Public Safety met here.

Robespierre was arrested here in 1793 by the patrols which he himself had instigated to safeguard the Revolution and which were in many people's minds the start of the Terror. In 1837 Carlyle put it in his own inimitable style: 'O Sea-Green Incorruptible, canst thou not see where this Patrollotism leadeth? O Patrollotism! O Patrollotism!'

In 1830 Louis-Philippe was proclaimed king from the steps of the **Hôtel de Ville**, then a seventeenth-century building. When he fled eighteen years later, the Second Republic was proclaimed from the same place. Baron Haussmann, prefect of the Seine, had his offices here when he was redesigning Paris into the city we know today. The Commune had their headquarters here in 1871 and, on departing, burnt the building to the ground. This was a habit they had.

The present town hall was finished in 1882, an example of Third Republic architecture, a blend of Renaissance and Belle Epoque. The outside is encrusted with 136 statues. Guided tours of the inside are available on the first Monday of each month, but numbers are limited and previous reservation is essential. We find a great staircase, chandeliers, coffered ceilings, statues and caryatids by the dozen; we can console ourselves with a Rodin bust ('La République') and some caricatures by Willette. At the river end of the building are the offices of the elected mayor of Paris.

Behind the Hôtel de Ville we find a remarkable church, **Saint-Gervais et Saint-Protais,** both Roman soldiers martyred by Nero. What we see is a vast classical façade which might be a lecturer's slide of the three orders of classical architecture, Doric columns at the bottom, Ionic on the first storey and Corinthian on the second. It is the earliest classical façade in Paris, finished in 1621, and behind it is a beautiful Gothic church which was not finished till 1657. Opinions vary on how well the two styles mix.

The inside is well worth a visit for its Gothic vaulting and its organ, built in 1601 and the oldest in Paris. Eight members of the Couperin family held the post of organist here and made the church famous for its music. Just off the north transept is a fine Flemish painting of the Passion from the sixteenth century. In the Lady Chapel, behind the altar, is a hanging keystone, eight feet in

136

diameter, like a floating crown. The church is now used by the Monastic Brotherhood of Jerusalem, who sing their offices in the Lady Chapel, their chanting replacing the playing of the Couperins. Saint-Gervais is built on a rise, with steps at either end. Its sixteenth-century belfry, floodlit at night, is another Seine landmark, visible from a considerable distance.

We return to the Seine at the nineteenth-century Pont Louis-Philippe, and continue along the quai. On our left is a long modern building (1965), the **Cité des Arts**. This provides accommodation and facilities for artists and composers, foreign as well as French. Nobody is allowed to stay there more than a year; by this time the artist is expected to have found a niche elsewhere. The Cité des Arts helps to combat the loneliness of the creative artist and provides opportunities for his work to be shown or heard by other artists and by anyone whom he can cajole into coming along. The underground art gallery is sometimes used by outside groups. The concrete façade, however, pleases nobody; fortunately in summer it is mainly concealed by trees.

Immediately beyond there is a large gravel area called Square Albert Schweitzer. Behind it we can see Hôtel d'Aumont, with Mansart's austere façade. On our right is the mediæval Hôtel de Sens, 1 Rue du Figuier (Metro Pont Marie). We are now skirting the area of old Paris called the Marais, full of big *hôtels* and narrow streets; but this requires a separate chapter. In the meantime we should continue along Quai des Célestins. At no. 32, now a modern office block, was once the Barbeau Tower, guarding the eastern entrance to Paris like the Tournelle on the Left Bank.

Continuing along the quai, we note the house on the corner of Rue des Jardins-Saint-Paul. Rabelais died here in 1553, as a plaque records. At the end of the quai is the little Square Henri Galli with a children's playground and the remaining stones from the Bastille prison, moved here from the original site. Their size gives some idea of that formidable fortress. To reach Place de la Bastille (Metro Bastille), where it stood, we must walk (or take a bus) along Boulevard Henri IV.

The Bastille is a legendary name in French and indeed world history. Frenchmen often say, 'I must do this or I shall be sent to the Bastille', hardly knowing what they are saying. The details of exactly what happened on 14 July 1789 have been overlaid by revolutionary propaganda, popular myth, romantic novels and historical films. Yet the words 'Quatorze Juillet' can still fire the

French imagination and the Fête Nationale is celebrated in France in a way which is hardly comprehensible across the Channel. Processions, bands, fireworks, dancing in the streets, balls given in fire stations and even in police stations – we can all take part in the rejoicing of a great city. The Place also has a lasting association with defiance and protest, and many demos and marches (*manifs*) begin or end at the Bastille. And all this because 633 men captured an almost disused and undefended detention centre.

The **Bastille Saint-Antoine** was built in 1370 as a fortress to guard Paris and provide a safe residence for the king, Charles V. Like the Tower of London, it served several purposes. It had eight towers and high walls, and its vast bulk dominated the whole area. Yet it was besieged several times and only once did it manage to hold out – it was not as large or formidable as it looked. In the seventeenth century Richelieu converted it into a prison, for which it was not very suitable as it held only fifty prisoners.

However, they were special prisoners, guilty of irritating somebody important, or of suspected insanity. Untried, they were sent to the Bastille by a *lettre de cachet,* a blank order signed by the king, the names to be filled in by anybody who might get hold of one. Voltaire's father filled one in to imprison his son and prevent his marrying a Protestant; however, he changed his mind and tore it up. But Voltaire was twice in the Bastille for impertinence and writing malicious verse. He whiled away the first time by writing a tragedy, *Œdipe*. The Marquis de Sade spent time there, before being transferred to the Charenton asylum. Nobody knows to this day the name on the *lettre de cachet* of the mysterious 'Man in the Iron Mask', though there have been many guesses.

The system of *lettres de cachet* was obviously a great abuse of personal liberty, a threat hanging over the head of every independent-minded citizen. It was much attacked and finally abolished in 1784, five years before the fall of the Bastille. But the *lettres* were revived in the Empire and Napoleon's police chief, Fouché, made use of them as never before – but not for the Bastille, which was no more.

The Bastille was not the Conciergerie. There was no shame attached to being there and no fearful death awaited its prisoners. They lived for the most part in considerable comfort. They had their own servants and entertained guests. One, the Cardinal de Rohan, gave a dinner party for twenty at the state's expense. Indeed, expense was one of the factors which made Louis XVI decide in 1784 to close the prison. In its place there was to be a big square to honour him, as Place Vendôme honoured Louis XIV. The Bastille was to be demolished, except for one symbolic tower. Beside it was to be a huge statue of the king, holding out his hand in mercy. The plans were never carried out; they can be seen in Hôtel Carnavalet. But the Bastille legend had started.

Early on 14 July the mob, of which only two hundred were Parisians, inflamed by Desmoulins' speeches, by the king's dismissal of the popular minister Necker, and by looted wine, marched to the Invalides where they captured a number of muskets, but little ammunition. A rumour went round that there were more than a hundred barrels of gunpowder in the Bastille. Shouting '*A la Bastille*' they marched off, thinking more of powder and shot than of liberating prisoners.

On arrival they burned the outlying buildings and fired at the walls. The governor, the Marquis de Launay, was in a dilemma. Though the walls were thick enough, he commanded only thirty-two Swiss guards and a larger number of French pensioners. Talks were held, followed by more shooting, more talks and an assault on the main gate. In the late afternoon the governor decided to surrender. The Swiss stacked their arms in the courtyard and the governor handed over the keys, which immediately became symbols of the people's victory; the key of the main gate was given by Lafayette to George Washington. Without their help the mob smashed its way in but, to its dismay, found no arms or powder. Somebody remembered the prisoners, but there were only seven there, forgers or lunatics. These were paraded round in carts to their great bewilderment. The governor and some of the Swiss guards were lynched.

Such were the events of the great day. The king wrote in his diary: '*Rien!*'– it had been a blank day's hunting. Charles James Fox wrote in a letter dated 30 July: 'How much the greatest event it is that ever happened in the world! and how much the best!' Both comments may seem to us somewhat exaggerated.

Forty-one years later, almost to the day, it was all to do again. In the Bastille area, Faubourg Saint-Antoine, there were three days of street fighting at the barricades in July 1830, at the end of which Charles X, the reactionary Bourbon king who had 'learned nothing and forgotten nothing' was dethroned and the bourgeois king Louis-Philippe put in his place, the so-called July monarchy. The fierce fighting, costing over six hundred lives, has been described by

Victor Hugo in the 'Petit Gavroche' episode of his novel *Les Misérables;* and by Delacroix in his picture in the Louvre.

Eighteen years later the Saint-Antoine barricades were up again, and this time the archbishop of Paris was among the casualties. Louis-Philippe was replaced by the Second Republic, which soon gave way to the Second Empire. There had been three revolutions here in sixty years and they had all led to autocratic dictatorships – as revolutions tend to do.

In the centre of the huge Place stands the July Column, a solitary spike 170 feet high surmounted by a winged and male Mercury (and not by 'La Liberté', as is sometimes said). It is closed to the public. There are a number of Frenchmen who regret the disappearance of the old Bastille; it would have made a fine historical monument, open to the public, probably with *son et lumière*. Paris has gained her National Day and a legend, but she has lost her equivalent of the 'Tower of London'.

Efforts have been made to provide other attractions in the area. There is a site for fairs and markets. **Opéra de la Bastille** (Metro Sully Morland) opened in July 1989, on the site of the old station. It was a surprise to Parisians when it was announced in 1982 that they needed a second opera house. The famous building by Garnier at Place de l'Opéra had been the largest theatre in the world, when it opened in 1875, and the problem had often been how to fill it. Paris was not a city of keen opera-goers. Although things were beginning to improve, audiences, even in the 1980s, were so apathetic that they tolerated a party of tourists who came in very late for *Tristan and Isolde*, making a whole row in the front stalls stand up to let them by, and then decided to leave during the opening notes of the *Liebestod*, causing noisy disruption the whole way out. In London, Vienna, Munich or Milan such philistines would have been lynched.

The official explanation of the Bastille building was that it was to be a 'democratic' opera, which would create a whole new opera-going public. The winning design, chosen by an international jury, was by Carlos Ott, a Canadian-Uruguayan architect, almost unknown in France. It was supposed to commemorate the bicentenary of the French Revolution. However, Carlos Ott, determined to be unlike Garnier has made no concessions to popular taste. On the outside, the front façade is curved but featureless. It has a smaller, curved, top storey. It is made of white stone, with a glass wall above. If the old opera house is a wedding cake, the new one is a blancmange.

The same materials are used on the inside, which emphasizes a high, three-tier staircase which looks like a fire escape. The auditorium has a glass ceiling, concealing 2,700 fluorescent light tubes, with a pale blue stripe across the middle. This and the steel-blue curtain are the only touches of colour. All the seats are covered in black. We begin to understand that 'democratic' means severely highbrow. Yet the repertoire here is similar to other opera houses. *Wozzeck*, of course was a natural. But who can picture *The Merry Widow* (in November 1998) in this setting?

As to numbers: this is the third largest building in Paris, not far behind the Finance Ministry, and seats 2,723, outdoing Garnier. It has very modern machinery which can alter the size of the stage or move it onto several different levels at once. The orchestra-pit, too, can be altered in size by pressing a button; its maximum is 110 players. More than a third of the building is below ground, reaching 100 feet below street level. Less than half the area is for the audience, the rest is backstage and used for rehearsals, workshops, storage and the Centre for Operatic Training opened in 1995. All this extends far to the back, along Rue de Lyon, and employs armies of decorators, costume-makers and workmen, plus a department known as 'Geniuses' who understand how to work the electronic machinery. Spectacle is thought to be important, and it is an advantage that nearly all the seats face the stage directly, unlike the old Opéra and Opéra-Comique, and have a clear view of it. An admirable decision to choose well-known contemporary painters and allow each to have a free hand to create his own set has produced excellent results.

Richard Strauss, in his last opera *Capriccio*, about the making of an opera, made clear the vital place of music. The result of this over-insistence on the site and its politics showed itself in early teething troubles. There were dissensions about the musical director and musical levels suffered. This gave the chance for opponents to argue that the whole project was a flop and opera should return to Palais Garnier, by then renovated. The decision to limit Garnier to ballet was revoked, under pressure from its friends, and it now stages some operas again. When the Bastille management was asked whether it was getting support from the public, the rather sulky reply was 'they'll come if we put on what they want. They know what they want'. It was this discovery which redeemed it all. In Europe a much more musically-aware public had for some time been growing up, especially in Britain and Germany, but spreading to France. No one who has been in the crammed, uncomfortable arena in Verona, watching a large part of the international audience following Verdi's *Nabucco*, note by note, the whole way through, with their own score, reading with hand-held candles, could doubt the seriousness of these young music lovers. Such an audience was there for the Bastille but insisted on getting higher musical standards.

Once this was grasped, and the Bastille decided to listen to the public instead of lecturing it, policies changed. Democracy worked wonders, when they discovered what it was. What the public wanted was the *best*, with star singers and guest conductors, because they were used to hearing the best music and nothing else would do. Since then, both at the Bastille and the Garnier, which are under the same management, the French National Opera has raised its standards considerably.

It has become hard to get tickets. If we wish to go, we should obtain from the opera house (well in advance) its programme and its list of dates when reservations can be made, for each opera. Of course we should apply on the *first* date. It's amusing to find that the dear old Palais Garnier is even harder to get into than the bleak Bastille.

A typical street of the area is **Rue de la Roquette,** leading off the main Place; narrow, winding, full of small businesses, the façades of the buildings restored. We should take the first turning right into **Rue de Lappe**. This is old and picturesque and we should note the wrought-iron balconies, some curved, some straight. The old *bal musette* dance-halls, with accordion bands can still be found on Sunday afternoons; also small restaurants and shops specializing in Auvergne food (sausages, tripe, cheese and Cahors wine). The clog (*sabot* or *galoche*) *is* the symbol of Auvergne and we shall see many in the street for decoration or sale. One small shop sells both clogs and Auvergne sausages.

Note the names of the boulevards which now meet at Bastille: Henri IV, rather off course, though the Hôtel de Sully in Rue Saint-Antoine may account for it; Richard Lenoir, an unknown workman (why, it was asked, should boulevards always be called after famous people?) and Beaumarchais, the playwright, whose handsome statue stands in Rue Saint-Antoine at the corner of Rue de la Bastille.

Beaumarchais would certainly have wished to be remembered in this area, but not for the obvious reason. His plays satirize the aristocracy and their way of life. In *The Marriage of Figaro,* the barber-turned-valet savages his master Count Almaviva with the words '*Vous vous êtes donné la peine de naître, et rien de plus*' (You took the trouble to be born and that is all) – hardly a respectful greeting from a servant to his lord. But then the dialogue of Beaumarchais was intended to attack the whole principle of aristocracy. Yet his revolutionary spirit was distinctly at odds with his personal life. A watchmaker named Caron, he changed his name to Monsieur de Beaumarchais. A middleman in the slave trade, an arms dealer in the American War of Independence, he had made himself one of the richest men in France. Shortly before the Revolution he built himself a sumptuous *hôtel* opposite the Bastille – the other Bastille, it has been called. Here he proposed to entertain the fashionable world in style, much like Theresia Cabarrus on Ile Saint-Louis. Although the mob on 14 July had the idea of sacking the place, boulle tables and snuff-boxes did not have the same attraction as gunpowder, and Hôtel Beaumarchais was spared and later forgotten. No trace of it now remains.

A few yards away is *Brasserie Bofinger*. It calls itself the oldest brasserie in Paris and it began as a small draught-beer house in 1864. In 1919 it was much enlarged and redecorated in Style Rétro of twenty years before, which it still retains, complete with coloured glass, leather banquettes and Art Nouveau storks.

Boulevard Beaumarchais is not a very interesting avenue, even though it is the end of the Grands Boulevards. But we might get as far as no. 21, where, through the railings, we can glimpse the fine classical façade of Hôtel Mansart, built by Hardouin-Mansart in the late seventeenth century for his own use. Otherwise we should take the metro direct to République.

We are now in the Temple area, once the stronghold of the Templars, the order suppressed and looted by Philip the Fair in 1314. Some of the land was given to the Knights of Malta, who were in turn suppressed in the Revolution. All that remained was the turreted Temple Tower, where Louis XVI and his family were imprisoned in August 1792. The following year the king was guillotined and his queen, Marie Antoinette, and his sister, Elisabeth, transferred to the Conciergerie. The young son, theoretically King Louis XVII, remained behind; in June 1795 a boy died mysteriously in the Temple, but it has never been established whether it was the young king (who was never seen again) or someone else. To prevent further investigations and possible pilgrimages, the tower was pulled down in 1808. Haussmann completed the work and all that remain now of the Temple are the street names.

The huge **Place de la République** (Metro République) is one of Haussmann's less happy inventions. It was part of his plan to open up Paris and discourage revolution and plotting, but it is now much used, like the Bastille and Nation squares, for demos and political marches. In 1958 de Gaulle proclaimed the constitution of the present Republic here. The enormous statue of *La République* in the centre is by Morice (1883) and the plaques round the base show events from the previous hundred years.

However, we are still on the Grands Boulevards. A little way down Boulevard du Temple is the **Cirque d'Hiver,** the last of many circuses which once abounded in the area. It is a permanent building, but it is on the small side and the more spectacular circuses have to go to Palais Omnisports at Bercy, the extremity of Paris.

Back in the metro, we take the train to **Père Lachaise,** Paris's famous cemetery (Boulevard de Menilmontant, Metro Père Lachaise), visited by thousands of tourists every year, as well as by those who have business there. Père Lachaise was the confessor of Louis XIV and gave generously to the Jesuit house of retreat, which became nicknamed after him. Under Napoleon it became a municipal cemetery and for nearly two hundred years it has been the fashionable place to be buried: marshals, politicians, writers, painters, composers, philosophers, singers, together with thousands of ordinary French people. There are nearly a million graves and the cemetery extends for more than a hundred acres; on undulating ground, it is landscaped with 12,000 trees. It was here that the survivors of the Commune made their last stand in May 1871, shooting among the graves. The 147 survivors were shot against the Federalists Wall, at the north-east corner, at dawn the following morning and buried in a common grave, now an object of political veneration.

However, as we wander along the cobbled paths of the cemetery, lined by thousands of tombs, like stone bathing-huts, our minds are less likely to be on revolutionary violence than on autumnal peace and melancholy. The best time to go is in October, when the chestnuts have turned and a grey light filters through the yellow leaves. On All Saints' Day (*Toussaint*, 1 November) French people flock to cemeteries to lay chrysanthemums on their family graves. The atmosphere of Père Lachaise is best appreciated at less crowded times, although visitors are constantly there.

The most romantic spot, undoubtedly, is Chopin's grave, with the falling ground and the trees meeting overhead; the tomb is beautiful too, with its mourning nymph. There will be many flowers and probably a group being eloquently lectured about the *Raindrop*

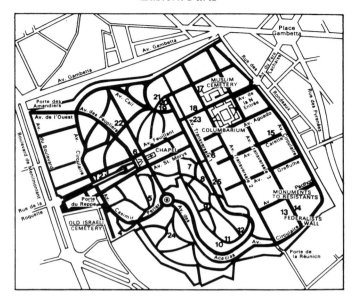

Père Lachaise Cemetery

1) Colette	10) Marshal Ney	19) Delacroix
2) Rossini (cenotaph)	11) Beaumarchais	20) Gérard de Nerval
3) Baron Haussmann	12) Murat and C Bonaparte	21) Balzac
4) Abelard and Héloïse	13) Modigliani	22) Bizet
5) Chopin	14) Edith Piaf	23) Allan Kardec
6) David	15) Oscar Wilde	24) Jim Morrison
7) Corot	16) Sarah Bernhardt	25) Sir Sidney Smith
8) Molière and La Fontaine	17) Marcel Proust	
9) Hugo family	18) Guillaume Apollinaire	

prelude. Chopin chose the site himself, near the grave of his friend Bellini, and a little of the earth here is soil from Poland, brought by the composer himself in a silver box when he left Poland aged twenty-one. He was always 'half in love with easeful death', half in love with his native land.

The biggest names do not always have the biggest tombs. Delacroix and Colette have simple slabs, Apollinaire a rough-hewn dolmen. The most lavish sepulchres have probably the least known names, but much of the sculpture is striking in itself: sad, naked ladies, holding flowers or books, sitting on the edge of graves or beds – in one case actually in bed. The withered flowers, the dog-eared books, the rumpled bedclothes are faithfully carved in stone or marble. At the Rond-Point there is an eerie piece, a veiled ghost beside a barred window; whether the spirit is trying to get in or out is unclear.

One of the most dramatic tombs is Epstein's monument to Oscar Wilde, donated by an anonymous lady admirer. The big sculpture shows a winged pharaoh, flying from one world to the other. Impressive indeed, though its connection with Wilde is not easy to see. On the reverse side is an inscription giving the bare facts of his birth, education and death and – in case we might have forgotten that he was a writer – four lines from *The Ballad of Reading Gaol*. The tomb has been marred by graffiti, and the pharaoh castrated.

We may be surprised to find the tomb of Admiral Sir Sidney Smith, a professional rival, but finally a friend, of Nelson. Despite having halted Bonaparte's triumphal march through the Middle East at the siege of Acre and, in the emperor's view, 'cheated me of my destiny', Smith was a Francophile. After 1815 he chose to live in Paris and, in 1848, was buried beneath a splendid marble monument, decorated with his portrait plaque after a drawing by Jacques-Louis David, which was restored and accorded a slap-up Anglo-French naval ceremony in 1999.

Under the gravestones lie many romances, some known only to their families, some to all the world. Abelard and Héloïse are here, together at last, though their grave is hard to find. (A map is essential, since the cemetery is not signposted, except for a few unhelpful 'street names' like Avenue des Peupliers.) But everyone will direct us to Edith Piaf's grave, surrounded by flowers. She lies there with her young husband Théo, for whose career she sacrificed her health and, indeed, her life.

Across the way lies Modigliani with his girlfriend, Jeanne Hébuterne, the mother of his daughter; we know her Gothic face and fair plaits well from his portraits. Modi died in 1920, aged thirty-six, killed by his bohemian life, by drink, drugs, tuberculosis and poverty. But recognition had come to him before the end and all Montparnasse was here at his funeral. But not Jeanne. Hearing of his death in hospital, she rushed to the morgue and covered his dead face with kisses, even though it was a mass of open sores. She was dragged away and went to her parents' home, from which she had been expelled some years before. After a bitter altercation she threw herself off the roof, even though she was almost nine months pregnant with a second child. Her parents refused to let her be buried with Modi; nevertheless they are together now. The slab has a touching inscription in Italian.

Chopin, Wilde, Piaf, but the greatest number of pilgrims are at the graves of Allan Kardec and of Jim Morrison of 'The Doors' – thousands of candles, flowers, notes. Kardec was the father of modern spiritualism and one by one they go round to touch the left shoulder of his bust, their eyes closed. After this experience we may find it a relief to see the down-to-earth features of Balzac a little way away.

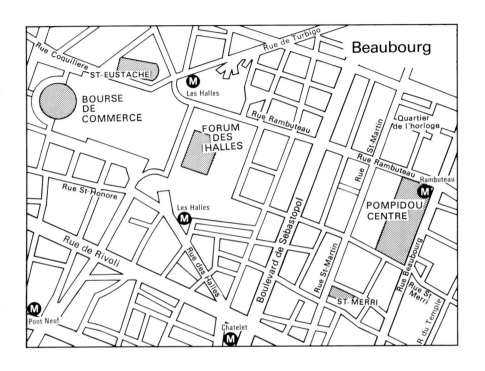

10

Beaubourg

BEAUBOURG, FIFTY YEARS ago, was an old, slummy village with narrow picturesque streets, squeezed between the church of Saint-Merri (78 Rue Saint Martin, 4me, Metro Hôtel de Ville) and Les Halles. Saint-Merri was once the centre of the haberdashery and clothing trades, while Les Halles was the great food market, the 'stomach of Paris', as Zola put it. Round the edge of Les Halles were restaurants which catered for local tastes at those hours of the night when food wholesalers normally work. These restaurants were discovered by a better-heeled class who had spent the night at a ball or a nightclub and wanted a bowl of onion soup before going to bed. The two classes mixed together very prettily.

Much of this has gone. Haberdashery and clothing have moved to the department stores, couture houses and boutiques. Beaubourg has been redeveloped into precincts and pedestrian areas; the new apartment blocks have been well designed to fit in with the old streets that remain and the original inhabitants have been rehoused in them alongside new and better-off tenants – not, it is said, without some conflict of lifestyles. And Les Halles have gone to Rungis, near Orly airport; their glass arcades have been demolished, despite protests that the arcades were themselves of artistic merit. In their place is a large shopping and leisure centre. Only the church of Saint-Eustache and the onion-soup restaurants survive – and thrive, despite the disappearance of the pork butchers and the oyster-sellers.

But the most spectacular innovation in the area is the **Georges Pompidou Centre** (Place Georges Pompidou, Metro Hôtel de Ville or Rambuteau). Designed by the then little-known Richard Rogers (British) and Renzo Piano (Italian), the simple parallelepiped of steel and glass encrusted on the exterior with the brightly-painted ducts, piping and vents necessary for its functioning, its façade enlivened by a rising diagonal of transparent escalators, provoked violent reactions when it was unveiled in 1977. It was perhaps the first gallery to present itself as architecture, as significant in itself as its potential contents, and, according to Brian Appleyard of *The Sunday Times* came into being 'through some fluke combination of French *gloire* and Anglo-Italian chutzpah'.

Despite or because of the controversy, it has become a beloved feature of Paris, a major attraction which has rejuvenated the area around it, in fact a victim of its own success as the flood of visitors was such that the building had to be closed for over two years of renovation in preparation for its relaunch with the new millennium. Renzo Piano and Jean-François Bodin were responsible for a remodelling of the interior which produced a world-class multi-disciplinary arts centre; the exterior, now mainly white with touches of red and gold, retains its exuberance while becoming less strident (unless we walk round the back where the wild blues, greens, yellows and reds of the past are retained).

Entry is from the piazza into an enormous foyer known as Le Forum. The ticketing and information area is overlapped on both sides, by a café on the right and a top-quality design shop on the left, while access to the lower floor is available via a large stairwell. This well provides, at the very heart of the building, a three-storey-high exhibition space which will be constantly renewed; at the time of re-opening it housed a gnarled olive tree and its supporting 8-metre-high earth block, a gentle hint at the age-old nature versus culture opposition by a young Italian artist, Maurizio Cattelan, which seemed to echo the only external exhibit on the piazza, a huge white cube supporting a gilded flowerpot by Jean-Pierre Raynaud.

The rest of the ground floor houses an exhibition gallery, a large book shop and the children's activities area where, through games and practical artwork, children are introduced to twentieth-century art. The library, open to all, occupies part of the ground and all of the second and third floors. Two cinemas offer contemporary and classic films, while two theatres on the lower floor house concerts, lectures, dance and discussion.

Within reach of the main building, beside and under the fascinating Stravinsky Fountain by Tinguely and Niki de St Phalle, is **Ircam**, where top-class musicians work with technicians and computer experts to create new compositional possibilities, while also taking contemporary music to the widest possible audience. On the piazza outside the centre the visitor can explore the **Atelier Brancusi**, a reconstruction of the sculptor's studio, left to the state on condition that it be faithfully re-erected. There, in a brilliant white setting, we can glory in a wide range of works in a variety of materials spanning his forty-year career. The display of his tools is magical, an artwork in its own right.

Combining the activities of all these areas, the centre's programme of events is breath-taking, mind-stretching and frequently multi-disciplinary. (It is well worth accessing the centre's website on www.centrepompidou.fr to plan your visit effectively.) Certainly the overwhelming sensation is of excitement, creativity, infinite possibility and richness, and every area is vibrant with life. Gone is the feeling of culture as something solemn and difficult and distant. This is a place to enjoy.

And so we shall, as we proceed, like most of the visitors, to the National Museum of Modern Art. As we progress up the escalators, the views of Paris broaden and it is certainly worth continuing to the sixth floor to enjoy an incredible panorama of the city, stunning by day or night. The spectacular restaurant is here, with a large outside sitting area, and there are three flexible galleries for temporary exhibitions.

But most visitors have come to see the wonderful modern and contemporary art collection, now housed on two complete floors. The permanent collection comprised more than 44,000 pieces at the time of reopening and will obviously continue to grow – 1,400 can be displayed at any one time. Discussion continues as to how more works can be available to the public, either by sacrificing the present multi-disciplinary nature of the centre or by dividing the collection or by the establishment of a 'downtown' gallery in outer Paris and a ring of provincial satellites to receive visiting exhibitions.

The entry point to the art museum is on the fourth floor and brings us straight into the contemporary collection. We are confronted immediately by a huge piece, a complex arrangements of cogs, belts and wheels, starkly black against a white wall. The different areas move according to their own rhythms so that the whole pulsates irregularly while light plays glancingly across it. On the right a tiny white leaf flutters frantically. *Requiem for a Dead Leaf* by **Jean Tinguely** is as musical as its name implies. The other major focus of attention as we enter is the recently-acquired *Giant Ice Bag* by **Claes Oldenburg**. Totally flamboyant, brilliantly orange, this example of Pop Art gradually inflates and rises, only to collapse back bathetically on itself again.

The stage is set for excitement, but, conscientious visitors, audioguide in hand, we will for the moment bypass the other attractions of this floor to head up to the fifth and tackle the exhibits in chronological order. Once again, our arrival does not disappoint. Straight ahead is one of the three roof terraces which so enliven this floor. Sculpture, in this case curvaceous female figures by Henri Laurens, is displayed in sheets of water and framed by the geometrical structures of the building and the Paris skyline.

The person responsible for the initial post-reopening layout was Werner Spies and the arrangement of the fifth floor, comprising canonical works, is broadly chronological. Two paintings, on our right and left as we reach the top of the stairs, set the theme of modernity. Douanier Rousseau's nightmarish *War* faces Picasso's *Little Girl Skipping*. Spies indicated that the motif of childhood in both symbolized to him the need to shake off academic values, so clearly demonstrated in Rousseau's naïve style and in Picasso's decisive rejection of previous norms, which marked the beginning of the modern period in artistic creation.

The fifth-floor collection, covering the period from the beginning of the century to 1960, is superb and the paintings are enriched by complementary displays of graphic art, photography, architecture, design, sculpture and film. Some of the major works are displayed in the central gallery which runs from end to end of the floor but most visitors take the logical, numbered route through the smaller galleries, snaking back to the main corridor as they progress through the years along passages which feature photographs, etchings and prints.

From the brilliant colours of the Fauves, we move into a stunning display of early Cubism, a wall of **Picassos** and **Braques** in warm ochres and gentle greys, the surface of the canvases a splintering of planes with only the barest links to reality. Facing them is a case of the primitive artefacts which, with Cézanne, were so important in inspiring the creation of this style. The development from this analytical Cubism to synthetic Cubism, with the introduction of colour, stencilling, pasted papers and other elements of collage is then shown – Picasso's *Portrait de Jeune Femme* is a supreme example of these techniques – with some emphasis on the works of **Juan Gris**. Much further on an outstanding room is devoted to later canvases by **Fernand Léger**, generally considered the fourth great Cubist but by then more influenced by Purism. These huge canvases, for example *Composition aux deux perroquets*, which glow with colour, show Léger's fascination with the machine and the mechanical nature of modern life. His monumental figures, still showing his Cubist bias, are flattened and geometric, apparently fashioned out of the same series of curved forms, and they gaze impassively and unnervingly at the viewer.

Emerging from the Cubists we find ourselves in the main corridor, facing the magnificent series of four *Nu de Dos* by Matisse, a calming moment before we plunge into the Dada section with an extensive display of ready-mades by **Marcel Duchamp**. Duchamp's lasting contribution to the evolution of art was his questioning of what, in fact, constitutes a work of art. He took prefabricated objects, such as the famous bottle-rack and urinal, signed them, exhibited them and declared them artworks on the basis of his selection of them. Neither beautiful, nor valuable, nor unique, they provocatively call into question the established order. A recent outstanding acquisition in the Dada section is **Francis Picabia**'s *Dresseur d'Animaux*, a large canvas in which a sinister dark figure with a whip is surrounded by a group of leaping dogs and observed by a mysterious owl on a perch.

We move on to a very international selection of Expressionists, whose general commitment to the emotive powers of colour is mediated through their different cultural traditions. Works by **Ernst Ludwig Kirchner** and **Marc Chagall** are particularly striking. **Georges Rouault**, to whom a whole room is devoted, was trained in the craft of stained glass and its dark outlines and luminous colours influenced his portrayals of human frailty, often personified in clowns or prostitutes, sometimes in violent and disturbing scenes. **Cobra**, the Expressionist group of northern painters, are represented by Asgar Jorn, Karel Appel and Pierre Alechinsky in a later room.

Artists whose careers span several decades recur throughout the exhibition and in Gallery 9 we have a particular treat, **Henri Matisse** from 1914 to 1917. These canvases are rather different from the usual colour, brightness and decorative elements we associate with Matisse; during these war years his palette darkened and his style simplified. *Le Violiniste*, playing with his back to us as he gazes out of the window is Matisse, a violinist himself, facing his canvas. Matisse used windows constantly in his search to solve the problems of depth and in *Porte-Fenêtre à Collioure*, the composition has simplified into four vertical stripes, with no distinction between outside and inside, no perspective, a complete flattening of the canvas.

The development of abstraction is illustrated in a wonderful series of **Kandinsky**s, together with works by Paul Klee and Frantisek Kupka. Subject matter is reduced until it ceases to be recognisable while colour, freed from imitation of reality, is at the service of the artist's sensations. The stunningly beautiful *Jaune-Rouge-Bleu* was painted by Kandinsky after his involvement with Bauhaus, and geometrical forms now coexist with brilliant colours and swirling curves.

Yet another path away from traditional art is exemplified in the work of **Kasimir Malevich**, the Suprematist who so famously painted *Black Square* in 1915. While this work may well have arisen as a stage direction, indicating the final curtain, it assumed for Malevich and for the artistic world the significance of a complete denial of all previous artistic activity, while at the same time symbolizing the beginning of a new aesthetic.

De Stijl, created by **Piet Mondrian** and **Theo Van Doesburg**, was an immensely influential movement, affecting the development not only of painting but of furniture and architectural design. Mondrian's gradual reduction of his paintings to plays of vertical and horizontal lines, his use of only primary colours, his search for formal perfection are mirrored in the architecture of the Bauhaus and the streamlining of forms demanded by the mass production of furniture which are displayed in a subsequent room. Notice **Marcel Breuer**'s *B3*, the first steel-tube armchair. A later room covers architecture from 1940 to 1960, featuring post-war reconstruction with the first use of prefabrication, and the development in furniture as flexible forms take over from right-angles.

Our progress along the central alley has now brought us to a series of **Pevsner** sculptures installed in front of the second terrace, on which *Femme* and *Femme-Oiseau* by **Joan Miró** and *Grande Grenouille* and *Grande Tortue* by **Max Ernst** dazzle us in front of a skyline which includes the Eiffel Tower. The full drama of such settings is even more apparent at night.

Passing through the joyous colours of Robert and Sonia Delaunay we arrive inexorably at Surrealism. The movement was defined by the writer André Breton in his 1924 *Manifeste du Surréalisme* and a section of his study is installed at the heart of the Surrealist exhibits, drawing in the dimension of literature, while visitors can also watch *L'Age d'Or*, the film produced by Luis Buñuel and Salvador Dali in 1930. Much influenced by Freud, the Surrealists wished to break the dominance of reason, free the subconscious and explore the world of dreams. Artistically **Giorgio de Chirico** was a decisive influence with such paintings as *Mélancholie d'un après-midi*, where irrational juxtaposition, distorted perspective and the ominous atmosphere so typical of his work create a palpable sense of unease. Their styles vary wildly, from the experimental techniques of **Max Ernst** to the minute detailing of totally irrational scenes by **René Magritte** and **Salvador Dali**.

Taking refuge on the main corridor, we encounter Matisse's truly delightful pair of découpés *Polynésie la Mer* and *Polynésie le Ciel*, 1946. In his final years Matisse, confined to a wheelchair, developed a new artistic method by which he cut out shapes from pre-painted sheets of paper and arranged them in largely abstract compositions. These two feature blazingly white birds, sea creatures and weeds, standing out against a vibrating background panelled in blue. The effect, as in many of these later works, is joyous, and we might skip across the corridor at this point to enjoy his magnificent *La Tristesse du Roi*, another découpé, this time vibrant with colour, incredibly completed when Matisse was in his eighties. This room also houses **Brancusi**'s magnificent bronze *Coq*. Mounted on a base of wood and stone whose patterns echo the stepped breast of the sculpture, the whole structure pulsates upwards in a surge of rhythm and reminds us not to miss the sculptor's studio when we leave the main building.

Both **Pierre Bonnard** and Matisse spent the Second World War years in the south of France, and from this period there is a wonderful Bonnard, *L'Atelier au Mimosa* in which the vibrant yellow of the flowers permeates the entire canvas.

We return to order with the painters of the Neue Sachlichkeit, a movement preoccupied with the horrors of war and the depravity of post-war society. *La Journaliste Sylvia von Harden* by **Otto Dix** is a remarkable portrait of a feminist Jewish intellectual.

Picasso and Braque resurface to amazing effect. *Le Duo* by Braque (1937), two female figures facing each other across a piano, has all the flowing lines and spatial play of his later *Studio* series. Picasso has moved on yet again, from his return to classicism so beautifully exemplified in the central corridor in *La Liseuse* to the blazing colours and fragmented planes of *La Muse*.

Progressing through the non-geometric abstraction of the fifties, we reach *Art Brut*, **Jean Dubuffet**'s term for the art of the young, the mad and the amateur, which he believed to be freer and more honest than the academic tradition. A room of more lyrical abstraction includes *Le Manteau (demeure 5)*, a 1962 work of **Etienne-Martin**, a montage of objets trouvés intended as a sum of memories, a bridge between the comfort of the womb and the childhood home and the outside world.

Alberto Giacometti and **Francis Bacon** are shown together as two artists working at the same time on the human figure. Their aims, methods and achievements differ wildly but the juxtaposition is thought-provoking.

By now we are at the very end of the corridor, facing the last terrace where a powerful **Alexander Calder** stabile, *Nageoire*, contrasts with his light-as-air mobile *Deux Vols d'Oiseaux* which we passed earlier, in which one yellow flight of birds and another red are fleetingly anchored at a black centre.

Lucio Fontana and **Yves Klein** were both concerned with the question of space. Fontana's slashed canvases are intended to draw attention to the infinite space behind the surface. Instead of creating illusionistic space, he dragged space into the work itself and his cerebral approach was influential in the development of Conceptual Art. Klein set out his views very clearly in *Ci-gît l'Espace*, a funereal tablet complete with artificial flowers and wreath. His canvases feature his 'International Klein blue', a strong deep shade which he patented in 1960. His monochrome pictures were intended to depersonalize and spiritualize colour.

While the Pollocks are rather disappointing, the Miró series *Bleu I*, *Bleu II* and *Bleu III*, huge canvases in a more restful shade than Klein's, punctuated only by vague black lines and hints of red, are a joy to meditate, as is one of the **Mark Rothko**'s featured in the corridor, *No. 14 (Browns over Dark)*, 1963

If you have survived until this point, the end of the fifth floor, you may well find it advisable to deposit your audioguide temporarily at the entrance to the museum and retreat to the mezzanine for a well-earned cup of coffee. While it seems worthwhile to take the audioguide, it covers only 100 of the exhibited works, all too often passing over those one most wants to hear about. There are cards available at the entrance to most of the major display areas, outlining the movement or artist featured.

After a break, we are ready for the excitement of the fourth floor. While the layout here also consists of a long central corridor with exhibits mainly concentrated on the right-hand side, there is from the beginning the feeling of a state of flux. Much of the art displayed is as yet unclassifiable, areas will be renewed annually and some spaces, specifically destined to showing the latest developments on the contemporary art scene, will change every six months. The Galerie du Musée will show new acquisitions, while the Graphic Art Gallery will profile individual artists or movements. Le Salon du Musée is a new teaching space, with enormous quantities of documentation in the form of videos, CD Roms, a database of museum holdings, Internet access and suchlike.

The movements featured in the initial hanging of the contemporary collection are Pop Art and New Realism (here applied to Pop Art's European offshoot), Op Art and Kineticism, Arte Povera and Conceptual Art. Much space is devoted either to single artists, many of them very recent, or to installations, some linked to the above, some highly individual. The integration of rooms on related disciplines continues and drawings, maquettes and representative objects illuminate contemporary art and each other. Among those featured are the architects Kahn, Foster and Gehry, the designers Panton, Pesce and Starck and the photographers Arbus, Struth and Bustamante.

Pop Art, a descendant of Dada in its rejection of the values of the established art world and its preoccupation with mass-produced objects, uses the imagery of popular culture to express the confrontation of the banal and the aesthetic and to protest against the desensitization of society as a result of repeated exposure to images of disaster through the mass media. **Robert Rauschenberg** launched into collage, developing the technique to produce what he called 'combines', often recycling discarded objects, as we see in *Oracle*. **Andy Warhol** used printing techniques to create multiple images – like his *Ten Lizes*, shown here, a five-by-two panel of identical versions of Liz Taylor's face.

Among the European works shown are a typical **Christo** wrap and **Sigmar Polke**'s *Pasadena* in which a press photo of Surveyor I's lunar landing is blown up to reveal the dots of the printing process with an effect close to Lichtenstein's comic strips. Another example is *Ben's Store*, from 1958 to 1973 an art and record shop, but also a gallery and avant-garde centre, in Nice. Covered now with objects and slogans by its proprietor, Ben Vautier, it has been re-erected here as a piece of sculpture or, as he preferred to call it, a *chose exposée*.

One striking example from the displays of **Kinetic art** – art incorporating real or apparent movement – is a recreation of **Yaacov Agam**'s ante-room at the Elysée Palace, created at the behest of M. and Mme. Pompidou. The nearest 'wall' of the room is made of sliding screens of differently coloured glass while the walls and carpeting are hectically patterned, the ceiling of tinted glass. As the spectator moves, he finds he is interacting with the complex rhythms of the work; colours and forms modify, while reflecting in *L'Oeil Cosmique*, a polished metal sculpture at its heart.

Conceptual art, another 60s movement, also questioned the status of the art object and tended to value the creative impulse more than the actual production of a work. Again, it is an extension of Dada but the final products, often deliberately lacking aesthetic qualities, tend to be rather unrewarding for the spectator. **Joseph Kosuth**'s famous *One and Three Chairs* consists of a photograph of a chair, an actual chair and a dictionary definition of a chair, three versions through three different media.

A more interesting Conceptual installation by **Dan Graham** is *Present Continuous Past(s)* of 1974. A combination of mirrors and a hidden camera which films the spectator as he enters the room and replays the sequence eight seconds later, leads to a confrontation with one's present, in the mirror and one's past, on the monitor, both reflected ad infinitum, which raises all sorts of questions of image, self-image, double and multiple vision, confusion of past and present. As well as being the spectator, the visitor becomes the subject of the gaze, his own and that of others, and his self-perception and sense of place is distorted.

The museum has a fine collection of **Arte Povera**, the movement which broke away from the mass culture symbols of Pop Art and the technological preoccupations of Op Art to establish a more poetic, more direct relationship with the natural world. Among works by Giuseppe Penone and Pino Pascali, is **Jannis Kounellis'** *Untitled, 1969*, a cascade of ten small interlocking balances, each heaped with spice – a reference to the unfairness of an economic system which pits the underdeveloped world against the more powerful West.

Jean Dubuffet's *Le Jardin D'Hiver* is a three-dimensional construction in polystyrene, a womb-like cave into which the visitor enters. The stark whiteness of the undulating floor and walls is woven over with black lines which rarely follow the contours of the walls and dislocate our sense of balance and perspective.

Side by side we see installations by **Edward Kienholz** – *While Visions of Sugarplums Danced in their Heads* is a grotesque assemblage of objets trouvés, a million miles away from *The Night before Christmas* – and **Dorothea Tanning**, the fourth wife of Max Ernst, a startling Surrealist whose *Chambre 202 Hôtel du Pavot* features soft sculptures of stuffed fabric, threatening female forms metamorphosing out of walls and furniture. **Arman**'s *Chopin's Waterloo* of 1961 is the end-product of a 'happening'. At a gallery opening he smashed a piano to pieces which were then reassembled on board like a colossal collage. The effect is oddly beautiful.

Just as Alain Jacquet's 1964 *Le Déjeuner sur l'Herbe* reworks Manet's picture in the idiom of Pop Art, so **Jeff Wall**'s *Picture for Woman* takes as its starting point Manet's *Bar at the Folies Bergères*. In the original, the woman in the foreground is seen rather oddly reflected in a mirror. In Wall's version, the 'reflection' is the artist himself, while rather than a mirror, the intervening space is his camera. Questions seem to be raised about different methods of recording images, and their validity.

Jean-Pierre Raynaud's *Container Zéro* is a white-tiled, room-like structure, into which he inserts his own work, that of others, or any object for display. In the early days of the new Pompidou, a French flag hung against the back wall. The cold, unemotional setting is an evolving work of art, a place for successive experiments, a gallery within a gallery.

Shortly before his death in 1986, **Joseph Beuys** completed *Plight*. Two interconnecting rooms are lined with enormous rolls of grey felt. In the first is a grand piano, on top of which lies a blackboard and a thermometer. The piano is sick, it produces no sound; the blackboard is not fulfilling its function either – it is bare. A second room opens out of the faintly felt-scented claustrophobic space, but there is no exit and the visitor must retrace his steps to break out of the closed environment.

Another powerful questioner of the status of the art work is **Claude Rutault**, whose *Toiles à l'Unité, 1973/Légendes 1985* consists of a series of simple forms, oblongs, circles etc. painted smoothly in the colour of the wall on which they are hung. Anyone who buys them is obliged to repaint them to match the wall against which they will be displayed. What price the 'artist' or the 'work of art'?

One of the more recent works is **Claude Closky**'s enormous fresco-like display entitled *1 à 1000* (1993). His material is cut from advertisements and catalogues, and each consecutive object costs exactly one franc more than its predecessor. Like Pop Art, it comments powerfully on the consumer society through the endless succession of goods arrayed.

Even newer, commissioned by the Pompidou Centre, is **Douglas Gordon**'s *Feature Film*, 1999. On a large screen in a very dark gallery reminiscent of a real cinema, we watch close-ups of different parts of the body of a conductor as he leads the orchestra through the soundtrack of Hitchcock's *Vertigo*. There are no images from the film. The artist is relying on the auditory memory of the viewer to sweep him back to the suspense previously conjured up by this score.

It is impossible here to do more than skim the surface and attempt to exemplify the diversity which is on show, but I hope I have managed to convey some of the excitement of this floor, the feeling of restless, questing creativity. (The magnificent fifth floor by now seems positively Old Master-like in its solid familiarity!) Perhaps the exhibits will have changed completely by the time you visit but the enormous wealth of the collection should ensure an experience which provokes, stimulates and thrills all over again with each new hanging.

However enjoyable any gallery visit, it is generally a joy to emerge into the open air. Perhaps we might now explore the **Quartier de l'Horloge**, a rebuilt area which lies just to the north of the museum. We pass through a shopping arcade, *le passage de l'horloge,* into Rue Bernard de Clairvaux. There, on the right under an archway, is **L'Horloge** itself, **'Le Défenseur du Temps'**. It is a remarkable piece of sculpture and engineering by Jacques Monestier, commissioned in 1975 and unveiled by the mayor of Paris, Jacques Chirac, in 1979.

Four metres high and weighing one tonne, it hangs from the wall, a rocky seashore made of oxidized brass. In the centre stands a lifesize man, wearing armour of polished brass (or is he naked?). Beside him is a brass clock on a pillar; round him are a dragon, a sharp-beaked bird and a crab, all also made of polished brass. The dragon breathes in and out regularly. Shortly before the hour, lights come on, drums roll and the Defender limbers up for action. A gong sounds the exact hour (quartz timing) and the man is attacked by one of the beasts, selected at random by the computer. This is accompanied by the noise of an earthquake, hurricane or rough sea, for whichever beast is attacking the man. He defends himself with his sword and shield, counter-attacks, and the beast retires. This happens every hour from 9.00 a.m. till 10.00 p.m. But at midday, 6.00 p.m. and 10.00 p.m. he is attacked by all three at once. It is an energetic fight, but he emerges victorious and the crowd of watching children cheer. Time is safe from nature for another hour. There is something intriguing about the mixture here of primitive terrors and modern technology. There is also something rather Wagnerian about the central figure himself; it is said that the clock was inspired by the Rathaus clock in Munich.

To the west of the Pompidou Centre, a little way up Rue Saint-Martin, at 51 Rue de Montmorency, is the oldest private house in Paris, built in 1407 by Nicolas Flamel, with angel musicians sculpted on the façade. West along Rue Rambuteau, we reach the vast area occupied formerly by the food market of Les Halles. Much of this is now taken up by a big shopping and leisure centre, the **Forum des Halles** (*le Forum* for short, or *le trou,* the hole) at 1–7 Rue Pierre Lescot, Metro Châtelet and RER Châtelet-les-Halles. It is indeed a big hole in the ground, the idea being not to obscure the view of the church of Saint-Eustache or the other buildings in the district.

The architects, Vasconi and Pencreac'h, have produced a pleasing symmetrical design in glass and steel, the entrances suggesting fountains, the sides waterfalls. The forum extends down four levels and at the bottom is a piazza where we can rest our feet and drink a cup of coffee in the company of a statue called *Pygmalion*, of a four-breasted woman and several strange beasts including a pig. (Pygmalion? Was the sculptor, Julio Silva, trying out an English pun?)

Of course, shopping is what we are here for, especially on Saturdays, when there will be crowds. Behind the glass walls are three tiers of boutiques, 180 altogether. The emphasis is on clothes, the most expensive and the smartest being on the top level (*quatrième niveau*). Leather is much featured, including coats, bags, shoes and accessories. Many established boutiques from elsewhere have branches here, often incorporating cafés or snack-bars. We can also buy scent, jewellery and watches. There is a small theatre, a branch of the Musée Grévin on the Grands Boulevards, which gives us a brief glimpse of the Belle Epoque and the can-can; and FNAC. This branch of FNAC is possibly the most popular part of the whole forum. Originally selling records and cassettes, it has moved on to electronic goods, sports, ticket reservations and a whole range of further possibilities.

The forum has direct access to the metro, the RER to Gare du Nord and Charles de Gaulle airport, also the underground car parks. On street level we can reach the surrounding streets. There is also access to the garden, which covers the rest of Les Halles district, a quiet place covering twelve acres in the middle of a crowded area. There was some argument about the design of this garden. The architects wanted an 'English' garden, but this was overruled by President

Giscard in favour of a traditional French garden, Tuileries style, complete with gravel pools. We enjoy a good view of the great **church of Saint-Eustache**, 2 Rue du Jour (Metro Châtelet-les-Halles).

It is an imposing building, immensely tall, with flying buttresses and steeply pitched roofs. Originally it was a small chapel dedicated first to St Agnes and then to St Eustace, a Roman general converted to Christianity by seeing, like St Hubert, a cross between the antlers of a stag. He was martyred, it is said, by being enclosed, with his wife and children, in a large bronze bull which was then heated – a very expensive form of martyrdom, we must think.

However, it is not of St Eustace that we think now when we look at the church, but of rich pork butchers and their families. The parishioners wanted a church worthy of their wealth, a building to rival Notre-Dame a short distance away. Indeed Notre-Dame was the model for the ground plan. But the church took so long to build that tastes changed; new benefactors gave lavishly, but there were often conditions. The original Gothic shape was retained, including the flying buttresses, lancet and rose windows. But the façade of the transept became much decorated in Renaissance style, covered with mouldings and grotesques, including a stag's head with the cross. The west front was remodelled into classical style, with Doric, Ionic and Corinthian columns. During the Revolution it was renamed, not unsuitably, the Temple of Agriculture. It was badly damaged by fire and restored by Baltard, who also designed the glass and iron food halls of the great market, now gone for ever, except for one, reconstructed at Nogent-sur-Marne, to the east of Paris. The church belfry too was partly demolished to suit a semaphore station. However Saint-Eustache remains an imposing building, better seen from a distance. It is well known for its music, a continuing tradition.

Entering the church through the west door, we are immediately struck by both the height and the light. There are several low dark churches in Paris, lit mainly by stained glass, but here is one with the full upspring of Gothic architecture; it is of cathedral stature and one thinks of Amiens or indeed of Notre-Dame – so to speak, its sister church. The nave is in fact 112 ft tall and the aisles are the same without galleries. The length of the church is also impressive. We should stand at the west door and look through the chancel towards the Lady Chapel, and see space behind space; or from the east end, look back at the rose window and organ. The church is 100 metres long, 330 ft.

One has to ask – did they not overdo it? Is there not too much decoration and ornament? The vaulting is a good example of Flamboyant Gothic with its hanging keystones. But is it not too florid and encrusted? Are soaring Gothic pillars made more beautiful by the addition of one or more Corinthian capitals?

The churchwarden's pew is eighteenth century, a gift from Philippe of Orléans. On the left of the Lady Chapel is Colbert's tomb; note the statue of Abundance by Coysevox. Inside the chapel is a statue of the Virgin by Pigalle. There are also an early Rubens, a sixteenth-century statue of St John in the south transept and a bust of the composer Rameau. As one might expect, such a big and important church, the parish church of Palais-Royal, was the scene of many ceremonial events. Among them were the baptisms of Cardinal Richelieu, Molière and Madame de Pompadour, the fishmonger's daughter; the funerals of La Fontaine, Molière, Rameau and Mirabeau; and, rather unexpectedly, the first communion of Louis XIV, who was living with his mother in Palais-Royal.

Back to the market, to the pigs and fish. Outside the church was the market pillory, used for the punishment of dishonest stall-holders. Somewhere here too was the 'Astrological Tower' built by Catherine de Medici for her doctor and adviser, Nostradamus. Nothing remains of it and we do not know what it looked like.

By now we will be thinking of our stomachs; indeed, it is hard to think of anything else here, what with the old market and the hundreds of restaurants, mainly medium-priced or cheap, which remain. We can, of course, eat in the Pompidou Centre or in one of the nearby snack-bars. Opposite the 'Defender of Time' clock is a friendly brasserie where we can eat or drink while waiting for the hour to sound. The forum is full of places to eat, mostly small. But we shall probably choose one of the 'onion soup' restaurants for which Les Halles is famous (Metro Châtelet-les-Halles). Some of these are open all day and night, every day.

Onion soup is known as a *gratinée,* as it is full of grated and melted cheese. It goes down very well on a cold day and is quite indispensable after a long night on the town. Once, after a ball, I was enjoying a *gratinée* at *Pied de Cochon*, 6 Rue Coquillére, at 5.00 a.m. when I noticed a wedding reception in full swing and I asked why they had chosen that hour for the great occasion. '*C'est normal,*' the waiter commented. And time, whatever its 'Defender' may feel, is of little consequence *aux Halles.*

163

Of course, it does not have to be onion soup. Those who prefer to eat at normal times will certainly choose pork. Other meat is available, but pork is the thing in Les Halles. We end, of course, with a pink sugar pig.

11

The Marais

THE MARAIS IS the 'lost' quarter of Paris. It is hard to find and hard to find one's way around; even taxis get lost here. Public transport (Metros Saint Paul and Chemin Vert) is remote and walking is the best way of getting about. Yet it is very rewarding. The Marais contains Paris's oldest square, which to many people, including myself, is the most beautiful. There are many fine seventeenth-century houses, with elaborate façades and courtyards, some of which we can visit. There are narrow, winding old streets and a population which has been there for centuries, probably the descendants of coachmen and housemaids and still looking like the jacquerie. And, permeating everything, there is the sense of history, the feeling that we may well meet a Guise or a Valois on the next corner, who will certainly challenge us to a duel.

The word *marais* means a marsh and that was what it was, a swamp on the right bank of the Seine, unhealthy and often flooded. Attempts had been made to drain it since the sixth century AD, with little success. In the twelfth century, King Philippe-Auguste enclosed it inside his great wall of Paris, of which a long section can still be seen here. In the following century, the marsh was finally drained and permanent building started.

Charles V (1364–80) was the first king to live here. He built more walls and two *hôtels,* the Tournelles and Saint-Paul, now both lost. He, and many of his successors, thought that the Marais, protected by city walls and the Bastille, was a safer place to live than Ile de la Cité or the Louvre. But it was in the seventeenth century that a great building boom began. Henri IV decreed a new square for the area on the site of the ruined Tournelles. When completed, in the reign of his son, Louis XIII, the square, Place des Vosges, became the fashionable part of Paris. The nobility and *nouveaux riches* built themselves imposing houses; indeed, the idea of an elegant town house, not a palace, not a château, but simply a house to live in, was

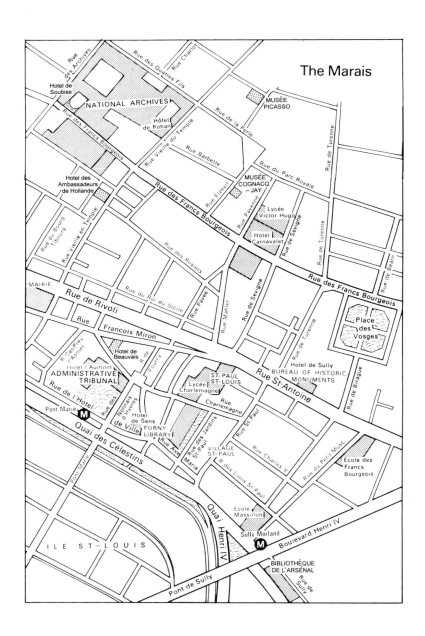

a novelty in itself. The architects of the time, Le Vau, François Mansart, Jules Hardouin-Mansart and others, excelled themselves in building beautifully proportioned houses which looked to the classical rather than the Gothic tradition.

Something else was emerging, a civilized, urban society distinct from the court or country estates. The seventeenth and eighteenth centuries were the great time of the *salons*. Conversation in these *hôtels* would be sophisticated, thoughtful, witty and often advanced in its thinking, much concerned with politics, philosophy and the arts; a long way indeed from Versailles' wars and hunting. Richelieu invited many of the more prominent members to join the French Academy, and among the names of those who haunted the *salons* over the years we may note Madame de Maintenon (Madame Scarron, as she was then), Madame de Sévigné, Ninon de Lenclos, Molière, Racine and Voltaire. For about a hundred and fifty years the Marais was the glittering intellectual centre of France.

All this ended with the Revolution. The Marais was too close to the Bastille for comfort and began to get a bad name as a rough district. The fashionable world moved further west and the Marais fell into a state of shocking dilapidation from which it seemed it would never re-emerge. However, Malraux's efforts to clean Paris had a noticeable effect with façades of ordinary houses as well as the *hôtels* cleaned and restored. Flats were modernized to attract a better class of owner or tenant. To walk along Rue François-Miron or Rue des Francs-Bourgeois is now a pleasure, even though some of the inhabitants may have preferred it the way it was.

The *hôtels* are more of a problem. Twenty-nine have disappeared over the centuries, but a hundred still remain. They are nearly all of historic or architectural interest, protected from redevelopment. Some house museums, libraries, the national archives, cultural centres and schools. Others are derelict.

Hôtel Salé, at 5 rue Thorigny, is thought to be one of the finest houses among the historic *hôtels* of the Marais, although its architect Jean Boullier, was little known. It was built between 1656 and 1659 for Aubert de Fontenay, who had salted away a fortune collecting the unpopular salt-tax: hence the nickname 'Hôtel Salé' (salted). It now houses the **Musée Picasso** (Metro St Paul). Many protested that this semi-derelict building was a highly unsuitable home for Picasso, but it became available just when this museum was looking for premises.

We may wish to continue in the seventeenth century and come back to Picasso on another occasion; or we can go in, and allow

Picasso to take over. If we are only able to make a short visit, we should concentrate on the ground floor, where we find the artist at his 'Picasso-most'. But the right way to appreciate the life and development of this genius is to take the lift to the top of the building and work downwards in date order.

Picasso hoarded his own work and this collection results mainly from donations by the Picasso family, accepted in lieu of French death-duties. We have the benefit of seeing works which the artist himself valued, but the selection is uneven, coming mainly from the 1920s and 30s. This is being partly remedied by donations and by purchases by the museum, notably *Portrait of Guillaume Apollinaire, wounded* (1916). But the early 'Blue Period' of 1881–1903 and the 'Rose Period' of 1904–1907 are poorly represented.

The top floor (the second) tries to fill this gap by arranging temporary, borrowed, exhibitions of Picasso's work and by rotating here his fragile prints and collages which must not be shown for long periods at a time. Here we may hope to catch some of his 'papiers collés', made of pieces of paper of various colours and shapes, pinned or pasted together to make a collage. These were first used in 1912, a time of friendship with Braque. They use sober blues, greys and buffs, plus white chalk and charcoal. The object was to avoid the use of paint and so to escape from the learned critics of the time, obsessed with brushwork and pigments. A comment made later by Tristan Tyard (in *Cahiers d'Art* no. 2931) announced that this medium marked 'the most poetic and the most revolutionary' moment in painting ... 'the sovereignty of the idea'. This makes joyous reading for artists of our own day, sick of hearing that the inspiration for their work must originate in the material itself. But Picasso could be 'poetic and revolutionary' in any medium he chose. This museum shows us the wide scope of his works. It includes, besides oil on canvas, sculpture in bronze, wood and even iron; gouache with lines in graphite pencil; drawings in black pencil, and oils on wood. In 1935 designs were made for tapestry; some of them were woven at Gobelin, long afterwards, in 1967 and 1976, by order of André Malraux. In every one of these media we find unmistakable Picasso, rejecting perspective and light-and-shade and revelling in 'the sovereignty of his idea'.

He offers us a wide range of subjects, too. In room 1 on the first floor are portraits, sad and Spanish-looking, with his famous one-eyed *Celestina*, 1904, thought to be a procuress, and a notable self-portrait in 1901, oil on canvas, painted in Paris. The sensual red mouth and red beard are the only points of colour, in contrast to the black eyes and hair. In 1909–17 he was painting oil on canvas, Cubist landscapes, influenced by Cézanne, of misty hill-cities among mountains. The word 'beautiful' is unfashionable, but to describe these it could be risked.

In room 2B we may notice a small bronze *Woman Dressing her Hair*, 1906, a figure almost as simplified into a rock as Matisse's *Woman's Back* or Rodin's *Balzac*.

In room 3 we find outdoors groups of figures, but they are a long way from this favourite theme among the Impressionists. In an oil, *Three Women under a Tree,* 1907 (a study for his *Les Demoiselles d'Avignon*, who were prostitutes), the tree, although understated in itself, dominates the nude figures posed under it. He has used the leaf-like shapes produced by the spaces between its trunk and branches and plastered these shapes in huge slabs of paint all over the canvas. So the figures and their similarly-shaped breasts are merged in the tree.

A shock among these drab-coloured works is a small breakout into brilliant colour, a study for *Baigneuses dans la Forêt*. This is a gouache over lines of graphite pencil, 1908.

Room 5 houses the 'Picasso Donation' of works by his friends and others which Picasso collected himself. There are some rather minor works by Dégas, Cézanne, Renoir, 'Douanier' Rousseau and Braque, but it is worth studying the vivid *Portrait of a Young Girl* by Derain, 1914, and a self-portrait by Miró (1919), far from his better-known style.

Picasso moved on in the twenties (or perhaps we may think he moved back) to almost conventional portraits and still-life, his 'Classical Period'. He shows us something very rare in any art: children who look like children, see his son Paul in *Paul en Pierrot*, 1925, oil. He must have loved children. But did he really love women? What many of us have come here to see are his female nudes and his bulls. These are what his name is apt to conjure up in our minds. He must earlier have been fond of Fernande, who was with him from 1904 to 1912, because he drew and sculpted her so often and tenderly (first floor) but did those bullfights end by getting confused with his sex drive? We move to the ground floor for these. In various versions, sometimes the bull kills the horse, sometimes the man kills the bull and sometimes the bull kills the man. In 1933 the bull even kills the woman in *The Death of the Female Torero*, oil on wood. In room 10 we see *Corrida – the Death of the Bullfighter*,

1933, oil on wood, and *Wounded Minotaur*. They are violent and effective. The theme of the minotaur (a legendary creature, half-bull, half-human) became very dominant, making one wonder if the sculpture dedicated to Picasso by César, in Saint-Germain-des-Prés, is perhaps mistakenly known as *The Centaur*. The importance of this subject had already appeared in 1927, coinciding, perhaps, with the deterioration of Picasso's relationship with his wife Olga, which evoked his violence and aggressivity towards women. Eluard wrote in 1926 'Picasso loves intensely, but he kills what he loves'. From then on (room 8) we see a series of tormented and fantastic nude studies – those typical Picassos. In his *Figures au Bord de la Mer,* 1931 the breasts are pistons, as they are in his bronze, nearby, *Baigneuse,* Boisgeloup, 1931. In his *Femme Assise dans un Fauteuil Rouge*, oil on canvas, Boisgeloup, 1932, the face and breasts appear as cannonballs. A sculpture of soldered and painted iron *La Femme au Jardin*, 1930–31, gives a wild effect of spikes.

In room 9 we have a complete change of colour-scale to green and mauve. These are larger oils on canvas, with much more exuberance than before. But Picasso can always surprise us: in room 10 there is a small oil on wood of 1930, *The Crucifixion*. In this, the central, crucified figure is white against a black sky, distorted and agonising but dignified. All round are crazily disordered figures, in garish colours, seeming to mock the stiffness of the Christ. If we have been visiting the Grand Louvre (and if we haven't we should go at once) we may remember that Veronese's *Crucifixion* (1555) has a very similar construction – the white figure against a black sky with a surrounding group in bright colours. But Picasso introduces an element of horror, which is distinctive, and quite appropriate to a scene of capital punishment.

We come next in room 11 to the great collage *Femmes à la Toilette* which covers a whole wall. A passage is railed off to allow us to see it from a distance. It shows three ordinary-looking women; one is seated in the centre, one stands behind her, combing her hair, and the third squats in front of her with her mirror. Did she have two maids, or two friends with nothing to do? It's a picture of idleness. It was made in 1938 and Picasso may have been thinking about the Spanish Civil War – the women seem completely unaware that all the walls are cracking and falling behind them. This design for tapestry was one of the ones later woven on André Malraux's instructions.

The other war and post-war works between 1936 and 1954 are shown on the lower level, but it is no use looking for *Guernica* here.

Instead, we may see the Sculpture Garden and the last ground floor rooms 19 and 20 which show the Cannes and Vauvenargues periods, 1955–61, and the last years, Mougins 1961–73. Even at the age of 88, Picasso could paint a convincing and passionate embrace, *The Kiss* (oil on canvas, 1969). Perhaps he had forgiven women, at last. He lived to be 92.

If we are sitting, after all this, in a café, trying to come to terms with Picasso, we may like to hear a true story set in a Paris café. An elderly French couple at one table are reciting yards of poetry to each other. A British visitor, at the next table, catches the phrase 'Hope is Violence'. Breaking in, he protests 'surely Despair is more violent?' 'Oh, yes, that too' they answer, 'but they are the two linked poles. To achieve happiness in life we have to accept the misery too. That is Apollinaire's philosophy.' They leave shouting 'Vive la Poésie'. How right the Picasso Museum was to buy his painting of Apollinaire. Their friendship explains a lot about Picasso's own philosophy.

Many of the *hôtels* have been cleaned, restored and put to good use and we shall see several of them during our visit. I suggest that our walk should begin at Metro Pont Marie, beside the Seine. Standing with our backs to the river, we see, across a playground and a formal French garden, the façade of **Hôtel d'Aumont.** This correct, though rather severe, *hôtel* was originally built in 1645 by Le Vau for Monsieur Scarron, one of the earlier enthusiasts of the Marais. It was altered and redecorated inside by François Mansart on the orders of Marshal d'Aumont, Scarron's son-in-law. The house is now occupied by the Administrative Tribunal and not open to the public, except for the main courtyard which we reach by Rue des Nonnais d'Hyères, the street on our right. The steep roofs with dormer windows are typical of Mansart and have been called after him. The courtyard itself is less severe than the façade, decorated with garlands and masks, as is the rounded entrance arch.

If we have plenty of time, now is the moment to walk up to Hôtel Aumont and along Rue de Jouy to look at **Hôtel de Beauvais** (no. 68 Rue François-Miron) which has a colourful history. It was built in 1657 by Lepautre for Pierre de Beauvais and his wife, Catherine Bellier. She was the daughter of a porter in Les Halles and chambermaid to Queen Anne of Austria, the queen mother of Louis XIV. Catherine Bellier had the duty, among others, of giving the queen her enema and, during this intimate activity, she became confidential enough to say with certainty that the young king, fifteen years old, was strongly sexed; she spoke from personal experience. The queen, recalling her sad years with her inadequate husband, was delighted by the news. Honours ('de' Beauvais and the lordship of Chantilly) and wealth enough to buy two adjoining houses were showered on Madame de Beauvais, who continued to enjoy a full sex life into old age. The queen had the pleasure of watching her son's wedding procession in 1660 from the windows and of knowing that all would be well.

A hundred years later the *hôtel* was the home of Count Eych, the Bavarian ambassador, and it was here that seven-year-old Mozart gave his first Paris recital.

Lepautre's problem, as architect, was to design a building to fill the seventeen-sided site, and he showed remarkable skill. A wide corridor leads to a circular vestibule with Doric columns and a cupola; this, in turn leads to a triangular court ending in a loggia. Unfortunately the building was split up in the nineteenth century, so that the complete effect can no longer be seen. Much of the decoration, too, was lost, but the main façade, doorway and richly decorated staircase remain. The pervading *motif* is of rams' heads (*bélier,* a corruption of Catherine's maiden name, is the French for ram). The *hôtel* is closed for extensive renovation.

Returning towards the river we find on our left **Hôtel de Sens.** This is in startling contrast to Hôtel d'Aumont, being Gothic in style. It is in fact much earlier in date, built between 1475 and 1507, and is one of the only two remaining Gothic secular houses left in Paris – Hôtel de Cluny on the Left Bank is the other. Even at the time it must have seemed something of an anachronism, with its turrets, gables and battlements. Perhaps the explanation lies in the fact that it was built as the Paris residence of the archbishop of Sens.

Outdated though it may have been, we can enjoy a glimpse of mediæval Paris, especially overlooking a very formal French garden. Every afternoon (except Sundays and Mondays) we can enter the courtyard through the Flamboyant Gothic porch to see the square tower with its *bretesse,* a kind of battlemented balcony. We can also go inside, since the *hôtel* houses the **Forney Library,** which is mainly concerned with the technology of art and architecture, including a good collection of technical magazines.

While thumbing through these, we can recall that it was in one of these quiet reading rooms that Cardinal Pellève, in 1594, died of rage while a *Te Deum* was being sung in Notre-Dame to celebrate Henri IV's entry into Paris. Eleven years later the king allowed his first wife, Margot de Valois, the daughter of Queen Catherine de Medici, to return to Paris after long years of exile in the Auvergne. Aged fifty-three, very fat and sexy, she resided here with her lovers. In 1606 the Count of Vermont, the current lover, jealously killed her young page, Dal de Saint-Julien, who was replacing him. The murder occurred in the royal carriage and two days later Vermont was beheaded in front of the *hôtel* on the queen's orders.

Later Margot built herself her own palace on the Left Bank, facing the Louvre, where she continued her scandalous and violent life. Hôtel de Sens at one time became the Paris terminal of the Lyons stage-coach, a journey famous for its danger. And from this glimpse of history we return to the present and put down our technical magazine.

We walk along Rue Ave Maria, past Rue des Jardins Saint-Paul and turn left into **Village Saint-Paul,** which is well signed. This is an example of the 'New Marais'; a cobbled pedestrian area of interlinking old courtyards with trees and shrubs. Below are antique shops and cafés, upstairs are flats. It must be a quiet and pleasant place to live in and one hopes that the antique shops will be successful, though they are rather off the beaten track. We emerge through one of the archways into Rue des Jardins Saint-Paul. Facing us, across a school playground, is a long section of Philippe-Auguste's wall, a formidable piece of masonry. At the end of the street is a fine view of the dome of Saint-Paul.

At the end we turn right into the delightful Rue Charlemagne and then left into Rue Saint-Paul. On either side there are pleasant glimpses of little streets, the impasses of old Paris. At the end is **Rue Saint-Antoine,** the main street of the Marais and for many centuries the widest street in Paris. It is in fact the eastern end of Rue de Rivoli, which we first met at Place de la Concorde, but it looks very different here, a busy workaday market street with pavement stalls.

However, it has a good deal of historical interest, going back to Roman Paris, when it was raised above the marsh, the only solid street in the town. Note the church of **Saint-Paul-Saint-Louis**, built in the seventeenth century by the Jesuits on land given to them by Louis XIII. Architecturally the fine dome is of interest, one of the first church domes since classical times. The façade, with columns, is also neo-classical. The twin water-stoups inside the entrance were given, surprisingly, by Victor Hugo. Who would have thought that a famous anti-clericalist would wish at any time to make gifts to

Catholic ritual! But Hugo was a man who moved on several different levels of thought and emotion.

At no. 62 Rue Saint-Antoine we find **Hôtel de Sully,** one of the finest of Marais *hôtels,* which has been well restored. The imposing street façade consists of a large gateway, with two large pavilions and a gallery. Inside we find a courtyard, a splendid example of Marais architecture. Beautifully proportioned, the courtyard has carved pediments, dormer windows, statues of the four seasons, the four elements (female nudes, of course) and two sphinxes. Less severe than some *hôtels,* it manages to avoid a feeling of clutter and the name of its architect, Jean Androuet du Cerceau, should be better known. Of note are the panelling and painted ceilings in Sully's study and bedroom, which look out on to the garden; the decoration is not strictly contemporary but thought to date from soon after his death in 1641. The floral tapestries are, however, thought to be contemporary with him and were recovered from his château on the Loire.

The *hôtel* was built in 1624 for a notorious gambler called Petit Thouars, who lost his whole fortune in one night. Ten years later it was bought by Sully, former minister of Henri IV. He was then seventy-five and no longer able to satisfy his young wife Rachel, who had nine children by various lovers. Sully tolerated all this with good grace, doling out money for his wife, the housekeeping and the lovers, provided that these last were kept away from the main staircase. He himself preferred more intellectual company. On a later occasion Voltaire, dining at Hôtel de Sully, was called to the main door by a visitor – only to find himself well thrashed by lackeys of the Chevalier de Rohan, whom he had insulted in his verses.

Hôtel de Sully often has temporary exhibitions, usually dealing with scenes from French city life. It also has the information office of the **Caisse Nationale des Monuments et des Sites** (Bureau of Historic Monuments). This helpful office will provide information and booklets about the Marais *hôtels* and much else.

Androuet de Cerceau was also responsible for **Hôtel de Mayenne,** further along the street at no. 21. This was built for Charles de Lorraine, the son of the Duc de Guise, who was the great enemy of Henri IV and Sully. But, architecturally, the two *hôtels* have much in common, in plan and in decoration. Hôtel de Mayenne's façade was restored in 1996.

In the sixteenth century this part of Rue Saint-Antoine was often used for tournaments and jousting, in particular by King Henri II.

The road was wide and strong enough for galloping chargers. But in 1559 the king, jousting with Count Montgomery, the captain of his guard, got Montgomery's lance through his eye. He was carried to his room in the nearby Hôtel de Tournelles, where he died. His queen, Catherine de Medici, in her fury, ordered the Tournelles to be destroyed. Montgomery managed to escape to England. But, fifteen years later, he rashly returned to France, leading a Protestant force to support the Huguenots. He was captured, imprisoned and beheaded. The Medici queen had waited a long time for her revenge, but she had it in the end.

From jousting to duelling is only a short step and the Marais became the favourite place for duels. And it was beside the ruins of the Tournelles that the most famous and terrible duel in French history took place. Henri III was the favourite son of Catherine de Medici, youngest of three decadent and childless brothers. It is said that he was brave in battle and interested in the arts; but he is best remembered for his sexual perversion. He often appeared in women's clothes and he filled the Louvre with his *mignons* (darlings or boyfriends). These young men behaved outrageously, with extravagant manners, screaming insults or compliments at each other, playing cup and ball, gaudily dressed as parrots – indeed, the palace resembled a parrot-house. Sometimes the *mignons* would flagellate each other for the king's pleasure. Many people could not stand them, especially the Guise family, but the king loved them all dearly, especially little Quélus, his favourite.

One day in April 1578 three Guises challenged three *mignons* including Quélus, a challenge which could not be refused. They met at dawn the following morning at the Tournelles. The Guises were in sober black, the *mignons* wearing their full finery, jewels, silks, velvet cloaks, the lot. They bowed elaborately to everyone and then the fight began. It was a sword and dagger affair and the Guises soon found that they had underestimated their opponents. The darlings fought with the greatest ferocity. Of the six duellists, four died *sur le champ,* Quélus, with nineteen wounds lived on for a month and the only survivor, a Guise, was crippled for life. The king was in tears and mourning until his own assassination.

Duelling was forbidden by Richelieu, but many felt that honour or self-defence were more important than the decrees of a not very popular cardinal. On 22 June 1627 François de Montmorency-Bouteville, seconded by the Comte de Chapelle, fought two other noblemen, Beuvron and Bussy d'Amboise in the Place des Vosges.

Richelieu was living at the time at no. 21 and the duel took place under his windows; it was indeed an act of provocation. Beuvron was killed and Montmorency-Bouteville and de Chapelle were arrested. Despite appeals by other members of the nobility, they were executed and their headless bodies taken to Montmorency-Bouteville's home, Hôtel Lamoignan in Rue Pavée.

Despite this, duelling continued and in the century which followed became something of an epidemic. A gentleman had to be a good swordsman to survive either formal duels with seconds or casual street brawls; nobody wished to be set on by the lackeys of another house. The vendettas gradually ceased with time, but duels for honour continued, although swords gave way to pistols and the preferred site moved to the greater seclusion of the Bois de Boulogne. The most recent duel, and probably the last, took place in the 1960s, when two politicians fired formally at each other in the Bois, much to the annoyance of President de Gaulle, who thought such behaviour unseemly in responsible men. Such is the changing code of manners.

We turn left off Rue Saint-Antoine into Rue de Birague and, passing through an archway under the King's Pavilion, we arrive in the splendid **Place des Vosges** (Metro Chemin Vert). It was the idea of Henri IV who wished to replace the ruined Tournelles and transform the Marais into a royal area. He would himself live in the big house on the south side (under which we have just passed) and his estranged wife, Marie de Medici, in a similar building on the other side. Building began in 1605, by the architect Clément Metezeau, and was finished in 1612, two years after the king's assassination, in the reign of his son, Louis XIII. It was named the Place Royale, though in fact no king ever lived there, Henri IV's sons preferring the Louvre and his grandson Versailles and elsewhere. During the Revolution it was renamed the Place of Indivisibility, and under Napoleon Place des Vosges, in honour of the first *département* to pay its taxes. Under the Bourbon restoration and the Second Empire it became Place Royale again, and then after 1870 reverted to Place des Vosges.

Metezeau's plan is totally symmetrical. The thirty-six houses or *pavillons,* nine on each side, are of brick and stone, with steep slate roofs and dormer windows. On ground level is a stone arcade running right round the square and here there are antique shops, art galleries and restaurants. In the centre is a garden, a French garden of gravel, lawns, trees and a statue – though some commentators have thought it not French enough; that the trees, particularly the four big central chestnuts, are too big, spoil the view and hide the statue. This statue is of Louis XIII, in Roman clothes on horseback, but the original was destroyed in the Revolution and the present statue, by Dupaty and Cortot, dates from the last century.

The garden is a very pleasant place, especially in spring and autumn when the maligned chestnuts are coming out or turning. Children hang upside down on the parallel bars of the playground, mothers knit, and young people read. Under the arches, or, in colder weather, inside, we can eat or drink. On the east side, the restaurant *La Chope des Vosges* has a pleasing three-level seventeenth-century décor. The west side is more modest. Inhabitants of the square like to breakfast here on Sunday mornings, especially in summer under the arcade; this is an agreeable and sociable occasion.

The square was officially opened in 1612 with a big tournament in honour of Louis XIII's marriage to Anne of Austria, and of his sister to a Spanish prince. The tournament went on for three days and was called the *Chevaliers de la Gloire*. According to contemporary prints, it was a lavish affair. Because of or perhaps despite such tournaments and duels, Place Royale became the fashionable place to live. The great king might be dead, his sad, near-impotent son elsewhere, but Richelieu lived there from 1615 to 1627. French society moved in to the magnificent new houses; *Tout-Paris* (as it is now called) had arrived.

The central garden became a parade of elegance and big receptions, the first *salons* were held in the large first-floor rooms. The sword was giving way to the pen, or at least to the tongue. Many receptions were held in no. 9, home of the Duc de Chaulnes and, later, of the actress Rachel. It is now the Academy of Architecture. Madame de Sévigné was born at no. 1 *bis* in 1626. More than two centuries later the house became the Paris home of the rich and eccentric Singer family – eccentric because the Marais was no longer a fashionable place. I recall dining there; a huge, dark, candlelit room with a minstrels' gallery running right round; the feeling that everyone ought to have been wearing clothes like the Three Musketeers and carrying swords. But in fact both the conversation and the food would have given more pleasure to Madame de Sévigné than to the Duc de Guise.

Place Royale was also the centre of a group who called themselves *Les Précieuses*. They practised an affected, mannered style of speaking and writing and laid down lists of words which might or might not be used. The French are fond of laying down detailed laws for literature, art, cooking, fashion and so on. When somebody breaks these laws, there is usually a scandal and the miscreant, whether deliberate or not, is abused. However, a new impetus has been given and possibly a new movement or fashion started. One of the reasons why Victor Hugo's tragedy *Hernani* came to grief in 1830 was that he used the forbidden word *mouchoir* (we may wonder how the *Précieuses* would have staged *Othello,* not that the occasion ever arose).

Hugo himself lived in no. 6 from 1833 to 1848, before his exile in Guernsey. The first floor of **Maison de Victor Hugo** is a museum; the second floor, where he actually lived, is now closed to the public. Nevertheless the museum is of great interest to admirers of Hugo, especially his drawings and self-designed furniture. Théophile Gautier, who lived next door at no. 8, has described how Hugo would take an ordinary household object, even an ink-blot, and make a drawing out of it. These 'doodles' are fascinating psychologically and they show us the black, Gothic side of his nature. They are nightmare fantasies of weird, twisted castles and towers, huge gnarled trees, everything seen in chiaroscuro against moonlight or storm. There is also an alarmingly prophetic giant mushroom. This is the dark night of Hugo's soul, the hunchback-and-sewers aspect of his character. It is a long way from his feeling for the sky, for the beauty of nature, for the great trees of Villequier and for freedom.

His furniture is equally weird. We do not know why he wanted to take cabinets and dressers and put them together, turning them into mock-Gothic court-cupboards of mixed style. The result is interesting rather than enjoyable. To see beautiful furniture we shall have to walk the few yards to **Musée Carnavalet** at no. 23 Rue de Sévigné.

Even without being a museum, Hôtel Carnavalet would be worth seeing as an example of Marais architecture. It was originally built for President de Ligneris in 1548. The keystone of the entrance and the porch pediment are the work of Jean Goujon, whose pupils sculpted the Allegories of the Seasons between the windows of the main building. The next owner was a Breton nobleman, Monsieur de Kernevenoy, a well-known horseman written about by Montaigne and Ronsard; but the Parisians, who like to re-spell everything their own way, changed his name to its present form. The carnival mask, a visual pun, over the main entrance, was added later.

François Mansart in 1655 altered the building a good deal, adding another floor both to the street and side buildings. More reconstruction was done in the nineteenth century; the Nazarene arch, which previously spanned Rue des Francs-Bourgeois, is now part of the *hôtel,* looking on to the street. Other façades, notably the Pavillon de Choiseul, were reconstructed. None of this much changed the appearance of the building, but important additions were made to the interior. Whole rooms were moved in from other *hôtels* in the Marais, preserving what might so easily have been lost. Note in particular the Gold Cabinet on the ground floor, the work of Le Vau and Van Obstal, which was originally in 14 Place des Vosges. From the same house comes the drawing-room with a ceiling showing Mercury introducing Psyche to the gods. The furniture has been collected from many *hôtels,* including the Temple, the apartments where the royal family were imprisoned. The statue of Louis XIV by Coysevox in the main courtyard comes from the Hôtel de Ville. The municipal council saved it from being destroyed at the Revolution by claiming it as their own property. The statue of Victory in front of the Pavillon de Choiseul was originally on top of the Châtelet fountain.

The museum is the municipal museum of Paris and devoted to the city. It is, incidentally, a good museum for children; models of the sixteenth-century Ile de la Cité, the Bastille and the guillotine are striking, as are old inn-signs which fill a whole room. The ground floor is concerned with the Revolution and Empire, the first floor with the eighteenth century.

In room 72 we cannot fail to be horrified by the portraits of three revolutionary leaders, which are hung together. Marat seems crazy, Robespierre mean and hard, and even idealistic Danton gross and brutal. Beside these portraits, and contrasting strongly, is a Louis XVI inlaid chest-of-drawers, a masterpiece of elegance and an example of the civilization which the revolution was trying to destroy. In room 80 we note the portrait of Madame Récamier by François Gérard (1805). Her sofa seems surprisingly small, almost a chair, unlike the famous one in her portrait in the Louvre.

On the first floor there is decoration and furniture from the reigns of Louis XIV, Louis XV and Louis XVI, though the building is of course older. These suites of rooms look much as they must have done at the time. The furniture includes some *chinoiserie,* as popular in France as it was in England. Madame de Sévigné's apartments are on the south-east corner. Some of her own belongings have been preserved, and the rooms remind us strongly of the witty and warm-hearted woman whose letters have helped us to appreciate her age and Marais life. She lived here from 1677 to 1696, with various members of her family (her husband had been killed in a duel), enjoying the Carnavalet and the *salons* of the Marais.

She has been called, rightly, the *grande dame* of the Marais. Born in Place des Vosges, christened in Saint-Paul, married in Saint-Gervais, she felt most at home in the Carnavalet. However, when she was seventy and very rheumatic, she went to live with her disagreeable daughter, Madame de Grignan, in Provence, where she died and was buried. During the Revolution her body was dug up, beheaded and the skull brought back to Paris, where it disappeared. The reasons for this atrocity are not known; perhaps some sort of witchcraft, perhaps political hatred, a feeling that she should not be allowed to escape decapitation merely by being dead.

The Carnavalet is her abiding memory. If we wish to end our walk here, we turn right at the main entrance, down Rue de Sévigné, one of the prettiest streets in the Marais with the dome of Saint-Paul dominating it, to Rue Saint-Antoine and the few steps to Metro Saint-Paul.

Our walk will have taken us through the most attractive parts of the Marais and shown us some of the best and best-known places. But there is much, much more to be seen in the Marais, some of it mainly for keen Marais-explorers. Within the limits of time and space available, we must be selective and brief. If instead of continuing to the metro, we turn right into Rue des Francs-Bourgeois, **Hôtel de Soubise** is at the far end, at no. 60. It belonged to the Rohan family and has a long history, with many architects and artists. On the corner are the fortified turrets of the original Clisson Manor (1380) which recall Hôtel de Sens. The manor later became the property of the Guise family, who enlarged it and renamed it Hôtel de Guise. In 1700 it was bought by François de Rohan, Prince de Soubise, for the enormous sum of 326,000 livres; and he commissioned Delamair to redesign it.

Delamair had ambitious ideas. He retained the old Clisson turrets, but created the great courtyard on the site of the old riding-school and added a majestic neo-classical façade to the Guise *hôtel*. This much-photographed façade is indeed imposing, with its double porticoes, its fifty-six double columns, the four statues of the seasons (only copies now) and reclining statues on the pediment, suitably named *Glory* and *Magnificence*. The distinguished sculptor was Robert Le Lorrain.

The prince was succeeded by his son, who lived in the Guise apartments behind the façade. But at the age of sixty he married a nineteen-year-old widow, Marie-Sophie de Courcillon. As a wedding present he gave her a new house, built on the site of the old Clisson keep. Boffrand, a pupil of François Mansart, was the architect and the best-known sculptors and artists, including Boucher, were employed. The result is a riot of rococo, especially in the princess's apartments on the first floor; the prince's on the ground floor are slightly more severe, as befitting his age (did they not live together?). We shall certainly enjoy the lushness of it all, the panelling, the ceilings, the chandeliers and, especially, the shape of the Oval rooms, Boffrand's original idea.

Round the corner are the **National Archives**, which contain about six thousand million documents kept on over two hundred miles of shelves (including subsidiary sites). Some of the more interesting can be seen in the **Historical Museum** in Hôtel de Soubise, which is open to the public every afternoon except Tuesdays. Here we used to be able to see, among other things, St Louis's Acts founding the Sainte-Chapelle and the University; the Edict of Nantes 1598, and its Revocation by Louis XIV, and Napoleon's will. These, however, have been placed in reserve, pending a new presentation.

We continue along Rue des Quatre Fils to Rue Vieille du Temple. At no. 87 is **Hôtel de Rohan.** This is sometimes called Hôtel de Strasbourg, because the three Cardinals de Rohan who lived here successively were also bishops of Strasbourg. The building dates from 1704 and has scarcely been altered since. The architect was Delamair and the cardinal an intelligent young man, a friend of the king. The *hôtel is* a little later in date than some we have seen and the great façade onto the garden shows this. With its tall windows, columned porticoes, pediment and rather flat roof, it is very different from Place des Vosges. The courtyard is more modest and leads to the stables. There, between the drinking troughs, we find Robert Le Lorrain's superb relief-sculpture, *The Horses of the Sun.* Against a background of the sun's rays, four horses rear or drink from shells held by men who may be heroes or even gods.

Inside, in the cardinal's apartments, the *grand salon* is the eighteenth century at its most splendid, and it contrasts with the little *Cabinet des Singes,* the Monkeys' Room, an entertaining example of popular chinoiserie, by Huet. The Aubusson tapestries in the suite, which also have Chinese motifs based on designs by Boucher, were not originally in the building. Of the smaller rooms the 'Fable

Room', with its medallions, dates from 1738 and was originally in Hôtel de Soubise. The other small rooms are decorated and furnished in the same style – rococo. Some people love this, the climax of baroque; others find it overdone, frivolous, decadent and likely to provoke revolutions. But probably we should avoid judgment and simply accept it for what it is – decoration de luxe. Those wanting something more severe can enjoy the towers of the next *hôtel*.

At no. 47 Rue Vieille du Temple is **Hôtel des Ambassadeurs de Hollande**, which has a misleading name. It never had any connection with the Dutch Embassy, though one of their chaplains may have been a tenant. Its most famous occupant was Beaumarchais, who wrote *The Marriage of Figaro* there, in intervals of organizing his arms traffic and slave trade business. The main portal is richly decorated by Regnaudin and covered with gorgons and allegorical figures representing War, Peace, Strength, Truth, Flora, Ceres and so on. Inside are two courtyards. In the first we should note the four painted sundials. The passage between the two courtyards is decorated with mock-Tuscan pilasters and a *trompe l'œil* painting hiding a blank wall. The *hôtel,* privately owned, is not open to the public and this is probably all the concierge will let us see.

Finally, away from the centre of the Marais, near Metro Sully-Morland is the **Arsénal**, at no. 1 Rue de Sully, which is one of the oldest *hôtels*. The arsenal of François I blew up in 1564 – the sound could be heard as far away as Melun – and Sully built a house for himself on the site. Sully's successor, Marshal de la Meilleraye, took over the house and redecorated it for his marriage to Marie de Cosse. These rooms are some of the finest surviving examples of seventeenth-century style on view. In particular we should note the Cabinet des Femmes Fortes. The panels show military scenes and pictures of famous tough ladies, whom the bride was to emulate; all rather intimidating for a girl to have in her bedroom.

The contrast in centuries can be seen clearly when we move to the Duchesse de Maine's music room. A hundred years later the proportions are equally pleasing, but decoration is infinitely more elaborate, especially the wood-carving. But, by using white, gold and pale colours, the rooms seem much lighter, if more artificial. The music room in the nineteenth century was the setting of the literary salon held by the librarian, Charles Nodier. Among the regular guests were Hugo, Vigny, Musset, Lamartine and Dumas.

The arsénal was first used as a library during the Revolution and grew in size and importance until it is now the second biggest in

France. Apart from over a million books, it has a large collection of manuscripts, many of them illustrated, engravings and a unique collection of theatrical books, plays and annotated scripts. It now forms part of the Bibliothèque Nationale, centred at Tolbiac.

We retrace our steps to Rue des Francs-Bourgeois and turn right and then left into Rue Elzévir, where we find the **Musée Cognacq-Jay** at no. 8. Unlike the hôtels of the Marais, of the seventeenth century, this museum, a collection formed by the founder of the *Samaritaine* department store, specializes in the eighteenth century, and has removed to this area. It is original in including the English painter Gainsborough. It also shows Fragonard, Greuze, La Tour, Canaletto and Watteau. There are over one thousand works, arranged, like the similar but larger Nissim Camondo Museum, with paintings, pastels and gouaches, and pieces of sculpture, plus furnishings and many *objets d'art*, set out, room by room, to complement each other.

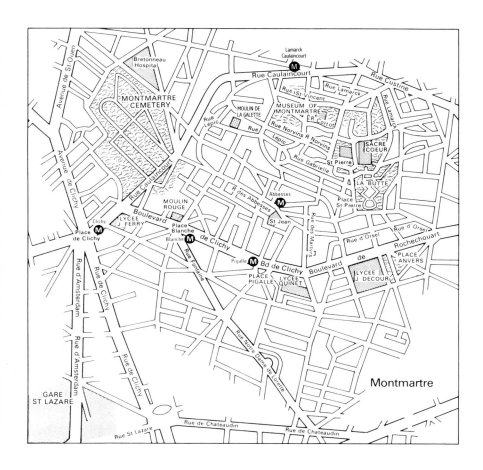

Montmartre

12

Montmartre

THE SKYLINE OF Montmartre is familiar to most people from their arrival in Paris – or even before, for those arriving by train at Gare du Nord. The domes and the campanile stand on the highest point of Paris – 424 feet high, Montmartre, the Mount of Martyrs and known generally as *la Butte*, the hill. It is a steep hill with winding, stepped streets, squares and terraces with tremendous views and a funicular to ease our ascent and descent. We walk to it from Metro Abbesses, asking for '*la Butte*'. Montmartre was a country village, a windy one, to judge from the windmills, and it still preserves a good deal of that atmosphere, despite the tens of thousands of tourists. We can either go in the middle of the day, see the church and the view, explore the streets and then have lunch, or we can go up in the evening, dine and make a night of it. Most people do the latter, and we shall find Place du Tertre very crowded at night.

Originally a sun-worship centre, it was later dedicated to Mercury, the favourite god of Gaul, and then to the martyrs who were beheaded there. The best known is St Denis (a corruption of Dionysius), the first bishop of Paris and later its patron saint. About AD 250 he was tortured and decapitated there, after which he picked up his severed head and carried it a long way to the part of northern Paris where his basilica now is.

The basilica now standing on the summit of Montmartre is, however, not named after him, but after the Sacred Heart, the **Sacré-Cœur.** This huge church, better seen from a distance floating above the river mists on an autumn morning, was begun in 1876 and only finished in 1910. It was not consecrated until 1919. Many architects were involved, the original being Abadie, a specialist in Roman and Byzantine architecture. The interior is full of mosaics, but the crypt is sometimes used for temporary exhibitions of modern religious art, of very different style. But the best thing about the basilica is the

185

view from the main steps and the terrace. Luminous or hazy by day, twinkling by night, it is seen most romantically at dawn.

Beside the Sacré-Cœur is **Saint-Pierre,** whose simple belfry is in great contrast to its neighbour's ponderous campanile. Saint-Pierre is all that remains of the big abbey of Montmartre and contains some old arches and stones which are said to have come from a Roman temple on the site. It also contains the tomb of Queen Adelaide, who had founded the abbey in 1133.

Many pilgrims still visit the area, especially on Good Friday, when the archbishop of Paris does the Stations of the Cross scattered around the Butte, himself carrying a cross. But the thousands of tourists who visit the Butte every year do not usually go for religious reasons any more. They go for the views, the picturesque streets, the night-life and the reputation of Montmartre as a centre of art, which it no longer is.

Artists arrived on the Butte towards the end of the nineteenth century, though many of them were already in Place Pigalle; painters, caricaturists, poets, singers, models, dancers, attracted by the bohemian life. From there it was only a short move up the hill to the Butte itself, which offered an easy-going village life, literary and artistic conversation in the *Lapin Agile* (café, later nightclub) and the studios at no. 13 Place Emile-Goudeau, later burnt down. It was here that Picasso, Braque and Gris created Cubism, encouraged by poets like Apollinaire and Max Jacob. Other artists who lived here (mainly in no. 12 Rue Cortot) were Renoir, Van Gogh, Dufy, Suzanne Valadon and her illegitimate son Maurice Utrillo.

Utrillo is the painter we chiefly think of when we visit Montmartre today. The little streets, the old houses which he painted so vividly, are still there. Rue Norvins and Rue Lepic still look much the same, apart from the crowds, as they do in his pictures. His walls glow with life, even if the occasional humans seem to be stuffed dummies. The famous *boulangerie* in Rue Norvins is still there. To look at, Montmartre has changed little since his day. But something has gone – the genuine artistic spirit. It moved in the 1920s to Montparnasse.

Nevertheless a great deal of artistic life still goes on and the main centre is **Place du Tertre.** This pretty little square, surrounded by old buildings and restaurants, still looks like a stage setting, the second act of *La Bohème.* In summer the paved centre of the square is full of restaurant tables, waiters and entertainers. Round the edge is a ring of colourful artists at their easels, and the occasional argument between an artist and a waiter adds to the operatic quality of the scene.

However, let no aspiring artist think that he can simply set up his easel and paint; the sites are as carefully guarded as booths in a fairground. Each artist is allowed to show two pictures, one which he has completed and one to which he is putting the final touches. These touches may take many months to complete and the artist working on it after lunch may not be the same as the one before lunch. Should we pause to consider a work which is simply standing on an easel, an artist, who has been eyeing us from the window of a café, will be instantly at our side, suggesting a price. The works are mainly landscapes (not necessarily of Montmartre), children and animals, and the fact that they are always complete, or almost, has prompted the ribald thought that they are imported from a wholesaler elsewhere. Better value are the caricatures, which are very much part of the Montmartre tradition. Often amusing and pointed, a good likeness of ourselves, they have the advantage of being done by the artist while we sit meek and still.

The local council has made an effort to raise artistic standards by placing its official stamp on the easels of painters who can show convincing credentials as professionals. We should look for these stamps, for information. But an art-buyer cannot be told what he likes; his own taste is the only important guide.

As for the restaurants, we can either sit outside in the square or, in cold or wet weather, inside – the restaurants are far larger than they seem. They are usually filled by coach tours and we shall overhear little French during our meal. *La Mère Catherine* has become a landmark. It is said to have been founded by the Cossacks in March 1814. The villagers of Montmartre, who have an independent nature, had put up strong resistance to the Cossacks in Place Clichy and at the Moulin de la Galette. But the Cossacks won and the Montmartre leader was crucified on the sails of the Moulin – one more martyr on the mount. In 1870 the villagers once again held out, this time against the Prussians. They formed an independent *commune* which became the Paris Commune, a brief and bloody episode which left its scars on the city, though not on the Butte. In 1940 Montmartre was again occupied; a vivid description of this can be found in Peter de Polnay's book *Death and Tomorrow*.

Those wishing to find something of the old cultural traditions of Montmartre should go to the **Museum of Montmartre**, owned by the Société du Vieux Montmartre, no. 12 Rue Cortot, the house where Utrillo and others lived, referred to earlier. The museum here is devoted to writers and painters who found their inspiration on the Butte. There were musicians here too; no. 6 Rue Cortot was the home of the composer Erik Satie.

For those in search of night-life the choice is wide indeed. Practically every restaurant and café offers some form of entertainment, either professional or spontaneous, and we may well wish to wander from one to another, as the mood takes us. Some of these have long histories and *Le Lapin Agile* and the *Moulin de la Galette* were painted by Utrillo – the outsides, of course, and in daylight. Utrillo's idea of a nightclub was very different from Toulouse-Lautrec's.

Descending the south side of the Butte, we can either take the funicular or, if it is a fine day, make our way on foot. Below *Moulin de la Galette*, in Rue Caulaincourt, we find **Montmartre Cemetery** where a number of famous writers, painters and composers are buried (Zola, Gautier, Dumas the younger, the Goncourt brothers, Stendhal, de Vigny, Heine, Guitry, Fragonard, Greuze, Dégas, Berlioz, Delibes, Offenbach).

We continue down the street until we meet the busy Boulevard de Clichy, a street full of cinemas, theatres, nightclubs, cafés and restaurants specializing in seafood (Metro Place de Clichy). Going eastwards, the main landmark of the Boulevard is at Place Blanche (Metro Blanche), where we find the much photographed sails of the *Moulin Rouge*. This famous cabaret was opened in 1889. Everywhere we find memories of La Goulue, Jane Avril, Yvette Guilbert and, of course, Toulouse-Lautrec who painted them.

A little further along we find **Place Pigalle** (Metro Pigalle). Jean-Baptiste Pigalle was a painter and sculptor, who was known for his pictures and statues of the Virgin, some of which hang in lady chapels, for example in Saint-Sulpice. We may find it ironic that the name of this pious, Virgin-minded artist should now have become almost synonymous with sex. And sex is what the Place Pigalle nowadays is about; the area and in particular the side streets leading off the boulevard are full of sex shops, porn films and books, erotic pictures, houses of pleasure, and girls of all ages and types. Once they were part-time, working in the daytime as artists' models or seamstresses, but now they are full-time professionals.

13

The Seizième Arrondissement

The Seizième (the sixteenth Arrondissement) is *le beau quartier,* the beautiful part of Paris, more even than the Septième, another *beau quartier.* Not that the area is all that beautiful; it is simply where the beautiful people live, and would be ashamed to live anywhere else. It is an area of good addresses, of streets people are proud to put on their visiting cards. And, incidentally, it is a quarter where some interesting people do choose to live.

It is a very large quarter, stretching from the top of the hill at Etoile down to Bois de Boulogne and the Seine. But it should not be called beautiful; architecturally it has little to offer. There are a few old houses which survive, and some modern blocks set in lawns with statues and possibly fountains. But, otherwise, it consists of long streets and avenues of buildings from the nineteenth century, all six storeys high, all about a hundred years old, all similar; you have to look at the street signs to know where you are. Behind elaborate but uninteresting façades are thousands of flats, all identical, all furnished with similar antiques or reproductions, all with portraits in large gold frames. They are inhabited by similar people, rich, class-conscious, traditional, hospitable and, to be fair, intelligent.

The Seizième is not an area for shopping or restaurants or hotels or theatres, although there are some important museums, about which more in a moment. It is an area to visit friends or go to a party, one of those small, select 'cocktails' which the French like to give. Only a carefully chosen few are invited and they usually know each other already. There will be a little champagne, or whisky, and plate after plate of 'eats'. The other guests will be expensively and quietly dressed, their conversation amusing or deadeningly polite – the one thing in this quarter which is variable.

The last of the old 'salons' used to be given, in the 1970s to 1990s, by the Duchesse Edmée de La Rochefoucauld in her large drawing-room overlooking Place des Etats-Unis. These were large

189

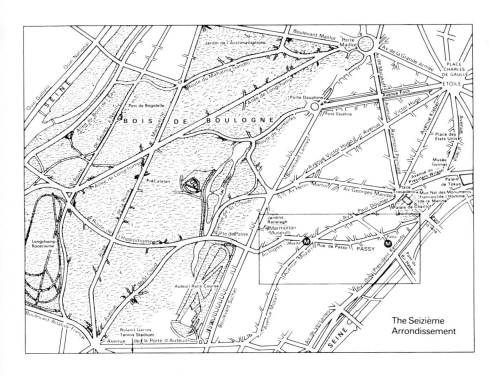

The Seizième
Arrondissement

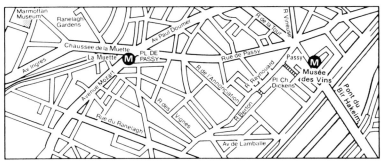

parties, centering on her own literary-feminist personality. Most of the guests were writers, though there would be a sprinkling of politicians, diplomats and artists. The duchess was an expert on Paul Valéry. A salon in the Seizième today is more likely to take the form of a formal lecture or debate.

We may be going to a private dinner in **Avenue Foch** (Metro Etoile). This wide tree-lined street, leading from Etoile to Porte Dauphine and the Bois de Boulogne, is still the most fashionable residential street in Paris and everyone here is very rich, or wishes to be thought so. A dinner party here will consist of many courses, served by waiters wearing white gloves. A fine series of wines will be offered to us, preceded by whisky and ending with champagne. And we may sit next to the daughter of the family, known to her fellow-Parisians as Mademoiselle Avenue Foch.

She is well brought up and well-off, though she never seems to have much pocket-money. She does not have a job, but is studying fashion design or *Science-Po*. She rides in the Bois, and is often to be seen at Longchamp, *Maxim*'s or the newest disco. She eats little and drinks less, being figure-conscious and afraid of a complaint called *cellulité*. She buys her clothes in Faubourg Saint-Honoré or even at one of the *haute couture* houses; she favours navy blue and a fawn raincoat. She lives at home and spends her weekends and holidays with her parents at their château in Burgundy. She has been a member since infancy of a *rallye,* a group of similar people of the same age, one of whom she is intended to marry. She has been schooled since childhood never to be *remarquée,* never to do or say anything interesting in public, especially if there are men present. We may feel that her total vocabulary consists of two words, '*Ah bon,*' which can be inflected in various ways.

This traditional image, the *jeune fille rangée,* has undergone some modifications in these trendy years, though they may not be noticeable at first glance. She is now more likely to be interested in the possibility of a television film part than in Science-Po. She goes further afield on her holidays and may even speak English. If questioned, she will readily admit that her baby is not by either of her husbands. But she still likes to wear navy blue and she still lives in Avenue Foch.

Apart from the parties and Mademoiselle, what are the attractions of the Seizième? Well, the village of **Passy** for one. The old village on the side of the hill overlooking the Seine still keeps an atmosphere of its own. Haussman overlooked Passy, and though many old houses and walled gardens have gone, some remain, together with narrow streets and sudden unexpected views. Passy provides us with a pleasant and interesting walk.

We should start at Metro Passy and walk a little way across the bridge (Pont du Bir-Hakeim) to look at the view: the Eiffel Tower, the new towers of Grenelle, the Maison de la Radio (which was the biggest single building in France when it was built in 1963); Passy on its steep hillside, the river full of petrol barges – this is not the typical Parisian view of the city. But it became more familiar with the film *Last Tango in Paris,* which became a classic, shot mainly in Passy. We can amuse ourselves by wondering in which flat all that sex-on-the-floor took place.

We return to Metro Passy (by the escalator) and make our way to Square Charles Dickens; the connection with the novelist is only nominal. At no. 5, at the corner of Rue des Eaux, we find the **Musée du Vin,** constructed in the cellars of the old Abbey of Passy. The monks were known as Minims, because of their poverty, or *bonshommes,* because of their age. They were, however, energetic and commercially-minded and, in warmer centuries, grew vines on the sunny Passy hillside. Their wine was sold in all the Paris taverns and some local street names, Rue des Vignes and Rue Vineuse, remind us of Passy's wine-producing past. In the seventeenth century mineral water was found there (hence Rue des Eaux); it contained iron and was supposed to be good for feminine sterility. A new and more fashionable crowd was attracted to Passy, which was beginning to lose its country feel. The abbey was closed during the Revolution, although it was not completely demolished until 1906.

The Musée du Vin, also called Caves de la Tour Eiffel, is rather a theatrical experience, with its audio-visual gimmicks and its waxworks. But it gives us a good idea of wine-making in a suitably dramatic setting, and we can taste some of the wines and buy bottles if we wish.

We walk to Place de Costa Rica and turn left into Rue Raynouard, which winds pleasantly along the hillside. Architecturally it is not of interest; it must have looked very different when Lauzun and Rousseau lived here. But **Balzac's house** at no. 47 still looks much as it did in his day, a comfortable country house with shutters. Balzac lived here from 1840 to 1847 and the house is open to the public. The walls are covered with caricatures of the novelist, so that we feel his personality strongly. Of interest is his study with his chair and table; we can imagine him sitting there, working in non-stop bouts day and night, pressed on by debt and fortified by black coffee; and then going to relax on Ile Saint-Louis.

Balzac wrote to a friend, Mme. Hanska, on 15 February 1845: 'Working means to me getting up every evening at midnight, writing until 8.00am, having breakfast in a quarter of an hour, working until 5.00pm, having dinner, going to bed, and then starting again next day'. In the France of the 35-hour week, this must seem a very odd letter.

The garden is charming, full of flowering trees and shrubs. On one wall is a bronze relief showing characters out of *La Comédie Humaine*, written here. On the other side we peer over into Rue Berton below us, an unexpected street with blank walls, ivy and old lamps; it is hard to believe that we are in Paris. Beyond, we have a good view of Château Lamballe, a fine eighteenth-century building, home of the Princesse de Lamballe, Marie Antoinette's best friend. Later it was a clinic for the insane; Dr Blanche tried to treat Maupassant's terminal syphilis here. It is now the Turkish Embassy.

At the end of Balzac's garden, no. 51–5, is a grim block built by Auguste Perret, the architect and town-planner. Here he lived and died (1954), much admired. His reinforced concrete pilasters still provoke controversy in art and architecture however.

Almost opposite, at no. 66, was the home of Benjamin Franklin from 1777 to 1785. During this time he was trying to forge an alliance between his new country, the United States of America, and Louis XVI's France. In between diplomacy and politics, he followed another of his interests, physics. On his house he installed the first lightning-conductor seen in France. It was not, presumably, his famous 'kite and key' but something more durable. The present building, about a hundred years old, has several television aerials, and it is difficult to see if it has a lightning-conductor as well.

We retrace our steps and at Rue de l'Annonciation turn left. We are in a quiet Passy street with little traffic and an old but much renovated chapel. At the end we arrive in **Place de Passy,** the old village square and hardly altered over the last centuries. We can sit under the trees of the open-air café or eat at the restaurant. Beside the square – a triangle, really –we find Rue de Passy, the old village street and one of the few shopping areas in the Seizième. One of its surprises, as it winds down the hill, is the way we keep seeing the Eiffel Tower almost in the street, although it is, of course, on the other side of the river. The shops are fashionable, as befits a rich neighbourhood, and we shall find smart boutiques with familiar names.

We can end our walk at Metro La Muette, but perhaps we would like to go farther, across Ranelagh Gardens to see the Marmottan Museum. The Ranelagh Gardens were originally created in the eighteenth century in imitation of the celebrated pleasure-gardens in London, owned by Lord Ranelagh. The present gardens (in Paris) were laid out in 1860, but they still have a very English feeling with their lawns and huge, unpollarded chestnuts. For children, there are donkey-rides, peepshows and sweet-stalls.

The **Marmottan Museum,** 2 Rue Louis Boilly, originally housed the collection, mainly paintings of the Napoleonic period, of Paul Marmottan, a civil servant and art collector, whose house it was. It is now known for its wonderful collection of Monets, most of them bequeathed to the museum by the artist's son in 1971. Here we can see the picture which gave its name to the movement, *Impression of Sunrise at Le Havre*; Gare Saint-Lazare in grey steam; the façade of Rouen Cathedral, one of the celebrated series, in bright sunlight; and Westminster on a murky evening. But most of the pictures are of his garden at Giverny on the Seine, a world of ponds, water-lilies, roses and trees.

The collection covers fifty years of Monet's life, from the *Impression of Sunrise* in 1872 to the final weeping-willow tree-trunks, those magical trees, in 1922. (Monet died in 1926.) We can follow his development from the time when Boudin suggested to him that he give up doing caricatures in Le Havre and look instead at the landscape and the sky. We watch him exploring light on water, or through mist or trees, until his final stage when he became more interested in the objects themselves, in the willow-trunks and the water-lilies. His pictures of these, dated 1920, are wild whirlpools, the lilies iridescent, painted in thick paint; full of energy, they are very different from his earlier quiet landscapes of the Seine valley. But they were sadly unsaleable; this at least has prevented the collection being dispersed.

Monet was once criticized for his lack of classical formalism, his lack of interest in perspective, his habit of leaving out the edge of the cathedral or the top of the palazzo. But then he also left out goddesses and plunging horses. Monet is now the public's favourite French painter; his greatness depends on his personal vision and his communication of it, rather than on having helped to start a new art movement.

There are other Impressionists in the Marmottan (which has 100 pieces): works by Renoir, Sisley, Caillebotte and Pissarro. But these are not their most luminous or famous works, for which we should go to the Musée d'Orsay.

The museum also houses the Wildenstein collection of European (mainly Flemish) thirteenth- and fourteenth-century illuminated manuscripts and miniature paintings (sadly, often cut from their original volumes). For lovers of this period, these are fine treasures, with startling, brilliant colours. But they make a weird contrast with the Impressionists a few yards away and one may feel that they would be better housed in the Louvre.

Our second walk is a shorter and simpler affair; just **Avenue du Président Wilson,** a dull street with a number of buildings by Perret. But it contains six important and varied museums and we shall need to be selective according to our interests. We start at Metro Trocadéro at the Place of the same name, on top of Chaillot hill.

This hill, overlooking the Seine, has always been thought a desirable place and many famous names are associated with it. Catherine de Medici built a country house here, later occupied by a licentious friend of Henri IV, who went to the Bastille for offending Richelieu. Later Henrietta of Orléans, daughter of Charles I of England, bought the house and turned it into a fashionable convent. Napoleon wanted to build a palace there for his son. Foch dominates Place du Trocadéro. The forgotten name is Trocadéro itself, an obscure fortress in Spain, besieged by the French in 1823; its capture was celebrated on this hill by order of Chateaubriand, minister of foreign affairs, who had organized the expedition into Spain.

The present **Palais de Chaillot** was built for the 1937 Paris Exhibition and consists of two curved low 'classical-style' buildings, wings to a central building which does not exist. The best that can be said for it is that it does not distract from the view, which is indeed remarkable. From the terrace we look across Trocadéro Gardens with their fountains and ornamental pool, across the Seine to the Eiffel Tower, the Champ-de-Mars and the Ecole Militaire. In the distance are the domes of old Paris and the high-rise towers of the modern age. The Trocadéro fountains are much admired, especially at night when they are floodlit; and the biggest displays of fireworks are let off here on 14 July and special festive occasions.

Apart from this scenery, Chaillot contains three museums and the Chaillot National Theatre which is underground, very large and modern, and is used for plays, concerts, operas, ballets and other cultural events.

The former Musée des Monuments Français (north wing) suffered a serious fire in the roof, caused by careless workmen. The contents were saved and the museum will reopen in November, 2000 as the **Cité de l'Architecture et du Patrimoine**, with the same contents as before, but in a new order. The reconstruction has been supervised by Jean-François Bodin, fresh from his revamping of the Centre Georges Pompidou. Over the museum door we read a quotation from Paul Valéry: 'The wonder-working hand of the artist is the equal and rival of his thought. The one is nothing without the other'. It is a remark much debated among artists.

Inside we find irremovable objects, such as frescoed ceilings, façades, arches, columns and portals, collected in replica from all over France, and we can enjoy many of the great treasures of the provinces.

The first sculptures of all (two great twelfth-century sculpted columns on either side as we enter the first room) are among the best. On the left, *Abraham sacrificing Isaac* defies any modern work in its vigour, terror and fantasy – yet the father and son cling to each other with real tenderness (central pillar from Souillac, Lot). On the right, *The Caryatids* (another central pillar, from Beaulieu de Corrèze) achieves another paradox: the weight seems too great for the figures to bear, yet the grace of the columns' lines gives a sense of calm strength.

The ground-floor rooms are well lit by skylights which allow daylight to play on the façades and figures. The works are shown in date order, but grouped by regions, so that we can get the distinct flavour of each time and place. We begin with the late eleventh century, the start of a great period of stone carving. Here we can see the huge portals of some of the twelfth-century cathedrals, still full of power and faith. Autun is here and the famous tympanum of the central narthex portal of Vézelay Abbey (c.1130). This great figure of Christ sending forth the Apostles seems to float as he stretches his (curiously big) hands towards us. Noteworthy are the carved foliage from Bourges Cathedral (1159) and huge Gothic figures from the west façade of Reims Cathedral (thirteenth century).

The Black Death (1348) and the Hundred Years' War ended this period; builders now built castles and sculptors made tombs. We next see a whole hall of tombs; a scale model shows us tombs of the kings at Saint-Denis, followed by replicas of some of them. Among them are two kings of England: Richard Cœur-de-Lion (d. 1199), a little unenthusiastically rendered, lies beside his mother, Eleanor of Aquitaine, and his father Henry II – an even more unflattering likeness. These come from Fontévault Abbey on Queen Eleanor's estates and perhaps the monks were admirers of Thomas Becket.

The famous soldier Du Guesclin (late fourteenth century) has two splendid tombs, an unusual achievement. The monks of Saint-Denis buried his body, but the enterprising church of Saint-Laurent-du-Puy-en-Vélay secured his entrails. The liver-and-lights tomb has the more vitality and shows Du Guesclin lying with a dog at his feet.

When prosperity returned in the fifteenth century, church building was resumed in a style which was beginning to be influenced by the Renaissance. The sixteenth-century sculpture is particularly delicate and beautiful, notably the carving from Limoges cathedral (1533) and perspective reliefs from the door of Beauvais south transept. Here are the well-known arch of the 'Grosse Horloge' in Rouen (1527) and a graceful fountain with dolphins and ribbons from Tours by François (1510). There are also works by the Renaissance sculptors Jean Goujon, Richier and Pilon; beautiful in themselves, they remind us how far art had moved from the fierce strength of the Middle Ages.

On the second floor (there are lifts) we can see seventeenth-, eighteenth- and nineteenth-century sculpture, including works by Pigalle and Houdon. They are mainly statues and busts in Græco-Roman poses and, if you wish to see a hundred togas, this is the place.

On the first and third floors are the frescoes. Whole vaulted ceilings and walls have been copied, mainly from churches of the fourteenth, fifteenth and sixteenth centuries, but including the oldest fresco in France, from the crypt of Saint-Germain Abbey, Auxerre (twelfth century). We may feel that frescoes transplant to a museum much less successfully than monumental sculpture, perhaps because they depend much more on their setting. Since the colours of the originals have faded with time, we have to make an effort of imagination to see these as they must once have been. However, they are worth studying, if we have time; they give us much insight into mediæval points of view.

Once again we feel the terrible impact of the Black Death, in a fourteenth-century fresco *Pestilence*, transfixing the congregation with a hail of arrows (Lavaudieu Church). There is also *Danse*

Macabre from La-Chaise-Dieu abbey church. We may contrast these with the fifteenth-century *Abundance*, showing a great feast. The most famous works are from Berzé-la-Ville, Vic and Cahors Cathedral. A long series, using the 'narrative-strip' teaching technique comes from Saint-Seine-l'Abbaye, near Dijon (1504). The most striking fresco is the huge *St Christopher* (Lassay, 1496), and the most charming the flying *Angel-musicians* from Kernascleden, Morbihan.

The **Musée de l'Homme** (south wing) presents the early remains of mankind and the cultures, from all over the world, of prehistoric and primitive societies, including present-day cultures still similar to the Stone Age. Diagrams and displays explain how men lived in ancient times and show their tools and earliest industries.

On the first floor, galleries deal with anthropology and fossils, early stone implements and so on. Here, near the entrance, we may see the skeleton of Cro-Magnon Man, the first European *Homo sapiens sapiens,* found in 1872 in the stalagmite grotto of the Grimaldi caves at Menton in the south of France. He is just like a modern Frenchman, except that the race may have been taller; he is 5 ft 10 ins, but was young and not fully grown; other skeletons found nearby were 6 ft 4 ins. He is at least 30,000 years old and lived at the time when the last ice age was receding. His body was covered with red ochre and he wore a crown of shells, and bracelets and anklets made of shells. He was buried with his tools and animal bones, suggesting a belief in life after death.

Homo sapiens skeletons of a similar date from Africa and Australia can be compared with Cro-Magnon Man. The museum points out that it was characteristic of them all to use artistic designs for their household objects and burial places, and to produce sculpture and mural paintings which indicate their religion.

Also on this floor are the *Hottentot Venus* and the ivory *Lespugue Venus*. There are fine collections of African art, of which the most exciting are probably the oldest, copies of prehistoric wall-paintings and photographs of rock-paintings from caves in the mountainous Ahaggar region of the Sahara. These are full of the same vitality as the rather similar Lascaux cave-paintings, of which small drawings and photographs are also shown on this floor, near the entrance.

The room of mediæval Christian Abyssinian murals is enjoyable. Figures of saints, somewhat Byzantine in style, have strong simple lines against a red background. Among the powerful Central African sculpture, we may note a huge drum carved with animals, from the Ivory Coast. It is in rich traditional local style, but must be fairly recent, since one of the figures carries a gun. The disappointing European section is at the end. It shows the survival of primitive art and customs through folk costumes, festivals and masks.

The second floor is mainly devoted to an excellent collection of pre-Columbian, Mayan and Aztec art, beginning on the staircase with a great carved stone relief from Mexico, the *Disc of the Sun* or *Aztec Calendar*, a wonderful work. Among figures of the god Quetzlcoatl, a massive statue from the Mayan civilization of Honduras dominates us; it seems curiously reminiscent of Asian styles, although so far away. Near it is the famous *Crystal Skull*, finely carved out of a single giant rock-crystal. Although this fascinates many people, we may feel grateful that the finders of the Koh-i-noor and Hope Diamonds did not feel a similar urge.

The most awe-inspiring exhibit in the museum is the gigantic replica of an Easter Island head, gazing upwards, originally carved in volcanic rock. The statue surmounted a platform for the lying-in-state of the dead. Also on the second floor are further exhibits from the Pacific and from the Arctic, but the Far East is poorly represented. There are also costumes from many lands.

Emphasis is on the homogeneity of mankind rather than on its diversity and notices are (perhaps deliberately) uninformative. But there is a completely individual work at the entry of the museum, a huge totem-pole carved from an entire British Columbian pine. This tells the legends of a North American chief's ancestors; one it seems, was hanged and another eaten by a crocodile. By any standards it is a splendid piece of sculpture.

The **Musée de la Marine** (south wing) is devoted to sea power, shipping, underwater exploration and the ports of France. These are shown by models, lifesize and scale, pictures, dioramas, souvenirs and films. French achievements are particularly emphasized, though the model of Columbus's *Santa Maria* is an obvious exception. Of special interest is a reconstruction of the removal of the Luxor obelisk from Egypt to Place de la Concorde. We shall also note Alain Bombard's sailing-raft *Hérétique,* if only for its name.

Following the museum's 250th anniversary in 1998, a new presentation was prepared for the year 2000 – *De la Gloire au Charles-de-Gaulle* – with emphasis on the modern French Navy, showing designs of the nuclear aircraft-carrier launched in 1997. The show is duplicated in eight naval ports such as Toulon and Brest. Further changes have been planned.

Leaving Trocadéro, we walk down Avenue du Président Wilson to Metro Iéna, the statue of George Washington and **Musée Guimet**. This was rebuilt for the year 2000, on the former site, and gained new acquisitions. It is the home in Paris of the art of Eastern Asia. It has 300,000 objects and related documents and a library of 100,000 works, plus 120,000 photographs and prints. Concerts are held here and there is a music department with listening booths. It is much visited by Asians as well as Parisians, and it was here that a group of Tibetan lamas came, when they were expelled from Tibet, to copy their sacred art and texts and re-establish their lost tradition.

This is a very carefully watched-over museum but, even so, some of the best items are considered too fragile or precious to be put on general view. If we are experts in this field and can produce convincing credentials, we should write in advance (English is spoken) to the conservator for permission to visit the reserve collection, especially the series of exquisite paintings of the life of Buddha, in the Tibetan Mandala.

We see Khmer gateways with carved pediments from North Cambodia. These date from the eleventh century. If we have seen the French portals of almost the same date in the nearby Palais de Chaillot, the different spirit of these carvings must strike us. Unlike the majestic but static French sculpture, the Khmer figures dance and clap. There are also Khmer heads of Buddha and a Shiva from Vietnam.

In the Lamaist collection we can admire very beautiful Tibetan and Nepalese banners, including the Mandala of Samvara. This is a mystic diagram, painted in gouache on textile, showing a square with four guarded doors within a double circle, presided over by the protecting but terrible god, Samvara. These banners cover a long span of time; one shows the Buddhist reforming monk Atisa (982–1055), another depicts the great fifth Dalai Lama (1617–82) receiving Chinese and Mongolian ambassadors. Among other objects we may note the dancing Dakini bronze.

Indian sculpture of many centuries is here from the third century BC onwards, including reliefs from North India and Hindu figures from the South. The museum attendants will point out to us the bronze sculpture of the Cosmic Dance (eleventh century) in the Dravidian style from South India. The god Shiva dances inside a circle of flames, symbolizing the Cosmos. With his foot he crushes a dwarf, symbol of the power chaining down souls.

The Chinese have an even longer history of art and their fine bronzes date back as far as 2000 BC. The massive gravity of the

Chinese style seems a constant feature of all periods, in contrast with the suppleness and rhythm of the Indian works. An interesting item is a great bronze ritual vase of the ninth century BC with intricate embossed patterns.

The *Bagram Treasure* from Afghanistan is a surprise here, because the small ivory or plaster figures and fragments are in the Hellenistic style of the first and second centuries BC, reflecting Greek influence at that date. They are Indian, not Afghan, but were dug up in 1937 on the site of the old Afghan capital, near Kabul.

There are fine collections of Chinese porcelain, mainly of the seventeenth and eighteenth centuries, and lacquer. The Buddhist banners are worth studying; the finest is a Korean fifteenth-century figure of Buddha, painted on silk.

In the Japanese section twelfth-century wooden figures and fourteenth-century paintings on silk have great dignity and severity. In a very different vein, a large painted and gilded *Screen of the Barbarians of the South* (end of the sixteenth century), depicts the arrival in Japan of a Portuguese ship, carrying gifts. The dignitaries are seen being received very stiffly by St Francis Xavier. The Elizabethan-style balloon-trousers and lace handkerchiefs evidently seemed very comical to the artist, who has caricatured the visitors.

Japan claims the oldest pottery yet discovered in the world, dating back to 10,000 BC. This find is too recent to be represented in Musée Guimet, because the works are kept in Japan, but a touring collection was shown in Paris in 1998, at the Japanese Cultural Centre, 101bis Quai Branly, Paris 75740 and aroused great interest. The French expert on ancient customs, Claude Lévi-Strauss, had already been fascinated by the prehistoric Jomon civilization, long before the present Japanese era, and wrote the preface for the catalogue, fully illustrated in colour, which may be seen at the cultural centre. He pointed out that these ancient people, who were hunters, fishermen and farmers and grew rice at a very ancient date, had, from the first, expert ceramics which were completely original. He called them 'exuberant-and-refined'. The development of their art can be followed, in rare isolation from other cultures, from its most primitive stage to its flowering in 2,500 BC. It was effaced by the later culture in about 300 BC, but handed on its tradition of using lacquer, extracted from trees, which later became such a well-known feature. Jomon art is notable for its jars decorated with flames; its enigmatic statuettes known as dogu, used in ritual, and its curious masks.

The **Palais de Tokyo** is the next museum we come to as we walk down Avenue du Président Wilson. A large double building built for the 1937 Exhibition, it resembles in design its contemporary, the Palais de Chaillot. On one side, it originally housed the National Museum of Modern Art, but its works were transferred to the Pompidou Centre at Beaubourg and the gallery was closed.

The left wing of the Palais de Tokyo, 11 Avenue du Président Wilson, is still called the **Museum of Modern Art of the City of Paris** (Metro Iéna) but only a small part of its permanent collection of late nineteenth- and twentieth-century art is now on view, in two ground-floor rooms, on a rotating basis. The rest of the building is used for temporary exhibitions, jazz concerts and so on, in an attempt to attract more young Parisian visitors. A 'Matisse Room' was opened in 1993. It has a collection of sixty paintings by Georges Rouault and rotates these. Sometimes it shows all sixty at once and we can then see that his talent was by no means limited to his well-known 'clown' style portraits of Christ.

We end our walk at Place de l'Alma, where we find the Seine and a metro station (Alma-Marceau). Here in one of the many cafés we can rest over a drink.

Our third and final walk in the Seizième is simply a stroll among the greenery of the **Bois de Boulogne** (Metros Porte Maillot, Porte Dauphine, Les Sablons, Porte d'Auteuil, Porte de Passy). Ideally it should be a ride but, if we cannot borrow a horse or a bicycle, we can always go by car or taxi and walk from our stopping-place. The bois is very large, over two thousand acres, and except for certain areas and certain days, we shall be able to find solitude, For many centuries it was a private royal park. Although it was opened to the public by Louis XIV, who hardly needed it, it did not become fashionable till later. The present bois is really the creation of Haussmann (of course!). He demolished the surrounding wall, landscaped the area with its lakes and riding tracks after the Hyde Park manner, and built some of the restaurants, the racecourses, and the main approach road, Avenue Foch (then the Empress's Avenue).

Those who like a *but de promenade* may like to visit the **Jardin d'Acclimatation** (Metro Sablons), an area for children with many amusements including a children's zoo, miniature railway, theatre and much else. Others may prefer the **Bagatelle** in the north-west of the bois (Metro Pont de Neuilly) with its shrubs, water-gardens, follies, rose-garden and glasshouses. The **Pré Catalan** area near the great waterfall attracts many people, not only for its café and restaurant, but for the copper beech, said to be nearly two hundred years old; and for the **Shakespeare Garden,** where all the trees and flowers are mentioned in his plays. Rather an academic method of gardening, one might think, but a remarkable example of Anglophilia. Shakespeare's plays, in English, are staged there. By ironic coincidence (given its plot), *The Comedy of Errors* was performed in 1983 while another performance in English was running in the gardens of the British Embassy, three miles away.

Or we may go there simply to eat. The tradition of dining in the bois has continued ever since the Second Empire. The most modest restaurant is in the middle of the Lac Inférieur, reached by rowing across. A romantic way to start and finish an evening.

The Bois de Boulogne is much associated with sport. At the southern end is Roland Garros tennis stadium, 2 Avenue Gordon Bennett (Metro Porte d'Auteuil), where the French Open Championships are held in May. A clay court tournament, it attracts all the big names and almost rivals Wimbledon in prestige. But it is easier to get into.

And horses. The bois is the headquarters of the Racing Club de France and the Société Hippique. But what bring the crowds are the two big racecourses. Auteuil (Metro Porte d'Auteuil) has the jumps, including a wide water-jump. Longchamp is the flat course, a blend of Epsom and Ascot, and the course is said to be hard (Metro Porte Maillot or Porte d'Auteuil). The big week of the year is at the beginning of October, the climax on the first Sunday with Prix de l'Arc de Triomphe. This is Europe's richest race and, unlike the Derby, it is not confined to three-year-old colts, so the choice is wider.

PART THREE

The Left Bank

14

The Latin Quarter

T HE LEFT BANK – la Rive Gauche – has a unique atmosphere and we are aware of it the moment we cross the river. The architecture (particularly nineteenth century), traffic and much of the to-and-fro may seem similar to other parts of Paris, yet we can tell the difference by looking at the shops and cafés and, especially, the people; they may not look happier than Parisians elsewhere, but they appear livelier and, in every sense, more colourful. The Left Bank is generally associated with youth, students, intellectuals, artists, books, poverty, freedom and a bohemian way of life – though in fact there are hundreds of thousands of people living on the Left Bank who have nothing to do with any of these things.

But the atmosphere remains, and with good reason. Anyone who has spent a term or a year at an art school or taken the short course in French Language and Civilization at the Sorbonne will always have nostalgic memories of that lost, unforgettable spring on the Left Bank. They will revisit their old haunts, look from the outside at their old window and wonder what has become of their one-time *copains*. For those of us who missed this experience, we can read and hear about it and, better still, try to rediscover its romance. As we stroll along the boulevards or the narrow streets, informally dressed and possibly munching pancakes, some of it will rub off on us. Henri Murger's novel *La Vie de Bohème,* and Puccini's opera based on it, not only publicized a lifestyle which had been going on for a very long time; both the author and the composer knew that they were on to a winner. (The word 'bohemian' in this connection comes from a double misunderstanding. The Left Bank 'bohemians' were vaguely identified with gypsies, who have a very different lifestyle; and all gypsies were thought to come from Bohemia.)

When the Roman city of Lutetia spread out from Ile de la Cité, it expanded mainly on to the Left Bank, towards the sun, towards Rome. Only a few ruins remain of this civilization and the real

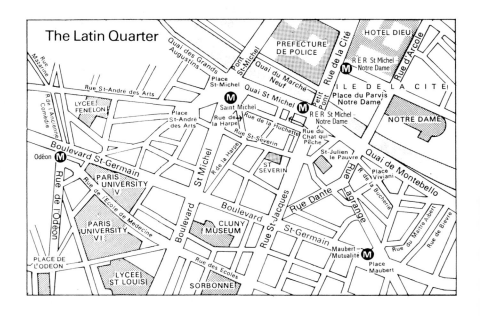

The Latin Quarter

history of the Left Bank began with the arrival of Christianity and the building of such abbeys as Cluny and Saint-Germain-des-Prés. It became the intellectual centre of Paris, of France and, arguably, of Europe. There were several causes: the removal of Abelard and his followers to the Cluny area; the foundation of the University of Paris (1215); the gift by St Louis of several houses to his confessor, Robert de Sorbon, for a theological college (1253); the first French printing works in the Sorbonne (1469); the founding of the Collège de France by François I in 1530. The whole area, the Latin Quarter, was ruled by the university (except the Collège de France, which has always retained a certain independence), and the university became a sort of autonomous state within Paris, strong enough to defy even the king, which it often did.

The university and printing press naturally attracted scholars, writers and in due course publishers, even if they had nothing to do with the university itself. Artists arrived at the end of the nineteenth century (whatever Murger may have imagined), attracted from Montmartre by the studios, art schools and cafés of Montparnasse. The musicians, however, remained faithful to the Right Bank, where they were nearer to the Conservatoire, the Salle Pleyel and the Opéra.

A good starting-place for our walk is Metro Maubert-Mutualité, on the edge of the most picturesque part of the area, the huddle of tiny streets between the Seine and Boulevard Saint-Germain and, east to west, between Place Maubert and Place Saint-Michel; the term Latin Quarter is sometimes applied exclusively to this part. Not that we are likely to hear any Latin here now. Apart from French, the most common languages spoken are from North Africa, the eastern Mediterranean and south-east Asia. Every other house seems to be a small restaurant serving the meals of faraway places. In between are small grocers (*épiciers*) selling exotic food and spices. The little streets reek of couscous. We could be in Tunis or old Saigon or, come to that, Soho.

Many of the streets are now closed to traffic and are a pedestrian precinct. This makes our exploration on foot pleasanter, though not necessarily safer. French policemen do not pound a beat and there has been a marked increase in pestering, drug-pushing and petty crime. But then there have always been perils in the Latin Quarter. The archetypal hero was not only the imaginary operatic Rodolfo, romantic, feckless and harmless; there are plenty like him still on the Left Bank and they are not always French; there was also the real François Villon, the fifteenth-century poet, violent criminal and master of arts at the Sorbonne. His poems and ballads were written in French, not Latin, and are extraordinarily vivid and direct, even today. But his memory should not deter us from our walk and we are unlikely to come to any harm in daylight.

Place Maubert was for centuries a place to be avoided, full of crime and such entertainments as public executions. Later it became the skid row of Paris, the haunt of drunken *clochards.* Now it is a respectable shopping area, architecturally uninteresting, but with a lively open-air market (mornings only on Tuesdays, Thursdays and Saturdays). The name Maubert is possibly a corruption of Maître Albert, a Dominican teacher at the university, who held his classes in the open air.

A number of small streets lead down to the river. In Rue de Bièvre was the private home of President Mitterrand. In Rue du Maître Albert we find a small animal clinic, the Paris branch of the PDSA and the gift of the Duke of Windsor to his adopted city. But we shall probably walk along Rue de la Bûcherie westwards to Square Viviani. This is a delightful garden with benches, truncated columns, acacias and a wonderful view of Notre-Dame across the river.

Behind the square is the small church of **Saint-Julien-le-Pauvre.** Many chapels have stood on this site; the present church is contemporary with Notre-Dame. It has no transepts, no stained glass or organ, but we can admire the Gothic vaulting in the aisles. The chancel, the east end, is rumoured to be very fine, but is shut off from our eyes by an iconostasis, a wall of icons and hanging lamps. For nearly a hundred years the church was the centre of the Greek-Catholic church in Paris, but it was originally intended as a church for the poor. It was named after the mediæval bishop of Le Mans, St Julien, who gave everything he had to the poor. Poorboxes abound in the church and it has for many centuries been the chapel of Hôtel-Dieu across the river; it is used especially for pauper funerals.

Continuing along Rue de la Bûcherie we find an English-language bookshop, Shakespeare and Company. This is named after (but not connected with) the celebrated bookshop in Rue de l'Odéon which no longer exists where Sylvia Beach provided a home-from-home, and often subsidies, for hungry British and American writers of the twenties and thirties.

We reach Rue Saint-Jacques, a big straight street built on the old Roman road, cutting like a knife through the Latin Quarter. Unlike most roads, which lead to Rome, this one was supposed to lead to Spain, to Santiago, Saint James of Compostela, hence the name. In fact it leads to Porte d'Orléans. Confusingly, the part nearest to the river, where we now stand, is called Rue du Petit Pont. We cross the street and, walking away from the Seine, find Rue de la Parcheminerie, a narrow street where parchment was made and sold. Leading off it is another pleasant garden, beside the cloisters of **Saint-Séverin.** The church, one of the finest in Paris, was for many centuries the parish church of the Left Bank and is now, officially, the university church. There is some dispute about which St Séverin it is named after; a hermit who lived on the site in the sixth century and who persuaded Clodoald (St Cloud), grandson of King Clovis, to become a priest; or a Swiss namesake; or the sixth-century philosopher Boethius, who was partly responsible for introducing Aristotle's works and thinking into Catholic theology. Some of his writings were translated into Anglo-Saxon by King Alfred. Boethius was eventually executed, declared a martyr and canonized as St Severinus.

The west façade is Romanesque, although the door comes from the thirteenth-century Saint-Pierre-aux-Bœufs on Ile de la Cité, now demolished. The church, however, is mainly late Gothic, complete with gables and monstrous gargoyles which overhang the street. It is a curious building, as broad as it is long, without any transepts. Inside, only the first three columns have capitals and some of the arches at the east end were transformed into rounded late seventeenth-century arches on the orders of La Grande Mademoiselle; she had quarrelled with Saint-Sulpice and had transferred her devotions and her wealth to Saint-Séverin. Happily her influence did not last long.

The great glory of the church is the ambulatory behind the altar. A double row of slender columns, the centre one twisted, rise into the tracery of the vaulted ceiling and we seem to be wandering through a garden of fountains made of stone. There are no distant views; we are lost in a Gothic forest. A jarring note, however, is introduced by the modern windows by Jean Bazaine, who also did some mosaics for the UNESCO building. His original sketches were much admired for the way in which he followed and complemented the Gothic columns. But the final effect is something else. The two blue windows, which can be seen from the nave, are dark and tolerable, but the four shocking-pink windows distract, I think, from the beauty of the church. A good time to see the ambulatory is late on a dark November afternoon, when the columns are lit and the windows have disappeared. But on a fine summer morning lovers of stained glass can console themselves by looking up from the nave at the fine late fifteenth-century glass in the clerestory. Bazaine, a leading figure in twentieth-century French glass, was more successful elsewhere.

The church has a good organ and is a centre for choral music. Concerts are often given by visiting choirs.

Returning to Rue Saint-Jacques, we turn towards the river and then left into the famous **Rue de la Huchette** – the 'Narrow Street' of Elliot Paul's famous book – though in fact an even narrower street turns off it, Rue du Chat qui Pêche, the narrowest street in Paris and a sad, almost windowless alley. Fortunately it is quite short and there is the quay at the end.

Rue de la Huchette, by contrast, was known for centuries for its luxury, though luxurious is hardly a word we should use about it now. But it is pretty enough and full of excitement. This is an area known for nightclubs and jazz cellars, making use, rather gruesomely, of the old dungeons. We find the small Théâtre de la Huchette, where a double bill of one-act plays by Ionesco (*The Bald Primadonna* and *The Lesson*) has been running non-stop since 1957, beating records for the world's longest run. We should also note no. 10 where a young Brigadier-General Bonaparte, unemployed and unpaid, existed for several months in 1795, not yet on the road to glory. At the corner of Rue de la Harpe we are in the heart of the souk; it is the moment, perhaps, for a cup of very black thick coffee.

We emerge on to the large Place Saint-Michel, a nineteenth-century square complete with a large statue and fountain of St Michael which students climb and plaster with posters. The square teems with people and traffic; it is the junction of the quay and Boulevard Saint-Michel, the main street of the Latin Quarter. Across on the far side we find a smaller square, Place Saint-André-des-Arts, a much older extension of the main square. It is a picturesque place, with its pavement cafés, and the restaurants provide French and Alsace food – we have left the Orient behind.

We follow the narrow Rue Saint-André-des-Arts, which is also a pedestrian precinct. At its end we are at a crossroads; ahead is Marché de Buci. On the right is **Rue Mazarine,** which has a nice view of the dome of the institute; on the left is Rue de l'Ancienne Comédie. At no. 12 Rue Mazarine the young Molière made his first stage appearance. With the help of an inheritance, he reorganized the existing small company, built a theatre on the disused tennis court and in effect founded the Comédie-Française.

After Molière's death (1673) the company continued under the direction of his widow, but in 1688 they were driven out by the teachers at the Institut college, who did not care for the near proximity of actors, and rather irreverent ones at that. Madame Molière found another tennis court at no. 14 Rue de l'Ancienne Comédie, which is really the same street, and in 1689 the theatre opened with Racine's *Phèdre* and Molière's *Le Médecin Malgré Lui.* The company remained there till 1770, when it moved to the Tuileries Palace Theatre. A notice outside no. 14 reminds us of Molière and the early days of the Comédie-Française.

Facing us at no. 13 is the old *Café Procope,* perhaps the oldest in Paris. It was for centuries the place where people went to hear the latest news and gossip and it was particularly busy during the years which preceded the Revolution. A plaque on the wall recalls some of the famous names, politicians and writers, who were clients of the café, and among them we may note Benjamin Franklin (the American envoy to France during the Peace of Versailles, 1783), Robespierre, Danton. Marat and Bonaparte. It was a centre of revolutionary thought. It was also a literary café, used by La Fontaine, Rousseau, Voltaire, Diderot and many others until the present day. A name missing from the plaque is Oscar Wilde, who drank there with the poet Verlaine. Poor old Verlaine, far over the hill, would sit there hoping that the prestigious Englishman would buy him another absinthe – something that Wilde unkindly sometimes failed to do. Later, after his own fall, Wilde would sit there hoping that someone would speak to him and buy him a drink. The *Procope* is now a restaurant. Its décor has been preserved in eighteenth-century style, and it has a mixed clientele.

We can stroll along the street to Carrefour de l'Odéon, the square where many streets meet Boulevard Saint-Germain. It is surrounded by cafés, cinemas, and bookshops selling medical textbooks; the Ecole de Médecine is at the east end. The *carrefour* is dominated by the bulky statue of Danton, calling in his best orator's style for more audacity and education and gazing enthusiastically towards the *Procope*.

Crossing the boulevard we continue up Rue de l'Odéon to Place de l'Odéon, a half-moon-shaped square of simple 1780 houses and several restaurants. Facing us across the 'half-moon' is the colonnaded façade of **Théâtre de l'Odéon,** one of the national theatres of Paris. It was built in 1782, in the neo-classical style then fashionable, to provide a more suitable home for the Comedians in the Tuileries Palace. The new 'Théâtre Français' was possibly the last artistic achievement of the reign of Louis XVI. The company did well for ten years, but the Revolution split it. Some became Republicans and moved to a new theatre on the Right Bank, the present Comédie-Française. The others went to the guillotine.

After the Revolution the theatre had a sad time. It was damaged by fire (and reconstructed), then used by failing companies for their productions. It was too far off the beaten track for the theatre-goers of the Belle Époque. Its revival started after World War Two, when it became the theatre of Jean-Louis Barrault, his wife Madeleine Renaud and their company. They produced modern plays, particularly by Claudel, Beckett, Ionesco, Genet, Albee, Sarraute – and Shakespeare. It was the most crowded theatre in Paris; the productions and acting were famous, particularly Claudel's *Partage de Midi* with Barrault and Edwige Feuillère.

All this came brutally to an end in the student riots of May 1968, when the theatre was occupied. The subsequent goings-on made good copy for journalists, but caused a good deal of damage to the theatre, scenery and costumes, and to the company itself, which was once again divided politically. It is now an ordinary theatre, belonging to the state, playing the French classics, mainly to school groups. What it really needs is a new Barrault – or Molière.

Beyond the theatre we are at the Luxembourg Gardens. We can either enter, or turn left along Rue de Medicis to Boulevard Saint-Michel. Or we can return, exploring various side streets on the way, to Danton's statue and the metro (Odéon).

214

15

Montagne Sainte-Geneviève

MONTAGNE SAINTE-GENEVIEVE (Metro Maubert-Mutualité) dominates the Left Bank. Not exactly a mountain, yet surprisingly steep in some streets, it was an obvious point both for worship and defence; in due course it became a centre of learning. On its north side, towards the Seine, we can number the Sorbonne, the medical and law schools, several schools devoted to technical subjects such as mining, the Collège de France, three large lycées (secondary schools) and the site of the Ecole Polytechnique, France's most prestigious centre of higher education. The summit of the mountain is the Panthéon, once the church of Sainte-Geneviève, patron saint of Paris. Soufflot's graceful dome, surrounded by a ring of columns, floats above the Left Bank and the city, a worthy crown.

Along the eastern flank of the Montagne runs the well-known **Boulevard Saint-Michel** – do not call it the 'Boul Mich', unless you want to sound very old. Metro Saint-Michel makes a convenient starting-place for our walk. This is the street of students, careworn young people in jeans and sweaters and raincoats, carrying large folders and paperback books. The boulevard is lined with bookshops, cafés and, surprisingly, shoe shops. The cafés, with their sandwiches and pinball machines are cheap and full of rather solitary young people, sitting and spinning out a cup of coffee in the warm while they write their papers; if we glance over their shoulders, it often seems to be algebra. For recreation they play at the pinball tables, which will cost them as much as another coffee or even a glass of beer.

The liveliest period is October, the *rentrée des classes,* when the street and the bookshops are full of people buying books and pencil-sharpeners, getting ready for the new academic year. They will have spent their summer with their families or lying quite broke on a sunny beach or, more probably, working in a restaurant. It is also the

Montagne Ste-Geneviève
& The Luxembourg

time of year for changing girlfriends. The idea of the *rentrée* has spread now to the whole of Paris – the party season, conversations about summer holidays in distant parts, autumn fashions, the vintage, cars, the new oysters. But it is not quite like that in Boulevard Saint-Michel.

The boulevard saw those famous riots of May 1968, when students burnt cars, broke shop windows, cut down trees as barricades and threw cobblestones at the police. Marxism and anarchism still thrive in the area, judging from the leaflets lying on the ground, but several 'students' afterwards admitted publicly that they were never at any college, and even at the time it seemed that some of them were rather elderly for the part. Anyway, the trees were replanted, the cobblestones covered with tarmac and the boulevard went back to its normal studiousness.

Leaving Metro Saint-Michel, we go southwards through the crowds, pausing perhaps to buy a newspaper from some other country, most of which are available in this area. Crossing Boulevard Saint-Germain, we have a garden, some Roman ruins, a sixteenth-century *hôtel* and museum, the Musée National du Moyen Age, Thermes de Cluny, to which we shall return at the end of this chapter.

At **Place de la Sorbonne** we can pause for a moment for breath. The square has been reconstructed for those on foot, lined with cafés, cleared of parked cars, and decorated with lime trees. At the end is the façade and dome of the Sorbonne Chapel, to which we shall also return. We can also consider the ornate statue of Auguste Comte (1798-1857), the Positivist (Humanist) philosopher admired by John Stuart Mill. His mottoes *'Famille, Patrie, Humanité'*, and *'Ordre et Progrès'* make the ideas of the nineteenth century seem more comfortable than our own. Surprisingly, he was dismissed from his post as examiner in mathematics at the Ecole Polytechnique for his 'revolutionary' theories.

Boulevard Saint-Michel meets the Luxembourg Gardens at a busy square (Place Edmond Rostand, Metro Luxembourg). On our left stood once the celebrated student café, *Capoulade*. We turn left here and climb Rue Soufflot to the **Panthéon.**

There have been holy buildings on the summit of the Montagne since time immemorial; since the sixth century they have usually been dedicated to Ste Geneviève. But in the eighteenth century her abbey and church were in ruins and Louis XV, who was seriously ill, vowed that, if he should recover, he would build a noble church in her honour. He duly recovered and the task was entrusted to

Germain Soufflot, who had royal connections through Madame de Pompadour. His ideas were grandiose indeed, in size and height: a gigantic classical temple with a dome under which the tomb of the saint would lie. But both time and money ran out and Soufflot never saw his dome. It was completed by his pupil Rondelet in 1789, the very eve of the Revolution.

It was soon declared a Temple of Fame, a great atheistic building fit to receive the bodies of great men who had died in the time of French liberty. It became a church again under Napoleon I, a necropolis in 1830, a church again in the Second Empire, and finally once more a necropolis for the great men of France who have been outside conventional religion. Auguste Comte's idea of replacing the calendar of saints with another dedicated to scientists and scholars finds its temple here, but politics tend to come to the fore. We can visit the tombs of Rousseau, Voltaire, Victor Hugo, Emile Zola, Braille, Jean Jaurès (left-wing politician and orator, assassinated in 1914) and Jean Moulin, the Resistance leader in the Second World War, tortured to death in the Occupation. André Malraux's remains were transferred here in 1996.

To describe all these men as atheists is much too simple. It would be more accurate to call them 'Free Thinkers', in the widest sense. Victor Hugo was anti-clerical, for political reasons in his time. Yet he wrote 'The religions pass. God remains'. André Malraux, too, was a man of many facets. He was thought to be a Communist because of his involvement in the Spanish Civil War, but many people supported the Republican side who were not Communists. Malraux accepted the post of minister of culture in General de Gaulle's government. He was also a faithful patron of the contemporary 'Salon d'Art Sacré' in Paris and went round the show every year, talking to the artists. He liked abstract meditations, and praised the salon in his memoirs.

Elaborate though some of the monuments are, they seem rather lost in the vast expanse of the building. The Panthéon received a boost to its prestige when President Mitterrand in 1981 on his Inauguration Day visited it to pay homage to Jaurès and Moulin. He left Notre-Dame till the following day. It was thought that he would be buried here, as he had said that he was an agnostic, but in his last years he acquired a grave-plot in a country churchyard, like de Gaulle, thus tacitly rejoining the church. His state funeral was held, with full pomp, in Notre-Dame, conducted by Cardinal Lustiger.

Renovation for the year 2000 was undertaken, to give access to the upper part of the building, leading to a terrace and a complete tour of the outside of the dome, with a view of Paris all round. Another innovation was the installation of 'Foucault's Pendulum', advertised as 'Come and see the Earth turn'. This is a metal ball, suspended from a height, which runs, by itself, round a wide circular track, demonstrating that the earth revolves on its own axis.

Below its dome the Panthéon is a grim building, better seen from a distance. The blank walls dominate the square like a prison and the super-colossal columns of the portico are of a grandeur which was never Rome. But standing under them, feeling dwarfed rather than uplifted, we can enjoy a fine view down the mountain, across the Luxembourg Gardens and palace to the Eiffel Tower. Framing the view are two symmetrical façades, also by Soufflot, now occupied by the local *mairie* and law school.

One of the great men of the area (and, indeed, of France) is not honoured in the Panthéon, though a street leading off the Place is named after him. **King Clovis of the Franks** (466-511) was without doubt the founder of France and of much else in Europe. He defeated the Romans at Soissons and so ended the Roman Empire in Gaul, though the Romans, compromising, gave him the title of proconsul. He fought off invasions from the East and incorporated dissident provinces into his new kingdom. Hard and ruthless, he gave France its own identity, based on Paris; a man of great ability, he organized the government and codified the laws. His conversion to Christianity by his wife, Clotilde of Burgundy, and Ste Geneviève, gave a new impetus to the young kingdom. His success in fusing the Teutonic and Gallic cultures started French civilization and finally produced, it can fairly be said, the modern Frenchman.

He built a large church on the summit of the Montagne, where the famous Lycée Henri IV now stands, and where he, his wife and Ste Geneviève were buried. The saint soon became the personality of the Montagne and there were big processions in her honour through the streets, with elaborate decorations, bells and a vast crowd. These processions continued for centuries, until they were firmly suppressed by the Revolution.

The church attracted a monastery and then became an abbey, so rich and powerful that it was ripe for looting. Nothing remains now except cellars and the belfry, known as Clovis's Tower, though it was of course built long after his time. The relics of Ste Geneviève were moved opposite to Saint-Etienne-du-Mont; the whereabouts of the remains of the king and queen are unknown.

The church of **Saint-Etienne-du-Mont** (Metro Cardinal Lemoine) is one of the finest Gothic churches in Paris. Originally the parish church of the abbey servants, it was rebuilt in the sixteenth century, starting with the belfry. A hundred years later in 1619, Queen Margot, the first wife of Henri IV, laid the foundation stone of the façade and the church was finally consecrated in 1626. The façade is indeed remarkable with its triple pediment. The east end, the chancel, is late Gothic in style; the windows of the nave were altered later to the rounded Renaissance manner.

Inside, it is tall, with elaborate late Gothic vaulting and a hanging keystone. The eye is immediately taken by the rood screen, the only one surviving in Paris because, being basically an arch, it did not cut off the altar from the congregation. On either side two beautiful spiral staircases (late sixteenth century) lead to the top of the rood screen and to the extensions towards the chancel. The organ is big and it makes a great sound at recitals, weddings and other big events. We should also notice the stained glass, particularly on the right side, where the gold and deep red glimmer in the dusk. The shrine of Ste Geneviève attracts much attention and many candles. Plaques also mark the burial places of the remains of Pascal and Racine. Marat, after a brief stay in the Panthéon, is buried in the charnel cloister, beyond the chancel. Before leaving the church we should also look at the wooden pulpit (1650), which is supported by a statue of Samson. Is he, we may wonder, about to pull down the whole church, or merely the pulpit and preacher? A slab marks the spot where an archbishop of Paris was killed by an unfrocked priest.

Re-crossing Rue Clovis, we are back at **Lycée Henri IV.** This is a pleasant building, dating from Napoleonic times, hardly integrated with its Gothic belfry. It was here, when it was a monastery under the rule of the abbot of Cluny, Peter the Venerable, that Abelard was given shelter after he fled from the Notre-Dame cloister and where he wrote his greatest works (see also p. 10). Dramatic though his private life may have been, it is his philosophical thinking which has given him his place in history. Neither the first nor last philosopher to be accused of blasphemy, he was certainly the first of the modern school.

Abelard, although himself a religious believer, contended that Reason cannot lead to results at variance with Revelation and that dialectics must therefore be used in the service of theology. This amounted to saying 'I understand in order that I may believe', in opposition to St Augustine's famous approach *'Credo ut intelligam'*

– 'I believe in order that I may understand'. By putting intellect first, before faith, Abelard became the founder of mediæval philosophy in France and was in line with later French thinkers, right through to the present day.

Farther down Rue Clovis we meet Rue Descartes. Whether **René Descartes** (1596–1650) ever lived there himself is doubtful; it was a street of brothels, la Rue des Bordels. But he was in Paris, on the Montagne, from 1613 to 1619 and again in 1625. His thinking, however, gained him no support either moral or in his livelihood, and he was forced to emigrate to Holland and finally to Sweden, where he had several admirers, among them Queen Christina. France, nevertheless, claims him as her greatest philosopher.

Descartes based philosophical reasoning on the principles and methods of mathematics, refusing to make any initial metaphysical assumptions. Instead, he took his own sense-experience as his *point de départ* in the well-known phrase: *'Cogito ergo sum'* – 'I think therefore I am'. He wrote three works in which he tried to prove by reasoning the existence of God (he was educated in a Jesuit college). This brought him under attack from both sides.

Forgetting philosophy for the moment, we turn right into Rue Descartes. On the left we can note the house where the poet Verlaine died in 1896; it is marked by a plaque and by a conspicuous sign, La Maison de Verlaine. Turning sharply left into Rue Thouin and immediately right into Rue du Cardinal Lemoine, we are at no. 74, where another plaque indicates that Hemingway and his first wife lived for several years here in the 1920s.

We are now in a picturesque little square, surrounded by cafés and shops. **Place de la Contrescarpe** (Metro Place Monge) has been cleaned up a good deal since Hemingway's description of it in *A Moveable Feast*. The bus stop, the public urinals and the *clochards* have gone, yet it and its frequenters still retain a certain atmosphere of seediness which some find attractive. Leading out of it is **Rue Mouffetard,** a narrow pretty street full of shops, cafés and art galleries, much painted and photographed. Many of the houses are old and marked by carved signs and two quiet passages lead off the street, where we can for a moment escape the bustle. The Pot-de-Fer fountain at no. 60, in Italianate style, was constructed for Marie de Medici as an overflow from the aqueduct which was to bring water to her new palace in the Luxembourg Gardens (see p. 234). At no. 53 a hoard of 3,500 gold coins was discovered in 1938, each bearing the head of Louis XV. They had been hidden there by the royal counsellor, Louis Nivelle, obviously an able and thrifty man in that extravagant age.

We return to Place de la Contrescarpe for a pause and a drink, probably at *La Chope*, two Hemingway cafés now joined together. Facing us is the site of the *Pomme du Pin* cabaret, mentioned by Rabelais and existing until the 1970s. Its songs, I recall, had a strong Resistance and anti-German flavour, long after the Liberation of France.

We walk back down Rue du Cardinal Lemoine. At no. 67, in an earlier house on the site, Pascal died in 1662. Next door is Foyer Sainte-Geneviève, a girls' hostel. This is a fine building and was for many centuries the **Scottish College**, the centre of Scottish Catholicism in France. The neo-classical chapel on the first floor once held, as its principal relic, the brain of King James II of Great Britain, who died in exile in Saint-Germain-en-Laye in 1701.

Turning into Rue Clovis, we find the pavement, narrow enough all the way, almost blocked by the ruins of King Philippe-Auguste's fortress wall. Over thirty feet high and thick in proportion, it reminds us that in the twelfth century Paris was indeed a fortified city and its walls were something invaders had to reckon with. On our right are the massive buildings of what used to be the Ecole Polytechnique. This is still France's prestige college; its members wear on occasions glittering uniforms and give an annual ball at the Opéra. Among its distinguished members we may note Auguste Comte, Foch, Jean Borotra the tennis champion and a great favourite at Wimbledon, André Citröen, the car designer, and President Giscard d'Estaing. Much attacked for its élitism, it moved to the suburbs, and the buildings on the Montagne are renamed Institut Auguste Comte, seeking, perhaps, a change of image.

We make our way back to the Panthéon. At the corner of Rue Valette we can see the Bibliothèque Sainte-Geneviève, a nineteenth-century building. Originally the Montaigu College, it was famous through the centuries for its learning, its collection of manuscripts and its lice, fleas and bugs. Only those with readers' passes are admitted.

Turning right down Rue Victor-Cousin or even Boulevard Saint-Michel, we are back again at Place de la Sorbonne (Metro Luxembourg), dominated by the **chapel of the Sorbonne.** It was built by Mercier for Richelieu, who had appointed himself chancellor of the university, and is a fine example of seventeenth-century architecture, the columns, pediments and the dome blending with the Gothic spirit which always lay underneath. More imposing is the north façade overlooking the courtyard of the Sorbonne, with its Corinthian columns, its pediment and, of course, the dome. Inside, the church is of neo-classical design and no longer used for services (except for one mass a year for the soul of Richelieu, but no one seems to know exactly when it is said). It is used mainly for exhibitions, which are usually well worth seeing. The cardinal's red hat hangs from the ceiling and will remain there, the story goes, until his soul is released from Purgatory, when it will fall to the ground. He was condemned to long purgation, it is said, for his sin in supporting the Protestants in the Thirty Years' War. The story is popular even among the ecumenically minded and no doubt the hat has been firmly wired up, to continue the legend.

The Sorbonne was strongly anti-Protestant until the Revolution; nowadays religion plays only a small part in student talk. Many of the students are Marxists, Moslems or Buddhists, or a blend of these beliefs. 'Againstism' has always been part of the Sorbonne: anti-Protestant, anti the king, anti-authority, in particular the civil power in Paris, and even at times anti-France. During the Hundred Years' War it supported the English and the Burgundians against the French, even to the extent of sending one of its best orators, Bishop Cauchon, to Rouen to prosecute Joan of Arc.

It is sad that nothing remains of Richelieu's Sorbonne, apart from the church. But it was, of course, far too small for the horde of students who now study there. The building, now unromantically renamed **Université de Paris IV,** has as its centre the big courtyard, where students talk and pass in the open or, if it is raining, under the arches. We are free to enter, walk about and talk to anyone we like. But, apart from the façade of the church, the nineteenth-century building is dreary indeed; as the main courtyard of a great university it can scarcely be compared with, say, the Great Court of Trinity College, Cambridge. The building manages to house a large number of amphitheatres, smaller lecture rooms, offices for the teaching staff, laboratories, an astronomical observatory and so on. The amphitheatres (large lecture halls) are rather sad places, difficult acoustically for both speaker and listener (I have been both).

Nevertheless the main courtyard has had its dramatic moments, and will no doubt have many more. During the 'events' of May 1968 when the university was occupied by the students and others, it was, so to speak, open to the public. It was a centre of revolution. When I had had enough of exploring, of reading leaflets on how to make

Molotov cocktails, of posters of Trotsky and Guevara and the scratched record of the 'Internationale', it was interesting to read graffiti on the walls. Two of them stay in my mind: 'Father a kid to carry on the struggle', and 'Invent new sexual positions'; which, between them, may explain the virtual disappearance of the girls from the riots after the first week or so.

We make our way through imposing corridors to the front of the building, down the main steps into Rue des Ecoles. In front of us is a statue of Montaigne, a pleasant garden where we can sit for a moment of quiet, and beyond it the old stones and plane trees of Hôtel de Cluny, which we shall soon visit. But, first, we should turn right, cross Rue Saint-Jacques and look at the outside at least of the **Collège de France.**

This has a long past reaching back into the Roman era, part of the Cluny establishment, but it sank during the Middle Ages in scholarship and reputation. It was revived in the sixteenth century by François I, who wanted a rival to the Sorbonne. Twelve King's Scholars, paid by the king, were free to study and teach whatever they liked, including such forbidden and pagan writers as Virgil. Thereafter it prospered, especially in the seventeenth century when many new subjects were added, including French, as contrasted with classical, literature.

The façade is mainly eighteenth century, by Chalgrin, and is pleasant enough with its statue of Claude Bernard and its unpollarded trees. Behind the façade there has been much rebuilding in the following two centuries. It is not primarily a centre for undergraduates and we may compare similar colleges in England, perhaps All Souls', Oxford. The collège has had many distinguished members: Claude Bernard, who did great research on the working of the human liver; Joliot-Curie, who split a uranium particle; Ampère, the physicist; Henri Bergson, the philosopher; Paul Valéry, the poet; and most recently Claude Lévi-Strauss, long-time professor of anthropology and one of the founders of Structuralism, a twentieth-century French philosophy.

If you think that there has been rather a lot of philosophy in this chapter, it should be remembered that philosophy plays a much more important part in French life than it does in British, where it is considered something of a specialist interest. Every schoolchild in France studies 'philo' as a normal part of education, often in some depth. Many have written essays on Descartes or Bergson, and Structuralism started naturally on the Montagne, though it later spread to many other countries, especially to Cambridge and Yale. This does not mean that the woman in front of you in the queue for cheese or fish and talking endlessly to madame is discussing post-Structuralism; she is probably giving the gory details of her sister's illness. But her children will be familiar with philosophy and we have only to talk to the local bookseller or overhear conversation in nearby *Brasserie Balzar* to get the point.

Paris is not only a city of art and architecture, of politics and revolutions, of people and good food and sex. It is also a city of ideas, as Athens was in its time, which at heart are the basis for all else. To understand Paris and the French people, and to converse with them, it is a good idea to have a little knowledge of 'philo', even if it is rather sketchy. And so – a quick look at Structuralism.

Structuralism, briefly defined as the search for 'structures' in human behaviour and institutions, applied recently developed mathematical structures to analyses of thought and behaviour. It was claimed as a blueprint for the future of the social sciences, while laying much stress on the past, studying the habits of primitive tribes still living in Stone Age cultures. Its trendy disciples enjoyed interpreting contemporary mores in terms of anthropology, in particular the habits of Brazilian Indians.

A clue to the attitudes of Lévi-Strauss may be found in his early enthusiasms for geology and Marxism. His 'structures' seemed to inherit a certain rigidity from both these disciplines, since developments of thought were claimed to be 'inevitable'. And so his followers saw the French intellectual tradition, traced through the thinking of Descartes, Rousseau, Auguste Comte, Durkheim and Bergson, as a continuous stream and producing inevitably (and with considerable hindsight) such philosophers as Lévi-Strauss and his fellow Structuralists, Jean Piaget, the child-psychology theorist, who had such an influence on modern education, and Roland Barthes, the literary critic.

Michel Foucault (d.1984), in his well-known book *Les Mots et les Choses,* followed the Structure theme. He decided, arbitrarily, that the essential functions of language (any language) are Articulation, Designation, Derivation and Attribution. These he depicted in the form of a diamond-shaped quadrilateral and then claimed that his diagram marked out the possible structure of any science, notably natural history, which is the main subject *of Les Mots et les Choses.*

Descartes and Comte would certainly have approved of Lévi-Strauss's and Foucault's zeal for mathematical method, but Structuralism was attacked during the upheavals of 1968 by the

225

Trotskyists and anarchists for attempting to find a pattern in life where none should exist.

Structuralism was already being undermined since Deleuze had brought Nietzsche back to the French scene in 1962. This appeared to offer an escape from the two traditional camps, simplified in the public's mind as 'It's all in the mind; what seems to be *is*' (sometimes leading students to drugs, where 'a good trip' became their only reality) and the mechanistic view, going back to Spinoza 'it's bound to happen anyway. One thing follows another – you can't stop it', which led many students to a sense of futility, and to suicide. Nietzsche appeared to bring back the possibility of individual intervention in the course of events. His theories were widely spread in the 1970s, influencing 'the post-Structuralist generation', who rejected Lévi-Strauss.

However, French post-Structuralism was too heavily influenced by Anglo-American ideas. As such it was not likely to last long in Paris, and Nietzsche's 'Will to Power' is not pleasing to everyone. With the slogan 'We are not Nietzscheans', students went back to Kant, popular fifty years before, and the next fashion was called 'Deconstructionism'. The debates continue, as in Paris they always will.

Enough of 'philo' for the day! Many historical and visual pleasures lie in store for us in Hôtel de Cluny a few yards away.

Hôtel de Cluny, 6 Place Paul Painlevé (Metro Cluny), was once residence of the abbots and, long before that, a centre of Roman civilization. The gardens facing Boulevard Saint-Germain are open to the public and, under the shade of great trees, beside Roman ruins and the sixteenth-century house, they are a pleasant place to read or while away an hour, traffic notwithstanding. On the side facing Boulevard Saint-Michel, we have remains of the Roman baths, the caldarium (steam) and the tepidarium (cooling-off) beside the railings, the frigidarium (cold water) further inside. They are best seen on an autumn evening, floodlit, covered with fallen chestnut leaves and with the smell of roasting chestnuts coming from the stall on the corner.

The present house was completely rebuilt at the end of the fifteenth century by the abbot of Jumièges in Normandy and may seem to us more like a country manor house than a Paris *hôtel*. It is, however, far more elaborate than an English equivalent. It has battlements and turrets, memories of the Middle Ages, purely decorative. We shall also see arches, mullioned windows, decorated friezes and balustrades. Under the balustrade there are beautifully carved grapes and vine leaves. On the dormer windows are elaborate, coats-of-arms and everywhere there are carved shells – *coquilles Saint-Jacques.* Shells are traditionally the emblem of pilgrims and Rue Saint-Jacques, the pilgrims' way, is only a few yards off. But when the decorators carved the shells, it is possible that they were thinking more of the taste of *coquilles,* that delicious seafood, than of the rigours of the long pilgrimage to Spain.

Comfort and luxury are the keynotes of the house. After long centuries of mediæval austerity, France was enjoying the taste for riches, which had come from Italy. It was the mood of the Renaissance, of Lorenzo the Magnificent in Florence and finally, of the Field of the Cloth of Gold (1520). The well-proportioned rooms are neither too large for heating nor too small for parties. The many tapestries give a vivid picture of the life of the well-to-do; the ladies in rich, ornamented clothes with plenty of jewels and servants (or alternatively naked, having a bath), the gentlemen setting out for a day's hunting. Wine (to be drunk out of gold goblets, also on view) is one of the themes of the building. Little of this luxury rubbed off onto the poverty-stricken peasantry, as Breughel made very clear in his pictures of life in the same century.

In 1945 it was decided to make the house into a museum devoted exclusively to the Middle Ages in France, the **Musée National du Moyen Age et des Thermes de Cluny**, though the word seems to cover the whole period from Roman Paris to the sixteenth century. It attracts a great number of visitors. A principal room now shows everyday life of the period, including a fine tapestry, *The Vintage* and a mediæval garden is being created.

We enter through the main courtyard in Place Painlevé, facing the Sorbonne, and we should notice the big turret containing a spiral staircase (no longer in use) and the well with its beautiful iron well-curb (fifteenth century). The ticket office is on the right. We begin among the tapestries. They are of the 'thousand flower' style and give a cavalcade of vigorous life, but with no attempt at perspective. However, we can enjoy them for what they are. There are five large tapestries of *la vie seigneurale.* One tapestry, *L'Embarquement* is in sharp contrast to the previous jollifications. One of the ships is sinking and there is much distress; it has also a primitive attempt at perspective, reminiscent, possibly, of Uccello in Italy.

There is no space here to list all the treasures of the museum, but certain ones may catch our eye as we pass through. Among them will

227

be the *Descent from the Cross* which dates from 1457 in Tarascon and is regarded as the most important painting in the museum. But it is not a picture gallery, and our attention will be taken more by vessels, plaques and other objects. Among these is a Byzantine-style *Christ in Glory* from the twelfth century, almost certainly made in Germany. An enamelled plaque, it shows a seated Christ within an oval enclosed space. Those who have seen the modern Sutherland tapestry in Coventry Cathedral may well find an artistic connection, eight centuries later.

The gold naturally attracts much interest, especially two double crosses (Crosses of Lorraine) from the thirteenth century. But the prize exhibit is a golden rose. Late thirteenth century, it was found in Basle and was probably a gift from the Pope to an important visitor. We also see a fine bronze gryphon, German, fifteenth century, one of the many heraldic beasts which abound in the museum.

We should linger for a while in the small **chapel**, which is an architectural masterpiece. A slender central column branches out, like a palm tree, into a roof of Flamboyant vaulting, intricately decorated with, once again, suggestions of vines, Around us are niches with carved canopies, which once contained statues of the Amboise family.

The chapel was the scene of a curious romantic episode. In October 1514 the king, Louis XII, married again. His first wife, Anne of Brittany, had died without producing an heir. His new wife was Mary Tudor, eldest sister of Henry VIII of England. He was in his fifties, she was a lively sixteen-year-old (and, as it happens, my ancestress). King Louis died three months later, exhausted by his young bride; the throne was seized by his twenty-year-old cousin, François I, and the queen was sent to mourn in Cluny. But François was naturally worried in case the young widow might be pregnant, which would probably cost him his throne. However, his spies reported that she was having an affair with Charles Brandon, a man-at-arms or perhaps a *chevalier-servant*. The king arrived late one night with an armed guard and a priest and, finding the young couple in bed together, ordered them to this chapel, where they were married on the spot, by consent. He then sent them straight back to England. There was some anxiety in case Brandon might be sent to the Tower, or even the block, for treason. But Henry VIII was in an indulgent mood; perhaps he was fond of his sister, or knew of the affair and did not disapprove – it would have been interesting to have had an Englishman on the throne of France. Anyway Brandon was created Duke of Suffolk and nobody knows who was the real father of their eldest child. François I remained firmly on the French throne and the two kings must have made some bawdy jokes about it at the Field of the Cloth of Gold.

In a more austere mood, the chapel also contains fine tapestries, originally in Auxerre Cathedral, showing episodes from the life of St Stephen, a popular saint in France. As we leave the chapel we see facing us a tapestry woven in 1490 of the saint's martyrdom. The dead body, with bloodstained stones, is being mourned by a lion and a unicorn. It is moving in its expression of grief, but without the artistic achievement which we shall find later. Lions, both winged and otherwise, abound in the museum; there is a historic connection between Christianity and lions, but these ones seem very friendly. We can find more carved on the Romanesque capitals of the stone columns from Ste Geneviève's church (twelfth century). A lion is also the main motif of a finely carved ivory hunting-horn (*Olifant*) from southern Italy, eleventh century. And, of course, there is the great stone lion in the garden outside (originally at Tour Saint-Jacques).

In the **Salle Archéologique,** we should note the column capitals from the nave of Saint-Germain-des-Prés; one of them is another oval *Christ in Glory*. There is also a good thirteenth-century Adam, from Notre-Dame, and in two adjoining crypts we can see the tombs of five grand masters of the Order of St John (or the Hospitallers; now generally known as St John of Jerusalem). Robed figures, they express both calm and strength.

We now descend into the **Salle Romaine,** originally the frigidarium. Built of stone with layers of brick, we may well find it a chilly place. Certain decorative designs suggest that it was built by the Boatmen's Guild of Paris; boatmen were an important part of Paris in Roman and mediæval times. Here we shall see the *Boatmen's Pillar*, Paris's oldest piece of sculpture, a column to Jupiter from the time of the Emperor Tiberius (AD 14–37) and originally in the temple where Notre-Dame now stands.

Against the back wall stand the heads of twenty-one kings, one of the great archæological finds of the century. They were discovered in 1977 during excavations in northern Paris and were originally on the façade of Notre-Dame. It was first thought that they were kings of France, including St Louis, as all were statues of kings, but it is now thought that they were the kings of Israel and Judah, claimed as the royal ancestors of the Virgin Mary. One of them is said to be Solomon, but it is hard to be sure. They are much battered by time, by venial canons who wanted the stone for their houses and, possibly, by revolutionaries. But even without their noses they exude a tremendous presence and dominate the big room with their personality. We feel humbler in their presence; they were truly kings.

But, the best till the last; we have kept the great treat for the end. We ascend to the rotunda on the first floor and there we find the six beautiful and mysterious tapestries, *The Lady and the Unicorn* (*La Dame à la Licorne*). Designed in France and woven, it is said, in what is now Belgium, they date from the late fifteenth century. They are part of a series and similar in design. A blonde lady, richly dressed and wearing a jewelled collar, stands in the centre with an attendant. On either side are a lion and a unicorn, and beside them are the banners and poles of the de Viste family from Lyons, white crescents on a blue band against a red background. The tapestry background is also red, of the thousand flower type, and teeming with rabbits, dogs, monkeys, birds and other wild life. She stands on an oval of blue-green grass, full of flowers and more animals.

The tapestries portray the five senses – it was a sensuous time. For 'Touch' the Lady is shown holding the banner-pole and the unicorn's horn; for 'Taste', she takes a sweet from a bowl which she is possibly going to offer to a parakeet on her left hand. For 'Smell' she sniffs a rose taken from a bouquet, while a monkey smells another one behind her. For 'Sound' she plays a portable organ, pumped by her attendant; the design in this one is especially fine. And for 'Sight' the unicorn lies with its paws in her lap, gazing at itself in a mirror. (Can unicorns see themselves in mirrors? Dogs cannot.)

It is the sixth tapestry which baffles us. The lady stands at the door of a tent, which has its flaps open; on the tent is the motto *A Mon Seul Désir*. She is taking off the jewelled necklace which she has worn throughout and placing it in a box. This is supposed to be a gesture of renunciation or sacrifice and the unicorn raises its horn in salute. What does it mean? Is she giving her jewels to the beast? There is much conjecture about this, even to the point of supposing the sixth tapestry to have come from a different series. But this cannot be so; she is the same girl, they are the same animals throughout.

The motto suggests a gift and the tapestries, it has been suggested, were a wedding present from Jean de Chabannes (whose arms included a lion) to Claude de Viste, his bride. But this is unlikely. A unicorn is a wild noble beast, a symbol of power, sex and purity, and it can only be tamed by a pure virgin. Claude de Viste was a widow, not a virgin, and moreover the lady never looks at the lion, although it is obviously begging for attention. Clearly she much prefers the unicorn. The museum supports the theory that the tapestries were made for Jean de Viste, Président des Aides et Seigneur d'Arcy, who died in 1500. But then, where does the motto come in?

Of course the lady does not have to be a Mademoiselle de Viste. She could be a saint, rather a luxury-loving one, or even the Virgin Mary, taming the noble savages round her. This idea is encouraged by a further six tapestries in the same style and possibly by the same artist, which now hang in the Cloisters, New York. These show the hunting of the unicorn, which, though wounded, savages the hounds with its horn, but finally lays its head meekly in the lady's lap.

In Chinese symbolism the unicorn is a rain-bringer and always fighting with the sun, the lion. This idea of the two beasts fighting each other also occurs in the English nursery rhyme, but not in these tapestries, or in the British coat-of-arms, where they tolerate each other.

I have a personal explanation of the sixth tapestry. It represents the sixth sense, which in this case is not extra-sensory perception, but quite simply Love. And in this I am supported by the motto A *Mon Seul Désir.*

But, intriguing though the subject is, and interpret them as we like, we cannot fail to enjoy their beauty. In design they are far superior to the tapestry mentioned earlier of the two beasts mourning the martyred St Stephen. The design is mainly triangular, the lady's head being at the apex of the triangle. On either side are upright features, banner-poles or trees, and below is the curved oval base. This use of the triangle is similar to the use of triangles in Italian Renaissance religious paintings. Contrasted with this geometry are the luxuriant landscape, abundant in flowers and animals, the swirling banners, the rich clothes of the lady. (Rabbits, which abound, are symbols of fertility, as are the crescents on the de Viste banners; so perhaps it was a wedding present after all.)

Anyway these tapestries are to be enjoyed and we can spend a pleasant half-hour or more studying them. What we shall chiefly recall is the splendid unicorn, a noble beast indeed.

16

The Luxembourg

THE LUXEMBOURG PALACE and Gardens* are the green heart of the Left Bank; the gardens are possibly the most enjoyable and certainly the most popular in Paris, thronged by children, prams, students, poets, sportsmen (of a sort) and strollers looking for fresh air, greenery and flowers in the bustling centre of the city. They are easily reached from the Latin Quarter, Saint-Germain-des-Prés and Montparnasse, but we should for preference enter them from Boulevard Saint-Michel (Place Edmond-Rostand, Metro Luxembourg). We walk down an avenue, pausing perhaps to buy a balloon or hot chestnuts, until we reach the balustrade, from where we can see the gardens stretching in all directions, the formal pond below us, all dominated by the façade of the palace, built between 1615 and 1625 by Salomon de Brosse on the orders of Queen Marie de Medici, second wife and widow of King Henri IV.

The first marriage of Henri IV (Henry of Navarre, as he then was) had been a disaster, after the murder of all his friends on the wedding day, in the Massacre of St Bartholomew (see p. 131), arranged by his mother-in-law-to-be, Catherine de Medici. The marriage was childless and finally annulled, and it is curious that for his second bride he should have chosen to marry again into the same family. But Marie de Medici, niece of the Grand Duke of Tuscany, had a dowry of 600,000 gold crowns and, after the civil wars of religion, France's treasury was very short of cash. Her appearance can only be judged by a series of pictures by Rubens in which she appears. These were in the Luxembourg Palace but now hang in the Louvre in a room specially redesigned to fit them. They show her as a stately red-head of considerable presence, and Rubens would not have objected to her ample figure; the pictures were painted in 1621 and the following years.

---

*A map of the Luxembourg Gardens appears on p. 216

Marie de Medici has been much criticized for her grossness, vulgarity, possessiveness of her son, her lovers and intrigues – though this was all part of the time. But the marriage produced children and she bore with her husband's infidelities. And we must be grateful to her for giving to Paris the Luxembourg.

When Henri IV was assassinated, her son (King Louis XIII) was only nine years old. Marie had brought with her to Paris her foster-sister and her husband, an uncouth bully called Concini, who rapidly became a duke and a marshal. The queen mother and Concini ruled the country, buying off the Guises and other important French families; the king was relegated to the nursery.

When he was fourteen the king became officially of age and one of his first acts was to authorize the murder of Concini, shot by the captain of the guard in the Cour Carrée of the Louvre. He then expelled his mother to Blois on the Loire. The new ruler of France was his chief falconer, Luynes, a man completely unfitted for the job. Fortunately for France his rule only lasted four years; he died, surprisingly for the times, of an illness. The queen and her son became reconciled. This was brought about by a little-known provincial clergyman, who had managed to become court almoner: Armand de Richelieu. For his services he was made a cardinal and president of the Council of State.

The Louvre was soon a nest of intrigue and counter-intrigue, as every reader of Dumas knows. Lovers, plots, ambitious hangers-on, whispering ladies-in-waiting; there were two queens, Marie de Medici herself, and her daughter-in-law, Anne of Austria, who, after ten years of marriage to Louis XIII, was still childless and probably a virgin. There was also the king himself: sad, sickly, pious, latently homosexual, easily influenced yet on occasions able to exercise his royal authority. His main recreation was hunting, and he built a hunting lodge at Versailles, later to become the great palace. He also took an interest in the arts and he and his mother encouraged the architects Le Vau and Marie (happily named) in the development of Ile Saint-Louis. He also completed Place des Vosges (see p. 176), begun in his father's reign, and he deserves his statue there. France, meanwhile, was ruled by Richelieu from the Palais-Cardinal, now Palais-Royal.

It was time for the queen mother to move out and she bought the house and estate of Duke François of Luxembourg. She ordered her architect, de Brosse, to build her a palace which would remind her of her native Florence – though the result may look very French to us. It was enlarged in the nineteenth century; in particular, the façade facing the gardens was rebuilt and two wing pavilions added, also the balustraded terrace with its statues. But the architect (Alphonse de Gisors) was faithful to de Brosse's original and the result with its simple design and harmonious proportions is very pleasing.

The main entrance is on Rue de Vaugirard (Metro Saint-Sulpice) and here we can see more of the Italian influence, with its Tuscan columns and, perhaps, the cupola. The ground plan, with its enclosed courtyard, is however in traditional French style.

Marie de Medici moved in in 1625 and herself supervised the final decorations and in particular the fountain, which still bears her name and about which more will be written later. She was also occupied by lovers and intriguers. On 10 November 1630, *la journée des dupes,* she made her son promise to dismiss Richelieu. Despite his nickname, Louis le Juste, the king revoked his promise the same day, and it was Marie de Medici who found herself in exile, in Cologne, where she died in 1642. The palace and gardens reverted to their original name, Luxembourg.

Abandoned for a while, it remained a royal palace and was the principal home of her granddaughter, another French personality. Anne-Marie-Louise, Duchesse de Montpensier, known generally as **La Grande Mademoiselle,** was the daughter of the brother of Louis XIII, the Duc d'Anjou; the Princess Royal of France and, through her mother, probably the richest woman in the world. She was a trump card in the game of royal marriages, but neither Richelieu nor later Mazarin, both expert in these matters, managed to find a suitable husband for her. They tried with Charles II of England, the King of Spain, the Holy Roman Emperor, the Archduke of the Netherlands, and even her cousin, Louis XIV. But there was no doing anything about her huge, ungainly size, her great feet, her Bourbon nose and her personality, sometimes capricious, sometimes obstinate.

She saw herself more as a man. During the Fronde rising, she was first up the scaling ladders at the walls of Orléans. She captured the Bastille and held it for a while. Twice she forced Mazarin into exile, but each time he, far cleverer than she, was back in power in a few weeks. After the second return, he exiled her to her estates in the south and there she remained for many years, until she was no longer a desirable bride.

After Mazarin's death she returned to the Luxembourg. She was forty-two and largely forgotten and then she fell hopelessly in love with the future Count of Lauzun. He was younger and far smaller, a penniless adventurer, a braggart not averse to duelling, touchy and a womanizer. He was, however, a captain of the Musketeers and not unknown to the king, Louis XIV. How his heart must have sunk when she first smiled lovingly at him, but he dared not antagonize such a formidable person. He dodged and evaded and the king did not approve of such a match. But somehow she obtained royal permission for a marriage, only a temporary permission, as it turned out. They were married secretly and Lauzun was immediately led away to prison, escorted by a company of his own musketeers, commanded by d'Artagnan, no less.

He remained there for ten years. Mademoiselle did her best to get him released. She begged, petitioned, intrigued and paid out much of her fortune in bribes. Typically inept, she always bribed the wrong royal mistress. But finally she got it right and the couple were reunited in March 1682 in Madame de Montespan's apartments at Saint-Germain-en-Laye. It seems to have been a silent reunion. Lauzun thanked her politely for her efforts, but was appalled by the elderly lovesick Amazon he found to be his wife. Mademoiselle herself was too moved to say a word.

The couple moved into the Luxembourg and Lauzun consoled himself with the thought of the probable advantages in being the husband of La Grande Mademoiselle, as she was still called. But, to his surprise, he found that they were not to live as man and wife. He was to lodge elsewhere, with Rollinde the intendant of her household, and to attend with many others her morning *levée*. He was also to pay her a longer visit in the evening, to play games. It does not seem that there was any question of a sex life.

Such an arrangement was unlikely to satisfy Lauzun for long and in August he bought the house on Ile Saint-Louis which still bears his name. Where he found the money for this is not clear; perhaps some of her bribes had found their way to him. Anyway Mademoiselle was not pleased by the new arrangement and still less by the goings-on in Hôtel de Lauzun, affairs and seductions (his mistress was Madeleine Fouquet), gambling parties at which the guests included such socially different persons as the Duke of Orléans and the butcher Tiber. It is said that she visited him secretly by boat, chasing him round the house while he escaped down secret staircases. But this seems unlikely. She was incapable of doing anything secretly. She did not visit, she commanded people to visit her, and his twice-daily visits now included a twice-daily scolding.

Obviously it could not last. Lauzun hoped that the king would make him an aide-de-camp and send him to the wars, but this did not happen. Mademoiselle ordered him to leave Paris and hide; he would look ridiculous in Paris, a captain of the Musketeers, when everyone else was at the wars. They would say it was her fault and this would make her very angry. The scene took place in the Luxembourg. Lauzun answered, 'I will go away as you wish, and I will say goodbye so as never to see you again in my life'. He bowed deeply and left the palace for ever. Mademoiselle lingered on for another nine years until she died. On hearing of her death Lauzun wore deep mourning, more out of panache, one must feel, than from grief.

Once the separation was public knowledge, Lauzun prospered. He was accepted back into royal circles, sold his house on Ile Saint-Louis and moved at last into Versailles. He was placed in charge of the musketeers who rescued King James II and his wife Mary of Modena from Whitehall and installed them in safety in Saint-Germain-en-Laye, a mission which he accomplished efficiently. The road from the Luxembourg to Versailles, as Madame de Sévigné put it, led through Whitehall. Two years later, in 1690, he commanded French troops, with much less success, at the battle of the Boyne in Ireland. However, he survived this and was made a duke. Aged sixty-three he was given a rich young bride of fourteen. He died at ninety, a respected old man who figures in eighteenth-century memoirs and later romances. But his only visible memorial is the *hôtel* on Ile Saint-Louis, which he occupied so briefly and boisterously.

The Luxembourg, still a royal palace, was neglected for nearly a hundred years, though it was used for a time as a monastery. At the Revolution and afterwards it was an annexe of the Conciergerie and several notable people were imprisoned there, including the aristocratic de Noailles family and Danton. Among famous trials held there were those of Camille Desmoulins (guillotined), Marshal Ney (shot by firing squad), and Louis-Napoleon Bonaparte, the future Emperor Napoleon III, who finally died in exile and is buried at Farnham, Surrey. In 1870 the Commune used it for the trials of those supporters who had become dissatisfied with the authoritarian regime and turned against it. During the German occupation it was a military headquarters. It is now the home of the Senate and is closed to the public, unless we have official political business there, and even then we may have to suffer long delays for bureaucratic and security reasons; there are guided tours on the first Sunday of the month. As the interior was completely transformed in the nineteenth century by Chalgrin (the architect of the Arc de Triomphe, among other things) little of Marie de Medici's time remains.

Some of the panelling and paintings from her private apartments survive in the Golden Book Room, while in the library are paintings by Delacroix of such personalities as Virgil, Dante, Alexander holding the epics of Homer and so on. There is also a Zodiac ceiling by Jordaens. But we may well prefer to spend our Sunday in the gardens themselves, like so many other Parisians.

The **Senate** is France's second chamber, like the House of Lords, and has equally little power, because it can be overruled by the Assemblée Nationale (parliament). However, it is a respected advisory body and the French were evidently attached to it as they voted against its abolition in a series of referenda between 1946 and 1969. Senators have prestige and their number has grown; a good deal of rebuilding has been necessary in the Luxembourg to give each of them his own office. But the Senate's electoral system and powers were again challenged in 1999, leaving its future in doubt.

The president of the Senate takes over the powers of the president of the Republic when the position becomes vacant. Monsieur Alain Poher twice did so, after General de Gaulle's retirement and President Pompidou's death. However, he has to call a presidential election within 35 days. With limited powers, he cannot make much impact on the nation but can run as a presidential candidate himself.

The gardens are a delight at all times of year, even in midwinter when mists and grey light shroud the bare trees. In the spring we go to see crocuses, daffodils, azaleas in flower and the first green leaves on the chestnuts. All these are near the Saint-Michel entrance, and in summer there is an open-air café, where we can sit under the trees and watch the world at play. We could be part of a picture by Manet, except that nowadays nobody is likely to be wearing a top hat.

But our first port of call must be the **Medici Fountain** which has inspired so much fiction and poetry. It is not exactly as Marie de Medici intended. Dominating it is a large grotto (built in 1863 by Ottin), inside which is a naked loving couple, said to be Acis and Galatea. Above them, peering over the rocks, is a great bearded giant, perhaps Polyphemus, watching them and awaiting his chance to destroy them or, more likely, to abduct the girl from her rather wan lover. The water flows out under their feet over three semi-circular steps into a long pool full of golden carp. This is the pool as Marie de Medici saw it, lined with big stone vases and very Italianate in design. From the far end there is a curious *trompe l'œil* effect that the water is flowing uphill to the fountain. The plane trees, for once unpollarded, meet overhead and there are plenty of benches and chairs where we can sit. It is a very romantic place, especially in the autumn when the leaves have turned, popular with loving couples and others, more solitary, reading or writing poetry.

I may perhaps recall my small personal contribution to the fountain. One day, sitting there, I noticed that the pool was covered with leaves, the fish were gasping for oxygen, and no water was flowing from the grotto. The fountain was dead and the fish would soon be dead too. Typically British, I went in search of a gardener, whom I found sweeping up leaves. After some discussion, not due to language problems, he got my point: I wanted the water turned on. He unlocked a wooden door in the side of the grotto; inside, along with the rakes and spades, was a vertical, rather wonky pipe with a tap in the middle. He turned on the tap. *Voilà, monsieur!* I thanked him suitably and returned to my chair and poem. Gradually the water began to overflow the first step, the second, the third into the pool. The leaves started to drift down to the grating, the fish stopped gasping, the fountain was alive again, though I do not think that the loving couples noticed. It is, at the moment of writing, still flowing.

Moving on reluctantly, we reach the terrace with its balustrade and view of the palace and the pond. This is the more formal part of the garden, where the trees are clipped and the flowers planted in regular municipal patterns. Behind us is a semi-circle of statues, erected in the nineteenth century, of eminent French women. They are not in themselves of great artistic interest, but we may note with some amusement two almost adjoining ladies of very different temperament: Ste Geneviève and Marie Stuart, Reine de France (Mary Queen of Scots).

Below us is the *Bassin,* the central pond with its fountain, filled with toy sailing-boats. These can be hired from a kiosk at hand and give great pleasure, not only to children. On the far side we re-enter the trees and watch games of *pétanque,* imported from the south and played on rough sand. Beyond, in fine weather, are tables for card-players and we can admire the ferocity with which the players throw down their cards. There are also tennis courts, a marionette theatre (times of performances are announced on posters), and an exotic garden. There is a large children's playground with a tree-house. They can ride ponies and donkeys. This part of the gardens, beside Rue Guynemer, is more in the English style. The trees are unclipped and some of them are very old.

We stroll back towards the palace where we find the **Orangerie** (not the one at the Tuileries) where delicate plants are housed in the winter. In summer it is often used for exhibitions of modern art. The choice of these is at the discretion of the Senate or, in French style, of an influential senator. Back in Rue de Vaugirard, we find the Petit Luxembourg, official residence of the Senate president. Across the street are some pleasant buildings of eighteenth-century origin, which are now part of the Senate. The doorway of no. 36 was built by Boffrand and has since been incorporated in a later building.

Beside the Petit Luxembourg is the **Musée du Luxembourg**, used for temporary exhibitions.

Bicycles are not allowed in the gardens, but there is access for dogs on leads at the junction of Boulevard St Michel and Avenue de l'Observatoire.

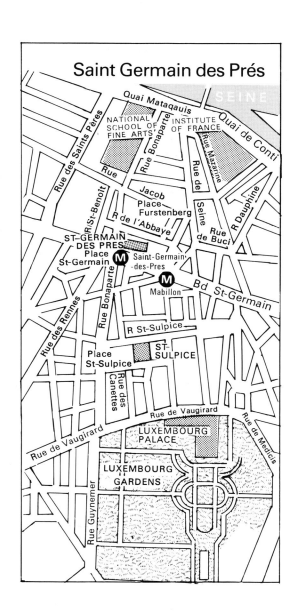

17

Saint-Germain-des-Prés

S AINT-GERMAIN-DES-PRÉS – Saint Germanus in the Fields –
is the intellectual and literary centre of Paris. This statement may
cause dissent at the Sorbonne or in Montparnasse, neither very far
away on foot. Yet it remains true. In Place Saint-Germain (6me),
under the steeple of the great church (Metro Saint-Germain-des-
Prés), in the narrow streets around and behind, much of French
thought has grown and been disseminated for several hundred
years.

To the modern tourist, and to journalists writing about intellectual
Paris, Saint-Germain-des-Prés means the decade or more following
the Second World War, the fifties, rediscovery of Paris after the
Occupation and, especially, the philosophy called Existentialism. It
started in Saint-Germain, partly because the whole area has always
been a think-tank, and partly because Sartre lived above the *Café
Bonaparte*. Its main areas of concentration were two cafés, *Deux
Magots* on the Place (and in particular the wall banquette nearest to
the window) and *Flore* on the next corner. Also involved were
Montana Bar (immediately behind *Flore*), where a rather obscure
philosopher, Merleau-Ponty, tried to teach the essentials of
Existentialism to the singer Juliette Greco, *Bar Rouge* in Rue Jacob
and the jazz-cellar, *Le Tabou*, in Rue Dauphine. The philosophy
attracted many followers, who became well-publicized for their
appearance, blue jeans, sandals, beards and a fierce, gloomy
expression. The leaders of the movement, the mandarins, held
themselves a little aloof. Sartre always dressed like a bank manager;
Simone de Beauvoir was concerned about her hairstyle. Many
Existentialists could scarcely understand the subtle difference
between Being and Existing, but jazz was a great common thread. In
Existentialist books many of the characters spend time listening to
jazz singers and clarinettists. When, near the end of Simone de
Beauvoir's very long novel *Les Mandarins,* we find Nadia listening

to César Franck rather than jazz, we are to understand that she has abandoned Existentialism in favour of family life.

Politics was also a common thread, in particular protest against atom-bomb tests. The slogan, 'I think day and night of the animals at Bikini', was plastered everywhere, even in the staid *Deux Magots*.

Existentialism is a difficult philosophy to explain in a few words. It has links with Germany (Heidegger's *Da-Sein* 'being there') but basically it grew out of the Resistance, the revolt against the German occupation. To put it briefly, everyone is in his own and separate hell; hell is also other people, who can impinge and torture us but with whom we can never communicate. The Existentialists produced a group of fine writers and playwrights, two of them Nobel prizewinners (though Sartre refused the award). They understood, like Plato many centuries before, that philosophy can often be better explained in fiction than in a thesis. And so, rather than slog our way through Sartre's monumental book *L'Etre et le Néant* (*Being and Nothing*), we would do better to read his short novel *La Nausée* (*Nausea*), his one-act play *Huis Clos* (*Vicious Circle*) or Camus's short novel *L'Etranger* (*The Outsider*) – the titles themselves give clues to this sad and lonely philosophy.

It was a passing phase, though some ageing Existentialists lingered around Saint-Germain-des-Prés. Anti-bomb protests still continue, but bikinis began to be worn, jazz gave way to rock, blue jeans became a symbol of American influence and Sartre himself moved to Montparnasse. The philosophy became a form of dissident Communism and was then superseded by Structuralism and post-Structuralism.

Saint-Germain, however, still continues, as it has done for centuries, and perhaps improved by the disappearance of the philosophic gloom. Never has it been fuller or livelier, its streets and cafés more crowded. To sit on one of the café terraces on Boulevard Saint-Germain for an hour or two and watch the world go by is to have a fashion display by people of all ages.

The centre of the quarter is **Place Saint-Germain** where Rue Bonaparte crosses Boulevard Saint-Germain, between the famous church and *Deux Magots*. It has recently been made more agreeable for strollers by wider pavements, the planting of many lime trees and the channelling of Rue Bonaparte traffic into a single one-way street.

On the terrace of ***Deux Magots***, business is mainly literary and *Deux Magots* calls itself the 'Rendez-vous de l'Elite intellectuelle'.

Most French publishers have their offices in the neighbourhood and the café is thronged by writers, publishers, agents, journalists and high-fliers who have little connection with literature or the arts – plus, of course, those who live locally and who like a cup of coffee (*un express*) in congenial surroundings – and a crowd of tourists. Inside, in colder weather, the café is brightly lit and crowded, especially at night. The two *magots* (mandarins) gaze down benevolently on those discussing contracts or politics or philosophy, or simply reading *Le Monde*.

The next café, at the corner of Rue Saint-Benoît, is **Flore,** which has something of the same reputation. It became some years ago a gay rendezvous for both sexes but their headquarters moved to the Marais, and this changed its atmosphere. Apéritif-sippers can enjoy the presence of pretty photographers' models, waiting to change their clothes yet again in the small lavatories upstairs, to be photographed outside the café.

Facing *Flore*, across Boulevard Saint-Germain, is the well-known **Brasserie Lipp,** one of the landmarks of the quarter, and of Paris too. Founded at the end of the last century by a refugee from Alsace (then under German rule), it quickly gained a reputation for Alsatian food. It has retained its décor and atmosphere, the ceilings covered by gigantic black, very full-bosomed, nude ladies, the waiters in old-fashioned black waistcoats and long white aprons.

The restaurant is a rendezvous for the world of literature, politics and art – the type of artist who can afford the prices and whose posters do not conflict with the décor. But we do not have to be famous to gain admittance; unknowns are welcome, if they seem to have the right personality and trendy appearance – ties are not important if we are the sort of people they want.

Or we can sit on the small terrace, now permanently glassed in, or at one of the tables just inside the door, and remember the days of potato salad and beer, described by Hemingway in *A Moveable Feast.*

Lipp's has its own life and is not a place for those who wish to sit and watch the passing scene on the boulevard. We can do this more cheaply and less fashionably at one of the cafés further along.

In a smart area it is not surprising that there should be plenty of boutiques. These come and go. In the men's shops, the accent is on casual dress, suitable for a cabin cruiser; but it is not every businessman who wishes to arrive in his office in short check trousers, a tight navy blue blazer with brass buttons and a silk scarf, so there are formal clothes too. For those wanting to browse among modern books (not only French) there is *La Hune*, next to *Flore* (open until late at night).

But Saint-Germain-des-Prés is not only the Place, the boulevard and the celebrated cafés. We must explore the little streets which lead to the river and, on the other side of the boulevard, to Place Saint-Sulpice, and beyond to the Luxembourg Gardens. These narrow streets are full of art galleries, publishing houses, both small and great, cheap restaurants, antique shops and cafés. Marché de Buci, at the corner of Rue de Seine and Rue de Buci, is a lively area (closed Sundays and, naturally, lunchtime). Rue de Seine (Metro Mabillon), which continues down to the river, is lined with art galleries. We are free to wander into any of them and see what is going on in the world of modern art in Paris. This does not necessarily mean French art; painters, sculptors and tapestry designers of many nations and continents show in these galleries. Rue Jacob and Rue Jacques Callot (which turn off Rue de Seine), Rue des Beaux-Arts which (behind a high wall and a courtyard) houses the famous art school, Rue Dauphine and other streets adjoining are full of galleries too. At no. 13 Rue des Beaux-Arts is 'l'Hôtel', the hotel where Oscar Wilde died. He remarked 'I am dying above my means'.

If there is a formal opening (*un vernissage* – a 'varnishing'), we are free to join in, look at the work, talk to anyone we like, perhaps drink a glass of wine. If we put our names and addresses in the visitors' book, we shall be invited to the next *vernissage* the following month. It is a good way of seeing modern art and of making friends.

Between Rue de l'Abbaye and Rue Jacob is a charming old square, **Place Furstemberg**. It has elaborate white-globed lamp-posts and old paulownia trees, and is often used by film-makers shooting backgrounds of old Paris. **Delacroix** had his studio at no. 6 (open to the public, a museum), but his greatest works are elsewhere. We should, however, recall the date 1830, high point of French Romanticism. It is sometimes said that this was a hangover from Napoleonic glory, but the year produced three remarkable works – Victor Hugo's *Hernani,* Delacroix's *Trois Glorieuses* and Berlioz's *Symphonie Fantastique*. They were received with little enthusiasm and *Hernani* provoked a riot (organized) in the theatre, which drove Hugo permanently out of playwriting. The other works survive and the symphony is now a popular work everywhere.

Returning to Place Saint-Germain, we should walk along **Rue de l'Abbaye**. Little remains of the original abbey, built by Pierre of Montereau in 1239, which was burnt during the Revolution, but it has been well rebuilt. The **Abbot's Palace** (no. 5) had a pavilion and later a Renaissance façade. These have been restored to something approaching their original appearance and the interior is now used for small concerts and lectures. In summer, perched among the trees which surround the church, we can listen to Bach or Mozart in delightful surroundings.

The church of **Saint-Germain-des-Prés** is the reason for the special existence of the quarter. It is the oldest church in Paris and all that remains of the powerful Benedictine abbey. It dates from Merovingian times (AD 542) and its builder, King Childebert, son of Clovis, King of the Franks, is buried there with St Germanus, bishop of Paris (496–576). Constantly destroyed by the Normans, it was rebuilt in 1163; the Pope himself attended the consecration but the bishop of Paris was not invited – Saint-Germain has always prided itself on its independence. But its rule eventually decayed and in the seventeenth century it turned to the austere Congregation of St Maur. It soon became a centre, not only of worship, but of scholarship and literature. Two of its greatest scholars, Montfaucon and Mabillon, were distinguished Greek scholars, historians and men of letters and left behind them a vast quantity of folios which happily were saved at the Revolution and are now in the Bibliothèque Nationale. Both men were attacked by the Trappists, who held that such work was not the business of monks; they defended their views splendidly and at great length. A bust of Mabillon (1632–1707) stands in a niche on the west wall overlooking the Place. The Maurists were also attacked for being secret Jansenists (near-Protestant) and there may be some truth in this. The church still has strong links with the Anglican church. And the literary and independent tradition continues. A 'Misa Criolla' concert attracted a large audience, and chanting by a Russian Orthodox choir packed the church.

The building itself has altered greatly. Only a few stones remain of the Merovingian church and the eleventh-century Romanesque monastery chapel has been much rebuilt. The north wall is still mostly of this date. The chancel at the east end was rebuilt in the twelfth century and there we can find the tombstones of Mabillon, Montfaucon and, surprisingly, Descartes. The outside was given its beautiful flying buttresses in the same century, more or less contemporary with Notre-Dame.

245

It was a three-towered building, but the two towers above the chancel were removed in the nineteenth century; the main tower with its rounded arches remains. The steeple which crowns it, and has become the symbol of Saint-Germain-des-Prés, is a nineteenth-century replacement. The building on the south side of the entrance is the presbytery, a pleasant eighteenth-century façade which enhances the attractions of the Place. On the north side is a little garden, where we can sit surrounded by flowering trees and some Merovingian stones. There is also Picasso's sculpture, a tribute to Apollinaire, and a reminder of the tolerance which Saint-Germain always shows to all kinds of thought.

The inside of the church, however, is a disappointment. Crudely restored with garish colours and glass and indifferent frescoes (by Flandrin, a pupil of Ingres), it has little feeling either of antiquity or sanctity. But parts of the chancel and ambulatory at the east end are still from King Childebert's church; we should note the columns with their Romanesque capitals. Apart from services, Anglican occasionally as well as Catholic, the church is used for concerts, discussions and lectures on contemporary subjects such as faith and anthropology.

Moving to the other great church of the quarter, we cross the boulevard and walk along Rue Bonaparte till we reach **Place Saint-Sulpice** (Metro Saint-Sulpice), a huge square with pink-flowering chestnuts and a big fountain with lions. All were destroyed to make an underground car park, but were carefully replaced, though it is doubted if the trees will ever have a sufficient depth of earth to grow large. The fountain, dedicated to the Four Cardinal Points, is a joke not only about geography but about the statues on it, of four eminent clergymen who never became cardinals – *point* in French means 'not at all'.

Standing there, we can consider the monumental façade of **Saint-Sulpice** which catches the evening sunlight, as it is no doubt meant to do. Originally founded by the Abbey of Saint-Germain-des-Prés as a parish church, the two soon went their separate ways, Saint-Germain with its independent and ecumenical outlook, Saint-Sulpice valuing its links with Rome. It was supported by a lay society formed to encourage more zealous and ascetic training of priests. The church has always been associated with the priesthood, training, ordination and subsequent councils. At one time the square was surrounded by little shops selling rosaries, crucifixes and little ivory images of the Virgin or the Pope (which were often given to the newly-ordained priest by his family), bookshops selling missals and other devotional books, travel agencies organizing pilgrimages to Lourdes and Rome. Many of these have disappeared with recent changes in thought, but some still remain.

The church has been rebuilt several times, most of it in the seventeenth century, but surprisingly ponderous for that time. By the eighteenth century, reconstruction had reached the portals and, especially, the façade. It was felt that 'classical architecture' since the Renaissance and particularly in the eighteenth century had not been faithful to Roman tradition; it was the time of the excavation of Pompeii and Herculaneum. A competition was held, won by the Italian architect Servandoni, and his plan for a vast Roman temple was accepted.

The design was much altered in building. The huge pediment was abandoned in favour of an equally huge balustrade. The towers, asymmetrical (the south one was never finished), were crowned by balustrades instead of Renaissance pinnacles. The effect of the façade is overwhelming for its size, if not for its beauty, and we may well prefer the south portal in Rue Palatine for its simpler, lighter design. Built by the eighteenth-century architect Delamaire (who also built Hôtel de Rohan, the stables at Chantilly, and Hôtel Matignon, where the prime minister officially lives), it is an example of the eighteenth-century classical architecture which Servandoni was trying to avoid.

We enter, however, from the west, up massive stairs. The interior is equally imposing for its size and heaviness. There are three points of interest, the first immediately on our right, the Delacroix Chapel. The two frescoes (of Jacob wrestling and the expulsion of Heliodorus) and the ceiling (St Michael and the Dragon) are full of Delacroix's usual energy and sense of line. He took a long time to paint them, as he only worked there during services; he said that the music inspired him, though the connection between Heliodorus and Monteverdi seems obscure.

In the chancel a metal band, embedded in the floor, runs due north and south, and it shows us the exact time at midday on the solstices and equinoxes – another indication that the church was, in its far origins, a sun temple. At the east end, in the Lady Chapel, we find a picture of the Immaculate Conception and note, with some irony, that the artist was called Pigalle.

Outside in the square we can pause for an apéritif. The quarter has a multitude of small restaurants where we can eat well or badly, expensively or cheaply, as we choose; and the choice is vast. On our left as we sit in the café, the narrow Rue des Canettes is full of bistros, some for people with special tastes. We might do better to return to Boulevard and Place Saint-Germain.

This area has been renamed Place du Québec and, as a gift to Paris, Québec presented it with a fountain by Charles Daudelin, called 'Embâcle' or Blockage. It keeps a low profile and shows what local people call a burst water-main throwing up some of the paving-stones. Straight lines, simplicity and destruction – three key themes of fashionable art. Revolution might be added. The sculptor has described it as a conflict between lateral and vertical pressures, another way of saying the same thing. *France-Soir* merely commented '*Ah bon*', but sculptors like it.

Across the boulevard, next to *Flore*, is Rue Saint-Benoît, another pretty street lined with restaurants; in warm weather we can eat on the pavements, probably being entertained by poets and singers. The *Petit Saint-Benoît*, at the end of the street, almost at Rue Jacob, is a haunt of writers and artists who cannot afford *Lipp*. An old-style bistro, it has carefully retained its 1901 décor. We should also notice the charming and celebrated blue-and-white-check washbowl in the lavabo; it should have a red towel hanging above it.

18

The Septième Arrondissement

THE SEVENTH ARRONDISSEMENT is another *beau quartier*, an area of good addresses, where smart people live and pay high rents. But there are some subtle differences between it and the sixteenth. The architecture is largely older and more pleasing; it has several historic monuments, which attract visitors; and it is on the Left Bank, although it has nothing in common with the Latin Quarter despite a street named, for historic reasons, Rue de l'Université.

It is a large arrondissement, shaped like a segment of a circle, with the Seine flowing along the northern, curved side. A number of long avenues or boulevards run across it north and south, among them la Motte-Picquet, Suffren, La Bourdonnais, Bosquet, Latour-Maubourg, Invalides and Saint-Germain. Running across them from side to side are four long streets: Rue de l'Université Rue Saint-Dominique, Rue de Grenelle and Rue de Babylone. These are rather narrow streets with big doorways suitable for coaches (*portes-cochères*). Behind them are courtyards and large hôtels, which are now usually embassies or ministries. There are many of both in the Septième, including the Soviet Embassy and Hôtel Matignon, the official residence of the prime minister.

The avenues and the streets are long and for this reason the area is not really suitable for a sightseeing walk; the sights are too far apart and it would be a pity to spend a morning tramping the length of the Avenue de la Motte-Picquet when we ought to be queuing for the lifts on the Eiffel Tower. For this reason we shall confine ourselves to major monuments, which can be reached separately by metro.

The area, however, is not only long avenues and embassies. For those who like a stroll and to explore pretty corners of old Paris, the Septième has something to offer. Rue Monsieur (Metro Saint François-Xavier) is an attractive short street; Nancy Mitford lived here for many years. Or, near Metro Ecole-Militaire, there is Rue Cler, a pedestrian area and open shopping market. The adjoining

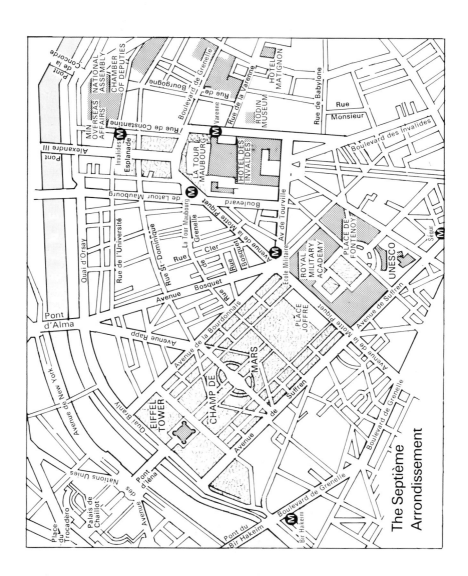

The Septième
Arrondissement

streets are agreeable – note Rue Bosquet. Another picturesque corner is the Fontaine de Mars, in Rue Saint-Dominique near Avenue Bosquet. In warm weather we can eat out under the colonnades surrounding the fountain. The nearby streets are, except for the Romanian Embassy, pleasant to look at.

However, most people do not come to the Septième to explore quiet corners. They come for the main tourist attractions, and we may as well start with Number One, the **Eiffel Tower** (Metro Bir-Hakeim). In less than a hundred years *La Tour Eiffel* became the symbol of Paris, the welcoming finger, the most easily recognized building in the world, even by those who have never seen it. Eiffel himself called it a flagpole three hundred metres high and in its *joie de vivre* and lack of function it is a festival in itself. Nor is it, as it turns out, useless; it is France's tallest radio mast and her big tourist attraction. Over half a million people visit the top in August, and lesser numbers through the rest of the year, over five million visitors in all.

Gustave Eiffel (1832–1923) was an engineer specializing in viaducts and pylons and the idea of a tall tower was a natural consequence of this. The occasion was the Paris Exhibition of 1889 – the centenary of the Fall of the Bastille. Although it was intended only as a temporary folly, it was at once a subject of controversy. A petition to have it removed immediately was signed by three hundred distinguished men, including Garnier (architect of the Opéra and the Monte Carlo casino), Gounod, Maupassant and the younger Dumas. Verlaine went out of his way to avoid having to see it.

On the other hand Cocteau called it the Queen of Paris, *Notre-Dame de la Rive Gauche*. (The tower is feminine, despite Freud.) It, or she, was also praised by Apollinaire, Pissarro, Dufy, Utrillo and others. A British architect has called it, on television, the world's most beautiful building, marred only by the second floor which added a tiresome horizontal line. He was admiring its graceful lines and proportion, and also the fact that it was uninhabited. We are a long way from Le Corbusier's idea of the *machine à habiter;* but he himself wrote: 'La Tour Eiffel est signe de Paris aimé et signe aimé de Paris'. A very different but equally remarkable view of the tower is from underneath looking upwards – an amazing perspective of lacework done in pig-iron. Gauguin called it 'Gothic'.

After twenty years the concession expired and the tower was due to be pulled down. It was saved by sheer difficulty and expense of dismantling a rusty pylon and by the fact that it was now of value as a radio transmitter. Later there was competition between it and the Empire State building in New York to be the tallest building in the world, each adding on further TV masts. Now both have been overtaken by buildings elsewhere. On its 100th birthday, an intrepid tight-rope walker, Philippe Petit, walked 700 metres from Palais de Chaillot to the tower.

For those who want the statistics, the Eiffel Tower is now 1051 ft high; the first floor is 187, and the second 377 ft high. The top only sways 4½ ins in the strongest winds, but the height can vary by six ins in extremes of temperature.

Friends of the tower have been sensitive about its weight. This was, at its heaviest period, 11,000 tonnes, but it was argued that its dead weight per square inch was only roughly the same as that of a man sitting on a chair. We were told that if we imagined a three-dimensional oblong which could contain the tower, the air inside the oblong would weigh more than the tower. This seems inconceivable, unless, like Pascal, we know the weight of air. However, when the mayor of Paris placed the tower under control of the SNTE, a government-owned body, in 1980, it was discovered that the tower was overweight for its frame and was showing its age by bulging at the belt, like many of the rest of us. (This was described as 'structural deformation at belt-girder level'.) A drastic slimming and tautening-up programme has reduced its weight by 1340 tonnes. The spiral staircases have been replaced by two straight staircases and 1000 tonnes of cement were removed from the first floor.

Other improvements reduced the fire-risk and also modernized the lifts, but we must expect queues, all the same. The tower claims to have more (paying) visitors than any other monument in the world. We should wrap up warmly in cold or windy weather; we queue in the open air. At the north pillar of the tower, we can buy queueless lift tickets if we are eating in the first or second floor restaurants, '*Altitude 95*' or the more expensive '*Jules Verne*'.

The view from the top extends almost fifty miles, but haze or cloud may reduce this. Paris too seems to get lost beneath us and, though we must of course go to the top at least once, we may prefer the view from the lower floors, from which we can recognize the familiar landmarks. The second-floor restaurant, *Jules Verne*, where I once signed a book contract, featured spectacularly in one of the James Bond films.

The first floor offers various places to eat, a post office where our cards can be franked by a special stamp, a souvenir shop, a cinema and a variety of other attractions which we are assured will be constantly changed. Some people revisit the tower often, especially the British, who are particularly fond of it. It now has its own Internet site, to keep us informed. The energetic, impatient or thrifty who wish to climb to the first or even the second floor on foot should be moderately free of vertigo and fit. Girls should wear trousers. There are 1665 steps. At night, 352 floodlights, pointing upwards, light the tower from the inside.

The **Champ-de-Mars**, at the foot of the Eiffel Tower, is a large rectangular park which is one of the pleasant features of the Septième arrondissement. Originally the parade ground of the Ecole Militaire (hence the name), it is now a playground for all. The façade of the Ecole Militaire stands at one end, the Eiffel Tower at the other, near the Seine. This part of the park is the most attractive; not only is there the soaring tower, of which we have a wonderful view, but the park has been landscaped with small cascades, shrubs, flowering trees and a pool. It is a delightful place in the spring when the blossom is out. Beside the tower is an organ-grinder who might play one of Paris's traditional tunes. We shall also, of course, buy a red balloon, to keep or release into the air. Ballooning has always been associated with the Champ-de-Mars. In 1780 a physicist called Charles launched the first hydrogen balloon here; it landed near Le Bourget. The following year the balloonist Blanchard floated away himself in the basket of a balloon, landing safely at Billancourt, near the Bois de Boulogne.

The Champ-de-Mars now has other attractions besides balloons. There is a marionette theatre and a children's playground. The Peripheral track is much used by joggers and those exercising dogs, while the transverse road, closed to traffic, has become a roller-skating and skateboard rink. There are also football grounds.

Unexpectedly, the Champ-de-Mars has religious associations. On the first anniversary of the Fall of the Bastille, Talleyrand, in his capacity as bishop of Autun, celebrated mass here in the presence of the king, Lafayette and a vast crowd who all took oaths of loyalty to the nation. Four years later, religion having been abolished in the meanwhile by the Revolution, Robespierre proclaimed his doctrine of the Supreme Being here. And, more recently, Pope John Paul II celebrated mass here before a huge crowd. Few noticed the irony, a Pope who preaches peace on the Champ-de-Mars.

We can now either take a moderately lengthy stroll on foot, or, if our next objective is the Invalides, return to the metro. If we decide to walk, we go down the length of the Champ-de-Mars and come to the **École Militaire**. The Royal Military Academy was possibly the brainchild of Madame de Pompadour, mistress of Louis XV. At any rate it was she who obtained grudging permission from the bored king, and some finance. Gabriel, the architect of Place de la Concorde, produced elaborate plans, which had for financial reasons to be much modified by Paris-Duverney, who was responsible for army finances. Nevertheless, the buildings are an elegant example of eighteenth-century architecture and lavish for an army school; they were finished in 1772.

From the Champ-de-Mars we can see the central pavilion with its Corinthian columns, pediment, statues and dome. The statue (1939) is of Joffre. Walking round to the opposite side in Place Fontenoy, we catch a glimpse of the main courtyard with its porticoes and columns in pairs, flanking the central pavilion. The rest of the building is nineteenth century.

Among the cadets who successfully completed the three-year course was young Napoleon Bonaparte, whose report said that he was likely to go far in favourable circumstances. The Ecole Militaire now houses the Staff College and the War Studies School. It is not open to the public except for Sunday morning services in the chapel.

The **UNESCO building** is across Place Fontenoy from the Ecole Militaire; it is the work of three architects, Nervi, Breuer and Zehrfuss, was completed in 1958 and is a typical example of twentieth-century architecture, except that it is not high-rise. Indeed, much of it seems to be underground. As the headquarters of the educational, scientific and cultural side of the United Nations, it is both busy and influential, particularly in the Third World, many of whose members we shall see in the corridors, looking for their conference rooms. There are up to sixty conferences here every day and (I write from experience) they tend to go on for a very long time. Folk music is apparently an unending topic of interest. Information about the organization's current activities can be obtained from the souvenir desk in the main entrance hall. UNESCO publishes a thoughtful magazine debating all the thorniest of the world's topical problems.

The UNESCO building is also a miniature museum of modern art, most of it First World. As we wander about we may see tapestries by Le Corbusier and Lurçat, frescoes by Picasso, a relief by Arp, a wall by Miró, a mosaic by Bazaine, sculpture by Giacometti and Kelly. The two biggest works are outside the main building; a huge reclining figure by Henry Moore and a swinging mobile by Alexander Calder.

From Place Fontenoy, Avenue de Lowendal brings us to **Les Invalides**. This is one of the most visited places in France. Most people go simply to see Napoleon's tomb and the beautiful dome above it which is visible from many parts of Paris. But the whole place is so full of historic and architectural interest that we should not rush our visit. The whole architectural ensemble, comprising Hôtel des Invalides, two churches, Cour d'Honneur, Army Museum, front garden and Esplanade, is one of the marvels of Europe.

It started, however, in a humdrum way. Louis XIV, concerned about the state of his old soldiers, many of whom had become beggars, ordered the architect Liberal Bruand to build a barracks for them, Hôtel des Invalides (we may compare the Chelsea Hospital in London of approximately the same date). The barracks were finished in 1676, financed by the pay of serving soldiers together with a levy on the local markets. The thoughts of the serving soldiers and stall-holders are not known, but it is the pensioners who are known as *grognards* or grumblers. Their barracks were lavish enough to look at, though probably not very comfortable inside. There is now only a remnant of pensioners left and they do not wear scarlet uniforms. Many are in wheelchairs and others act as guardians or odd job men.

The ideas of Louis XIV grew more glorious, and in the following year he commissioned Jules Hardouin-Mansart to build a second **church** with a dome and a semi-circular colonnade, like St Peter's in Rome. The colonnade was abandoned in favour of an avenue (Avenue de Bréteuil), but the rest of the church is as Hardouin-Mansart planned it, one of the masterpieces of the seventeenth century, the *grand siècle*. With his innate sense of form and line, which we have noticed elsewhere, allied to his technical expertise, he produced a baroque church of great beauty and simplicity. The façade has Doric columns and a single pediment. Above it rises the drum with forty columns and windows; and above this the dome, crowned with a lantern and spire. The dome is decorated with trophies and garlands and the spire rises to a height of 351 feet, a little lower than its contemporary St Paul's in London, but equally imposing.

The dome was first covered in gold leaf in 1715, an eye-catching and sun-catching effect. The gold leaf has been replaced several times since. But did Hardouin-Mansart see it as a golden dome? He died in 1708, and the church with its gilding was finished by his brother-in-law, Robert de Cotte. There is a statue of Hardouin-Mansart near the main door; but if you seek his monument, look up!

The inside of the dome is elaborately painted by distinguished artists of the period and shows the Evangelists, kings of France and Apostles, in that order. At the top is St Louis presenting Christ with a sword, thus striking from the very start a military note. It is quite possible that both the king and the architect had martial glory in mind all the time; after all, the *grognards* can hardly have wanted a second church.

> *Louis Quatorze*
> *Was addicted to wars.*
> *He sent Turenne to the Palatinate*
> *With orders to flatten it.*

Louis XIV would have been very happy to know that Turenne was the first soldier to be buried in the Dome church. He was re-interred here in 1800 on the orders of Napoleon, and from that moment the Invalides became the French Valhalla. It was separated from the other church, Saint-Louis-des-Invalides, and no longer used for services, but a notice reminds us to remove our hats and speak in low voices. We are in a shrine. Those entombed here include Turenne, Vauban, Bertrand, Duroc, Foch and two Bonaparte brothers (rather out of their element, we might think). In the centre, dominating everything, lies the emperor himself.

Napoleon died in St Helena in 1821. In 1840, after years of political negotiations, the British agreed to his body being brought home to France. He himself had said, 'Paris will still cry "*Vive l'Empereur!*"' A party went to St Helena including Louis-Philippe's son, General Bertrand, the writer Las Cases who had helped Napoleon to write his memoirs, and his valet Marchand. In their presence the coffin was exhumed and opened. To general astonishment it was found that, after nineteen years in the warm damp earth, the body was still perfectly preserved – a tribute either to Napoleon's personality or to the skill of the local undertakers.

The body was brought home to Le Havre, the Arc de Triomphe and finally the Invalides. The present **tomb**, however, was not ready until 1861. It was designed by Visconti and is one of his finest achievements, both majestic and simple. Napoleon lies inside seven coffins: the first is of iron, the second of mahogany, the third of lead, the fourth of lead, the fifth of ebony, the sixth of oak and the seventh, the visible sarcophagus, of red porphyry. It reads like a verse from *Revelation* and indeed there is something apocalyptic about it all. As we gaze down on the tomb, the charisma reaches us through the years, through the coffins. Whether we think of Napoleon as a man who spread revolutionary enlightenment, law and order through Europe, or as an ambitious soldier who brought war and death to unfortunate millions, one thing cannot be denied: few men in history have aroused such fervent hero-worship.

Napoleon spent his six years on St Helena recreating his image, with the help of the sycophantic Las Cases. The image now was the benevolent ruler, wise law-giver. Julius Cæsar had been replaced by Justinian. Round the tomb, on the lower, crypt level are wall-plaques illustrating this; one shows Napoleon with his arms outstretched, one hand touching the Laws of Justinian, the other the Code Napoléon. There is a quotation from his memoirs which may be translated, 'In every country where I ruled, the permanent trace remains of my good deeds'. Other quotations emphasize the Code Napoléon, his work for education, restoration of law and order and the suppression of dishonesty in the public services. There is not much about liberty or fraternity, nothing about the Grande Armée. But on the marble floor of the tomb are the names of his chief battles. Against the pillars are twelve huge classical figures, by Pradier, representing the campaigns from Rivoli to Waterloo; dignified and sorrowful, their laurel wreaths are lowered in mourning. Whatever Las Cases may have thought, we are in the presence of a commander-in-chief.

In a niche beside the tomb is the grave of his young son, the King of Rome – not that he ever saw Rome. He died aged twenty-one in Vienna and was buried in the Habsburg crypt, but his body was returned to France in 1940, an unexpected present from Hitler to Paris. He lies beneath a dominating statue of his father and there are often fresh flowers on his grave.

The other church, **Saint-Louis-des-Invalides,** once shared a sanctuary with the Dome church. It is now completely separated and we enter it (free) from the far end in the Cour d'Honneur. The work of the original Invalides architect, Liberal Bruand, it has been criticized for its severity. But in fact it is a pleasantly proportioned classical church with an interesting ceiling; the more intricate organ-loft is by Hardouin-Mansart and a plate-glass window over the altar allows a glimpse into the Dome church. The most conspicuous features are the captured banners which hang from the upper gallery; many of them were burnt by the governor of the Invalides in 1814 to prevent them falling into the hands of the Allies, but plenty still remain. It is called the Soldiers' Church and services are held here on Sundays; but it is best known for its military funerals and memorial masses – Berlioz's *Requiem* was first performed here. In the crypt (not open) are the tombs of more soldiers, including Joffre, Leclerc and Juin.

We emerge into the great **Cour d'Honneur,** Bruand's best achievement and a fine example of *grand siècle* architecture. Completely formal and symmetrical, it has arcades below and pitched roofs above. But Bruand has broken up the horizontal lines with four pavilions and pediments, prancing horses on the corners of the roof, oval dormer windows and sundials. Under the arcades are a number of captured cannon of great size and weight, most of them with names and histories. The south wall is also the church façade and in the middle of it is a large statue of Napoleon by Seurre, which at one time stood on top of the Vendôme column.

The cobbled courtyard is the scene of many parades and military occasions. It was here that Captain Dreyfus was publicly disgraced. On a pleasanter note we may like to recall the select number of men, some of them foreign, who have been publicly honoured here with the traditional kiss on the cheek bestowed by a Frenchman of equal rank. It was here that Churchill was kissed by de Gaulle, Montgomery by Juin. I do not know who kissed Eisenhower.

On either side of the courtyard, occupying three floors, is the **Army Museum,** which we should certainly visit. If we are short of time or energy, we should concentrate on the east side of the courtyard. This part of the museum is devoted to the French Army from Louis XIV to the Crimean War and of course includes Napoleon's own campaigns, which will be much in our mind.

On show are many uniforms, much armour, a great deal of it mounted on realistic models; also swords, daggers, harnesses, pistols and rifles. The uniforms are tight, elaborate and much covered with lace; the weapons richly chased or engraved and signed. As we look at them, it is hard to realize that we are seeing material from a bloody battle, and indeed there is nothing in the museum to suggest that war is an unpleasant business – except perhaps the bullet which killed Turenne, and this is hard to find. There is also an absence of models or sand-tables which would help us to understand the tactics of the various battles. We seem to be in a gunsmith's shop or a military outfitters, wondering how on earth it was possible to move, let alone fight, in such tight clothes.

Several things remain in the memory, chiefly relics of Napoleon. His death-mask, taken by a British doctor in St Helena, was only later presented to the museum. Also eye-catching are his solid portable desk; his big white dog, which was his companion on Elba (stuffed), and the well-known portrait by Delaroche of him at Fontainebleau in 1814 after his first abdication, a brooding figure.

We leave the Cour d'Honneur on the north side, emerging into the garden, full of clipped yews and cannons and surrounded by a dry moat. This is a good point from which to see the façade; long, sternly classical, emphasizing the flat horizontal lines. Impressive rather than attractive, it looks like a barracks – and indeed that was what Bruand was ordered to build. However, he provided some variation with the two end pavilions and fine central portal. Above this is a statue of (by way of a change) Louis XIV on horseback, assisted by Justice and Prudence, not qualities with which he is generally associated. The statue dates from 1815, the original by Coustou having been destroyed in the Revolution. The dormer windows are decorated with helmets, which gives them a grotesque, semi-human appearance.

Beyond the garden stretches the **Esplanade** which reaches to the Seine. It was planned by Robert de Cotte, who completed the Invalides dome, and provides another of those magnificent perspectives which the French admire so much. The trees are kept low and indeed with underground car parks and transport terminals they have little depth of earth. The only building actually on the Esplanade is the Air France Terminal (Metro Invalides, also RER) and this keeps a deliberately low profile. Nothing must be allowed to spoil the view from the Seine and Pont Alexandre III. Five hundred yards away the dome seems to float over Hôtel des Invalides.

If we leave the Invalides from the courtyard by the Eglise du Dôme, and walk down Boulevard des Invalides past the church of St François Xavier, we reach **Musée Rodin** at no. 77 Rue de Varenne, on the corner of Boulevard des Invalides (Metro Varenne). It is a must for lovers of sculpture, housed in the house and the garden of Hôtel Biron. It would be hard to imagine a more perfect setting for the works of a sculptor. Rodin's (1840–1917) works would seem impressive anywhere, but it is a joy to have them in a classical setting which is neither overwhelming nor cramped.

Hôtel Biron would be worth a visit for itself alone; it is possibly the only *hôtel,* in an area noted for its fine houses, which is open to the public. Eighteenth century, with columns and pediments, it was designed by Gabriel for a rich wig-maker, and was later the home of the Duke of Maine, illegitimate son of Louis XIV and Madame de Montespan, who married the granddaughter of Le Grand Condé. Biron, a general in the Revolution, occupied it briefly before being guillotined. Later it became a convent and unfortunately the mother superior had the white and gold eighteenth-century panelling ripped out for being both materialistic and baroque. However, the panelling in the two end rotundas survives, a beautiful example of eighteenth-century décor, even though it is now plain wood-coloured; this provides a better background for marble statues.

Later the house became an official home for those connected with the arts, an earlier Cité des Arts. Among those who lived there were the German poet Rilke, the British dancer Isadora Duncan, and Auguste Rodin from 1908 until his death in 1917. They paid for their lodging by presenting their works to the state, though it is not clear what Madame Duncan presented. But we must be permanently grateful for the Rodin collection, which also includes works by other artists, which he possessed.

Coming to his own sculpture, we may well be amazed at its strength and vitality, by the mastery with which he handled the change from the classical to the modern idiom, and by the variety of themes which he studied. One of the principal themes is emergence – hands and heads emerging from rough rock or water, the creation of humanity. In *The Hand of God*, a hand emerging from limbo holds Adam and Eve in a gentle grasp. In one of his most celebrated works, *The Cathedral* (1908), two large hands emerge from rock, the tips touching in a prayerful attitude, forming a sort of chancel arch. The close observer will note that it is not a pair of hands, but two right hands. Indeed, with one exception, all his studies of hands are right hands, sometimes sensitive, sometimes stubby-fingered, as in *The Secret* (1910), usually holding something or someone; the left-handed exception is *La Main du Diable,* the devil's hand crushing humanity.

Feet were another of his themes. His walking men, his barefoot figures, when they have legs at all, have large muscular feet with strong toes. But his main theme was the torso, the human body, usually nude. Even in marble or bronze, the women are soft, the men have well-muscled backs. This is especially noticeable in his famous marble, *The Kiss*, which is remarkable both for its delicate eroticism and for its harmonious design. The bodies are beautifully shaped, but the faces hardly exist. The same applies to many of his imaginative works and also, of course, to his headless torsos; one might be forgiven for thinking that Rodin was not much interested in the human face. And then we look at his heads of Balzac, Hugo and Clemenceau, so full of life and character, Balzac's with almost a Dionysiac twinkle, and we see that Rodin was a fine portraitist. But it was a different facet of his art.

The Hugo busts and the Balzac statues are on the first floor. Rodin made several statues of Balzac, including a nude. But Balzac's portly figure hardly looks at its best nude, despite a resemblance to a middle-aged Bacchus, a resemblance perhaps justified by Balzac's own lifestyle. But a great novelist should not appear thus to the passing crowds and we must feel that it was right to choose a clothed, cloaked version for Boulevard Montparnasse.

The gallery of marbles was renovated in 1995 and now shows forty marbles protected from the elements.

In the garden are some of Rodin's largest and best-known works. Look carefully at the bronze *Le Penseur – The Thinker*. This was at one time in a park in Lübeck, Germany, where it was painted by the Norwegian Expressionist Edvard Munch, a picture which is now in the museum. The sculpture was bought back, with money raised by public subscription, and is now on the right of the entrance. *The Thinker* sits, chin on hand, elbow on knee, legs crossed, his body present, his mind far away. The dominating features are, once again, the great hands and feet; the head, by contrast, seems rather small. Perhaps the artist's model was not a great thinker – a problem which confronts many sculptors.

On the other side is the well-known group *The Burghers of Calais*. Rodin made several versions of this in plaster and we may well prefer the more homogeneous one, on the first floor of the museum. Against the east wall is a vast, extraordinary work, *The Gates of Hell*. This shows writhing bodies, Michelangelo-style, being sucked down, while over them sits a smaller version of our old friend *Le Penseur*. Above him, over the doors, are three shades, the same figure in three different positions. In this work, the symbolism eludes me, nor can I imagine Rodin's purpose, except that sculptors like writhing bodies. It was commissioned for the portal of a museum but the project was dropped.

Before leaving we may well dawdle for some pleasant minutes in the garden, where there are sometimes temporary exhibitions. But even if not, we shall enjoy the garden for itself. In many ways it is the quintessence of much that is best and most typical in Paris. There are no long perspectives or picturesque old corners, but it is the sort of place which the French themselves enjoy; the pool, the statues, the lime trees, the overshadowing dome, the classical façade of the house, the quietness. We might be in the eighteenth century.

Further down Rue de Varenne, we turn right into Rue du Bac for **Fondation Dina Vierny – Musée Maillol** (Metro Rue du Bac) in Hôtel Bouchardon, 59–61 rue de Grenelle. Dina Vierny puts her name first on the museum's brochure and perhaps she deserves it. She emerges as the personality of the sculptor Aristide Maillol's (1861–1944) later life and career, and the founder of this museum, now state-approved, as well as its chief curator. She was only fifteen when she walked into Maillol's life. His friends told him 'This is the woman you've been sculpting all this time without knowing it'. He accepted her at once as his Muse and from then on she inspired all his best later work. His paintings and drawings of her are of high quality. He even lent her out to his friends Matisse, Bonnard and Dufy, whenever their inspiration flagged. She was not only a woman of splendid physique which we can admire in the works here, but showed, after Maillol's death, that she was a very capable person, by running an art gallery in St Germain in its artistic heyday and making this collection. The eighteenth-century building, with its imposing façade behind an even more grandiose fountain by Bouchardon (built between 1739 and 1746), may not seem a suitable home for the first modern sculptor to break with the gesticulating allegoric nineteenth-century tradition and search for pure form. But the building had an artistic tradition of its own. Alfred de Musset was brought up there and Garnier designed his Paris Opera in the studio of his friend the architect Baudry, who lived there.

It has 27 rooms, but they are not large and cannot show all the 2000 works by 36 leading artists of the twentieth century which Dina Vierny collected. These are rotated in temporary shows, but many of them are drawings, which deteriorate if exposed for long. Much of the space is rented out for other temporary exhibitions. What we are likely to see, therefore, is mainly limited to Maillol's own work, with its monumental pieces, as we enter, on the ground floor; his paintings, drawings and ceramics on the first floor, among works by his circle of friends, notably Bonnard (1867–1946), and his tapestry and paintings, as well as smaller sculpture, on the second floor.

There we have the happy surprise of discovering Marcel Duchamp (1887–1968), Wassili Kandinsky (1866–1944) and Serge Poliakoff (1900–1969); some excellent paintings collected by Dina Vierny. We may decide to start our tour at the top of the museum, to see them first. There is a splendid Poliakoff in grey, red and dark blue (1951), an all-yellow (very unusual) of 1956, and an all-blue (also rare) of 1961. Kandinsky (an almost exact contemporary of Maillol) is there with *Angles Rouges*, 1928, oil on canvas. Items float against a dark ground, with a zig-zag of red dividing them from corner to corner. We should not miss these rooms.

Going down, to the first floor, we should look for Pierre Bonnard's *Le Grand Nu Sombre* oil on canvas, painted between 1941 and 1946, one of his last and finest works. Dina Vierny was his model for this. The seated woman and the background glow with warm light.

Back on the ground floor we see *Leda* (bronze, height 29 cms). In 1901 Maillol had one of his first successes with this piece. It may seem to us now that it shows a very squat model with fat legs. But that is not how Rodin saw it; he exclaimed 'It is absolutely beautiful!' He realised that Maillol was setting a new trend, in his search for 'Pure Form'. This was very well followed up by *La Méditerranée*, 1902–5 bronze 110 x 120 cms, a restful, sitting nude, well composed. André Gide wrote 'She is beautiful. She signifies nothing. This is a silent work'. It is in great contrast to *Action in Chains*, 1905, a monumental bronze over two metres high. This is a great striding woman, struggling to free her wrists which are chained behind her. It was a commissioned monument to a revolutionary called Blangui. We may think it odd that he did not use a male figure for this, but Maillol confined himself to female nudes. Almost his last work *The River* (lead, 124 x 230 cms, 1943), is again a very long way from his peaceful 'pure form' of 1902–5. It suggests a girl thrown down, and fighting against rape. The explanation of this tormented work is that in 1943 France had been invaded and occupied; we may see it (as no doubt André Malraux did) as a Resistance symbol.

These monumental works may seem familiar to us. Some of us have seen them, cast in bronze or lead, in the Tuileries Gardens. These are versions of the same works. In 1964 André Malraux accepted 18 of them as a donation, and placed them in the gardens of the Carrousel, fulfilling Maillol's wish 'Give me a garden and I will fill it with sculpture'. In 1995 they were moved to the Tuileries Gardens.

If we go down to the basement to the cafeteria, we must look for the work of Emile Gilioli (1911–1977) particularly a great bronze head (height 90 cm) *La Grande Babet*, 1966. This is a very good likeness of his wife, as well as being a striking piece.

19

Montparnasse

MONTPARNASSE MAY FAIRLY be called the cradle of modern art. All contemporary art is, of course, 'modern', but Montparnasse was the forcing-house of ideas which had been germinating in our civilization and which came to harvest in the first forty years of the twentieth century. In the plastic, visual arts, its influence was worldwide; generally referred to as 'modern art', it was also called the Ecole de Paris, though its influence soon spread. Many of its leading figures were not French in origin; sometimes they were refugees from foreign tyrannies, sometimes simply enjoying freedom of expression, the general café *ambiance* and meetings of sympathetic minds, all of which they found in Montparnasse. Nor was it confined to the plastic arts. Some were writers, political thinkers, composers, dancers, theatre designers or those connected with the new art form, films. Many of their successors are still there and can be seen in the evenings in the *Coupole* or the *Select*. There were also many hangers-on, with less talent, and a good picture of Montparnasse in the 1920s can be read in the first half of Hemingway's early novel, *Fiesta (The Sun Also Rises)* and in his memoir, *A Moveable Feast.*

We can start our walk with Hemingway, at the eastern end of Boulevard du Montparnasse (14me, Metro Vavin) but first we can pause for a cup of coffee while we consider the life of Montparnasse and its fascinating history.

It was not concerned specifically with painting, originally. In the seventeenth century poets and students, finding Pont Neuf too noisy and the near presence of Queen Margot discouraging, took to the nearby countryside to declaim their works. The 'mountain' was hardly worthy of the name; it was merely a heap of stones from disused quarries, covered with grass, but it was given the nickname of Mount Parnassus. It has long since disappeared and the area was built over, becoming a lively centre of Paris, with cafés, cabarets and

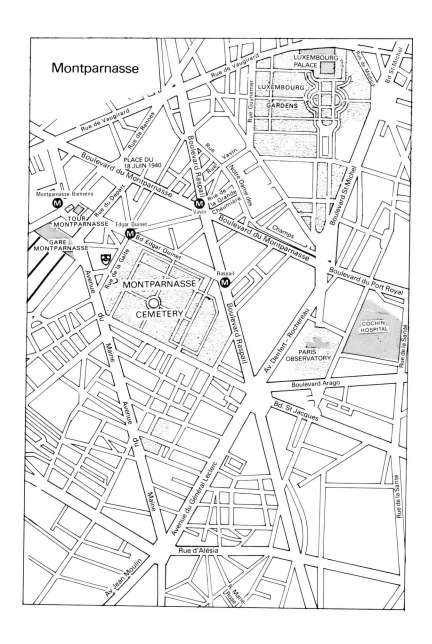

dance-halls. The can-can was danced here, before it ever appeared at the *Moulin Rouge*. Much of the quarter was rebuilt by Haussmann in the nineteenth century, in particular the two wide boulevards, Boulevard du Montparnasse (which preserved the colloquial name) and Boulevard d'Enfer, now Boulevard Raspail, a very long street which Hemingway's 'Jake' 'could not stand to ride along', though he did not mind walking along it (Metro Denfert-Rochereau). An interesting building is no. 26 Rue Vavin, a block of flats built in 1911 and covered almost entirely in white tiles. The flats are stepped back from each other to give each one an open-air terrace, very unfashionable in these glass-tower days. But as a piece of Art Nouveau it is remarkable. Otherwise, the quarter is of little interest architecturally; atmospherically it is fascinating.

The first writer to move into the area was the satirist, Alfred Jarry; the first painter, Rousseau 'le Douanier'. After the 1900 Exhibition, the wine pavilion was reconstructed to provide modest lodgings and studios, known informally as the *Beehive* (*La Ruche*), and among its first tenants were Modigliani, Chagall, Léger, Soutine and Zadkine. Apollinaire, the poet who coined the word Cubism, arrived early on the scene, followed soon after by Picasso, Braque, Juan Gris and Van Dongen, who had previously been centred in Montmartre, but were attracted by the liveliness of the new quarter.

We may drop some further famous names: Kandinsky, Klee, Matisse, Rouault; Scott Fitzgerald, Gertrude Stein, James Joyce, Hilaire Belloc, Ford Madox Ford, Max Jacob, Henry Miller, Samuel Beckett; Stravinsky, Satie, de Falla, Milhaud; Cocteau, Eisenstein. There were some 25,000 Russians living in Paris during this time, many, but not all, refugees from the tsarist régime, and they would argue with each other all evening in the Montparnasse cafés. Among them were Lenin and Trotsky.

Unless we have other transport, our walk is reached from Metro Vavin, along Boulevard du Montparnasse, eastwards towards Boulevard de l'Observatoire. When Hemingway came to Montparnasse from Place de la Contrescarpe, he and his family lived at no. 113 Rue Notre-Dame-des-Champs, just round the corner from **Closerie des Lilas.** This was the literary café of the area and, as he liked writing in public, he would sit at a table on the pavement, writing in his notebooks, greeting his friends, sometimes snubbing them, sometimes, absorbed in his work, not even seeing them. In the evening, according to some who later remembered him, he would stroll along the boulevard to the *Dôme* café, where he would join a table and from then on dominate the conversation, although he was not yet the world figure he later became.

Closerie des Lilas is no longer a café, but it still has literary associations, one of the places where established writers and aspiring winners of the Prix Goncourt should be seen. The atmosphere is not quite the same as at the beginning of the century, when the writer Paul Fort held his rowdy Tuesday evenings there; or when Lady Duff-Twiston (Hemingway's 'Brett') danced the Charleston.

Outside the garden of the *Closerie* we find the celebrated **statue of Marshal Ney,** French tactical commander at Waterloo, brandishing his sword among the trees, only a few yards from the place where he was executed. Responsibility for his trial and death (7 December 1815) lay with the Duc de Richelieu, who ruled France in the name of the Bourbon king, Louis XVIII. The king, rather out of his depth in a country divided between Royalists and Bonapartists, was accused by both sides of weakness and only too glad to leave politics to Richelieu, a close friend of the tsar.

We are now at the meeting of four boulevards and there are fine views through the trees of the Observatoire, the dome of the church of Val-de-Grâce and, down the Observatoire avenue, a distant façade of the Luxembourg Palace.

However, we shall stroll (*flâner*) with many others along Boulevard du Montparnasse. The first part is not very interesting, but opposite is a small street, Rue de la Grande Chaumière, which we shall certainly look at. The **Grande Chaumière** was a cabaret and 'dancing', a rather noisy one, which started during the Revolution. It became a well-known private art school and, as there was no entrance examination, anyone from anywhere could enrol on payment. The students sat in crowded rooms, doing charcoal drawings of plaster saints or female figures, clothed and nude. Watching young people emerging for their lunchtime break and coffee in *Select*, we might try to guess who were serious artists and who were merely passing a year or two in pleasant, artistic surroundings. The academy still continues and is proud of its tradition.

Almost opposite is an excellent artists' colourman, Gattégno, a shop which sells canvases, paints, brushes and so on in almost unlimited sizes and shapes to everyone, professionals and students alike.

Returning to the boulevard, we are at Carrefour, the crossroads with Boulevard Raspail. There we find Rodin's famous **statue of Balzac,** which certainly deserves our attention. Rodin's basic idea was that a statue was both a figure and a rock, one emerging from the other, and the Balzac statue combines both. Rodin worked long on it, making many sketches, and the result has been hailed as a masterpiece, though some have found it over-praised. It is certainly a dominating tribute to two great men, near contemporaries.

At Carrefour, back at Metro Vavin, we are in the heart of the quarter, crowded with people and life, not much connected with art. Two well-known cafés, *Dôme* and *Rotonde*, face each other. Neither are what they were in the days when tables stretched down the street to the next café. Here Modigliani would hawk his pictures from table to table, with moderate financial success; there must be many people alive now who wish that their grandparents had disbursed a few francs on those occasions. Both cafés are now mainly restaurants, full of nostalgic reminders of the 1920s, but with small, glassed-in terraces, and filled by the better-off bourgeoisie.

Beyond Rue Vavin is *Select*, which appears in many novels. The café is the same still but there is now a restaurant as well. We find a crowd or artists or pseudo-artists drinking and talking. Artists are convivial people and we shall have no trouble in making friends. We may well be asked to see their studios and their work in the hope, of course, of selling us a picture. If we are lucky and choose right, our grandchildren may find themselves millionaires. But it is a long-odds gamble.

Opposite is the **Coupole,** a large café-restaurant and the artistic and literary heart of the quarter. It is a place where we go to see who is there, especially in the late evening. Here there are posters on the walls; every artist having a show has to have his poster in the *Coupole*. More and more it is being turned over to food, mere drinkers and talkers restricted to the glassed-in terrace. But it is crowded every evening.

Moving on down the boulevard, past cafés, cinemas and small shops (and even a church, Notre-Dame-des-Champs, neo-Byzantine, on the site of an old country church), we reach the crossroads with Rue de Rennes, Place du 18 Juin 1940 – the name recalls the date of de Gaulle's historic broadcast from London. Facing us is the Maine-Montparnasse Building Complex, dominated by the tower.

Montparnasse Tower (Metro Montparnasse-Bienvenue) indeed dominates, not only the quarter but the whole of central Paris. It was completed in 1973 and was part of the plan to renovate a rather decaying area with new business facilities. From the point of view of transport and the metro, it was ideally situated and the tower has many qualities. Nearly seven hundred feet high (two hundred metres) it was the tallest office block in Europe. It has 39,000 square metres of glass. It is a beautiful skyscraper, the work of a team of French architects, Cassan, Beaudouin, de Marien and Saubot. Unlike some new North American towers, it has a curved shape, not over-severe, and reminiscent possibly of the Pirelli building in Milan. One could almost call it a piece of giant sculpture. But whether it is placed in the right city is a matter of continuing debate.

Seven thousand people work there. But we shall ignore them and ascend to the 56th floor by a fast lift, well signposted. Here we have a panorama, not only of Paris but of twenty-five miles of the Ile-de-France. This is on fine days; on wet days the clouds swirl round the windows, romantically. At night we have a million twinkling lights below us.

It is a view which should be seen, though personally I think Paris looks better from lower down. What we see from the top of the tower are the other high-rise buildings, La Défense, and the new apartment blocks which now encircle Paris. The famous avenues, domes, palaces and churches which we have come to see are lost far below us and we shall have some trouble in identifying them, even with the help of the painted encircling map.

Two flights higher (on foot) we find ourselves on the open-air terrace able to see, if we wish, the distant airports and Mont Valérian. On a windy day we may have the feelings of a main-topman furling the sails in a westerly gale or a mountaineer who has continued the ascent against the advice of his guide. There are careful precautions against suicide, one of the problems of high-rise architects and one to which Eiffel did not, perhaps, give enough attention.

Returning to the ground, we find ourselves in the big building complex, the commercial centre. This is on eight levels, six of them underground and served by lifts or escalators. There are two department stores (Galeries Lafayette and C & A); about sixty boutiques; cafés; snack-bars; a sports centre; swimming pool; and the export offices of over two hundred companies. France Telecom has a large office there. It was originally intended that the complex should be an art centre, revitalizing the artistic life of the quarter, and for a time this seemed to be coming about. A huge tent was erected in the piazza behind the tower, where several exhibitions and salons were held. But then the plan was dropped in favour of Beaubourg and the Montparnasse Centre was given over wholly to business and businessmen, who rarely live in the quarter. In a bustling area traditionally devoted to art and entertainment, the biggest architectural feature is largely empty at night.

The tower and the commercial centre are built on the site of the nineteenth-century Gare Montparnasse and our walk ends here. In August 1944 General Leclerc and his armoured division arrived from Porte d'Orléans and made their headquarters in the station; no trains were of course running. On 25 August, he accepted the surrender of the German military governor there, as is recorded by a plaque on the left side of the commercial centre. The rebuilt **Gare Montparnasse** is now a few hundred yards farther down the line. It was the most modern railway station in Europe, following Rome and Euston, when it opened. The trains run into a tall canyon of glass, steel and concrete, and every possible amenity is provided for the traveller, including a chapel and a statue of St Bernard, carved from an old railway sleeper. But the station only serves Brittany, lower Normandy and the Atlantic coast. It has no long-distance or international traffic, which bring so much glamour to the ageing stations elsewhere, and is mainly used by commuters, who are always in a hurry.

Nevertheless, Montparnasse remains a centre of attraction. Many artists may have been forced by rising rents to live farther out, but they return frequently for the *ambiance* and one another's company. Many people come for the night-life, which goes on till all hours and is centred, suitably, on Rue de la Gaîté (Metro Gaîté). This was originally an old country road lined with cafés and cabarets, and it continues the tradition with nightclubs, cinemas and restaurants, with a mixed crowd of visitors and local inhabitants. The street also has two 'straight' theatres and the Bobino music-hall, the Left Bank equivalent of the Olympia on the Right Bank. Many prominent pop singers appear here, and it was the favourite theatre of the modern troubadour, Georges Brassens. There are more nightclubs in Rues Vavin and Bréa, near the intersection with Boulevard Raspail. The 'discos' for dancing have been driven out of Rue de la Gaîté by sex shops but there are others nearby.

Lest it may be thought that Montparnasse is, and has always been, just a place for fun and revelry, we can pause for a moment to consider the more serious side. The places of interest are scattered and can be reached by metro from Montparnasse-Bienvenue.

Lenin lived from 1909 to 1912 at no. 4 Rue Marie-Rose (Metro Alésia). His apartment, and the adjoining one, are now a museum which we can visit by previous arrangement with the Association Musée Lénine.

The three-room flat is modest, fifty-nine square metres, but an ample lodging by modern Paris or Russian standards, and it had central heating, its own lavatory and a kitchen with an old-fashioned range. Lenin worked in the front room which overlooked the small street, the trees and the wall opposite (the hideous red-brick church which now dominates the street was not there in his time). The flat, which he shared with Kroupskaya and her mother, has been re-decorated to look much as it did in 1909, comfortable but not luxurious. His and Kroupskaya's bedroom has no outside ventilation and he was short of furniture, writing at a kitchen table and keeping his books stacked on the floor.

He had other problems too, apart from politics. His printer went bankrupt, leaving him short of money, like any other bourgeois. His correspondence was hindered by a postal strike, about which he expressed himself forcefully. His letters were also watched and he was forced to adopt clandestine and rather romantic methods; Kroupskaya's mother would copy out old and harmless texts and, between the lines, her daughter would write Lenin's manifestos in invisible ink, schoolgirl-style. However, he also managed some more public events: political meetings in *Puits Rouge* café, since demolished, at the corner of Avenue Jean-Moulin (then Avenue de Châtillon), facing the church at Metro Alésia. The area was then part of the Montrouge district, and the word and colour *rouge* must have been much in his mind. The fifth Communist Party congress was held in a dance-hall at 99 Rue d'Alésia in 1909.

On the centenary of his birth, 1970, moves were made to rename the street Rue Lénine, but there was fierce opposition and the flat was sacked by right-wingers. Behind the smashed mirror over his writing-chair a piece of the original wallpaper was found. This relic was sent to Russia where it was copied and printed and now the whole flat is papered with it, a design of laurel sprigs in pinkish-buff. This and the oil lamps give an idea of the time and, in a sense, of the man. The apartment next door contains books, manifestos and photographs, among them the British Museum Reading Room, more identified in our minds with Marx than with Lenin. The plaque outside was erected in April 1945, before the end of the war, and obviously prepared well in advance by the Resistance.

In 1912 Lenin decided to leave Paris, no longer a suitable headquarters for his work. In June of that year, he said goodbye to his colleagues at Pavillon du Lac in the nearby Parc Montsouris and started on the long, fateful journey through Switzerland and Germany to the Finland Station in St Petersburg, which he reached in 1917.

Revolutionaries, however, continued to exist in Montparnasse, though Lenin might not have approved of their dissenting ideas. In recent times Sartre lived his last years near the main Montparnasse-Raspail crossroads, and often lunched late in *Coupole*, speaking to nobody except his adopted Algerian daughter, to whom he talked incessantly. She never replied. It has often been thus in Montparnasse.

At the east end of the boulevard was Port Royal convent, a centre of the Jansenist (near-Protestant) movement so cruelly persecuted in the reign of Louis XIV; it is now part of Cochin Hospital (Metro Saint-Jacques) next door. We see the big hospital itself, where de Gaulle was operated on for prostate. Or we may pass the Santé prison (Metro Glacière) where the guillotine blade fell for the last time. And then on to **Montparnasse Cemetery** (Metro Raspail), which at least we can enter, from Boulevard Edgar-Quinet. Here we find the graves of several artists previously mentioned, plus those of Baudelaire, Maupassant, Citroën, César Franck and Saint-Saëns. Jean-Paul Sartre and Simone de Beauvoir share a joint grave on the right of the gates; a strange *huis clos* for such an independent pair. Then, to cheer ourselves up, we cross Rue Emile-Richard (the longest street in Paris without houses) to the eastern part of the cemetery. There, beside Boulevard Raspail, we find Brancusi's statue *The Kiss*, which will remind us that Montparnasse has always been a place of romance. A simple monolithic gravestone, it conveys in the modern idiom a touching devotion, and it invites comparison with Rodin's famous work on the same subject.

Perhaps it is our last night and we have decided to stay up late. If we are heading back to Montparnasse for a long, multilingual evening, we go back to Metro Vavin. But there are many other possibilities.

The night-life of Paris has long been famous. Indeed the whole idea of 'Gay Paree' is based on the city's night-life rather than on attractions discussed in previous chapters. Paris is a city which never seems to sleep. If we happen to be out in the middle of the night, we shall find people going about, on pleasure or unimaginable business. Unlike French provincial towns, which firmly turn out all the lights at ten o'clock, Paris goes on all night, *la ville lumière*. For those who do not wish to go to bed, Paris offers a wide choice. Whether we are wanting a show or a poetry-reading, a glamorous gala, billiards-club, jazz-club or casino, or a tramp along the boulevards in Henry Miller style, we can find it.

The traditional way of ending a night out in Paris is to drink onion soup at Les Halles, and it is still the right way, even though the great market may have gone. We may even have a last bottle of champagne with it.

It has been a long night. We have dined and wined, listened to fast, brilliant dialogue, we have danced or walked miles along the boulevards or beside the river. And now it is dawn, the Paris sky is growing pink, the pigeons are beginning to coo on the rooftops. It is time to part; you have a journey ahead of you, I am thinking of my bed.

But you will certainly come back. Hemingway wrote that Paris is a moveable feast; wherever you go for the rest of your life it stays with you. So we shall certainly meet again, next year or even sooner – in front of your favourite building or masterpiece, strolling down a wide boulevard or narrow street, sitting on the terrace of your favourite café. Together we shall look at the flying buttresses of Notre-Dame and at Monet's water-lilies. We shall window-shop in Saint-Germain-des-Prés and picnic beside the Seine. And we may even stand on the star of Kilomètre Zéro.

Yes, we shall certainly meet again. But in the meantime it is Goodbye. Or, as a modern French novelist has put it, 'Au, dit-il, revoir'.

Appendices

Outer Paris

La Défense
Suburb between Pont de Neuilly and Nanterre. Boulevard Circulaire
(Exit 7, right) metro, RER and railway station

La Défense is Paris's biggest business suburb. It is a rival to
London's Barbican, and the name has a similar meaning: a
monument commemorates the defence of Paris in the 1870 war.
Many of the major public utilities and commercial enterprises of
France have their offices here, particularly American firms. It is too
far out to be a good headquarters for visitors to Paris, but, if we have
come to do business, we shall find that the district is self-contained,
with its own hotels, motels and amenities. Some businessmen arrive
straight from the airport, do their business and fly home, without
realising that they have not been to Paris.

Although the area can be reached by metro or RER, it is much
better to arrive by car or bus tour, if we can, taking Exit 7, right,
from the Boulevard Circulaire. Parking is provided; we should
follow signs for 'Parking de la Grande Arche'. To arrive on foot is a
desolate experience; it is a long, gritty trudge from one skyscraper to
another, signposts are few and it is very easy to get lost. Sightseers
should start at 'INFO Défense', 15 Place de la Défense, Défense 4,
where useful maps and booklets can be obtained. This is at a central
point, near to the metro and RER arrival, and in sight of the great
arch.

There is no habitable centre, like a traditional city, but some good
motels make an attempt to humanize the district, and there are a few
little restaurants, but a simple steak-and-chips costs more here than
in central Paris, suggesting that rents are too high.

La Défense was planned in 1958 with the chief object of keeping
skyscrapers out of Paris; this was not the only object in which it
failed. Building has gone on ever since and the ups and downs of

277

this still unfinished project have made town-planning history. It was at first conceived as an avenue of high-rise blocks, a sort of triumphal way continuing the Champs-Elysées beyond Pont de Neuilly.

This image soon gave way to the 'group of towers in a park' idea, made fashionable by Le Corbusier in the 1950s. It was to be a mixed residential and commercial centre where 'a new vision of the town' would 'enforce on the world a conception of life in total rupture with humanity's past'. A huge open space described as an 'architectural silence' was to cut pedestrians off entirely from traffic, so that the inhabitant would never even hear a car. But Parisians, who are attached to their way of life and to their cars, decided not to live there. There are still only 40,000 inhabitants. Three times as many are commuters. They took a great dislike to the whole project, especially when the first towers began to dominate the Paris skyline and the famous view up the Champs-Elysées. Even the popular Salon de Mai was boycotted when it was held at La Défense, although the CNIT Exhibition Hall was a remarkable place, shaped like an up-turned shell. The art gallery later closed and became a defence museum (AD 1600 to present-day).

Office building went ahead, but on such purely profit-oriented lines that in the 1970s a major public outcry broke out. The towers, it was claimed, were outmoded before they were built and paid scant respect to French aesthetic and town-planning standards. Staff refused to work in them until something was done about ventilation, lighting and soundproofing. Office blocks stood empty, sites were left vacant and finances plunged into a huge deficit. Resources were diverted to Créteil, the newer new town, where high-rise development was rejected.

This crisis was a turning point for La Défense. The planners at the governing body EPAD must be congratulated on having reacted with a new initiative which took La Défense into its third and more varied stage, taking public opinion into account at last. It then took shape in a real sense and became, finally, a success. Visually the later towers were more elegant, and their edging with more imaginative lower buildings along the motorway gave the quarter a new cohesion. Modern sculpture is a feature (note Calder's last work, a huge red stabile *The Spider*) and a giant workman's thumb by César (bronze), and fountains and gardens were laid out. The change proved to be financially rewarding and the area since then has paid its way and expanded. There has been a return of big-business tenants, led by IBM, which has its European registered offices in Tour Descartes.

The Manhattan Tower was bought by Kuwait. Even Parisians have softened towards La Défense: 'We have got our Brasilia without realizing it'.

Those like myself who enjoy a good skyscraper will think these towers rather small by US standards, but we can find a number of buildings to admire as well as some to regret. The succession of styles, already spanning more than a generation, begins with a tower with an all-metal frame. The shining 45-storey Framotose (formerly FIAT) Tower belongs to the much-criticised middle period, but it has its qualities and still dominates the whole district; the green GAN Tower came next. The Aurore Tower, with bronze-tinted glass layers followed. The twin-towers 'Les Miroirs', with only 16 floors, showed the trend of the 1980s and most buildings since then have been normal office blocks.

The great arch, which was supposed to be the last building, instead gave a new impetus to high-rise. The black glass twin towers of the Société Général (1996) and the Europlaza (formerly Septentrion) will not be the last skyscrapers; two more are under construction, Cœur Défense and Tour Heinz, 165 metres high. But the future is uncertain because further expansion is not being welcomed by the neighbouring area, Nanterre, where they had their own high-rise experience a long time ago. Their huge block of council flats (HLMs), decorated with holes and known locally as 'gruyère-cheese', is the only landmark we can distinguish at all clearly from the roof of the Arche, and it must be admitted that it has more character than anything seen yet in La Défense.

The Grande Arche de la Défense

This government-funded project was intended to complete the whole plan and give La Défense a less purely commercial image. The huge cost was justified to the taxpayers by the announcement that it would be 'an International Communications Exchange, resolutely oriented towards the 21st century'. This was to 'keep France to the fore in video, telecommunications and cinema'. As no one understood this, there has not been too much disappointment about the use, in the end, of one side of the arch for government departments and the other side for offices. In an age which has made a religion of football, the public-relations men might have made it much more popular if they had hailed it as a giant goalpost.

The building is extremely severe – just straight lines and right-angled corners. It would not be remarkable except for its size (height 110m – 35 floors). If we ask French people why it is feminine, when Carrousel and Triomphe are masculine, they will usually just shrug and say it is 'obvious'. But some will tell us that Triumph is for men and Defence is for women. The Arche's femininity has not softened its lines, but the heavy structure is lightened by a mirror surface and a white interior, cambered inwards. This simplicity is ruined by the off-centre lift, which clutters the view through the arch. If the beautiful Saint-Louis bridge in America can conceal its lift inside, even on a curve, surely the Défense lift could have been built inside one of its thick legs.

A huge flight of stairs leads to the base, like the most inconsiderate cathedrals, but if we are cunning we do not climb them. We go down into a small arena in front and get access by escalator. This is well thought. But at the top of the lift we get a sad surprise: it does not go to the roof, but leads only to an enclosed area with a restaurant and an art exhibition. If we want to see the view, we have to go outside and climb a very steep, high, staircase. It can be cold, windy and wet. If we have a handicapped pass, there is an ingenious wheelchair, worked by an attendant, which will climb the steps with us inside it, along a rail.

We are told that we can see ten kilometres on a clear day. But the view is disappointing. Apart from La Défense itself, with a rather jolly giant green globe near us, we only look out on a wilderness. Paris is too far away to appear as more than a few molehills on the skyline. Behind us, the arch leads nowhere, but a passerelle takes walkers into some gardens. This view cannot compare with that from the roof of the Arc de Triomphe, looking down into Etoile all round, or the Eiffel Tower or Tour Montparnasse, showing Paris like a map below us.

Our height of 110 metres overtops, no doubt deliberately, the Arc de Triomphe which is only 70 metres high, at the other end of the long avenue. But as we go down in the lift, the Arc de Triomphe rises up over us. It is on higher ground.

If we leave at dusk, we can see La Défense at its best. Floodlighting softens the Arche and the skyline of the buildings frames the lights rising over us in the towers. This un-Parisian city has its own magic, after all.

Basilique de Saint-Denis
1 Rue de la Légion d'Honneur, Saint-Denis, Metro Saint-Denis-Basilique

The abbey of **Saint-Denis** now lies in an unattractive northern quarter of Paris. Once it stood outside the city walls, just as Westminster Abbey was outside the City of London. St Denis, the apostle and first bishop of Paris, was said to have been buried after his martyrdom in c.250 in a Gallo-Roman cemetery on the site; the monastery later erected in his memory was patronized by the last great king of the Merovingian dynasty, Dagobert, during his brief reign of ten years from 629. The new Carolingian dynasty in the eighth century continued this patronage, and, like Dagobert, chose Saint-Denis as their burial place, but with the massive expansion of the empire under Charlemagne and his preference for Aachen, Saint-Denis was temporarily eclipsed. It was not until the accession of the Capetians that Saint-Denis became the accepted royal burial place: after 996, only three kings were ever buried elsewhere.

The monks of Saint-Denis were in close touch with the royal court, and during the fourteenth century acted as the official chroniclers to the monarchy, compiling the *Grandes chroniques de France* under the auspices of Charles V. They were the guardians of the royal regalia and of the sacred banner of France, the *oriflamme,* the great scarlet flag which in peacetime hung over the tomb of St Denis. It was first used by Louis VI in 1124, and its last appearance was at Agincourt in 1415. Mediæval writers claimed that when it was unfurled it was a sign that no quarter was to be shown. The war-cry of France was also derived from the abbey: in the fourteenth century it was '*Montejoie, Saint Denis!*'

For their part, the kings of France encouraged and rewarded this devotion to their dynasty with wide grants of lands and revenues. Indeed, ambitious monks in the thirteenth century forged a charter to prove that Charlemagne had given the kingdom of France itself to Saint-Denis as a fief, and the king himself was the abbey's vassal. But even St Louis's generosity did not go this far: his most enduring contribution to the abbey was the commemoration of his ancestors. The royal tombs had been placed at random throughout the abbey, with a group before the altar of the Trinity. St Louis commissioned a series of effigies and new tombs to be placed below the rebuilt crossing of the church; the kings and queens are all portrayed in thirteenth-century clothing, including St Louis himself. Even though his arrangement of the tombs was soon disrupted, and at the Revolution two of the effigies were destroyed, fourteen still survive, replaced under the crossing. They are a remarkable witness to the mediæval idea of a royal dynasty and to the awakening of a royalist nationalism in France which was to survive the disasters of the fourteenth century.

Of the other mediæval effigies, the most striking are André Beauneveu's masterly portrait of Charles V, the figure of Bertrand du Guesclin, and Pierre de Thoiry's effigies of Charles VI and Isabella of Bavaria. Beauneveu's likeness of Charles V brings out the practical and austere nature of the man who rebuilt the kingdom after the debacle at Poitiers in 1356 and the wild years of the peasant rebellion known as the *jacquerie,* while his great commander, du Guesclin, youngest son of a poor Breton knight, is portrayed with the utmost realism. The same realistic vein recurs in the effigy of Charles VI, whose madness plunged France once again into chaos: the sculptor is clearly trying to present a favourable image, but the result none the less hints strongly at a disturbed mind.

The church itself has been rebuilt many times since Ste Geneviève's first edifice on the site in the fifth century. Yet the bulk of the surviving architecture represents the work of two men: Abbot Suger and Pierre de Montreuil. As one enters the church, the immediate impression is that the entire building is a unity, in High Gothic style of the thirteenth century. In fact, substantial portions of the twelfth-century fabric of Abbot Suger's day survive. The façade and west porch date from this period, but have suffered so severely over the centuries as to be almost unrecognizable as Romanesque. At the east end, the lower storey of the apse, one of the earliest examples of the new Gothic style, is from Suger's period.

In Christopher Brooke's words, 'Suger was a monk, an administrator, a royal minister, a notable author and a great patron of artists and architects. The combination is at once unique and characteristic of the age'. Indeed, 'royal minister' is an understatement, for Suger was effectively regent of France in 1145–7 while Louis VII was on the Second Crusade; it was he who laid the foundations of the French royal administration and consistently acted as chief adviser until he died in 1151 – Suger's own account of the rebuilding of the abbey is a vivid glimpse of the problems involved in an ambitious project of this kind. Faced with a crumbling church whose fabric had to stand up to hordes of pilgrims to the shrine of St Denis, he had to find his own sources of stone and timber; but merely to reconstruct was not enough, and what Suger created was the first Gothic church. He claimed to have desired above all to harmonize old and new work, but after the construction of the west end he seems to have turned to a new architect for the choir, an architect whose designs included the earliest known Gothic vaulting, supported by slender pillars which give the effect of space and light for which Suger strove. His new church was to be full of light, but not the austere white light of the Cistercians: Suger sought light coloured by stained glass, reflected from precious stones or sparkling from golden vessels. Some of the church furnishings survive, adapted from antique treasures: a porphyry vase mounted on an eagle, a water-jug and another vase in the Louvre, a chalice of sardonyx in the National Gallery at Washington and a copy of the base of Suger's great cross in the museum at Saint-Omer. He himself appears as donor in a stained-glass window in the central chapel of the choir, a window made to his order between 1140 and 1144 and thus among the earliest stained glass to survive, ranking with that of Chartres. Sadly only fifteen panels of the original series, which included a depiction of the First Crusade, have survived.

Pierre de Montreuil's rebuilding of the upper part of the choir, the crossing and the nave is entirely in the spirit of Suger's original concept of light and space, albeit in the fully developed Gothic idiom. The large dimensions of the transept were specifically designed to contain the royal tombs, but the nave, too, is generous in scale, lit at all three levels instead of allowing all the light to come from the clerestory, as in Romanesque designs. This gives the nave a unity which, with the quality of the details and refinements such as the gradual increase in the size of the pillars towards the choir, make the late-Gothic work at Saint-Denis a masterpiece in its own right. But it is the presence of the royal tombs and the inheritance of Abbot Suger that makes Saint-Denis what it is –a monument to one of the outstanding figures of the Middle Ages and a focal point for the cult of the French monarchy.

Palais Omnisports de Paris à Bercy – 'POPB'

12me, Right Bank, on the opposite side of the river from the Bibliothèque Nationale. Metro and RER Bercy.

The POPB, as it is called even on the road signs, is a huge stadium for great sporting events, of almost every kind except football.

Television viewers know Bercy well for holding the big French Open Tennis tournament every November. But they also hold skating events, making their own ice for them; an annual wind-surfing contest, for which they fill the area with water; and 'Moto-Cross' (cross-country motorcycle races) for which they bring in earth and build terrifying obstacles. They are thoroughly enterprising people, and don't stop there, staging spectacular operas and ballets and big pop concerts. Something called 'Danse Sportive' has its 'Lalique Trophy'; they show 'Les Dieux du Gymnase' and karting races. For these transformations, building contractors are brought in, bulldozing the whole centre area, and even the POPB's own staff are not allowed to enter it while the work goes on.

The POPB was part of a redevelopment plan which included the surrounding area, formerly an old district of wine cellars. These were once cheerful places where Parisians tested the new wine, like the now touristic Grinzing in Vienna. But they had become derelict and the wine-depot is now at Charenton. They had been stone buildings, something like stables to look at. One of them is preserved, as the 'Ecole de Boulangerie' in Rue des Pirogues de Bercy. The rest were razed and replaced by a large park and a mixture of HLM's (blocks of council flats) and 7-storey blocks of private flats. These are in a deliberately unostentatious 'Right-Bank' style, which, it seems, appeals to the buyers more than the imaginative earlier styles, like the Horlage district. They are comfortable and slightly cheaper than flats in central Paris. But their inhabitants have to endure the sight of the vast new Finance Ministry, spread along the river nearby. This, no doubt, houses the refugees turned out from their previous stronghold in the Louvre. It was a costly building, larger even than the Bastille Opera House, and one of its expensive features was its roof, designed as a landing-area for helicopters. But this was never used, because flights over that part of Paris were forbidden before they began. How quickly the future becomes the past.

The Omnisports Palace had three architects, Andraud, Parra and Guvan. Building began in 1983. It holds 17,500 spectators. Like the Bibliothèque Nationale at Tolbiac, opposite, the site is between the river and the railway. From the start they cared about local opinion and took trouble not to make their mammoth building appear a monstrosity. Many people might have objected to a stadium on their doorstep, but everyone likes mountains. So they covered the huge flat-topped mound with earth and grass, and it took the fancy of its neighbours at once. They tell us with awe that it is REAL GRASS! And that it has to be cut like a lawn. In this formerly slum district, perhaps some of them had never seen grass before. The sides of the mound are so steep that even the hardiest farmer in the high Alps might quail at the thought of making hay there. But an ingenious mechanical cutter, like a very long saw, is fixed at the top and bottom and cuts it in vertical swathes. There are trees in the grounds, but no flowers and a French-style garden. A roller-skating area is free, for juveniles.

Visitors have been considered rather less. The principal entry is at 'Porte 1' opposite the Finance Ministry. Here we are faced with three great flights of steps, one above the other, which are unavoidable if we wish to get in. Like the other great building projects of President Mitterrand's era, the POPB makes no concession to the ageing population, for whom such staircases can be an ordeal. There are no handrails, either. It was perhaps thought that retired people stayed at home in their armchairs. In fact, they are hardy travellers, culture-vultures and great sport enthusiasts, an important element in tourism. Escalators should be provided in all such buildings. Meanwhile, for serious or wheelchair cases the POPB has a special 'handicapped' lift which can be reached directly from 'Porte 38' on the far side.

Stade de France

A huge new football stadium, the Stade de France, was erected at public expense in 1998 with 80,000 places. It is reached (to the north of Paris) by the RER, Line B, at the stop 'La Plaine St. Denis – Stade de France', or Line D, 'St Denis – Stade de France'. It opened just in time for the 1998 final of the football World Cup, in which France beat Brazil, who were hot favourites, and won the cup. Since then the stadium has been described by French TV as 'sacred soil'.

The Avenue Daumesnil
12me. Metro Daumesnil

The suburban railway line used to run along here over a high bridge of arches, from the Bastille to Nogent-sur-Marne and on to other towns. When the line closed, the arches for 1½ kilometres were boarded up and looked very run-down and dirty. These have been imaginatively transformed into boutiques of good-quality art-objects, china, decorative furniture, etc., giving the avenue a new luxury image. Neighbours will tell us that the goods are so expensive that no shop-keeper dares to put price-tags on them. Certainly there seem to be rather few customers. But the main sales, we learn, are made to agents from the Far East, often buying back treasures from their own countries.

The railtrack overhead has been turned cleverly into two kilometres of gardens, called the Promenade Plantée. In these we find ourselves at tree-top level, looking down on the avenue. We walk down the straight central path between flowering bushes of oleanders and syringa on either side and young trees, including sweet-smelling limes. The ground is close-planted with lavender, rose-beds and other flowering plants. It is well designed not to require too much gardening.

We hear birds, see loving couples walking out and joggers trotting by. There is a long pond, shallow enough to be hard to drown in, with bridges across it and a trellis-arch at the end, with benches for us to sit on. In fact it's so pretty that it seems sad to find so few people there, even on a fine summer afternoon. The reason for this is simple: the lift is locked. The people who enjoy sitting or strolling in gardens are usually pensioners or young mothers with pushchairs and toddlers. None of these can get up the steep, high stairs. Perhaps one day a lift-attendant can be afforded and then we can all enjoy this oasis.

The Parc André-Citröen
15me. Metro Balard

During the 1970s to 1990s, two very different currents were at work, transforming Paris. While monumental buildings were being put up by President Mitterrand (e.g. Arche de la Défense, the Bibliothèque Nationale with its towers at Tolbiac, the Grand Louvre with its Pyramid, and the Bastille Opera), his rival and next president, Jacques Chirac, at that time mayor of Paris for 20 years, had his ear to the ground and was laying out gardens. He responded to a very strong 'back to nature' movement. Unlike Londoners, so many of whom have their own gardens or live near big parks, Parisians have been flat-dwellers for centuries. Unless they lived near the famous Luxembourg Gardens, they seldom saw anything green except some severely pollarded trees. Chirac, and his successor as ayor, laid out a hundred and fifty new parks and gardens in Paris. This was made possible by a sweeping slum-clearance programme by which higher-density buildings were provided for rehousing, leaving spaces free for planting. This is such a novelty in Paris that guided tours are taken to see them and films of them have been made for the Videothèque de Paris. Flowers have been the latest discovery.

The most notable is Parc André-Citröen. The main entrance is at the corner of Rue Balard and Rue Saint-Charles (Metro Balard). This park covers a very large area reaching down to the river. It was originally used for market-gardens, which explains why the earth is so fertile, but in 1915, in an emergency drive to produce more arms for the 1914 war, it became the site of the Citröen armaments factory. In 1918 this was turned over to making the well-known Citröen cars, but the works has since been removed to a more suitable site outside Paris. The area is now defined by an overhead railway along one side, with a very pleasing arch, and a line of glass buildings, including a huge ultra-modern hospital, on the other. It is quiet, except for occasional trains; we hear many birds and we have more a sense of being in the country than in Paris. There are trees, flowering shrubs and yew hedges in the English style. Dogs are not allowed, but we may walk on the grass. Staid grown-ups usually walk along the paved path, which is wide enough for prams, but children love grass and there is a sculptural rockery which is fun for them, because they can hop from one boulder to the next, arriving in a secret garden with some picnic-tables.

Great imagination has been used in making this park. There is an open central square with benches for people to sit quietly in the sun, but, apart from this, the space is divided by thick planting of bushes and hedges into a whole series of different 'secret' gardens, each with its own theme, exotic scented flowers and colour-scale. These are known as 'the white garden' 'the blue garden', 'the shady garden' and even 'the dark garden', enclosed by greenery. The best surprise is the double waterfall among fountains which you come upon suddenly. The water comes down two great stone slabs, rushing on one side and rippling smoothly on the other, and you walk between them: a very original effect.

Off-Beat Paris (Paris Insolite)

The Sewers
7me. Metro Pont de l'Alma

The sewers are one of Paris's big attractions and it is worth being ten minutes early to avoid queuing (in the open). We find the entrance sign close to the southern end of Pont de l'Alma in front of 93 Quai d'Orsay. Full-length cruises are no longer allowed, since a famous bank vault robbery via the drains. We are shown historic details and a 'Spectacle Audiovisuel'. This is followed, when possible, by a tour, guided by the *égouteurs* themselves. There is a boutique and we can buy posters.

The sewers have been described as Haussmann's finest achievement, and are still considered unique; they enlarged and modernized the earlier system, built in 1740, which replaced the mediæval open drains. They now reach to 65 ft down and the big tunnels are 18 ft high, 14 ft wide, with a raised path on either side. Every street in Paris has one under it, and a map of the sewers would also be a street map of Paris. Knowing Paris, Jean Valjean, the persecuted hero of *Les Misérables,* was well able to find his way among the sewers, although, if laid end to end, they would reach from Paris to Istanbul.

They all have to be cleaned all the time, by *égouteurs* who wear waders and helmets; they walk behind special machines and drive special boats, and take great pride in their work. They remove enough rubbish – sand, obstructions and such unlikely objects as bedsteads – to fill six hundred barges a year. The stink is appalling but nobody, *égouteur* or visitor, is so poor-spirited as to mention it.

The sewage moves entirely by gravity. After thirteen hours it reaches one of the four sewage-farms outside Paris – the largest is in the Forêt Saint-Germain. Here it is allowed to settle and then bio-degraded and pumped back into the Seine, theoretically clean. The sewers also carry, hooked to the tunnel roofs, the clean water pipes of Paris, telephone wires, traffic-light cables and the pneumatic postal network. We used to be able to send a billet-doux to a girl-friend by *pneu,* which travelled through the sewers on its way. But the system was closed in 1984.

In the Marais
Metro St Paul

Some of the picturesque old streets of the Marais have acquired a special character of their own. In one of the narrowest, Rue des Rosiers, and also in Rue Pavée and Rue des Tournelles, we find specialist Jewish food on sale and in restaurants, and other Jewish-made products in the shops, for example clothes, reminding us that the garment industry has a long Jewish tradition in many countries. This has earned the district the title 'the Jewish Quarter'. There is a Jewish school in Rue des Rosiers and we may see boys walking by wearing black caps. There are three synagogues in the 4me arrondissement. Many people come here to buy kosher delicacies.

The **Museum of Judaism** was opened in one of the splendid Marais *hôtels*, at 71 rue du Temple, 3me, in December, 1998. It records the life and faith of Jews living in France since the thirteenth century. We may see many intricate *objets d'art* of great value, both religious and secular. There are also portraits, of various dates and varying quality, and there is much which is of historic interest.

Nearby, with a totally different atmosphere, are two other streets of old Marais houses, Rue Vieille du Temple and Rue des Archives. These have now taken over from St Germain the reputation of being Paris's 'Gay' headquarters for homosexuals. There are many bars and restaurants. At the end of these streets we can see the fine old arches of Porte St Martin and Porte St Denis, the last remains of the Gates of Paris.

Canal Saint-Martin
Boat Trip

This canal is an old cut, near République, which was originally made for barges. It still has the wide paths, on either side, which were made for the towing carthorses. It is lined with plane trees and is now used for 'Bateaux-Mouches' boat-trips.

Unlike such voyages along the Seine, it does not give us much view of Paris and its landmarks, but it is a pleasure in itself, its Seine-coloured water making a green cavern at one point where it reflects the overhanging chestnuts and the passerelle (footbridge) at République. The bridges open, like Tower Bridge in old London, to let the boats go underneath.

The City of Paris has linked the canal with its gardens called the Promenade Richard-Lenoir, making a water-garden with irises.

The Chinese Quarter

13me, Avenue de Choisy and Avenue d'Ivry. Metro Place d'Italie

Asiatic people, from many regions, like to come here to do their shopping, because there are so many shops owned by Asians which provide oriental specialities of every different sort. The architecture itself is not picturesque, but the cheerful restaurants, some offering tempting take-away dishes, and the forest of signs, many of them in Chinese lettering, make it look attractive. There are delightfully mixed idioms like 'Tang Frères Supermarket' or 'Prêt à Porter' with Chinese signs below. Thailand and Vietnam have their own food-shops. This is a business quarter, too, and we find the International Commercial Bank of China and an insurance company, indicating that there is money about. The owners of the businesses live in premises over the shops and in tall blocks of flats nearby, so there is a resident community.

The Catacombs

14me, entrance at 1 Place Denfert-Rochereau. Metro Denfert-Rochereau

The catacombs were once quarries, and extend for many miles under Paris. Often attributed to the Romans, they are certainly much older, going back to prehistoric times and Cernunnos. Single visitors are not allowed because, once lost, you would never be found again. A torch and a warm coat are essential, at all times of year. No photography is allowed.

Since 1810, skeletons from Paris cemeteries have been taken to the **ossuary** under Montrouge. There are six million there, if we enjoy that sort of thing.

Passages Couverts

There are several little alleys without traffic in Paris, known as Passages Couverts. The most picturesque is Passage de la Cour de Rohan, which runs between Boulevard St Germain and Rue St André-des-Arts. It has a tea-room (Metro St Michel). Others include Galerie Vivienne, 4 Place des Petits-Champs, Galerie Colbert, 6 Rue des Petits-Champs, Passage Choiseul, 44 Rue des Petits-Champs, Galerie de la Madeleine, 9 Place de la Madeleine, and Galerie Véro-Dodat, 19 Rue Jean-Jacques Rousseau.

Another, uncovered, passage is between Rue Royale and Rue du Faubourg St Honoré. This has little shops and a bar with tables outside. Not luxurious but 'insolite' (Metro Concorde).

Musée Français de la Carte à Jouer
Galerie d'Histoire de la Ville, 16 Rue Auguste Gervais, Issy-les-Moulineaux. Metro Mairie d'Issy

At the far end of line 12 of the metro we find a 'far-out' museum founded in 1995, concerned entirely with playing cards, 4,996 packs, no less, all collector's pieces, some of them beautiful miniatures, other curios. These come from all over the world and date back to a sumptuous pack of Italian tarot cards of the fifteenth century. In the twentieth century this form of art was taken up by some famous artists (for example Sonia Delaunay) and we may see here a pack designed by Jean Dubuffet, and one by the respected Flemish artist Simone Lacour. There are also drawings and posters and over 1,000 objects, such as porcelain, and model-dresses, all using designs inspired by cards. There are four ballet-costumes, two kings and two queens, created by André Derain in 1919 for the Russian Ballet of Diaghilev. All this is shown in a pleasant old château once owned by the Princes de Conti. (Matisse had his studio in Issy between 1909 and 1917.)

Museum of Public Assistance
5me, 47 Quai de la Tournelle. Metro Maubert-Mutualité

Museum maniacs may like to know of this little-visited Paris museum. Set in a pleasant seventeenth-century house with some good period chests-of-drawers, it is devoted to the history of hospital life and public assistance in Paris. Most of the exhibits are documents, engravings, portraits of doctors or benefactors. However, it is always interesting to see a picture of a surgeon performing a mastectomy, wearing a top hat.

How to Get About

Paris, now with over nine million inhabitants, is divided into the Ville de Paris and the suburbs. The Ville de Paris, which is what this book is concerned with, is divided into twenty arrondissements or districts. Each of these has its own mayor, town hall and a limited amount of self-administration. Each, too, has its own atmosphere and lifestyle; to know the number of someone's arrondissement is to get a rough idea of his social position and interests. Arrondissement No. 1 is right in the centre of Paris, including part of Ile de la Cité, Hôtel de Ville and Palais de Justice. After this the arrondissements spiral out clockwise to No. 20 which is on the eastern city limits.

Very useful little books can be bought at any newsagent or *tabac*, giving maps of Paris, the suburbs, the metro, detailed maps of each arrondissement, the location of every street in Paris with arrondissement number and nearest metro station, and also diagrams of all the bus routes. Even lifelong Parisians find these invaluable.

Streets are numbered from the end of the street nearest to the river, odd numbers on the left. If the river is at both ends, as on the islands, then the numbering starts from the southern end, the end nearest to Rome. If the street runs parallel to the Seine, then the numbering goes downstream, with the flow of the river. It must, however, be admitted that this information is useless to many people, particularly if they happen to be far from the Seine. Some streets too, after redevelopment, do not obey the rule – for instance, the long Rue de Vaugirard. But the principle holds.

On foot. Walking still remains the pleasantest way of getting about and exploring the areas which appeal to us. Many of the chapters in this book have been based on a walk, which can be shortened or altered according to wish; everyone likes to make his private discoveries and this is best done on foot. However, there are some hazards. The pavements may be cluttered with parked cars or motorcycles; cars may drive forwards or backwards along them, or

293

shoot suddenly out of or into underground car parks; dog-dirt is a hazard, since French dog-owners usually walk their dogs off the lead, and the dogs are understandably reluctant to go out into the road; we may be run into by boys on roller-skates or skate-boards, their ears deafened by walkman headphones. We should use traffic-lights or pedestrian crossings to cross main roads, but even here we should be careful; strict obedience to regulations is not something the French pride themselves on. Nevertheless, despite all this, a summer's day stroll along one of the great boulevards can still be one of the most enjoyable experiences to be found anywhere.

Driving. Many people bring their cars to Paris on their way to the south and have the interesting experience of driving in this city. The obvious resemblance is to a chariot-race. We should resign ourselves to bumps and dents; Paris cars carry their scars proudly. French drivers change lanes abruptly and without signalling – this adds to the excitement. They also have an interesting theory that you can go the wrong way down a one-way street provided that you go backwards. We should treat this theory with caution.

But we should obey carefully the 'Rule of the Right'. Unless lights or signs say otherwise, the car coming in from the right has right of way over the car going straight ahead. Many British drivers used to go across Paris, and indeed Europe, without knowing this, with inevitable results.

Traffic lights should be obeyed, whatever other cars may choose to do. However, should there be a policeman on point-duty as well (for instance, in rush-hours) then we should obey the policeman rather than the lights. Should there be two policemen on duty, the position becomes more complicated and we should follow the cars round us.

Parking is a problem in Paris, as in other cities. If possible, we should use one of the underground car parks. These, however, are not guarded and so cars should be locked. Kerb parking, being free, is universal, though free places are increasingly hard to find. Many drivers find manœuvring into a too-small gap a good sporting event and, having succeeded, leave again; it is estimated that a third of Paris cars are not going anywhere in particular, and they disappear in bad weather. Should we find a gap, we should of course reverse into it; if, while we are doing this, another car nips in forwards in our place, a lively scene will certainly ensue – one of the features of Paris street life ('Have you bought the street, Monsieur?') We should never park in front of a courtyard gateway (*porte-cochère*), on a pedestrian crossing or on a corner. Infringements bring a fine (*contravention*), the piece of paper we find under the windscreen-wiper after dinner. Cars with foreign numbers, which cannot easily be traced, may get away with it for a time, but they can be towed away or clamped. Getting a clamp removed is a slow and expensive business. If we do not already belong to a club, we should have cover from Europ Assistance which provides a breakdown service.

The Metro. The Paris metro, which celebrated its one hundredth birthday in 2000 with extensive station renovations, is one of the best in the world, and the normal way of getting about. Trains run frequently – almost nose to tail in rush hours – and there are many stations. Nowhere in Paris is very far from the nearest metro station. The authorities have attempted to make the metro a way of life by providing festival weeks, concerts, art exhibitions, cafés, restaurants, shops, and information and reservation centres. It is possible to spend all day and much of the night (until 1.00 a.m.) below ground, all for the price of one metro ticket.

However, I assume that we are using the metro mainly for purposes of transport, and the first thing to know is how to find our way about. Every metro station has maps, both outside and inside and some even have electric push-button maps to tell us which way to go. The secret is to ignore the ostensible number of the line, which nobody knows, and concentrate on its final station, which gives its name to the line. This will be marked 'Direction Mairie des Lilas' or similar. Should we have to change lines (*correspondance*), we follow another Direction towards a different and distant destination, which we shall certainly never reach (like characters in an Anouilh play). For example, if we want to go by metro from Gare du Nord to the Arc de Triomphe, like many people, we first study the map. Then we take Direction Porte d'Orléans as far as Châtelet, where we change, taking the tunnel marked 'Correspondance'. Then we follow the signs marked 'Direction Neuilly' as far Etoile-Charles de Gaulle, where we emerge. All very simple, quick and cheap.

We can buy metro tickets at every station, and in some *tabacs* too. We should buy them in blocks of ten (*carnets*), which are almost half-price. If we plan to be in Paris more than three months and to use public transport regularly, we might consider buying a *Carte Orange*, which offers further reductions. Both it and ordinary metro tickets are also used on buses. To stamp the ticket, we put it through an electric gate, which will then let us through. (Never try to jump the gate, like many young men.) To open the train doors we press a button or raise a lever. The doors close automatically when the guard decides that there are no more travellers getting off or on. In crowded rush-hours it is usually easier to push yourself on backwards: if, on leaving the station, you should find our way blocked by glass doors, you should remember to push the glass panel and not the metal rim. The Meteor line, opened in 1998, is automated; its trains have no drivers.

The RER. This is the suburban network, providing fast travel to the suburbs, including Versailles, Saint-Germain-en-Laye and both airports. It interconnects at several *correspondances* with the ordinary metro, but stations are much less frequent and ordinary tickets are only valid inside the city limits. We need our tickets to get *out*, as well as in.

Buses. These are one of the pleasantest ways of getting about Paris in daylight, but they take time and do not usually run after nine o'clock in the evening, except for a special night service. On Sundays they run only occasionally. There are diagrams of bus routes, not only in the little red guidebooks, but also at every bus stop. These are often sheltered; some have telephones. The system, which takes some mastering, produces enjoyable travel. We clip our ticket ourselves (the same ticket as for the metro) beside the driver and gradually make our way down to the exit door, pressing a button on our way to ask for the door to be opened. There are no conductors. A single ticket (unlike the metro) will not necessarily take you all the way. For a journey beyond inner Paris you will have to clip more tickets. The driver will advise you, monosyllabically. Bus stops are hard to find, especially in one-way streets, and you are advised to concentrate on one route until you are familiar with it, before tackling another. Personally I use Paris buses a good deal, but only on one route. Unlike other cities, the drivers do not leave you standing at the stop because the bus is nominally 'full'.

Taxis. These are increasingly hard to find, especially in rush-hours or on wet days. However, we may be lucky. Our hotel or restaurant can normally telephone for one. Cruising taxis rarely stop; we find taxis at railway stations or at taxi-ranks (*têtes de station*) which occur throughout the city. The driver will ask us where we are going – he or she is not obliged to carry anyone anywhere, and hopes we are going a long way, preferably to an airport. If he refuses to take us, we should try the other taxis behind him – this is the normal practice. On leaving, we should tip, usually about 15% of the fare.

Guided Tours (or with an official guide in our own car): details from Office de Tourisme, 127 Champs Elysées (Metro Etoile).

Helicopters. Over Western Paris only. Reservations needed. Heli-France, 4 Ave de la Porte de Sèvres, 15me, for departure from heliport outside Paris; Delta-Lima, 37 Ave. Mac-Mahon, 17me, for thirty-minute tour, take-off from Toussus-le-Noble (15 minutes from Paris), round trip transfer by shuttle bus (Metro Etoile); 'Paris Helicoptère', Le Bourget Airport: 25 minute flight.

River Transport. Cruise boats offering a variety of hourly cruises, with longer lunch and dinner excursions, leave frequently from Pont de l'Alma (Metro Alma-Marceau), Quai de Montebello (Metro Saint-Michel), the Eiffel Tower (Metro Bir-Hakeim), the Square du Vert Galant (Metro Pont-Neuf) and Port de Suffren (Metro Bir-Hakeim). It is also possible to cruise along the Canal Saint-Martin and a section of the Seine between the Musée d'Orsay and Parc de la Villette.

A newer service, called Batobus, operating from April to November, aims to help us get about in Paris. We can pay for just one stop, or buy a one- or even two-day ticket. This allows us to get off at one of the stops and then complete our journey on a later 'bus' without paying again. If our hotel is close to any of its stops, it gives us a pleasant journey to see the *Mona Lisa*, the d'Orsay Museum, or Notre-Dame (for example), arriving and leaving in a relaxed way, by river. Or we can just sit in the 'bus' all the way and see Paris from the water. They call it 'Paris in six stops'; these stops are Eiffel Tower, Musée d'Orsay, Saint Germain-des-Prés, Notre-Dame, Hôtel de Ville and Louvre.

Bus Tours. 'Parisbus' ('Car-Rouges') 3–5 Rue Talma (Metro La Muette) offers a 2¼ hour tour, with nine stops, commentaries in French and English, 15–21 departures daily; a 2-day ticket allows us to break our journey and go on later. Other companies include Cityrama, 147 Rue Saint-Honoré and Parisvision, 214 Rue de Rivoli.

Motorcycles and Scooters. Can be hired from 'Easyrider', 144 Boulevard Voltaire (Metro Voltaire).

Bicycle Hire. Numerous firms, including 'Bike 'n Roller', 6 Rue Saint Julien-le-Pauvre, Metro Maubert.

Guided group cycle-tour. 'Paris à Vélo', 37 Boulevard Bourdon, (Metro Bastille). Offers some lively tours every day.

How to Live in Paris

Many people come to Paris for several months or a year on a sabbatical, research project, or because they have a job here. They often feel lost and lonely, and may like some advice.

How to find a flat. Choose the quarter where you wish to live and go to the local agencies (*Immobilières*). Also read the small ads in *Le Figaro* and *France-Soir*. These can be divided into *appartements de grand standing, deux pièces* (more than one room), *studios* (large one-room flats with mod. cons.), *studettes* (bed-sitters) and *chambres-de-bonne* (garret rooms, with shared WC, formerly occupied by living-in maids). Rents vary according to area, number of stairs and quarter. Except for *chambres-de-bonne,* flats are usually unfurnished. Furniture can be bought economically at Samaritaine, BHV, or Habitat in the Montparnasse shopping centre.

You have to pay two months' rent in advance as a deposit, plus the normal one month in advance, plus agency fees (about a month's rent). This can add up to a lot of money, but you cannot sign the lease (*bail*) until it is paid. The deposit is refundable, but there are somehow always deductions.

If you are hard up, *chambres-de-bonne* are cheap and, with their views of the roofs of Paris, romantic for the young and strong-legged. Make sure that there is a communal WC on the same floor, with light; that the room has running water and an electric socket where you can plug in a drink-heater, a small cooking-ring or even a small bowl-fire, should no heating be provided.

How not to starve in a garret – for students on insufficient grants, artists, etc. Use the electric socket in your *chambre-de-bonne*. There's no need to live on cold cooked chicken (expensive) and keep warm all day in a cinema, as many visitors do.

Fresh sardines, mackerel, or chicken livers (bought from the greengrocer), are very cheap and flavour a large quantity of ready-cooked rice (also easy to get). Guests can be impressed by apparent luxuries: oysters, artichokes, slices of seafood *pâté* are much cheaper in Paris than elsewhere. The latter also make good sandwiches. Shop in side streets, always much cheaper than the main thoroughfares. A hot *plat du jour,* sold 'to go' in *triperies* and many small restaurants, is delicious and would cost double in a café. Overcome your prejudices and try tripe or hamburgers from the local horse-butcher – cheaper and tastier than in other shops.

Doctors. The best way of finding one is a recommendation from a friend or, failing this, your chemist (*pharmacien*). There are health centres in many places which are excellent and do lab tests and X-rays on the spot. A free booklet giving details of Paris hospital services is available at any hospital, clinic or health service. The maternity services of the Saint-Vincent-de-Paul and Hôtel-Dieu hospitals are thought to be particularly good. But, in any event, your own doctor will advise you. For urgent cases, the emergency ambulance is SAMU, telephone 15. There are 'SOS Médecins' (doctors) too. The police, telephone 17, can give us the local number for these.

Hospitals. If you are entitled to Social Security (compulsory for all workers in France after the first year), you will pay very little, and nothing at all if you are in hospital for an operation or illness for more than a month. Otherwise you should have some private insurance of your own, valid in France. While on holiday (only), those covered by the British Health Service are covered in France too. Ask for 'Form E.111'.

If you must have an English-speaking hospital, both the British and American Hospitals are available, but expensive. The Franco-British Hospital, 5 Rue Barbès, Levallois-Perret, 92300, Metro Anatole France, has ninety beds, maternity and general and also out-patients. If you have French Social Security, this covers you in the British Hospital, but only pays 20% of the bill in the American Hospital at 63 Boulevard Victor Hugo, 92202 Neuilly, Metro Sablons. This is a general hospital with 187 beds.

French private clinics come under the Social Security scheme. If you are of executive grade (*cadre*), you will get a private room without extra charge. Authors are not '*cadre*'.

Carte de Séjour (Residence Permit). This is compulsory for all foreigners, even members of the EC, after three months. This is issued by the Prefecture of Police on Ile de la Cité, even if they pass you on to a local sub-office, but it is as well to get a statement of address from your local police station, and to take a paid electricity bill if you have one. You will need your passport, two photographs, proof of means such as a bank letter or a form from your employer and stamped addressed envelope. You should allow some six afternoons for appointments and interviews, after which you will receive a temporary card. When this expires, you do it all again, for a longer-term card.

Schools for your children. Much depends on how long you mean to stay and whether your children are heading for the British or French system, the *baccalauréat* or A-levels. For infants, the Montessori Bilingue at 65 Quai d'Orsay provides happy play, if not ambitious education. The American School is tougher physically. The British School of Paris, 38 Quai de l'Écluse, 78890 Croissy-sur-Seine, prepares for GCSE and GCE 'A' levels. So do many others (48 when last counted) including Mary Mount School, founded in 1923, and the International Lycée at Saint-Germain-en-Laye, which is bilingual and takes pupils from many countries, but has a British school programme. The Ecole Bilingue is at 117 Boulevard Malesherbes, 8me, and there are several other branches in Paris. These are mainly French-speaking and preparing for the *bac* and French universities. The British Council has a leaflet about schools.

There are also a large number of private French-speaking Catholic schools in all parts, which are cheap and where your child will learn, among others things, perfect French. Teenagers, with a year to spare, usually find the Sorbonne summer course in French culture and civilization enjoyable and rewarding (for advice, see the British Institute, below). The American Library in Paris, 10 rue du Général Camou, 7me, has books in English; so has the British Council Library, 9 Rue Constantine, 7me (see below).

Meeting the British community. The Cercle Interallié in Faubourg Saint-Honoré is expensive and you have to be proposed by two members. Squash and swimming are available. The Country Club at Meudon, the 'Standard Athletic Club', Au Clos Obœuf, Route Forestière du Pavé de Meudon, 92360 Meudon La Forêt, provides tennis and swimming and is a haunt of British businessmen and their families. Children especially enjoy it. It is best reached by car but is ten minutes walk from the rail station Meudon-Bellevue (Gare Montparnasse) or twenty minutes walk from Metro Issy-les-Moulineaux. The Franco-British (Junior) Chamber of Commerce and Industry, 'young executives', 31 Rue Boissy d'Anglas, Metros Madeleine or Concorde, organizes lots of social functions, to which wives may be brought. All applicants are accepted and the parties are usually fun and youthful. After the age of forty you move to the Senior Chamber. The two Anglican churches also organize many meetings and events; St George's also has the Cardew Club, 50 Avenue Hoche, Metro Etoile, for lost au pair girls in Paris. St Joseph's RC Church is English-speaking. The Scots Kirk is at 17 Rue Bayard, Metro Franklin D. Roosevelt.

The **British Community Committee**, 17 Villa Chaptal, 92300 Levallois-Perret, publishes a most useful *Digest*, listing British associations, clubs and societies in Paris, and their social activities. Through this we may get in touch with the 'Mothers' Support Group' if we have children. More and more British families are coming to live in Paris and the group already has 1,000 members. Their experience may help us about choosing schools.

Tearooms. *Angelina's*, 226 Rue de Rivoli, Metro Concorde

Pubs. *Sir Winston Churchill Pub*, 5 Rue de Presbourg, (Metro Etoile). This is an interesting hybrid of a Victorian pub, with engraved glass and brass rails, and a French restaurant, with plush banquettes on a higher level, for those who wish to eat and be served by waiters. It is a popular rendezvous for the British, both visitors and locals, especially on Saturday nights. Opening times are very far from British licensing hours. *The Long Hop* is at 25–27 Rue Frédéric Santon (Metro Maubert-Mutualité).

The Brasserie of Ile Saint-Louis, Rue Jean du Bellay (Metro Pont Marie), on the corner beside Pont Saint-Louis footbridge to Ile de la Cité, has been nicknamed '*The Oasis*' by the British. It is inexpensive, informal, crowded and fun. Its warm (in both senses) hospitality has made it a rendezvous for the British, especially at weekends – and for other nations too. It is difficult to leave the old wooden bar without having found an old friend or made a new one.

The **Centre Culturel Britannique**, which is also the elegant and imposing offices of the British Council, is at 9 Rue de Constantine, Metro Invalides, overlooking Esplanade des Invalides. The British Council arranges lectures in English, with distinguished guest-speakers. They advise about schools, for British students in Paris and for French school-children visiting Britain. Otherwise, the main attraction is the English-language library where, on weekdays, we can borrow books, videos and tapes. We must, of course, pay a subscription and also give a Paris address which is not a hotel. They have periodicals and 20,000 books. We should take an identity card and a photograph.

The **British Institute** is at the same address as the British Council, but next door. A link between Paris and London universities, it organizes courses in English literature and current affairs, and French language courses which can be combined with courses at the Sorbonne in Visual Arts, History or Political Science.

A private organization, the Association France-Grande Bretagne 183 Avenue Daumesnil, 12me, organizes occasional lectures in French on some aspect of British life.

Meeting the American Community. Several rendezvous of the American Community have already been mentioned: the Cercle de l'Union Interallié (see above); the France-Amérique Club (see p. 78); the Crillon Bar (see p. 84); Harry's Bar (see p. 96); the American Hospital (see above); and the American Library in Paris (see above). The American School is at 42 Rue Pastens, St Cloud.

The **American Cathedral** (see p. 76), known for its good music, welcomes a congregation drawn from many countries which values its traditional, reverent, services. These, known to Americans, and others worldwide with American links, as 'Episcopalian' are based on what British people call 'the King James prayer book', dating back to the seventeenth century. The worldwide community which has had links with Britain calls this 'Anglican'. It adds up to a great many people, visiting Paris or now living there, and the cathedral is always full.

They have a Eucharistic Service once a week for 'Disadvantaged people' (the polite word for 'poor') after which a meal is provided. A new 'outreach' initiative is the 'Francophone Ministry' which has French-speakers on the cathedral staff and makes radio broadcasts in French on 'Fréquence Protestante' and 'Radio Notre-Dame'. A Eucharist Service in French is held on Saturdays. They also have a Taiwanese Episcopal priest who ministers to Paris's Chinese-speaking communities.

The **American Church**, 65 Quai d'Orsay, (Metro Alma-Marceau) corresponds to the British idea of 'Free-Churches' and has a great variety of social activities.

The **American Embassy** is at 2 Avenue Gabriel, Place de la Concorde, opposite the Hotel Crillon (Metro Concorde). The **American Consulate** is at 2 Rue Saint-Florentin (Metro Concorde). The **United States Ambassador's Residence** is at 41 Rue du Faubourg Saint-Honoré, next to the British Embassy (Metro Madeleine or Concorde).

Lost Property Office The 'Service des Objets Trouvés' is at 36 Rue des Morillons (Metro Convention).

Opening Times

Most attractions are closed on public holidays and many museums are free on one Sunday per month. Before visiting, as opening times change constantly, it is wise to refer to current local publicity material, such as the weekly *Pariscope* or the monthly *Paris Free Voice*. The main branch of the Paris Tourist Office is at 127 Champs-Elysées, close to Etoile, and open daily 9.00–20.00, with a useful website at www.paris-touristoffice.com.

1. Ile de la Cité

Archaeological Crypt, Place du Parvis de Notre-Dame, Metro Cité
Open daily: 9.30–18.30, April–September; 10.00–17.00, October–March.

Mémorial de la Déportation, beside Passerelle Bridge, Metro Cité
Open daily, except last Sunday in April: 10.00–12.00, 14.00–19.00, April–September; 10.00–12.00, 14.00–17.00, October–March.

Museum of Notre-Dame, 10 Rue du Cloître Notre-Dame, Metro Cité
Open Wednesdays, Saturdays and Sundays: 14.30–18.00.

Palais de Justice, 4 Boulevard du Palais, Metro Cité
Open daily, except Sundays: 8.30–18.00.

Sainte-Chapelle, 4 Boulevard du Palais, Metro Cité
Open daily: 9.30–18.30, April–September; 10.00–17.00, October–March.
Guided tours through the Caisse Nationale des Monuments Historiques et des Sites, Hôtel de Sully, 62 Rue Saint Antoine, Metro Saint Paul.

Conciergerie, 1 Quai de l'Horloge, Metro Cité
Open daily: 9.30–18.30, April–September; 10.00–17.00, October–March.

2. Notre-Dame

Notre-Dame Treasure, Place du Parvis de Notre-Dame, Metro Cité
Open daily, except Sundays: 9.30–11.30, 13.00–17.30.

Notre-Dame North Tower, Place du Parvis Notre-Dame, Metro Cité
Open daily: 9.30–19.30, April–September; 10.00–17.00, October–March.

3. Ile Saint Louis

Hôtel Lauzun, 17 Quai d'Anjou, Metro Pont Marie
Apply to Caisse Nationale des Monuments Historiques et des Sites, Hôtel de Sully, 62 Rue Saint Antoine, Metro Saint Paul. Tours are for groups only and must be reserved months in advance.

4. The Seine

The Zoo (La Ménagerie du Jardin des Plantes), 3 Quai Saint-Bernard, Metro Gare d'Austerlitz
Open daily: 9.00–18.00, April–September; 9.00–17.00, October–March.

Institut du Monde Arabe, 1 Rue des Fossés Saint-Bernard, Metro Sully-Morland or Jussieu
Open daily except Mondays: 10.00–18.00.

Musée de la Monnaie, 11 Quai Conti, Metro Pont Neuf
Open Tuesdays–Fridays, 11.00–17.30, Saturdays and Sundays 12.00–17.30.

Institut de France, 23 Quai de Conti, Metro Pont Neuf or Odéon
Guided tours on Saturdays and Sundays, 10.00 and 15.00.

Palais Bourbon, 126 Rue de l'Université, Metro Assemblée Nationale
Visits on Saturdays, unless the House is sitting, at 10.00, 11.00 and 15.00. Assembly point: 33 Quai d'Orsay, carrying identification.

5. The Museé d'Orsay

Musée d'Orsay, Quai d'Orsay, Metro Solférino
Open Tuesdays, Wednesdays, Fridays and Saturdays, 10.00–18.00; Thursdays, 10.00–21.45; Sundays, 9.00–18.00. Daily opening at 9.00 between 20 June and 20 September. Frequent guided tours to highlights or aspects of the collection.

6. The Champs-Elysées

Arc de Triomphe, Metro & RER Charles de Gaulle-Etoile
Open daily: 9.30–23.00, April–September; 10.00–22.30, October–March.

Palais de la Découverte, Avenue Franklin Roosevelt, Metro Champs-Elysées-Clemenceau
Open Tuesdays–Saturdays 9.30–18.00, Sundays 10.00–19.00.

Musée Jacquemart-André, 158 Boulevard Haussman, Metro Saint-Philippe-du-Roule
Open daily: 10.00–18.00.

Musée Nissim de Camondo, 63 Rue de Monceau, Metro Villiers
Open Wednesdays–Sundays: 10.00–17.00.

Musée du Petit Palais, Avenue Winston Churchill, Metro Champs-Elysées-Clemenceau
Open daily except Mondays: 10.00–17.40. Closing indefinitely for works at the end of 2000.

Galerie Nationale du Jeu de Paume, 1 Place de la Concorde, Metro Concorde
Open Tuesdays 12.00–21.30; Wednesdays, Thursdays and Fridays, 12.00–19.00; Saturdays and Sundays, 10.00–19.00.

7. The Opéra District

La Madeleine, Place de la Madeleine, Metro Madeleine
Open daily: 7.30–19.00. Closed some Sundays between 13.30 and 15.30.

Musée Edith Piaf, 5 Rue Crespin du Gast, Metro Ménilmontant
Visits by pre-arrangement: Mondays–Thursdays, 13.00–18.00

Opéra Garnier, Place de l'Opéra, Metro Opéra
Open daily, 10.00–17.00, unless performances are taking place.

Musée Grévin, 10 Boulevard Montmartre, Metro Grands Boulevards
Open daily: 13.00–19.00, school holidays 10.00–19.00, April–September; 13.00–18.30, school holidays 10.00–18.30, October–March.

La Bourse, Palais de la Bourse, Metro Bourse
Open Mondays–Fridays: 13.15–16.00

Bibliothèque Nationale, 58 Rue de Richelieu, Metro Palais Royal
Médailles Collection open Mondays–Fridays 13.00–17.45; Saturdays 13.00–16.45; Sundays 12.00–18.00.

8. The Louvre

Musée du Louvre, Rue de Rivoli, Metro Palais Royal
Open Thursdays–Sundays, 9.00–18.00; Mondays 9.00–21.45 (certain sections); Wednesdays 9.00–21.45 (whole museum). Closed Tuesdays. Tickets are valid for one day and re-entry is permitted within that time. Variety of tours available.

Musée des Arts Décoratifs, 107 Rue de Rivoli, Metro Palais Royal
Medieval and Renaissance collections open Tuesdays, Thursdays and Fridays 11.00–18.00; Wednesdays 11.00–21.00; Saturdays and Sundays 10.00–18.00. Full reopening is scheduled for 2001.

Musée de la Mode et du Textile, 107 Rue de Rivoli, Metro Palais-Royal
Open Tuesdays, Thursdays and Fridays, 11.00–18.00; Wednesdays 11.00–21.00; Saturdays and Sundays 10.00–18.00.

Musée de la Publicité, 107 Rue de Rivoli, Metro Palais Royal
Opening hours are as for the Musée de la Mode et du Textile, and a combined ticket covers both collections.

9. Eastern Paris

Hôtel de Ville, 29 Rue de Rivoli, Metro Hôtel de Ville
Open for pre-booked guided tours on the first Monday morning of each month.

Opéra de la Bastille, Place de la Bastille, Metro Bastille
Open Mondays–Saturdays for guided tours at 10.00, 13.00 and 17.30.

Père Lachaise Cemetery, Boulevard de Ménilmontant, Metro Père Lachaise
Open Mondays–Fridays, 8.00–18.00; Saturdays 8.30–18.00; Sundays 9.00–18.00 (mid-March–5 November). Winter closing at 17.30.

10. Beaubourg

Centre Georges Pompidou, Place Georges Pompidou, Metro Rambuteau or Hôtel de Ville
Open daily except Tuesdays: 11.00–22.00. Entrance includes access to the Brancusi Studio on the piazza. Innumerable guided tours of aspects of the collection.

11. The Marais

Musée Picasso, Hôtel Salé, 5 Rue de Thorigny, Metro Saint Paul
Open daily, except Tuesdays: 9.30–18.00, April–September; 9.30–17.30 October–March.

Hôtel de Sens, Forney Library, 1 Rue du Figuier, Metro Pont-Marie or Saint-Paul
Open Tuesdays to Fridays, 13.30–20.00, Saturdays 10.00–20.30.

Hôtel de Sully, 62 Rue Saint-Antoine, Metro Saint-Paul
Open Tuesdays to Saturdays: gardens 9.00–19.00; Caisse Nationale des Monuments Historiques et des Sites 9.00–18.00, Saturdays 10.00–13.00 and 14.00–17.00.

Maison de Victor Hugo, 6 Place des Vosges, Metro Chemin-Vert
Open Tuesdays–Sundays: 10.00–17.40.

Musée Carnavalet, 23 Rue de Sévigné, Metro Saint-Paul
Open Tuesdays–Sundays: 10.00–17.40.

Hôtel de Soubise, 60 Rue des Francs-Bourgeois, Metro Rambuteau or Hôtel de Ville
Open Mondays, Wednesdays, Thursdays and Fridays, 12.00–17.45; Saturdays and Sundays 13.45–17.45.

Hôtel de Rohan, 87 Rue Vieille du Temple, Metro Hôtel de Ville
Open daily during temporary exhibitions – details from Hôtel de Soubise.

Arsénal, 1 Rue de Sully, Metro Sully-Morland
Open Tuesdays–Saturdays, 10.00–18.30, Sundays 11.00–19.00. The library is open only to occasionally-scheduled guided tours – details from Caisse Nationale des Monuments Historiques et des Sites.

Musée Cognacq-Jay, 8 Rue Elzévir, Metro Saint-Paul
Open Tuesdays–Sundays: 10.00–17.40.

12. Montmartre

Sacré Coeur, Parvis du Sacré-Coeur, Metro Anvers
Open daily: dome and crypt 9.0–19.00, April–September; 9.00–18.00 October–March; basilica 6.45–22.30.

Musée de Montmartre, 12 Rue Cortot, Metro Lamarck
Open Tuesdays–Sundays: 11.00–18.00.

Montmartre Cemetery, Avenue Rachel, Metro Blanche or Place Clichy
Occasional guided tours.

13. The Seizième Arrondissement

Musée du Vin, 5 Rue des Eaux, Square Charles Dickens, Metro Passy
Open Tuesdays–Sundays: 10.00–18.00. Closed over New Year period.

Balzac's House, 47 Rue Raynouard, Metro Passy
Open daily except Mondays: 10.00–17.40.

Marmottan Museum, 2 Rue Louis Boilly, Metro La Muette
Open daily except Mondays: 10.00–17.30.

Musée National des Monuments Français, Palais de Chaillot, Place du Trocadéro, Metro Trocadéro
Closed until late 2000 when it will reopen as Cité de l'Architecture et du Patrimoine

Musée de l'Homme, Palais de Chaillot, Place du Trocadéro, Metro Trocadéro
Open daily except Tuesdays: 9.45–17.15.

Musée de la Marine, Palais de Chaillot, Place du Trocadéro, Metro Trocadéro
Open daily except Tuesdays: 10.00–17.50.

Musée National des Arts Asiatiques – Guimet, Place d'Iéna, Metro Iéna
The museum is closed for renovation until November 2000. Until then, the Guimet collection is on show at the Panthéon Bouddhique, 19, Avenue de Iéna.
Open daily except Tuesdays: 9.45–18.00.

Museum of Modern Art of the City of Paris, Palais de Tokyo, 11 Avenue du Président Wilson, Metro Iéna
Open Tuesdays–Fridays, 10.00–17.30, Saturdays and Sundays 10.00–18.45.

15. Montagne Sainte-Geneviève

The Pantheon, Place du Panthéon, RER Luxembourg
Open daily: 9.30–18.30, April–September; 10.00–18.15 October–March.

Saint Etienne du Mont, Place Ste-Geneviève, Metro Cardinal Lemoine
Open Tuesdays–Sundays 9.00–19.30; Mondays 9.00–12.00, 14.00–19.30. Closed on Mondays in July and August.

Scottish College, 65 Rue du Cardinal Lemoine, Metro Cardinal Lemoine
Open weekdays, 9.00–11.00, 14.00–16.00; Saturdays, 14.00–1600. Closed Sundays, July, August and last week in December.

Sorbonne Chapel, Rue des Ecoles, Metro Cluny La Sorbonne
Temporary exhibitions.

Hôtel de Cluny – Musée National du Moyen Age et des Thermes de Cluny, 6 Place Paul Painlevé, Metro Cluny La Sorbonne
Open daily except Tuesdays: 9.15–17.45.

16. The Luxembourg

Luxembourg Palace, 15 Rue de Vaugirard, Metro Saint Sulpice
Guided tours on the first Sunday of each month. Contact the Caisse Nationale des Monuments Historiques et des Sites, Hôtel de Sully.

17. Saint-Germain-des-Prés

Eugène Delacroix Museum and Studio, 6 Rue de Furstenberg, Metro Saint-Germain-des-Prés
Open daily except Tuesdays: 9.30–17.00.

Church of Saint-Germain-des-Prés, Boulevard Saint-Germain, Metro Saint-Germain-des-Prés
Open Mondays–Saturdays 08.00–19.45, Sundays 9.00–20.00.

Church of Saint-Sulpice, Place Saint-Sulpice, Metro Saint-Sulpice
Open daily.

18. The Septième Arrondissement

Eiffel Tower, Champ de Mars, Metro Bir Hakeim
Open daily: 9.00–24.00, 11 June–31 August; 9.30–23.00 during rest of year.

UNESCO Building, 7 Place Fontenay, Metro Ségur
Open Mondays–Fridays: 9.00–18.00.

Les Invalides, Napoleon's Tomb, Esplanade des Invalides, Metro Latour Maubourg
Comprises Hôtel des Invalides, two churches and three museums.
Open daily: 10.00–18.00 April–September; 10.00–17.00 October–March.

Musée Rodin, Hôtel Biron, 77 Rue de Varenne, Metro Varenne
Open daily except Mondays: 9.30–17.45 April–September; 9.30–16.45 October–March.

Fondation Dina Vierny – Musée Maillol, 59–61 Rue de Grenelle, Metro Rue du Bac.
Open daily except Tuesdays: 11.00–18.00; 23 June–22 September 10.00–18.00

19. Montparnasse

Montparnasse Tower, 33 Avenue du Maine, Metro Montparnasse Bienvenue
Open daily: 9.30–23.30 April–September; 9.30–22.30 October–March.

Musée Lénine, 4 Rue Marie-Rose, Metro Alésia
Open Mondays–Fridays, 9.30–17.00, by previous arrangement. Closed for one month during the summer.

Montparnasse Cemetery, Boulevard Edgar-Quinet, Metro Edgar Quinet or Raspail
Guided tours available.

Outer Paris

La Grande Arche, Esplanade de La Défense, Metro Grande Arche de la Défense
Open daily: 9.30–20.00 April–September; 10.00–19.00 October–March.

Basilique de Saint-Denis, Saint-Denis, Metro Saint-Denis-Basilique
Open Mondays–Saturdays, 10.00–19.00 April–September; 10.00–17.00 October–March; Sundays 12.00–19.00 April–September; 12.00–17.00 October–March

Off-Beat Paris (Paris Insolite)

The Sewers, intersection of Quai d'Orsay and Pont de l'Alma, Metro Pont de l'Alma
Open Saturdays–Wednesdays: 11.00–17.00 April–September; 11.00–16.00 October–March. Closed last three weeks of January and in the event of storm, flood etc.

Museum of Judaism, Hôtel de Saint-Aignan, 71 Rue du Temple, Metro Rambuteau
Open Mondays–Fridays, 11.00–18.00, Sundays 10.00–18.00. Closed on Saturdays and Jewish holidays.

Canal Saint Martin
Canal sailings leave from 13 Quai de la Loire, Metro Jaurès

The Catacombs, 1 Place Denfert-Rochereau. Metro Denfert Rochereau. Guided groups Tuesdays–Fridays, 14.00–16.00; weekends 9.00–11.00, 14.00–16.00.

Musée de la Carte à Jouer, Galerie d'Histoire de la Ville, 16 Rue Auguste Gervais, Issy-les-Moulineaux, Metro Mairie d'Issy
Open Wednesdays, Saturdays and Sundays, 10.00–19.00, or by appointment.

Museum of Public Assistance, Hôtel de Miramion, 47 Quai de la Tournelle, Metro Maubert Mutualité
Open Tuesdays–Sundays: 10.00–18.00.

Restaurant Vocabulary

Paris restaurants often use 'codewords' to describe a number of standard dishes, which we shall often eat. The descriptions may not always be exact or adequate. The dishes may well be elaborately prepared and with variations; every cook likes to improvise on occasions. But a short glossary may be helpful.

à l'ancienne	anyhow, using up stock and leftovers
anglaise	plain boiled or fried
sauce anglaise	Worcestershire sauce, unpronounceable in French
armoricaine, now usually spelt *américaine*[*]	a sauce of shellfish, white fish, tomatoes, white wine and brandy, often tinned
basquaise or *catalane* or *espagnole*	with tomatoes and sliced red and green peppers
bercy	a white wine sauce with shallots (onions)
bordelaise	a red wine sauce with beef stock and marrow, for steak
bourguignonne	stewed in red wine until it is thick and dark, for beef and kidneys
Caen, à la mode de	cooked with calvados (apple brandy), usually for tripe
catalane	see *basquaise*
chasseur	a thin brown sauce, with mushrooms and herbs, usually for rabbit
dieppoise	with shrimps and sometimes mussels
dijonnaise	with a mustard sauce
espagnole	see *basquaise*

---

[*] The Armoricae lived in west Normandy, before the Norsemen arrived in the eighth century.

311

financière	with a thick white sauce, for sweetbreads
florentine	with tinned spinach
grand-mère	a thick brown sauce, with bacon and mushrooms
grenobloise	with capers
herbes de Provence	with thyme, rosemary etc., not garlic
jardinière	with diced, mixed vegetables, probably tinned
lyonnaise	with tomatoes and onions
maison	how we always do it here
maître d'hôtel	a parsley-butter sauce
meunière	dusted with flour and fried
milanaise	with spaghetti
à la mode	with tinned carrots
mornay	with a cheese sauce
niçoise	with olives and anchovies, usually a salad
normande	with a sauce of butter, cream, egg-yolks and calvados (apple brandy)
printanière	with grated raw carrots, usually an egg salad
provençale	with garlic
Provence, herbes de	see above
rouennaise	game cooked in its own blood and giblets
suprême	an almost tasteless white sauce, for chicken
toulouse	with sausages, whole or sliced
viennoise	coated with breadcrumbs and fried
vin, marchand de	a red wine sauce with chopped shallots and lemon juice, for steak

Index

Note: page references in **bold type** indicate major references. Page references in *italic type* indicate opening times.

Index

317

Index

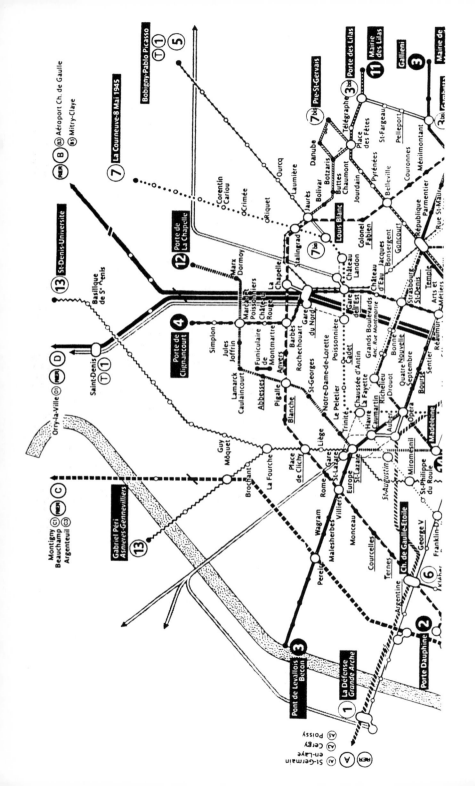

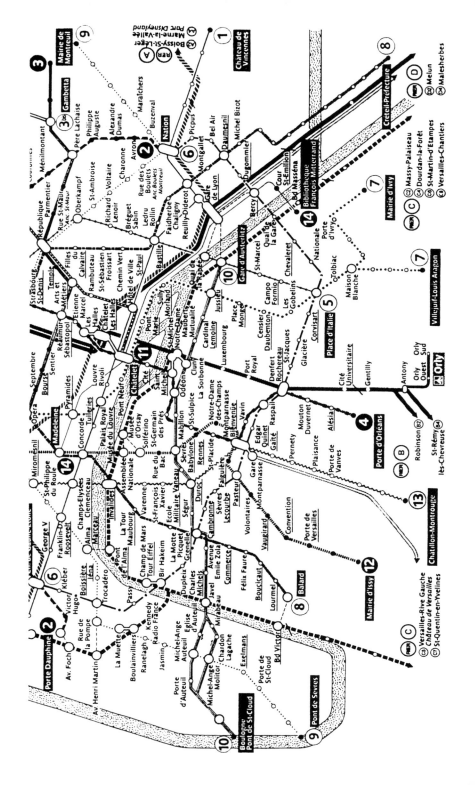